CW01664415

HOW TO BE A GOD

A GUIDE FOR WOULD-BE DEITIES

Richard. A. Bartle

First published in Great Britain by NotByUs, 2022

Orchard House, Queens Road,
West Bergholt, Essex. CO6 3HE

http://www.notbyus.com

ISBN 978-0-9556494-9-3

To gods-who-are and gods-to-be.

CONTENTS

Virtual Worlds as Virtual Worlds 5

1. REALITIES AND GODS 6

Definitions..7

History 20

Unrealities.. 35

The Central Conceit...46

2. CONTENT TO CODE 52

Dramatis Personae 54

Software..62

Engines..69

Content 75

Resets...84

Real Content...92

Replications 105

Reboots...120

Virtual Worlds as Realities 133

3. REALISING DREAMS 134

Making it Real 135

Origins of Reality....147
Origins of Sub-Realities....154
Realities Determined....157
Getting Personal....168
Self-Modifying Systems....183
Granularity....195
Simples....208
4. EXISTENCE....218
Ontology....219
Representing and Absenting....228
Copying....237
It's All Relative....242
Coincidence....248
Perspective....252
5. IMMERSION....257
Our Own Image....259
The Fiction....271
Realisticness....285
Physics and Causality....294
Realities as Realities....309
6. SAPIENCE....310
Mobiles....311
The Bots Among Us....327

Freeish Will....334
Theory of Mind....343
Speculation....356
Keeping Up Appearances....364
7. MORALITY....376
Changing People....378
Mortality....385
The Soul of an NPC....398
Being Moral Beings....414
Religious Places....438
Creation Destruction....449
Realities as Virtual Worlds....457
8. CONNECTIONS....458
Consequent Realities....460
Gods and Governments....469
9. POINT OF YOU....480
Motivation....482
A Lens....507
Answers and Unanswers....520
Well How About That....531
Reflections....538

Acknowledgements

This book would not be as it is without the input of:

My daughter, Jennifer Bartle, who told me bluntly that the entire text needed to be completely restructured.

Veteran game designer Eric Goldberg, who concurred with Jenny but was less blunt about it.

Computer Scientist Pat Parslow, who found multiple bugs both in my text and in my arguments.

Game designer Zoë O'Shea, who demanded more diagrams and got more diagrams.

Philosopher Hazel Speed, who survived the first draft all the way to the end.

My student Rachel Lowe, who suggested that I drop the words "to conduct" from the subtitle.

The dozens of people who pronounced on early ideas for the cover. Without their comments, you would never have even looked at this book.

My wife, Gail Bartle, who could have stopped me but didn't.

PROLOGUE

This is a book about philosophy, theology and computer games.

I myself am a computer game designer. In common with all other computer game designers, I am an expert in neither philosophy nor theology. That said, the number of philosophers and theologians who are able to claim they're experts in computer game design can be counted on the fingers of no hands, too. This lack of intersection isn't perhaps surprising, because what could one group possibly have to say that would be of any interest to the other?

Well, that's what I aim to set out in the coming chapters.

The kind of game I specialise in is the *virtual world*. Also known as Massively-Multiplayer Online Role-Playing Games (MMORPGs for short) (MMOs for shorter), virtual worlds are among the largest and most expensive games yet created. *World of Warcraft* is probably the best-known of them, but there are thousands of such games around, boasting hundreds of millions of players worldwide. They're basically pocket universes –

pocket *realities* – cut off from the world we live in precisely because their players *want* to be cut off from the world we live in every once in a while[1].

The folks who design and build virtual worlds are often referred to as the "gods" of those games, and for good reason: MMO designers entirely control the functionality of the realities they construct. That's exactly what makes a god a god: absolute control over a reality. Philosophers and theologians debate in depth the nature of the reality in which we live, but they've never had cause to design and implement a reality themselves. MMO designers have. They can profess *actual experience* of being gods, and of making those decisions that only gods typically have to make. This puts them in a position to help answer some of the questions that have been bothering students of Metaphysics since forever – and to bother them further with questions that they haven't yet considered. This is largely what I shall be attempting to do in this book.[2]

My approach will be broken down into four unequal parts.

---

[1] Where "every once in a while" typically means two to four hours a day. Some people watch TV in the evenings; some people play MMOs instead.

[2] I was going to add "Wish me luck.", but I suspect you're going to need it more yourself.

- *Part 1:* Virtual World as Virtual Worlds
  I'll start off by explaining what virtual worlds are and whence they came. This will have the additional effect of enabling you to judge whether I may know what I'm talking about or not.
- *Part 2:* Virtual Worlds as Reality
  Next, I shall consider some problems that philosophers have identified regarding the nature of our own reality and outline how these are tackled in virtual worlds – where solutions actually have to be implemented.
- *Part 3:* Realities as Realities
  After this, I'll change focus from looking at virtual worlds as purely physical (well, virtual) spaces, and instead concentrate on their inhabitants – the non-player characters with which[3] we populate them. Assuming that the field of Artificial Intelligence eventually gets its act together, we could end up with virtual worlds containing simulated beings as smart as or smarter than we are.
- *Part 4:* Realities as Virtual Worlds
  Finally, having thought about how we, as gods, feel we ought to treat the denizens of the realities we make, I'll shift the perspective up a level: if our own reality has one or more gods, is the way that they

---

[3] Or with whom.

apparently behave towards us the same as or different to how we propose to behave towards the beings of our own creations?

The narrative thread therefore goes something like this: explain what realities are; describe how we create realities; discuss what responsibilities those who create realities have; assess whether any creator of Reality lives up to these responsibilities.

The title of this book is *How to Be a God*. It's not *How to Become a God*, because in time anyone who wants to be a god (of a virtual world) will be able to become one. Neither is it *How to be a God*, with an uncapitalised *be*, because that would emphasise power over responsibility. It's *How to Be a God*, because it concerns how people should behave once they become gods (regardless of whether or not they *want* to become gods – this isn't a power fantasy).

As for what "should" means there, well that's for you to decide. I'm no demagogue: as I said, I know how to design realities, and I know some of what does and doesn't work with them, but I'd have to be even more arrogant than I am already to suppose that how *I* think things "should" be is indeed how they should be. That's a decision for the bulk of humanity to make; all I can do is point out that humanity does need to make it.

So yes, that means it's a decision for *you*.

Right, then! Shall we begin?

Part 1

Virtual Worlds as Virtual Worlds

Chapter 1

REALITIES AND GODS

I am a god.

It's great! I love being a god!

Three or four seconds ought to do it.

So, having despatched to social media those readers who are more interested in indignation than in explanation, I should now be left with those of you who thought "What does this mean?" rather than "What's the meaning of this?!".

Hi, folks!

Although of course there was an element of trolling to my opening remark, I do stand by it: I am indeed a god. Naturally, I don't mean that I'm a god of the physical reality in which we live, which is fortunate both for me (because that kind of attitude tends to spawn angry mobs of pitchfork-wielding villagers) and for you (because you needn't worry that I might strike you down with a thunderbolt). I *especially* don't mean that I'm the particular and popular god called God, although I do acknowledge that it would be cool if I were.

Nevertheless, I am a *bona fide*, literal-not-metaphorical god; this book is my shot at sharing with you some of what I've learned from being such over the past four decades, so as to help prepare you for the day when *you're* a god (if you aren't one already).

Definitions

Indulging me for a moment, under what definition of the word "god" could I possibly be one?

Well, I'm one under the very first definition of the term in the *Oxford English Dictionary*: A.I.1.a. It describes a god as being:

> *A superhuman person regarded as having power over nature and human fortunes; a deity (Oxford English Dictionary, third edition, 2014)*

OK, so it's not *immediately* apparent how the *OED*'s definition could apply to me. The word "nature" usually refers to the phenomena of our own physical reality, yet I've explicitly stated that I'm not a god of this reality (leastwise if I am, I haven't noticed). However, you don't *have* to bind the word "nature" only to the context of *our* reality: all realities have their own natures. Given a different reality, a god of that reality would therefore be someone who has power over that reality's nature.

That's the kind of god I am.

Sadly, merely asserting this statement isn't on its own enough to make it true. If I'm to persuade you that I really am a god, I need to explain: what I mean by a *reality*; what is meant by the *nature* of a reality; and what it means to have *power* over that nature. Only then can I point at a reality over the nature of which I have power and thereby justify my claim.

What's a reality, then?

Well we're all familiar with at least one reality: the objective, physical reality in which we are presumed to exist. The consensus is that this existed before each of us was born and will continue to exist after each of us has died. In this book, I shall be referring to it using the proper noun *Reality*, to distinguish it from all the other realities that I'll be discussing. Yes, there are other realities. For example, if you believe that when you die, your consciousness goes to another plane of existence, that plane of existence would qualify as a reality – just it's not Reality.

I'm calling these places "realities", rather than "worlds" or "planes" or "universes", because I want to keep them absolutely distinct both from Reality and from each other. A reality is a self-contained space of existence; I hope not to give the impression that one reality can be part of another reality (although, as we shall see in due course, one reality can be *implemented* in another reality).

A reality isn't a free-for-all space where anything goes: each one adheres to a set of physical rules[1] individual to it that define its characteristics. Collectively, these characteristics are a reality's *nature*. The rules themselves are its *physics*. Reality unquestionably has physics, because otherwise physicists would be out of a job, but other realities also have physics – it's what *makes* them realities. Note that I usually talk in terms of a reality's physics rather than its nature, as the latter derives from the former; it's like algebra, with physics being the equations and nature being the solutions.

The rules pertaining to realities in general don't have to be the same as the rules pertaining to Reality in particular. If, for example, you believe that some people who die go to a place of punishment where they are burned for all eternity in a lake of fire, well clearly the way that fire works there is different to how it works in Reality[2]; therefore, its physics must be different to Reality's.

The physics of a reality affects[3] its nature in three ways:

---

[1] Or laws; I'll be using the terms pretty well interchangeably. Besides, what makes a law a law is the subject of some disagreement even among philosophers (Carroll, 2016).
[2] Contact with it is still likely to hurt, though.
[3] The word here is "affects" rather than "affect" because the noun "physics" is singular. Well, it is except when referring to

1. It determines what the components of the reality are. Everything in Reality is either matter, energy or (quite possibly) both.
2. It manifests these components in an ongoing configuration[4]. The atoms in Reality that comprise your body[5] were doing other things a thousand years ago.
3. It determines how the current configuration is transformed to give a new configuration. In Reality, gravity encourages objects to move towards each other, meaning their positions tend to change dynamically.

The consequences of a reality's physics are the nature of that reality. Gods of a reality have power over its nature, so that's equivalent to saying they have power over its physics. What, then, in practice, can they do?

Well, a god of a reality has the ability to change any and all aspects of physics for that reality. If you were the god of a reality made up of bottles of soda water[6], you could decide to allow it also to contain ping-pong balls. If you were the god of a reality

---

several different physics, a situation brought on because "physicses" isn't a word.

[4] The configuration may well be of components that are entirely manifested as fuzzy balls of probabilities, but there's only one of it.

[5] Roughly 10^{26} of them for each kilogram you weigh.

[6] If this sentence refers to "soda water", that means the sponsorship deal didn't come through.

made up of sounds, you could spontaneously create (or, if your composition skills aren't great, recreate) a symphony within it. If you were the god of a reality with colours, you could make their saturation automatically cycle every Sunday.

The non-god inhabitants of a reality can perform none of these activities. They *can* make changes to the reality's configuration if its physics allows them to do so, but they can't change the physics itself[7]. For example, I am able to bring a sandwich into existence because the transformative rules of Reality's physics allow me to make gradual changes to the way that Reality is configured such that the result is a new configuration in which I have a sandwich. Only a god could make it a stegosaurus sandwich, though (notwithstanding future advances in paleobiology).

The physics of a reality encapsulates the laws of nature for that reality. Unlike regular laws that are enforced by police, they're self-enforcing; as such, they're unbreakable by non-gods. Laws of the land operate within the laws of nature, and *can* physically be broken (not that I'm advocating this). For example, it isn't a law of nature that you must drive on the left in Britain; you'd be risking your life and the lives of others if you drove on the right[8], but you could, physically, do it. You could

[7] "I can't change the laws of physics." (Scott, Stardate 1704.2).

[8] Except along Savoy Court in London, where it's the other way round.

not, however, drive both on the left in Britain and on the right in France simultaneously; this is because Reality's physics makes it incredibly difficult to be in two places at the same time. It's possible to conceive of a reality in which this kind of thing would be a breeze, but Reality is not such a reality. It does readily allow you to be in two times at the same place, though.

So to summarise: a reality is a self-contained space of existence that's defined, maintained and continually modified by its own physics. A god of a reality is an individual with control over the physics of that reality.

Notice how I seamlessly segued back to the topic of gods, there.

I should mention that I'm using the term "god" in a gender-inclusive fashion in this book – and not only for the purely pragmatic reason that I don't want to have to write "god or goddess" every single time. The thing is, some gods have no or multiple genders (the concept of gender fluidity is not a modern one), so even "god or goddess" doesn't always work; it might be "god and goddess" or indeed something else entirely[9].

I make this point because of an important convention that I have adopted throughout this text: *all Reality's gods exist.* I don't want to offend

---

[9] I could have used the more gender-nonspecific term *deity*, and almost did, but you wouldn't have bought this book if I'd called it *How to Be a Deity*.

anyone by suggesting that their deeply-held beliefs are wrong[10], so I treat all of them as if they were right. If I say that Apollo is both a healer and the bringer of disease and death, but you think that Apollo is just a pretend person that the Ancient Greeks made up, well it's for you to field complaints from angry Apollo-worshippers – I'm staying out of it. Thus, I'll talk about *accounts* rather than *myths*, even though in all cases more people think they're myths than think they're accounts.

This will undoubtedly come across as weird on occasion. I'll sometimes support my statements by referencing as fact what no human being alive regards as being anything other than fiction. For example, I might say that some gods can't control the physics of Reality themselves but do have a veto on other gods' actions; I could illustrate this by pointing to the Slavic gods Zorya (she's two gods in one) who prevent the doomsday hound Simargl from destroying the universe. It's irrelevant that this description carries the distinct whiff of having been invented: what's important is that my subsequent argument (about whether having power over a god makes you, too, effectively a god) hasn't come out of nowhere. It's not a straw man: it's based on an assertion that either was or is widely accepted as being true. It's

[10] Although I do realise that I may still cause offence by suggesting that all gods are of comparable validity.

therefore legitimate to ask whether, if Zorya can do what she can do, there is an equivalent situation in virtual worlds, and if not, why not[11]. Taking it further: if, in Reality, you are the boss of a virtual world's boss, can you yourself also be considered a god of that virtual world even if you never play it?[12]

I'll sometimes refer to accounts of gods' behaviour as *evidence*. This may also come across as weird. For example, consider the observation that in popular books and films featuring a "chosen one", the chosen one is often a teenager[13]. I might point out that there is scant evidence that gods choose teenagers as their chosen ones, the implication being that it's a bad idea. In support of my argument, I could mention that Abraham was aged 75 when called by God[14]. This would definitely count as admissible evidence for debating what, in theory and practice, gods *can* do, *don't* do and *do* do – regardless of whether you, personally, believe there's any truth to it or not.

Although my definition of the term *god*[15] is basically the same as the *OED*'s, it does differ in one important respect: I don't connect *being* a god

---

[11] I don't actually ask this question, but the short answer is that there can be such a situation but usually isn't.
[12] I do look at this briefly in Chapter 8.
[13] Not always: Neo from *The Matrix* is not a teenager, for example.
[14] It says so right there in Genesis 12:4.
[15] To wit: an individual with control over the physics of a reality.

with being *regarded* as a god. Using my definition, you can be a god without being regarded as a god, and you can be regarded as a god but not actually be a god. When it comes to practicalities, what's important is whether you *have* control over the physics of a reality, not whether someone else *thinks* you have it.

Of course, most established gods of Reality satisfy both these criteria anyway. Perhaps the best-known example of a god of Reality is the one known in English as God[16]. God is clearly regarded as a god (he's worshipped as one), but he can also back up the contention with action: stopping a burning bush from being consumed by its flames; turning a woman into a pillar of salt; bringing flood waters to destroy all flesh wherein is the breath of life (except that on a 300-cubit ark); the list of examples is long. With such physics-defying abilities at his command, God definitely qualifies as a god (of Reality).

Other candidates may be lacking, however. For example, you might regard one of Reality's rivers as having control over nature because it floods each year and deposits fertile silt that helps your crops grow. Now while helping crops grow does indeed look like a power over nature, it's one that a river only possesses as a consequence of its own

---

[16] The word "God" is a proper noun in this context, hence its capitalisation. To be fair to other gods, however, I won't be capitalising the associated pronouns, so "he" not "He".

place *in* nature. Sure, you may believe that your river has power over nature, but actually nature has power over your river. Your river therefore wouldn't qualify as a god by my definition, but it would by the *OED*'s.

Conversely, it's possible that someone does have control over Reality's nature, but isn't regarded as a god simply because they've kept a low profile. It's even conceivable that they don't *know* they're a god. I confess that one of the hopes I have for this book is that it will alert people who are gods of realities other than Reality to the fact that they *are* gods of those realities, thereby dissuading them from doing anything horrific by accident[17].

Adopting this tighter definition of what makes a god a god doesn't help me in my quest to show that I myself am a god[18], but the reason I nevertheless chose to go with it is that it removes opinion from the equation. If I'm to bring my practical experience of being a god to bear, I need a definition that's less to do with psychology and more to do with engineering. You can therefore assume that when I refer to a god of a reality, I mean that the individual in question actually *has*

---

[17] They can, of course, still do something horrific deliberately; not every god is a paragon of all that's good. Yes, Whiro-te-tipua, Māori god of darkness, I'm calling you out.

[18] Under the *OED*'s definition, I could show it merely by bribing people to regard me as having power over nature.

power over that reality's nature, irrespective of whether they're *regarded* as having power over it.

From what I've said so far, it would seem to follow that the gods of a reality must be equal in standing: either you have power over that reality's physics or you don't. It's true[19], too: a reality's gods are indeed all equal in terms of what they can do to that reality (if not necessarily to each other) – but this doesn't mean that they all have the same status. There's a qualitative difference between the Mongolian god Esege Malan (who created Reality) and his sons (who created the flying serpents, giant dogs, invisible spirits and multi-headed beasts that are manifested *within* Reality). I'll be discussing later why this distinction is important, but for the moment I'll simply note that some gods are creator gods and some aren't.

It's also worth pointing out at this stage that there are accounts in Reality of beings who, while they're not exactly gods, are nevertheless in possession of some pretty serious capabilities. It's clear that the gods of a reality can change its physics and that the ordinary people of that reality (who are bound by its physics) can't, but between the two are what are generally called *supernatural beings* (if they're entirely spiritual) or *demigods* (if they're not). These individuals remain bound by their reality's physics, but a *different* physics applies to them than applies to ordinary people.

[19] Trivially so if the reality has one or fewer gods.

For example, in Reality ordinary people are statistically very unlikely to be able to walk through walls (believe me, I've tried). Ghosts, however, can walk through walls whenever they feel like it. This makes ghosts supernatural beings: they can't control Reality's physics, but they do have a special, permeable-to-walls dispensation. Similarly, the Ancient Greek hunter Orion was a demigod who could walk on the sea, a talent he inherited from his father, Poseidon[20]. When it came to water-walking, different rules of physics applied to him than applied (or indeed apply) to ordinary folk. Apart from that one difference, though, the same rules applied to him as apply to you and me[21].

Wielding my definition ruthlessly, it turns out that some so-called gods are actually just very powerful demigods. Hermes, for example, the Ancient Greek messenger of the gods, can fly very quickly because of his winged sandals; if he had full command of the physics of Reality, he wouldn't need the sandals. Either he's not a god, or he has some explaining to do.

OK.

So if you're a physicist, a philosopher or a theologian, for some time now you'll have been ranting to anyone who will listen about what

---

[20] Do not attempt this unless your father is also Poseidon.

[21] You, too, could be killed by a giant scorpion and made into a constellation of stars.

you've been reading herein. It will seem to you that I'm presenting a naïve, unsophisticated view of How Things Are that has been thoroughly understood (or possibly misunderstood) for a long, long time.

That's fair enough. I'm neither a physicist, a philosopher nor a theologian, so entirely accept that people who have studied these topics for their entire academic careers are going to look upon my words with a mixture of amusement, impatience, pity and "he hasn't even read Hegel!".

What I *am* is a game designer.

This means *I* know some things that, regardless of how long and distinguished their careers may be, physicists, philosophers and theologians *don't* know. They may have described, analysed and speculated about realities, but I've *actually made realities*. What's non-obvious to those who use a product can be obvious to those who make it[22].

This book recounts lessons I have learned from doing such, and points out some of the inferences that this knowledge allows us to make regarding the implementation of Reality.

I suppose I need now to explain what kind of games I design and why these qualify as being realities.

---

[22] See the short section on paper manufacture in (Updegraff, 1916).

HISTORY

In October 1978, at the age of 18, I began my studies at the University of Essex, England. Just because I'm a game designer, that doesn't mean I can't be old.

Some time that month – our best guess is October 20th – an undergraduate in the year above me, Roy Trubshaw, began work on a computer game he called *MUD* (short for *Multi-User Dungeon*, but we only ever referred to it as *MUD*). I met Roy a few days later when I joined the university's Computer Society (Roy was its secretary). He showed me *MUD*, I described some games I'd designed myself, and we rapidly became friends.

I realise that this sounds as if I'm about to lay out my credentials so as to enable you to judge my level of expertise, and to a large extent that's true; however, what I say here will turn out in much later chapters to have further relevance, so it's not *entirely* an exercise in self-aggrandisement.

At this point, *MUD* was just a test of technology, but Roy had already started work on the fully-fledged game itself. He began with the physics (you can see where I'm going with this, right?) and had something playable by Christmas. He then added more of what nowadays is called *content*[23], along

---

[23] There's a detailed section on content in Chapter 2, if you're not sure what it is and don't mind skipping ahead to find out.

with additional physics[24] to widen the range of content that could be supported.

Although Roy undertook all the programming himself, he let several other interested students help with occasional acts of content-creation. I was one such student; we didn't add much, but we got a handle on what he was doing and discussed at length its possibilities.

Work on *MUD* proceeded apace, however it gradually became clear to Roy that its program was becoming somewhat unwieldy. He'd written it in an assembly language, which runs fast but is slow to program. Also, he'd implemented it such that the functionality to add content to the game sat within the game itself; it occupied so much memory that it significantly reduced the amount left available to store the content that it was meant to be being used to add.

After about a year, Roy snapped and began work on a third version of *MUD*. He separated the game's content-creation from its physics and rewrote everything from scratch in a systems programming language called BCPL[25].

This was an ambitious project, and by Easter 1980 Roy had only managed to rewrite about 25% of the game. Noticing that his finals were

---

[24] Like water, physics is uncountable. That's why this word isn't "physicses" either.

[25] As historians of computers will attest, BCPL was the language that the language that the language C was based on was based on.

impending, he passed the baton to me. Because I was (and still am) younger than Roy, I had another year before my own finals would loom, during which I duly completed the remaining 75%.

Unlike Roy, however, I didn't leave Essex University when I graduated. I was the only student in my cohort to achieve first-class honours[26], and because of this won a grant to do a PhD (in Artificial Intelligence, for reasons I'll touch on later).

Over the next few years, I kept adding bits and bobs to what (notwithstanding its actually being the third version of *MUD*) came to be known as *MUD1*. Inevitably, though, I too finally hit my frustration limit, and in 1985 rewrote it all yet again as *MUD2*. We'll stick with calling it just *MUD* for now, though.

OK, so this is all very[27] interesting, but why am I telling you about a game from the dawn of time that today is little more than a museum piece? It's pretty obvious I'm going to claim that *MUD* is a reality and that I, as one of its designers, am therefore a god of it, so why not just cut to the chase? Why the history lesson?

Well, I *shall* soon be explaining how *MUD* qualifies as a reality, yes, but I'm going to keep

[26] They were much less common back then. Some years, nobody got one. Nowadays, around a quarter of students in the same department graduate with a first. Modern teaching methods are just so much better than they were in the 1970s.
[27] For certain charitable definitions of the word "very".

going with the history for just a little longer so that I don't have to re-undertake the whole process again half a book from now. *MUD*'s history, you see, is its origin myth.

These days, around half of British 18-year-olds go to university. Back in the 1970s, it was more like one in seven. The vast majority were from middle-class backgrounds and studied History, or English, or Medicine, or Economics, or (if they weren't especially bright) Sociology. Few middle-class parents wanted their children to be engineers, because engineers mend broken railway locomotives, climb up telegraph poles and (horrors!) consort with mathematicians.

The country did *need* engineers, though; in particular, because these new-fangled "computers" looked as if they might one day be beneficial, it needed software engineers. So it was that exceptionally-clever working-class children with sufficient flair to pass their exams could find places at university on courses that involved Computer Science.

Flair *was* required, too, because most of us had completely the wrong impression of how examinations were marked. Surely, if asked to calculate the integral between 0 and $\pi/2$ of x cos(x) with respect to x, you'd be awarded more marks for writing simply $\pi/2$ -1 than for showing a step-by-step solution? You'd managed to work it all out in your head – that *had* to be worth more marks! It didn't occur to us that if there were five marks for a question, you could nevertheless obtain four for getting it wrong and only one for getting it right. With flair, you'd at least get that one mark, though, and so could pass overall (albeit with an indifferent grade); without flair, you'd get nothing.

Those of us who found ourselves studying Computer Science at Essex University were therefore often pretty smart cookies, either from underprivileged backgrounds or from more privileged backgrounds in defiance of our parents. Either way, we were social outcasts. All other students at the university looked down on us. We were the lowest of the low[28].

In all fairness, we *were* a little different. To study Computer Science in its early days required a certain mindset. Those who were drawn to the subject needed to have a systems-oriented way of thinking, coupled with natural creativity – an unusual combination[29]. The requirements were the same in Computer Science departments across the globe: they were populated by people who saw the enormous potential afforded by computers to change the world for the better and who found joy simply from playing with them. They didn't want

---

[28] A situation which prevailed until the Psychology department was founded in 1991.

[29] This remains the case for all designers of *MUD*-like games. Indeed, Mike Sellers (who was one of the designers of the early graphical world *Meridian* 59) persuasively advocates using a systems-thinking approach for game design in general (Sellers, 2018).

to be told what to do; they wanted to be shown how to use tools, which they could then employ however they liked in ways that no-one else had yet imagined.

In *Dungeons & Dragons* alignment terms, we were Chaotic Good[30].

This collective viewpoint came to be known as *hacker culture*, but it wasn't a culture in the sense that when you arrived at university it was inculcated in you by those already there. Rather, it was that Computer Science selected for people with a particular world view, who upon arrival discovered that everyone else doing Computer Science had that same world view. They shared notions of freedom, of fairness, of the limitless possibilities of computers – all of which informed the creation by Roy and I of *MUD*.

The thing is, we didn't *like* being bottom of the pile. We didn't like poverty. We didn't like being judged by how we dressed[31] or by our accents, as if we were uneducated, unsophisticated yokels. We didn't see ourselves as losers *at all*. We railed against it! We particularly disliked the smug, paternalistic, patronising attitude of middle-class students who paid lip service to equality of opportunity but who fully expected to go on to jobs

---

[30] Chaos is officially opposed by Law, but it always seemed to me that Law only existed because of Evil. If everyone was Good, we wouldn't need Law.

[31] In general, shabbily, which was nevertheless quite smart by 1970s undergraduate standards.

in which they would boss people like us around for four times our salary. We didn't like being trapped by the way we looked, by the way we sounded, by whatever particular hand of gender, sexuality, ethnicity and physical form Reality had dealt us. We wanted to be judged by our actions and by our character, not by other people's uninformed interpretations of how we were – or worse, of how we must be. The world of 1970s Britain was not a pleasant place for people like us. Frankly, it sucked.

We were, therefore, as is so often the case when it comes to instigating social change, Angry Young Men. We'd have said Angry Young People ourselves, but as Roy and I are indeed both male, let's go with Men.

When Roy started work on *MUD*, it was because a fun piece of operating system functionality had provoked in him a visionary idea. As he continued, he – and those of us he discussed it with – soon concluded that what he was writing was not only a game, but something else. It was our way out; or, if not ours, then a way out for people like us in the future.

MUD, you see was unlike any computer game yet invented. It was its own, separate-from-Reality reality, what would today be called a *virtual world*. Virtual worlds are the kind of computer game that I design.

Annoyingly, the term *is* "virtual world" rather than "virtual reality". Virtual reality is a technology that presents physically-immersive interfaces to computer-maintained environments[32], whereas virtual worlds comprise one particular sub-class of such environments. Given how much I talk about realities in this book, I really wish I *could* call them virtual realities instead of virtual worlds, but the VR people called dibs on the name first. Whatever, I digress....

We didn't know at the time that there weren't hundreds of games just like *MUD* running in universities elsewhere, but we didn't particularly care. We knew what *we* had, and what *we* could do with it.

When you ran *MUD* for the first time, it would ask you by what name it should call you and (for reasons of English-language pronoun usage) what sex you wished to be. It would then drop you into its world, to join everyone else who happened to be playing at that moment. You could talk to them, explore with them, work together with them, attack them, or of course simply ignore them – all in a strange, fantastical setting in which the older something looked, the more powerful and dangerous it was likely to be.

Because who you were in the game world both was and wasn't who you were in the world of objective reality (that is, Reality), you were able to experiment with your identity. You could cast off whatever social and psychological chains were holding you in place and be someone else. More to

---

[32] In the terms of this book, then, it would be "virtual Reality".

the point, through doing this you were freed to become and to be *yourself*.

All of this was quite deliberate. I told you I was a game designer, and *MUD* was very much designed. Never think that nerdy, teenaged computer programmers only know and care about computer programming (or teenagers) (or nerds). Just because *you* are acquainted with plenty of well-read, rounded individuals who are technologically illiterate, that doesn't mean that the technologically literate can't be well-read, rounded individuals. All you're doing by treating them as if they're culturally-unaware, one-dimensional dweebs is giving them an axe to grind. Roy and I obligingly ground our axe.

MUD was[33] a program that its players connected to and played concurrently. That made it *multi-user* (hence the first two letters of its name, although the modern preference with regard to games is *multi-player* or *multiplayer*). There were plenty of other multi-player games around at the same time, of course – *Monopoly* is a multi-player game, as are team sports – but *MUD* differed in several important respects. Unlike anything that had come before it, it simultaneously satisfied all the following criteria (which double as a definition of the term *virtual world*):

---

[33] Well, as with many ancient virtual worlds that haven't yet closed, perhaps still more "is" than "was".

- The game world operated by using an underlying automated rule set – its *physics*.
- Each player was represented by an individual "in" the game world – their *character*.
- Interaction with said world took place in *real time*.
- The world was *shared* with other players.
- The world didn't end when you yourself stopped playing – it was *persistent*.

Actually, there *was* something like *MUD* that had come before it: Reality. Indeed, of the properties listed above, all but the first were bounded by Reality. Even so, *MUD* was nevertheless a self-contained space of existence that was defined, maintained and continually modified by its own physics; in other words, *MUD* was also a reality.

Because that first property – *MUD*'s physics – was not dependent on Reality, it was the only one over which the game's programmers (Roy and I) had full control. We couldn't do much about the other criteria (not if we wanted people from Reality to play our game), but we could – and did – both formulate and change *MUD*'s physics.

That was enough to make us the gods of the reality that was *MUD*.

This is why I can honestly say that I'm a god. I've been a god of *MUD* since 1978.

So now you know the rather unintuitive rationale behind the creation of *MUD*. It was written as a response to the British class system. We really, *really* didn't like how the world worked, so we did something about it: we wrote our *own* world.

Bear this in mind should you manage to stagger to Chapter 9, where I discuss why gods commonly create realities.

To be honest, when people ask me what our discussions about *MUD*'s design were like, the answer is a little disappointing. We didn't have long, philosophical conversations that went on deep into the night. Our chats were mainly ideas-oriented. There were no grandiose debates about what we were trying to achieve – or even why we were trying to achieve it. Much of our resentment about our lot in life was unspoken. See, when someone thinks the same way that you do, you don't *need* to know why they think what they think; there's little to deliberate. You know already that they have similar goals to you; your conversations therefore concern suggestions regarding how to achieve those goals – they don't concern what those goals should be.

Roy started constructing *MUD* in earnest for the same reason I joined him constructing *MUD*: to make our world better by making a better world.

So, we're now just about done with the history of *MUD* – but we're not *quite* done with the history of virtual worlds in general. It remains for me to outline how we got from where we were to where we are today. This is because the second half of the book is mainly about certain aspects of where we're going.

Now I mentioned earlier that Roy and I didn't know that what we were creating was the first example of a new kind of game. I later discovered that it was, although feel free to disagree if you have a broader definition of what a virtual world is than the criteria-based, bullet-list one I provided just now.

As it happens, the concept of a virtual world was invented independently multiple times. Just because *MUD* was first, that doesn't mean all subsequent virtual worlds owe anything to it. The full list of original, invented-from-nothing virtual worlds that I know of is:

- *MUD* in 1978 by Roy Trubshaw and Richard Bartle (wave).
- *Sceptre of Goth* in 1978 by Alan Klietz.
- *Avatar* in 1979 by Bruce Maggs, Andrew Shapira and David Sides.
- *Island of Kesmai* in 1981 by Kelton Flinn and John Taylor.
- *Habitat* in 1985 by Randy Farmer and Chip Morningstar.
- *Monster* in 1989 by Rich Skrenta.

That said, almost all modern virtual worlds *do* ultimately descend from *MUD*. There's a reason for this.

Roy and I wrote *MUD* because we wanted to give people the freedom to *be*. We didn't write it to make money. When anyone asked me for the source code, then so long as I could be persuaded that they weren't merely players looking for an edge over other players, I sent them a copy. We *encouraged* people to write new virtual worlds, either by using the *MUD* engine itself or by writing their own.

Several people did write their own games based on *MUD*. Some such games were worse, some were better; most were at least different. People played these games; inspired, several more wrote their own. So it continued. New ideas were tried out, discarded, amended, incorporated, refined; in short, new virtual worlds evolved from older ones. The class of such games as a whole came to be known as MUDs; this is why *MUD* itself was later referred to as *MUD1* – to make it distinct from the genre that now bore its name.

The number of MUDs grew and grew, helped by the free availability of newly-written, customisable source code that you could adapt to your own requirements. There were so many of them that in March, 1991, MUDs accounted for 11% of all transatlantic Internet traffic (Wakeman, et al., 1991).

These MUDs were primarily text-based; there wasn't enough bandwidth for graphics back then[34]. This in part explains why those early games with a graphical element to them – *Avatar*, *Habitat* and to some extent *Island of Kesmai* – didn't spread to the Internet at large from their host systems. The text-only *Sceptre of Goth* wouldn't have done so either, but its source code was ripped off by a disgruntled programmer, prompting the franchising of the game (Alberti, 2010). As a result, a visible thread of *SoG* does run through the otherwise *MUD*-woven fabric of virtual worlds from the past to the present day.

We always knew that there would be 3D graphical MUDs, just as today we know there'll be virtual reality equivalents once the technology is up to it[35]. It took longer than we expected, but in the 1990s commercial game developers finally did decide to try making graphical MUDs for entertainment and profit. Naturally, they sought to employ people with existing expertise in the area, and through sheer force of statistics almost all of these designers and developers turned out to have a *MUD* heritage (outnumbering as they did those of other heritages hundreds to one).

---

[34] Besides, we started off using teletypes. Graphics don't go well with what are essentially typewriters that write slower than you can type.

[35] Traditionally, the time when the tech will indeed be up to it is always "ten years from now", or five years for optimists.

The term "graphical MUD" didn't stick. Today, the virtual worlds these pioneers created are known as Massively-Multiplayer Online Role-Playing Games (or *MMORPGs*, although the abbreviated acronym *MMOs* is usually preferred[36]). The genre went on to become wildly popular and incredibly lucrative. *World of Warcraft*, which launched in 2004, still has more players than most countries have population, and continues to rake in billions of dollars a year. It's not the only virtual world that does that, either – it's just the one that's best-known.

Almost all modern MMOs therefore have an ancestry that tracks back to a single progenitor. That progenitor is *MUD*.

This is why I'm writing this book and you're not[37].

In Britain, if you develop an idea that makes you billions of dollars, you get a seat in the House of Lords. If you develop an idea that makes other people billions and billions of dollars every year for decades, you get to be an Honorary Professor of Computer Game Design at a provincial university. Now I realise that this perhaps sounds rather bitter, but it's not: Roy and I didn't do what we did for personal gain; we wanted the idea of virtual

---

[36] It turns out that some people find unpronounceable six-letter acronyms cumbersome to use.

[37] Unless you're Roy Trubshaw (hi, Roy!), in which case the reason is that I need the money more than you do.

worlds to spread far and wide, and to change people's lives for the better. If we hadn't wanted this, we wouldn't have written *MUD* in the first place[38].

We achieved our goal, too, although the pace of change is frustratingly slow. There's so much *more* that could have been done by now! Nevertheless, I'm relatively content. I don't see visiting a virtual world as a *retreat* from Reality; I see it as movement to an *improved* reality[39]. At the very least, virtual worlds give Reality some competition.

So now you know the following: what I mean by a reality; how I define what a god of a reality is; why I myself am such a god; what drove me to create a reality; and why it is I feel qualified to write about creating realities.

I may, however, be wrong.

Unrealities

I've argued quite strongly that the virtual worlds we create are realities in the same sense that Reality is a reality. However, those of us who develop virtual worlds do not speak with one voice

---

[38] Don't get me wrong, though: I still think that the British establishment treats game development disgracefully in comparison to other creative industries.
[39] Gratifyingly, I'm not alone in this view (Kania, 2017).

on the subject; in fact, there are long-standing differences of opinion among us as to whether virtual worlds are indeed separate from Reality, or whether they're simply part of or an adjunct to it.

Three main positions are argued. The most idealistic one is what might be called *optimistic-exclusive*. This says that virtual worlds are separate from Reality (that is, exclusive) and that they can for the most part fend off attempts to bring Reality into them (that is, optimistic). Because of the need to visualise virtual worlds in advance of their being made, most designers tend to think this way.

The second position is *pessimistic-exclusive*. This says that although virtual worlds are in theory separate from Reality, in practice too much Reality is brought into them for the proposition reliably to hold except in short bursts. This is the popular view among most of the non-designers who work on building virtual worlds; they're sustained by a vision of hope, but know in their hearts that it won't survive contact with the players.

The third position is *inclusive*. This simply says that virtual worlds are part of Reality, and denies that they can ever be independent realities themselves. Yes, they are venues for play, and as such afford their players a release from quotidian life; nevertheless, they themselves exist firmly in Reality. This is the predominant view of those who design or create virtual worlds for other people to exercise their own creativity within.

The disagreement, then, is not over whether virtual worlds can be treated as if they were realities[40]. Rather, it's over whether the reality they're being treated as collapses to Reality. In this book, I shall be taking the optimistic-exclusive position: that it doesn't actually matter how much Reality impinges on a virtual world, it always remains a reality in its own right. To explain why, let's consider the two other competing views.

For game worlds, such as all MMOs and most text MUDs, the players readily take on board the idea that they're visiting a separate reality. When people play *World of Warcraft*, *Final Fantasy XIV* or *Black Desert Online*, they know intellectually that they are merely interpreting pixels on a screen, just as you know that this book is merely marks on a page. It takes a minor act of will to accept that the pixels represent a view from within a virtual world, but the players are happy to comply because of what they gain from it.

What if they don't perform that minor act of will?

Well in social worlds, such as *Second Life* and *Sansar*, that's largely what happens. Although players *can* still treat the virtual world as a reality if they care to, there's no incentive for them to do this. Social worlds aren't billed as being fictional,

---

[40] Unsurprisingly, because the word "virtual" is being used in the very sense of "that which isn't, having the form or effect of that which is" (Bartle, 2003).

they're billed as being venues populated by interesting people where you can do interesting things. A security guard interprets the images on a CCTV screen as showing a piece of Reality, and the players of a social world typically interpret the images they see on their own computer screens in much the same way. To them, the virtual world is just a visualisation of more Reality.

This is why the designers of social worlds tend to think of them as adjuncts to Reality rather than as separate realities in their own right – it can be a genuinely more useful perspective for them[41].

Routinely thinking of a virtual world as being part of Reality doesn't mean it *is* part of Reality, though. The fact that virtual worlds are *not* part of Reality is substantiated by one, simple observation: they have different physics.

If you advocate the inclusive argument, then, you're abstracting away the differences in physics because they're not important to you. Nevertheless, while it might be useful in some contexts to think of your virtual world as if it were part of Reality, objectively it isn't.

If the inclusive argument concerns absorbing the virtual into the real, the pessimistic-exclusive

---

[41] Many academics take this point of view, too, for example (Hammer, 2005). In some cases, this may be because much of the early, foundational research on virtual worlds all but entirely concerned social worlds (most notably, *LambdaMOO*).

argument concerns absorbing the real into the virtual.

Even if we restrict ourselves to game worlds, a great deal of Reality does ooze into them. Indeed, some of the people who play do so precisely because they wish to exploit this potential. Examples include: social scientists studying those who play virtual worlds; journalists looking to interview players for a story; gold farmers, systematically collecting in-game currency to sell to players for you-can-buy-food-with-it currency; and designers of other virtual worlds, checking out how this particular virtual world hangs together.

Such players are in a minority, but the pessimistic-exclusive argument is that their activities have disproportionate weight. If every time you try to will yourself into the virtual world there's someone there talking about the current sorry state of either politics, their favourite sports team or their love life, you're repeatedly snapped back to Reality. It's like the virtual world is coffee and Reality is water: how many drops of water can you add and still call it coffee?[42]

The claim being made here is that so much Reality is being dumped in virtual worlds that for all intents and purposes they're pretty well part of Reality regardless of how wonderfully-independent

---

[42] Homeopathy answer: all of them, whereupon it will cure you of all the ailments that resemble the effects of undiluted coffee.

their physics is. Having myself experienced bombardments of offers to buy *World of Warcraft* gold for United States dollars, I can well see how it might look that way to players; that said, how it looks to players isn't actually relevant here. Players' views are subjective; my definition consciously removes subjectivity. Although it's legitimate to talk about whether intrusions from one reality can change the character of another reality[43], it doesn't alter the fact that they're both realities.

A simple way to demonstrate the point is to deny all players access to the MMO that they've supposedly transformed into a near-as-makes-no-difference simulacrum of Reality. OK, so the immediate effect might be that the virtual world loses all financial viability, but be that as it may, there won't remain one iota of Reality in it; it's therefore clear that whatever the player experience might indicate, the virtual world's fundamental nature is not that of Reality. Players aren't gods: they can't make the changes to the physics of a virtual world that would be necessary to incorporate it into Reality[44]. Transient changes to how a reality is interpreted don't stop it from being a reality.

---

[43] I do this indirectly in later chapters.

[44] For example, by giving the non-player characters in a virtual world control of killer robots in Reality.

Having successfully seen off the main objections against it, the optimistic-exclusive argument looks to be sitting pretty. It's not, however: unfortunately, elements of the pessimistic-exclusive argument can be employed to amplify the inclusive argument in a powerful way. The basic line of attack, which draws on theories both from Game Studies and from Philosophy, suggests that virtual worlds aren't realities because Reality isn't one either. Realities are just constructions of the mind.

Here's how the argument goes.

So, although there will often be people who are playing an MMO for ulterior reasons, those who are playing it straight nevertheless usually make up the vast majority of its player base. When designers talk about the "players" of such games, these are the people they generally mean. The reason such players play is that doing so gives them something they want; that something (despite the best endeavours of academics to label it as *engagement*), they call *fun*[45]. To achieve this, however, requires a certain outlook.

For any game, players must adopt what's called a *lusory attitude* (Suits, 1978), which is the acceptance of the game's rules and fiction as being

---

[45] At a conference in Germany, I once asked what the German word for "fun" was, genuinely wishing to know. I was told there wasn't one – much to the pained amusement of the (almost wholly German) audience.

limiting and true, even though the players know they're contrived. In *Chess*, for example, you could, on your first move, take your opponent's king and declare yourself to be the winner. That you don't, and play by the rules instead, is due to your adoption of a lusory attitude. The rules are there to enable the conditions under which you'll find playing the game fun; *Chess* wouldn't be much fun if players didn't play by the rules[46]. When all players in a game have a lusory attitude, it's called a *magic circle*[47] (usually "the" magic circle in the abstract).

The magic circle is porous, though. People bring things into the game from Reality (and every so often, the other way around). The language you speak in a virtual world is a language from Reality. You yourself are real, come to that; only the character you play is virtual. Players can choose to ignore these intrusions up to a point, but Reality can always break in and end proceedings. "It's all

---

[46] Indeed, it's debatable whether the resulting activity could still be referred to as *Chess*.

[47] The origin of the term is a book by Dutch historian Johan Huizinga (Huizinga, trans. 1949), but it appears only as an element in a list of examples. It was chosen from this list as a synecdoche for the overall concept by US game designers Katie Salen and Eric Zimmerman (Salen & Zimmerman, 2003), who in so doing popularised it.

fun and games until someone loses an eye. Then, it's just fun."[48].

So far, the argument is pure pessimistic-exclusive. This is the point at which it changes tack.

Suppose the reason the magic circle is porous is that virtual worlds are indeed part of Reality. For the purposes of play, the players wishfully maintain the idea that they're separate realities, but in truth (as can be seen by what happens when the bubble of the magic circle is popped) they're just kidding themselves. If you remove the players, you don't have a reality: all you have is a sophisticated computer program.

This suggestion – that virtual worlds live all in the imagination – is a seductive one. I would nevertheless argue that the word "reality" does remain appropriate here. Yes, all you have may well be a sophisticated computer program – but it's still a reality. It may not be a reality for us, but it's one for those characters we create to inhabit it.

That's not the end of the attack, though.

What these examples have in common is the notion that for you, a reality is a conceived space that your consciousness can inhabit. Even my engineering-oriented line of argument accepts this as the truth; where it differs from the more

[48] I believe this is a quote from Wednesday Addams, but all my attempts to find confirmation have to date been frustrated.

human-oriented line of argument is that mine doesn't treat the statement as a definition of what a reality is, whereas the other one does.

If we nevertheless accept for the moment the "virtual worlds live all in the imagination" argument, it follows that there's a single *paramount reality* (Schütz, 1945) – what I'm calling Reality[49] – and then many strata of other realities depending on where people are currently projecting their thoughts. "The world of science" would be a reality in this light – as would "the world of athletics", "the world of philately", "the world of Robin Hood" and so on. This way of couching what realities are has quite some philosophical heft to it, too, as we shall see later.

So, that's the combined argument: virtual worlds aren't separate from Reality because your mind constructs and interprets them the same way it does Reality. If they're separate realities then so's Leicester.

To be honest, I do have some sympathy with this approach, because it's satisfyingly reductionist: all you really know is *that* you know; everything else is speculation[50]. When it comes down to it, though, I side with objectivity over subjectivity. It's not *believing* that something is real

---

[49] Tolkien called it the *primary world* (Tolkien, 1964), which I'll bring up again in due course.

[50] This is Descartes' "I think, therefore I am", only less well put. I'll bring this up again in due course, too.

that makes it objectively real[51]; it's the possession of certain *physical properties* that makes it objectively real.

We could both work in "the world of high finance" and yet have completely different ideas regarding what is and isn't part of it; a virtual world, on the other hand, is necessarily the same for both of us. Likewise, "the world of 1980s pop music" fades into and out of existence depending on how many people are talking or thinking about it; virtual worlds continue to exist independently of whether anyone is playing them or not.

The way to decide if a candidate reality is part of or separate from Reality centres on how you access it from Reality.

If, to access a reality, you have to attach to an entity operating under a different set of physical rules to that of Reality, how can you legitimately claim that this reality is Reality? It *must* be separate from it. If you don't have to access it this way, how can you legitimately claim it is anything other than Reality? It *must* be part of it.

So it is that for the remainder of this book I shall be referring to realities as if they were physical spaces[52] rather than perceived spaces – albeit physical spaces which may be contingent on

---

[51] Actually, it is for some gods – it's how Ptah created Reality, for example. Yes, you guessed right: I'll also bring this up again in due course.

[52] Which is to say *places*. I briefly discuss the difference in Chapter 7.

the existence of other physical spaces to support their own existence. *MUD* qualifies as a reality, but the hardware that runs it is in Reality.

That said, there is a way to reconcile these two definitions of a reality (that is, as physical or as perceived spaces); I briefly alluded to this earlier. The key is that you define a space to be a reality if it is (or at least in principle could be) a paramount reality for an individual native to it. It doesn't matter whether we, as visitors to a space, think of it as a reality or not: it's what that space's programmed-in characters think (or would think, if they had the smarts) that make it a reality.

Virtual worlds, then, are examples of realities.

THe CenTraL ConCeIT

Thank you for your patience.

I've spent most of this chapter blithely touching on topics that are relevant to what I want to say, but aren't themselves what I want to say. I had to present them in a certain order, so that I didn't use any technical terms before I explained them. The result is rather more impressionistic than it is expressionistic; I hint at where I want to go, but I veer off in other directions, too. Really, you probably could do with a signpost.

So, here's the signpost. It has two parts: where we've been and where we're going.

First, where we've been.

Several decades ago, I co-wrote the progenitor of a class of computer games known variously as MUDs, MMORPGs and MMOs, which here I've been calling "virtual worlds". These worlds share enough properties with the world we live in, which I've been calling "Reality", that it's worth investigating whether conjectures about the former could apply to the latter. I'm calling the kind of thing that virtual worlds and Reality are "realities", because I need an umbrella term and this one fits (at least from the perspective of someone who has made one). I'm calling the people who design realities the "gods" of those realities, which is indeed what the players of MUDs called them until the worlds became so large that said gods stopped making appearances.

Second, where we're going.

Although not all realities are examples of virtual worlds, virtual worlds are all necessarily examples of realities. If you're a god of a virtual world, you're a god of a reality; you can speak with some authority about what it means to be a god of such a reality. Sure, that doesn't mean you know anything much about being a god of *other* kinds of reality, but it does mean you're better qualified to talk about the practicalities of being a god than are people who have never been one at all[53].

I know what decisions those who create realities have to make. I know why realities are created, how they are designed and who gets to visit them. I also have questions regarding how to treat the population of characters that we install in them.

The central conceit of this book is that if I know these things about creating realities, that's practical advice which may be useful for anyone pondering the creation of Reality.

I am an academic[54], but (despite its having a references section) this isn't an academic book. There have been thousands of works written about gods, belief systems, religions and multiple worlds, and the people who have studied them know more about the subject than I possibly ever could. There's no shortage of research papers even on the specific sub-topic of religion in computer games, with special issues of journals devoted to it[55]. My aim isn't, therefore, to support some hypotheses and to debunk others; how could it be, when I have only a superficial understanding of them at best?

No, my aim with this book is to say how things are *in practice* when it comes to creating realities.

---

[53] Post-modernism is all well and good for understanding a reality, but it's next to useless for creating one.

[54] You can tell by the presence of all these footnotes, right?

[55] Such as (Heidbrink & Knoll, 2014).

Philosophers and theologians can do what they will with this information, and that's fine; the only thing they can't do is dismiss it. It may be mainly opinion, but it's well-founded opinion.

Suppose a professional historian has spent the bulk of their adult life to date studying, say, the way that folk tales were adapted for different audiences in 1400s Ireland. If a monastic archive was found to contain an old text, written by an Irish bard, explaining exactly how tellings and retellings of ancient stories were achieved from the perspective of a practitioner, the historian would be somewhat remiss not to treat this as potentially useful information.

Likewise, if you're a career theologian (or even if you merely have an interest in the origins of Reality), you should at least take some note of what a practitioner of reality-creation says. Hey, if the practitioner is speaking nonsense, maybe you can explain exactly *why* it's nonsense so they can update their knowledge accordingly? I for one would certainly be interested if a theoretician were able to tell me how to design better virtual worlds, because the end result would be something I passionately want: better virtual worlds.

Creating virtual worlds is not science. It's art expressed as engineering. Whether your culture roots its philosophy in reason (Ancient Greece), karma (Ancient India), harmony (Ancient China), emotion (Ancient Africa) or anything else may speak to the art, but the engineering is deaf to it. Engineering and science are related, however.

Scientists decide what to research by alternating between theory and practice. They make an observation about the world that they can't explain ("Why is there gravity?") then they develop hypotheses to come up with answers ("Maybe there's a fundamental particle that carries it"). They design experiments to test these ideas ("Let's smash billions of large hadrons together underneath the France/Switzerland border") and either these produce evidence in support of the hypotheses ("Yay, Higgs bosons!") or they don't (so one of "I guess we were wrong" or "We're going to need a bigger collider...").

There's an old joke in academic circles concerning which university department is the least expensive to run. A mathematician claims that it's Mathematics, because mathematicians need so few resources: just a notepad, a pen and a waste-paper basket. A theologian counters that no, it's Theology, because theologians don't need the waste-paper basket.

What this joke is saying is that theologians are all theory and no practice. Unlike mathematicians, they can make statements but they can't prove them; unlike scientists, they can construct hypotheses but they can't test them.

Well, with virtual worlds we *can* now at least test some of these hypotheses: we have the ability to look at, to reason about and to experiment on objective realities in ways that are simply not possible with Reality. What previously has been a matter of faith can now become a matter of, if not necessarily fact, at least factually-informed faith.

What if Reality is to its sub-realities (such as MMOs) as some super-reality is to Reality?[56]

That's what this book is ultimately about: using what we know about reality-creation to inform what we don't know about Reality-creation.

---

[56] As Charles Babbage rather ponderously put it: "The notions we acquire of contrivance and design arise from comparing our observations on the works of other beings with the intentions of which we are conscious in our own undertakings." (Babbage, 1838).

Chapter 2

CONTENT TO CODE

If I'm to address questions regarding how Reality *might* work by making reference to how virtual worlds *do* work, I should perhaps begin by devoting some time explaining the latter, rather than by simply diving right in.

As a designer, I'm mainly interested in how virtual worlds are designed. That's only part of the story, though. Ideas and plans don't make programs: someone actually has to implement them.

In software engineering terms, design takes place during the *pre-production* phase of development. The process of turning a design document[1] into an executable program takes place during the *production* phase of development. There are two other phases: *roll-out*, in which the product

[1] Indulge me, please, programmers. I don't want to have to alarm non-programmers with the full truth of how incomplete, inconsistent and at times incomprehensible these collections of badly-written specifications really are.

is released; and *operation*, in which it is run, maintained and operated as a service. For virtual worlds, there's a further, final stage known as *sunset*, during which the service is closed down in an orderly manner (usually because it has too few players to break even).

I'll be touching on all these phases in this book[2], but I'm going to begin with production because that's where the machinery of virtual worlds is brought into being.

The designer of a virtual world can't simply produce their design and expect to see it materialise exactly as written: there are limitations on what it's possible to program, and the design as envisaged could well have flaws[3]. Also, the process of manufacturing a virtual world will itself affect the design: there will inevitably be aspects that the designer hasn't considered which will only come to light when the program intended to match the design is being written; there will also be other aspects that the designer has considered but which the programming exercise exposes as impractical. The general rule is that design dictates 80% of the final product and implementation dictates the other 20%. The trouble is, you don't know at the

---

[2] In the case of pre-production, probably more like thumping than touching.

[3] I may be kicked from the designers' union for suggesting this, but here goes: we aren't *entirely* perfect.

outset which 80% of the design is the part that's fine and which 20% is the part that isn't.

This is the fault line where reality design and program design collide: it restricts what you want to what you can have. In line with the aims of this book, it will in due time present us with new ways to think about what both might mean for Reality. You're safe from that for the moment, though.

All this implies that I'm first going to have to talk a bit about the construction of virtual worlds if much of what follows is to make sense[4].

Dramatis Personae

Let's begin by looking at the various people involved in the creation and playing of virtual worlds.

The vast bulk of humanity has never had any contact with a virtual world (yet). For those of us who have, there's a relationship between who we are in Reality and who we are in any given virtual world. The principals are:

- Designers.
- Developers (programmers and artists).
- Customer support representatives.
- Players.

---

[4] Note how I carefully avoided saying that it *will* make sense.

- (Also another category that isn't exactly ... oh, wait and see.)

Designers are the people who plan out what a virtual world will be like. As such, they are the gods of these realities.

Modern MMOs are rarely designed by just one person, though: there's a *design team.* Team members specialise in particular systems (such as the game's economy) or particular spaces (such as a specific zone of the game world); they all qualify as gods, but most design in accordance with the design of someone else. This person, who has full overall creative control, is called the *lead designer* (or, for very large projects, the *game director*).

The lead designer also operates within constraints, any of which could quite possibly change during the production phase (so entailing a redesign). Uppermost among these are the project's business requirements, covering aspects such as the budget and the scope of the game. These can at times be quite prescriptive, for example if you're designing a virtual world for an existing intellectual property then much of its lore will be imposed upon you externally. Even so, in the general case it's the lead designer whose artistic vision is being realised[5] by the rest of the design team and by the programmers, artists, musicians and everyone else involved in developing the virtual world (there could be

---

[5] Strictly speaking, I guess this should be "virtualised".

hundreds of them). Thus, it's the lead designer who is definitively responsible for how the virtual world will be.

That's not quite the same as saying that lead designers are gods, though.

My basis for asserting that the designers of virtual worlds are the gods of those worlds is that they control the physics. Do they, though? Don't the programmers control the physics? With *MUD*, it didn't matter because Roy and I both did both jobs[6]. However, for modern, large-scale MMOs, designers design and programmers program. So ... are an MMO's gods its designers or its programmers?

Well, ultimately the designers are, because the programmers program to the designers' design. Programmers nevertheless do have a meaningful level of creative input, so you could argue that they are indeed gods, just lesser gods. Artists often undertake design work, too, as a lot of the world-building can be (and indeed is) handed over to them. They aren't able to change the physics of the virtual world, but they do get a say in how its local geography is set up, so also make a god-like contribution[7].

---

[6] That said, this can itself lead to internal conflicts when a single individual has the roles of both designer and programmer (Farmer, 1993).

[7] The graphics themselves, like the music and voice-acting, are purely interface elements present for the benefit of the

If you're alert to mappings, you may well have noticed a correspondence here. Lead designers are like ruling gods such as Zeus, with the rest of the design team being specialists in either particular systems (in the same way that Hephaestus is the god of crafting) or particular spaces (in the same way that Athena is patron of Athens, Sparta and Syracuse). Programmers and artists are like nymphs: divine beings who form and animate nature at the behest of gods[8].

To keep things simple, in this book I'll tend to refer generically to "designers" as being the gods of virtual worlds. I thought I'd give programmers and other developers a shout-out, though, so they know I haven't forgotten them[9]. They rarely get the creative credit they deserve. Formally, they're the supernatural beings of virtual worlds.

Customer service representatives are not developers. Their position involves dealing with the flak that is inevitably thrown up by the people playing the virtual world. CSRs are effectively demigods: they can't define or change the physics of the virtual world in any way, but they are able to perform tasks that players can't by using tools and commands that are not available to customers. For

---

people who play the virtual world; as they're used at the moment, they don't contribute to its physics.

[8] The difference is that programmers and artists wear more clothes when at work and nymphs don't subsist on pizza and Red Bull.

[9] Not producers, though: those, I *have* forgotten.

example, they may be able to advance a quest for you, or to teleport you back to civilisation if you somehow fall through the virtual world's architecture[10]. Note that although CSRs (and this also applies to playtesters) aren't gods themselves, they do have the ear of the gods: they can tell them what damn well needs to be fixed right now if Terrible Things aren't going to happen, and expect the gods to hear if not necessarily to listen.

The people who play a virtual world are its players. They are individually represented within the virtual world as *characters*. Because the gods and demigods are also represented by characters when they make an appearance in the same reality, sometimes a distinction is made between *immortals* and *mortals* – a relic from the days when regular player characters could die and stay dead. Players themselves (as opposed to their characters) can also be legitimately referred to as *heroes*, for reasons I'll explain in Chapter 5. No-one does refer to them as heroes, though; I really only mentioned it to manufacture a paratextual reference to the title of the fourth supplement to the original set of *Dungeons & Dragons* rules: *Gods, Demi-Gods and Heroes* (Kuntz & Ward, 1976).

---

[10] This has happened to me as a player in *World of Warcraft*, *The Secret World* and *The Elder Scrolls Online*. Only in *WoW* did a CSR actually rescue me – I had to quit and reset in the other two (and no, to those *TSW* and *ESO* CSRs reading this, the /stuck command didn't work).

Some players refer to their characters as *avatars*. The term, which was borrowed, loaned, imported, appropriated or stolen (your choice[11]) from Hinduism, has a long history in virtual worlds, its having been used as the actual name of one of the first such realities[12] and to refer to the graphical appearance of player characters in another[13]. Designers continue to use it in the appearance-only sense, but the novel *Snow Crash* (Stephenson, 1992) popularised it among players to mean the character itself, which has led to some confusion[14]. I shall be avoiding its further use in this book (except in the context of Hinduism), but have mentioned it here because it is a term that still has currency – especially in social worlds – and I would be remiss if I didn't.

Sometimes, by the way, players can play characters who are "gods" in the fiction of the game world. This was the major selling point of an early MUD called *Lap of the Gods* (or *Gods* for short), and is also the premise of the rather more recent MMO, *SkyForge*. However, players are only *actually* gods of a virtual world if they can change its physics – something impossible in both these

---

[11] If you want help deciding, see (De Wildt, et al., 2019).

[12] The one called *Avatar*.

[13] The one called *Habitat*. It's generally recognised that *Habitat* first introduced the term this way, although it was also introduced independently by other games.

[14] See (Carter, et al., 2012) for evidence of this with regard to *EVE Online*.

examples, because if they could then they would and the game would inevitably crash as a result[15]. Some players may have god-granted access to different physics, but that only makes them eligible to be thought of as demigods, not as gods. That said, if the gods no longer bother with the game then the demigods may well have sufficient powers to run it as ersatz gods (Lawrie, 1991) (Lawrie, 2003).

So: we have gods (designers), supernatural beings (developers), demigods (administrators) and characters (players). I did, however, suggest that there was another category of person involved in virtual worlds, but that there was something fishy about it.

Well, this other category is comprised of the ordinary inhabitants of the virtual world who have no player controlling them: the *non-player characters*, or *NPCs*. NPC is an old role-playing[16] game term which came about in opposition to the characters played by players – *player characters*, or (less commonly nowadays) *PCs*[17]. NPCs, along with

---

[15] See Chapter 3's section on self-modifying systems for an explanation as to why *"a virtual world based on unconditional but consequential magic cannot exist"* (Bainbridge, 2010) (italics original).

[16] I used to spell this *rôle-playing*, but reluctantly had to move with the times.

[17] Some social worlds call the player characters *players* and the players *typists* (Hess, 2003).

monsters[18] and everything else, are handled entirely by the physics of the virtual world of which they are ingredients. They aren't played by people from Reality, but it's not unimaginable that they could be the people of their own reality (as we'll consider extensively in Part 3).

Figure 1 summarises all this as an easier-to-follow-than-the-text table[19].

Rank	**Virtual worlds**	**Ancient Greece**
Ruling gods	Lead designers	Zeus
Specialist gods	Designers	Athena
Supernatural beings	Developers	Maia
Demigods	Administra-tors	Hermes
Heroes	Players	Heracles
Everyday folk	NPCs	Ancient Greeks

Figure 1 – *Dramatis Personae* Examples.

[18] NPCs and monsters are examples of what are called *mobiles*, or *mobs* for short. The differences between them are discussed in Chapter 6.

[19] Contrary to custom, I don't number tables and figures separately, because in my view that makes them harder to find. What can I say? I'm a rebel.

I should perhaps point out that although Athena, Hermes and Heracles are all children of Zeus, and Maia (the eldest of the Pleiades) is the mother of Hermes, such a degree of nepotism is not normally evident among those who work with virtual worlds.

Anyway, now that we've covered who does what and vaguely why, let's look at the virtual worlds themselves. What *are* they?

Well, they're a collection of pieces of software.

Software

I won't be delving into great levels of detail in this section, because the result would be a stodgy mess[20].

The consequences of this decision are sure to annoy those readers who know about software[21], but by providing a somewhat simplified overview I can spare those readers who *don't* know about software from undue suffering. Therefore, if I make a statement and you want to shout "Duh! Firmware!" at me, be assured that I *am* actually

---

[20] I can say this with some certainty, because I did initially delve into great levels of detail and the result was a stodgy mess.

[21] I can say this with some certainty, too. because I know about software myself and said consequences do annoy me.

aware of what I'm glossing over, but that from the perspective of this book the cost of precision outweighs its value.

So: computers are pieces of hardware which follow instructions presented to them as software.

The hardware is a physical machine. If you want to change how it works, you have to change the wiring[22]. You can't replace a memory card by running a program: you have to switch off the machine and do it manually.

Software constitutes the data for hardware. It encompasses whatever programs run on the hardware, along with whatever ancillary data they use. It can *control* the hardware, but it can't change it. It *can* change the software, albeit not freely: while running[23], programs are usually considered to be invariant and inscrutable, for reasons I'll explain anon. Indeed, programs (the stuff of which is called *code*) are often loaded into a specially-protected area of computer memory precisely to *prevent* them from being modified while they're running.

Regardless of whether or not a program is running, changing it will usually require the attention of a programmer – that is, a human

---

[22] Ah-ah-ah, programmers and electronic engineers! No shouting at the author, remember?

[23] The technical term is *executing*. Fortunately, executing a program is not the crime that executing people is. That said, see Chapter 7....

being[24]. Programmers and computers are in the main mutually unintelligible. Programmers write programs in high-level languages, which are meaningful to programmers but meaningless to computer hardware. A program called a *compiler* translates high-level language *source code* into binary *executable code* that is meaningful to computer hardware but meaningless to programmers. The computer can then load this binary form into its memory and run it directly.

To make changes to a program, a programmer must: edit the source code; recompile it; stop the program if it's currently running (they may indeed need to do this before the recompilation); start the new version running from the beginning.

The reason the program must be stopped if it's currently running is that otherwise its behaviour would almost certainly cease to make sense. Imagine you were reading a book on an e-reader and, mid-sentence, the entire text was replaced by an updated version. You could now be looking at a completely different word, and even if you found your old place (assuming it still existed) you wouldn't know if everything you'd read up until that point still held. This is what it's like when you overwrite a running program with a new version: it's almost certainly going to result in garbage behaviour.

---

[24] Despite what media stereotypes of programmers might have you believe, programmers *are* human beings.

You can sometimes safely modify the code of a running program from another program, as anyone who has poked bytes in a 1980s home computer will be aware, but even then you'd really want to suspend the program while you did it (unless screwing yourself over was your goal).

Refreshingly, non-executable data *can* arbitrarily be changed (or looked-at) (or both) while the program using it is running, so long as it stays within whatever limits the program expects[25]. Right now, I'm entering this text using a word processor (Microsoft Word, because often it works just fine[26]). When I started the program up, it loaded the text into computer memory (as data) from a file. The keyboard characters flowing freely from my fingers are being used to direct changes to said data; the end result will be stored in a new version of the file.

In terms of this example, then: the word processor is a program – a piece of software; the text of this book is data for this program; the program's executable runs on hardware, which at the moment is my personal computer[27].

---

[25] For example, if the program is expecting to see an integer between 0 and 6 that represents the day of the week, it's going to complain should you change a 3 to 4.7, -6 or "Sunday".

[26] Hmm, maybe I'll save, just in case.

[27] I use the word "runs" for reasons of convention only. Despite the fact that I have a high-end games machine,

Data can be fiddled with using programs, but there's not always the need. For example, a word processor's dictionary qualifies as data, but it won't *usually* be changed except perhaps if the user switches it out for a different dictionary (an English one isn't going to be much use if you're writing in Spanish[28]).

Some data will absolutely *never* be changed, though. If your program uses the mathematical quantity π (pi), there's no sense in keeping it in a separate data file to load in every time you run the program: its value is fixed[29]. Constant quantities such as π can therefore be embedded in program code directly.

When data values are written straight into the code, they're said to be *hard-coded*. If they're initialised from or stored in files external to the program, they're said to be *soft-coded*. The latter term isn't actually used very often, because the default assumption is that data values *are* soft-coded; it's mainly employed when referring to soft-coded *code*.

Ah, yes. I said earlier that computers are pieces of hardware which follow instructions presented

---

"walks" would be a better description of its behaviour. Thanks, Windows 10.

[28] I intend one day to write a general English-to-non-English dictionary that has each word in English translated into that same word but IN CAPITAL LETTERS.

[29] Approximated in binary (because it's an irrational), but nevertheless fixed.

to them as software. This is indeed correct. However, it's also possible for pieces of software to follow instructions presented to them as data. Programs can handle data in a manner analogous to that in which hardware handles software. The meaning of the ones and zeroes in a program's memory is determined by the program: if the program chooses to interpret them as instructions then that's what they are.

When this happens (and it happens a lot), it's as if we have two programs running. One, running on the hardware, is an *interpreter*. The other, running on the interpreter, is a *script*. It could also just be a program, though: whether to call an interpreted program a script or not is largely a matter of taste and context.

Scripted code is of special interest from the perspective of this book because it can *self-modify* much more easily than can regular code. The designers of computer hardware and operating systems go to great lengths to stop code that's currently executing from being accidentally overwritten, and they also put barriers in place to prevent programs from stomping on one another's data. They aren't at all bothered by the possibility that a program might run riot over its own data, though; that is, after all, what many programs are meant to do. To an interpreter, its script constitutes its data; as such, the script is already in a form amenable to program manipulation, so it can in principle be changed by itself relatively easily while it's executing. Whether that's a good idea or not is beside the point.

To summarise, then: scripts are interpreted by interpreters, and can readily (if not necessarily advisedly) be modified while they're running; programs (including interpreters) are executed by hardware[30], and are very difficult to modify while they're running; hardware operates according to the physics of Reality, and can't be modified programmatically at all while it's running[31].

Fundamentally, then, the basic model of a digital[32] computer involves parts you can't change (hardware) and parts you can change (software). Software that is run (programs) is harder to change than software that isn't run (regular data).

Figure 2 illustrates this diagrammatically.

---

[30] You *can* script interpreters to script interpreters, but happily that isn't germane to this book.

[31] Other methods for modifying hardware remain possible: I once took a sledgehammer and a power drill to a hard drive, for example. It had it coming.

[32] Analogue computers don't even have the programs. In effect, for the task they do, the code is constant and can be embedded directly in Reality. This means that analogue computers can only really do one task, but that this can involve continuous quantities rather than discrete (that is, digital) quantities.

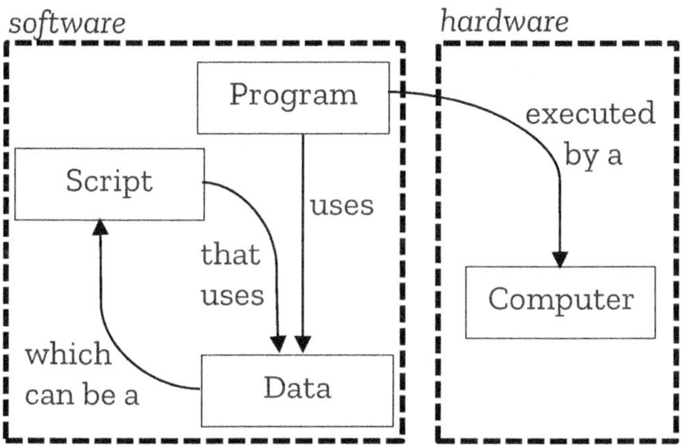

Figure 2 – Hardware and Software, Somewhat Simplified.

Let's consider what this means for the implementation of virtual worlds.

ENGINES

Right! So, virtual worlds! Fascinating though the foregoing overview of basic computer architecture was in its own right[33], I did undertake it for a reason; well, for several reasons actually, of which I shall now relate the first.

[33] Especially if you forewent it.

Virtual worlds are programs. One of their primary functions is to implement the set of physical laws governing their reality. These laws are embodied in the virtual world's software.

So far, so good.

There are three main ways a virtual world's physics can be so embodied:

- *Hard-coded*. The physics of the virtual world's reality never changes and can be implemented directly in an efficient systems-programming language. Only the current state[34] of the reality needs to be stored as data.
- *Soft-coded*. The physics can't itself be changed, but some of its properties can be. Gravity's strength (represented as a number) could be increased or reduced, or even made negative, but gravity will always have the same functionality. It can't be made to apply only to liquids, for example.
- *Interpreted*. The physics can be changed even while being applied. The laws of physics are objects of the virtual world, and could themselves be subject to laws of physics if the designer so decided.

Virtual worlds can be implemented using any of these approaches. Given the complexity of modern

---

[34] This is actually a technical term, but it means what it looks as if it should mean. I go into more detail about states in Chapter 3.

MMORPGs, they're probably going to use all three of them in various capacities; however, there will always be one that dominates the others. Crucially, this central approach determines what supernatural powers the reality's gods (and to some extent demigods) have while the virtual world is running.

If a reality is hard-coded, the only powers its gods have are the ones explicitly coded-in. In such a situation, the gods will be able to do some things that other beings can't, but they don't have much flexibility. If they want to make a permanent change, they have to carry out the appropriate alterations to the reality's source code, then compile it into a new executable, shut the reality down, then restart it using this new executable. From within such a reality, if you asked a god to do something for you, OK, well the god *could* do it, but they'd have to stop and restart the reality for it to happen. Such a reboot would annoy the players and could have major implications for the NPCs; I'll be discussing these in Part 3.

If a reality is soft-coded, gods have more extensive powers at their fingertips. They can create new objects at will without interrupting the operation of the reality (so long as those objects aren't too dissimilar to existing objects), and they can tweak the settings of what in a hard-coded world would be a constant value (such as the atomic mass of gold, say). What they can't do is add new functionality to an object. They couldn't make it that if you now put two gold coins next to each other then they will melt together and form a single gold coin with the same volume as one coin but double the mass. The physics software would have to be rewritten and recompiled to do that, entailing a reboot.

If the reality is interpreted, well, anything goes! The virtual world will run more slowly in Reality[35], but the NPCs won't notice and the prize is that their reality's god or gods will be able to make whatever changes they desire, on the fly. Of course, were one of the gods a feeble programmer then we'd see a few extra crashes this way, and the more that physical laws were changed then the harder it would become to keep track of what such laws currently pertained. It's a very, very flexible technique, though.

For the most part, virtual worlds today take the soft-coded approach. Interpreters are less efficient, and although designers would appreciate the flexibility, live updates to a virtual world's functionality aren't a good idea (for soon-to-be-discussed self-modification reasons). The soft-coded solution, which endows the ability to make extensive tweaks to object properties without kicking everyone out for a reboot, is still pretty good, though – especially when fire-fighting bugs

---

[35] As a general rule of thumb, interpreted code runs about ten times slower than the same code would if compiled and executed directly.

or stomping on exploits[36]. Hard-coding is only worth it if you know you're not going to make any changes. Thus, the soft-coded approach is usually preferred.

This division between what should be coded-in and what should be stored as data brings us to the topic of *game engines*.

Game engines are basically portable pieces of software that can be employed to create games (of which most virtual worlds are examples). They typically have functionality covering graphics, physics, artificial intelligence, audio, networking and the popular "much, much more". There are often several specialist engines available for each of these components, and to some extent developers are able to mix-and-match between them; for the sake of simplicity, though, I'm just going to use the term "game engine" to refer to the general software platform upon which the game is built, whether it's all-in-one or made up of middleware stitched together in a bespoke fashion.

The developer's choice of game engine affects the character of the resulting game (which in our case will be a virtual world). Things the engine makes easy to implement have a far better chance of appearing in the final release than things it makes difficult. If the engine has rag doll physics, for example, this offers the designer options

---

[36] An *exploit* is a design or programming bug that a player consciously takes advantage of for their own ends.

regarding combat that would otherwise be tricky to include; furthermore, the designer may be more tempted to pursue these options because of this. If, on the other hand, the engine is poor in its handling of, say, shadows, then the designer will probably want to avoid heavy use of strong lighting rather than waste programmer time trying to improve matters for little material gain.

In the text days, the differences between engines[37] were more pronounced than they are today. For example, if an engine had magic hard-coded into its physics then that would make it a good choice to implement a virtual world that used a similar magic system. It would be a bad choice to implement a virtual world set aboard a starship. If you wanted to construct an original magic system, there were game engines that would make it easier for you to do so. If you wanted players to be able to create their own, independent magic systems within the virtual world, there were game engines that would accommodate this desire, too. Several major game engines existed, each with their own offshoots[38], so designers weren't overly dictated-to by engine availability.

That said, some textual engines came with predefined sample worlds (which is easier to do in

---

[37] They were called *codebases* back then; only the hard-coded part was referred to as the game engine.
[38] For a late contemporary genealogy of MUD codebases, see (Keegan, 1997).

text than in graphics). These were often incorporated into the final games, as anyone who knows Midgaard from playing a DikuMUD can doubtless confirm. After all, if it's already written, why throw it away?

As a result, we wound up with a group of virtual worlds with similar content that were much of a muchness (a phenomenon known as *stock MUD syndrome*).

You may have noticed that I used the word "content" again there. This is an important concept in virtual worlds.

CONTENT

What's the point of restaurants?

The owners, the chefs, the kitchen staff, the wait staff and the customers may all have different answers to this question, but ultimately it comes down to food. A restaurant without food isn't a restaurant.

Food is the *content*[39] of restaurants. It's different in each restaurant (or at least each chain of restaurants), but it's what makes a restaurant worth visiting as a restaurant. It doesn't matter

[39] Pronounced CONtent, not conTENT.

how good the restaurant's location, ambience, menu or chef is if there's no food.

In computer games, content is that which the players consume while they play.

You could create a vast virtual world, with beautiful scenery, exotic creatures, a fully-realised populace of NPCs and an enticing character-creation system, but if there's nothing for players to *do* in it, it lacks content[40]. They might spend some time looking at scenery, or admiring the wildlife, or stalking NPCs, or creating a character who looks just like their favourite pop star might after falling down an elevator shaft; all of these count as content. The player is soon going to tire of it, though, because whatever they do will rapidly get repetitive. It's content, sure, but there isn't *enough* of it. In a virtual world (well, an MMO, anyway), you need *gameplay*.

This is from the perspective of the players. From the perspective of the NPCs, there may be quite enough content to keep them occupied. They have people to see, places to be, giant spider legs to purchase, undead horses to be tormented by: they don't *play*, they *live*[41].

NPCs don't pay the bills, though: players do. Well, some players do: in virtual world with a

---

[40] The best-known example of this is *No Man's Sky*, which launched with 18,446,744,073,709,551,616 different planets (Murray, 2014), all basically the same. It's improved since then.

[41] Not necessarily for very long.

subscription revenue model, sure, they all do, but under the free-to-play model that most MMOs use today it's mainly the stupidly rich or the richly stupid who do. The majority of players either hardly pay anything (in Asia) or never pay anything (in Europe and North America).

This suggests that smart MMO developers should target their games at high-rollers (known as *whales*, a term originating in the gambling industry); after all, these are the only players likely to hand over money in noticeable amounts. Doing that would be a mistake, though: the non-paying players will leave if there's not enough content for them. As for why you might *care* if non-payers ceased to sponge off you, well the answer is simple: if they go, so do the whales. This is because players *themselves* are content for each other.

If you have a virtual world, you therefore need sufficient content to keep all your players happy, not just the whales. Otherwise, you'll have an empty world. This is fair enough if that's what you want, but if not then there has to be a range of activities that players can do with, to and independently of each other.

So, here's the thing you need to know about content: it's expensive to create. In its basic form, some designer has to sit down and think up things for players to do. They have to think up lots of these things. Lots and lots of them. They need other designers to be thinking up lots and lots of them, too. MMO players typically play for two to four hours every night for months, years. That's a great deal of entertainment they're going to require to occupy their time. *World of Warcraft* launched with 2,600 quests; its *Burning Crusade* expansion raised this to 5,300; its *Wrath of the Lich King* expansion took it to 7,650. Six expansions later, it surpassed 32,000[42].

That's just the quests. Content also comes from the raiding, the exploring, the guild drama, the player-*versus*-player (PvP) combat, the role-playing and the myriad other opportunities players have to engage with the virtual world and with each other for extended periods[43]. In a modern MMO, it's mainly driven by the quests, though.

Virtual worlds don't actually have to have quests in the sense that *World of Warcraft* has them. *WoW*'s quests are an example of *explicit content*: content that is flagged explicitly to the players by the game's design as being content. Virtual worlds can also have *implicit content*: content that emerges implicitly from the rich interactions of the various systems that make up the virtual world's reality. Most MMOs have some of both, but will favour one over the other. The

---

[42] The first three figures are official, having been cited by *WoW*'s former director, Jeffery Kaplan, on a panel at the Game Developers' Conference in 2009. The figure of 32,000+ comes from (Wowhead, 2021).

[43] In my case, when I cancelled my *World of Warcraft* account in 2012, the total time I'd spent playing came to a few minutes over 5,400 hours, or about 225 days.

ones that favour implicit content are called *sandboxes*; the ones that favour explicit content are called *theme parks*.

Yes, I am indeed aware that "explicit content" sounds as if it ought to be racier than it is, but that's technical terms for you. It's therefore somewhat ironic that non-game worlds such as *Second Life* have entirely implicit content (in the technical sense) which at times can be quite explicit (in the ye-gods-how-many-penises-do-you-need?! sense).

Because content is expensive to create, a number of different methods have been employed over the years to reduce the cost. Their availability depends on the game engine used, but the main ones that have found favour are as follows:

- *Game-mastered content* (GMC). This is both the most high-quality and the most expensive kind of content, involving as it does live interactions between select groups of players and game masters (a bit like in tabletop RPGs such as *D&D*). It doesn't scale well and requires both talent and flexibility, so it tends to be the province of text MUDs rather than graphical MMOs[44].

---

[44] In the best-known MUD that does this, *Achaea*, the game masters have actual physics-changing abilities so qualify as gods. Indeed, they're formally referred to as "gods" in the game. See (Iron Realms Entertainment, 2021).

- *Hand-crafted content* (HCC). This is also expensive, as it requires each element to be constructed individually by a designer. It's generally high-quality and can carry layers of meaning that are rarely found in cheaper types of content. Formal tutorials invariably use HCC.
- *User-created content* (UCC). This is content overtly created by players, for players, usually employing in-world tools. It's inexpensive (for the developer) and can be fun (for the player). In a game context, however, unless the player doing the creation has some design ability, the result will be content that either gives away loot for next to no effort or is a death-trap[45].
- *User-generated content* (UGC)[46]. This content emerges from interactions between players. Competitive, PvP combat is a good example of it, but UGC can also be co-operative. In general, UGC is relatively inexpensive to implement but can be expensive to manage if relied upon too heavily.

---

[45] I briefly explain why in (Bartle, 2016).

[46] UCC and UGC are often confused. People will routinely use the terms interchangeably, or just stick with one and employ it for both types.

- *Procedurally-generated content* (PGC[47]). The content here is created algorithmically to programmed specifications[48]. It's popular because it's cheap and can produce new and individualised content in great quantities dynamically. Sadly, in most implementations to date it has tended to get very samey very quickly.
- *Systems content*. This doesn't really have a formal name, hence its lack of an acronym. It's the default kind of content, which emerges from interactions between players and the virtual world's systems and environments.

Systems content is implicit and underpins all the others, thereby forming the basis of a virtual world's gameplay. The sandbox ideal is to have all content be of this nature, but for it to work the virtual world has to have multiple, complex interacting systems that provide players (and possibly NPCs) with a variety of objectives that they can define for themselves and which they can pursue either alone or in groups. Few MMOs achieve this (*EVE Online* is perhaps the best-known one that does), but most don't try anyway as an immediate wall of possibilities can overwhelm

---

[47] The act of creating PGC is sometimes referred to as *procedural content-generation* (PCG).

[48] Not so much intelligent design as artificially-intelligent design, then.

newbies. Systems content, hand-crafted content and game-mastered content are sometimes described as *designed content*, as they're created by designers.

These different forms of content-creation can usefully be classified as being either direct or emergent, freeform or contextual:

- *Direct* content is content created explicitly. Hand-crafted content and user-created content are examples.
- *Emergent* content is content created implicitly. Systems content, user-generated content and procedurally-generated content are examples.
- *Freeform* content is content that can potentially break the context of the virtual world. User-created content regularly delivers this (sports cars in medieval worlds, that kind of thing), but user-generated content can too (players discussing the current president of the USA in a fantasy setting[49]).
- *Contextual* content is content that fits the fiction of the virtual world[50]. Game-mastered content, hand-crafted content, procedurally-generated content and some

---

[49] I'm aware that on occasions the fantasy may be more believable than the reality.
[50] Such content is called *diegetic* by scholars of Game Studies. The term crops up again in Chapter 5.

user-generated content are examples.
Systems content also formally goes here.

The most apposite of these relationships are summarised in the table that is Figure 3. From this, we can see that all contextual content is either designed, emergent or both. Given that we have no evidence that Reality contains anything other than contextual content, we can therefore deduce that it's either designed, emergent or both.

Put another way: if Reality was created by one or more gods, they knew what they were doing.

Content Type	**De-signed**	**Emer-gent**	**Con-textual**
Game-mastered (GMC)	yes	can be	yes
Hand-Crafted (HCC)	yes	no	yes
User-Created (UCC)	can be	no	no
User-Generated (UGC)	no	yes	can be
Procedurally-Generated (PGC)	no	yes	yes
Systems	yes	yes	yes

Figure 3 – Content Creation Features.

Having thus explained how virtual worlds do content-creation, the natural question to ask is how Reality does it. I shall indeed be asking that in the next-section-but-one, however before I do so I have one more concept to describe that wraps up my discussion of how virtual worlds work (or at least how the parts relevant to reality-creation work).

Resets

For reasons of expensiveness, most virtual worlds today have content that is consumed much faster than it can be created, the few exceptions being those that have a very high level of emergent PvP content-creation (such as *Crowfall* and *Albion Online*) or of very-slow-to-consume content (such as *Black Desert Online*)[51]. This means that, periodically, either new content has to be added, or consumed content has to be made available again for different people to consume. Otherwise, the players won't have enough to do and will leave.

Non-emergent new content comes in the forms of *patches* and *expansions*.

[51] When content involves repeatedly doing very similar things over and over for little appreciable gain, it's known as *grinding*. Some players like it, but most don't; the latter will only (grudgingly) tolerate it for occasional, limited stints.

Patches are updates performed to a regular schedule (usually weekly[52]) in which bugs are fixed, gameplay balance is adjusted, and, occasionally, new quests or enemies are added. A patch is basically like any other kind of software update, except because it applies to an MMO (or other game) it can include new content.

Expansions are large-scale changes, having more of a revolutionary than an evolutionary feel. The whole point of them is to add great swathes of new content[53], perhaps at the expense of some existing content which may be sacrificed to serve the overall narrative; this most memorably happened with *World of Warcraft*'s third expansion, the aptly-named *Cataclysm*.

As I said, though, new content is usually added at a slower rate than that at which it is consumed, so most MMOs also recycle content to ensure that there's enough for the players to do. There are two ways of doing this: *sudden resets* (also known as *full resets* or the *Groundhog Day* approach) and *rolling resets* (also known as *respawning*).

Most modern MMOs use respawning to recycle content. A monster is killed, its treasure is looted, then the player goes off to do something else. A few minutes later, the monster pops back to life (that

---

[52] If a big hoo-ha is made over them then they'll be months apart and the weekly updates will just be called *updates*.
[53] Cynics might argue that the whole point of them is to make money, which may well be true but the *way* to make the money is by adding new content to keep players engaged.

is, it *respawns*) and the next player to wander past can take it on. Alternatively, if the player doesn't leave, the monster is killed again by the same hand; this tends to happen if the monster is wealthier than usual (meaning its risk/reward ratio is lower than for comparable monsters), or if staying in the same place is less bother for the player (comparable monsters could be far away), or if the player desperately wants a particular item of loot that the monster drops only very, very infrequently[54].

Figure 4 illustrates the difference between reset and replacement strategies in the form of a handy-dandy table.

	Reset	**Replacement**
A bit at a time	Rolling resets	Patches
All at once	Sudden resets	Expansions

Figure 4 – Reset and Replacement Strategies.

Respawning isn't exactly realistic, in that Reality doesn't work this way (don't test it out, kids!), but players accept it for its convenience. It's

[54] I once needed a particular tailoring recipe in *WoW* and killed the same NPC more than 300 times in a row before finally obtaining it. Because the NPC respawned faster than its corpse despawned, I was standing in a sea of 30 identical dead bodies for most of that period.

only suitable for creatures and maybe some destroyable objects, though. Complicated pieces of interrelated content can't easily be reset one component at a time. For example, suppose nixies[55] inhabit the ruins of temple that's submerged in a lake behind a dam: if you were to destroy the dam, the waters would subside and you'd gain access to the nixies; you could then proceed to give them a good telling-off for their policy of enslaving humans. While so engaged, you wouldn't want the dam and the water suddenly to respawn and drown you. You'd probably rather that it held off awhile until after you were done with the quest.

MMOs that have this problem will *instance* the content. This means that a special copy of the content is created that's private to the individual or group experiencing it. Anyone else experiencing the same content will be in their own instance. For you, the nixies guarding the dam may be still alive and putting up a fight to save it; for someone else, these could be dead and the dam is starting to crumble from the effects of multiple fireball spells; for a third person, the dam is down and there's a fight going on in the temple to kill the unreasonable nixie queen.

An instance, then, is like a pocket universe that's created to a template when the player enters, only to disappear when the player leaves.

---

[55] These are water sprites, ripped off from Germanic folk tales by generations of RPG designers.

A related feature is *phasing*. This is where the world changes as a result of your character's having consumed content, so that in subsequent visits to the area it's no longer the same as it was before. Other people, though, who haven't consumed the content, will still see it as (for you) it was.

A good example of this appears in *WoW*'s second expansion, *Wrath of the Lich King*, in which a battle is about to take place at a location known as Angrathar the Wrathgate. When the player's character arrives there for the first time, two armies are laying siege to it. A number of quests are given that help prepare for the combat to come. These culminate in the start of the battle, the outcome of which is shown as an extended cut scene. Afterwards, whenever the player character visits Angrathar the Wrathgate there will be no armies present but there will be some wounded. This is because the area is phased. If two player characters enter its vicinity, one of whom has previously fought in the battle and the other of whom has yet to experience it, they will be placed in different phases and will no longer see or be able to interact with one another (communication excepted) until either they both leave or the one behind in quests catches up.

When the virtual world is simply too complicated for either a rolling reset or localised phasing to work, it has to be reset as a whole, suddenly. The "suddenly" is because it involves unceremoniously kicking everyone out so the virtual world can be rebooted. With instanced content, you can wait until everyone has left until you reset the instance; with the virtual world in its entirety, there's almost always someone playing it, therefore there's almost always someone who's going to be kicked out when it shuts down.

All early MUDs reset using this method (it was/is timed to occur every couple of hours for *MUD2*), but it slowly lost popularity. No-one likes the inconvenience of being evicted mid-quest several times an evening, and it can be dispiriting to enter a game that's close to being played-out. Because of this, rolling resets have become the norm.

That said, all virtual worlds have a sudden reset when they're brought down for patches or maintenance. The forthcoming reset is advertised well in advance, so people are aware that it will happen; nevertheless, they'll often continue to play right until the moment that the server actually disconnects them. Sometimes, it might be possible for one geographic area of the game to be taken down while another remains playable, but usually it's just easier if the whole shebang is halted and the players are all locked out while the programmers do their jobs.

Sudden resets also occur if the programmers haven't done their jobs and the game crashes.

Most MMO operators run multiple, simultaneous instantiations of their virtual worlds;

these are known as *shards*[56]. Basically, the developers just duplicate their software on separate server[57] clusters or cloud configurations. This means that if a virtual world has only enough content to service ten thousand players at once but a hundred thousand people want to play, overcrowding can be avoided by creating ten separate shards that serve ten thousand players each. All shards can use the same program, but there will necessarily be differences in their data because their players will not be performing the exact same actions in each one.

Over time, the popularity of virtual worlds can rise and fall. It may be necessary to add more shards or to merge shards together. The latter tends to happen more often than the former, and is known as a *server merge* (because for historical reasons, players tend to call shards *servers*); when a nigh-full shard is split into two half-full copies, that's a *server fork*. Players don't usually like server merges as it disrupts the social *status quo* and is an indication that the virtual world is in decline. Some of them may have to change their character name,

---

[56] The term originated with *Ultima Online* as a fiction to explain why there was more than one copy of Sosaria (the game's world). The evil wizard Mondain trapped Sosaria in a crystal which was then shattered; each shard contained a refracted copy of the world (Garriott & Fisher, 2017).

[57] A *server* is a computer or piece of software that provides functionality for another computer or piece of software (a *client*) upon request.

too, if it clashes with that of a character on the other shard[58].

To avoid the problems of server merges, and to help spread the computational load more efficiently, many modern virtual worlds use an approach called *layering*. In this, it's as if every shard is its own phase. As an individual player, you will usually be placed in the same layer every time you enter the virtual world, but layers are dynamic and you can be switched between them spontaneously (and imperceptibly); this would happen if you grouped up with other players from different layers, for example.

Layering isn't going to work when the shards of a virtual world diverge substantially (such as in *Ultima Online*, where the location of your house is shard-specific). It can also be a problem if you don't require player characters to have unique names. In general, though, layers are a good way of managing access to a virtual world that has little or no user-created content, so long as its players can communicate and group up across them.

Figure 5 illustrates the ways of replicating virtual worlds in the form of a second handy-dandy table.

---

[58] Character names are often, but not always, unique to a shard. If they weren't, 50% of mages would be called Gandalf.

	Base	Overlay
Specific subset	Instance	Phase
Whole world	Shard	Layer

Figure 5 – Ways to Replicate Virtual Worlds.

These implementation approaches I've described fall into two broad areas: replicating parts or all of a reality (instances, shards, phases, layers); and reset/replacement strategies (rolling resets, sudden resets, patches, expansions). It's interesting to speculate whether any of these might apply to Reality – and what kinds of content Reality has in the first place.

OK, so let's speculate.

Real Content

Up until now, I've spent this chapter outlining several concepts related to how virtual worlds are designed and implemented. I haven't examined any of them in much depth, because you only need to be reasonably clear about what they are and what affordances come with them. I don't expect you to go away and code them in C++.

Those of you who nevertheless *could* go away and code them in C++ might well be wondering why I picked up on the particular aspects that I did. I'm likely to bring more into play later on, yes, but why start with these ones? Why am I at pains to discuss the rather obscure topic of reset strategies instead of maybe security, or account management, or how to handle floods of asynchronous commands?

Well, the reason I chose these specific topics to open with is that they put us in a position where we can think about what the implementation of virtual worlds might have in common with that of Reality. The promise of this book can now start to be delivered: using what we know about the nature of virtual worlds to gain insights into the nature of Reality.

There are two directions from which we can come at this, both summarisable as questions. What do we see (or have we seen) in Reality that rules out some of the approaches used by virtual worlds? What, if Reality did adopt one of the approaches used by virtual worlds, could we expect to see but don't (or haven't)?

When I say "what we see" here, I'm essentially suggesting that we look at *evidence*. What counts as evidence, though? The kind of observations that scientific disciplines accept are definitely admissible, of course, but they're not much help when it comes to the kind of physics-breaking events that gods can bring about. In addition, therefore, and in line with my assumption that all Reality's gods exist, I shall also accept as fact any historical account of supernatural incidents in a non-fictional context (even when contradicted by other such accounts[59] or by science).

I'm happy to do this, because it enables me to accord each proposal as much support as can be mustered for it. Whatever conclusions I might then draw can't subsequently be dismissed by appealing to an account that denies them. For example, if I only accepted hard science then I couldn't argue that looking at the right metal snake can cure you of the effects of snake venom, whereas if I accepted supernatural accounts then I could[60]. Being open to such possibilities from the outset means that any conclusions I draw will be far more robust – and far more useful, too.

I'll begin this exercise by first examining content generation, then moving on to reality partitioning, before finishing the chapter with a look at reset strategies.

So, as I said earlier, virtual world designers create content for players rather than for NPCs. This doesn't mean that Reality has to be that way, though: it could contain content designed for NPCs

---

[59] Few explanations of how Reality was created tend to agree, for example, but that's no reason to discount them.
[60] Numbers 21:4-9 in *The Bible*, if you're wondering.

(which is to say, us) rather than exclusively for players (which is to say, beings from the reality where Reality's hardware can be found). I'll therefore examine the subject of content-creation from both these perspectives.

The first point of view I shall consider is that of a player of Reality. We, as I slyly noted in the previous paragraph, are *not* players of Reality: we're Reality's non-player characters[61]. How might we recognise these "players" of Reality, then?

Although there are plenty of recurring examples of gods and demigods visiting Reality, accounts of players doing so are much more clustered; we haven't had any for many centuries. Indeed, Christianity has had no players at all visit Reality from God's reality except (if you take a very bold line) just *maybe* those playing as prophets[62]. The Ancient Greeks, by contrast, describe scores of players who have visited Reality – they're true standard-bearers for the cause. For example (using the terminology of virtual worlds), the player character Heracles[63] was the son of the non-player

---

[61] "Though you may think of the world as God's play, you are not God." (Riezler, 1941).

[62] You could view saints as player characters, but given that many of them met very sticky ends it's more likely they were just exceptional NPCs. You or I could conceivably become a saint if we did the right things (well, you could, anyway) but we could only become prophets if we were sent as such by God.

[63] Hercules, if you're from Ancient Rome.

character Amphitryon and the designer's player character Zeus. There was an abundance of such characters around in the Ancient Greeks' heyday.

That doesn't seem to be the case these days, though, as far as we can tell. Nevertheless, it remains legitimate for us to ask: what type of content is provided for such player characters to consume in Reality?

As a reminder, the types of content available are: game-mastered, hand-crafted, user-created, user-generated, procedurally-generated and systems.

Well, some but not all of these have been used. Historically, the player characters of Ancient Greece (or of anywhere else) didn't seem to find Reality interesting enough to experience in and of itself. They were, however, regularly entertained by game-mastered content (that is, gods or demigods overtly intervened to make life interesting for them); there's also some evidence of what might be hand-crafted or procedurally-generated content (explicitly-authored or narrowly-algorithmed quests to go find a golden fleece or golden hind or golden apple). That said, none of the usual geographic indicators that content is designed – areas gated to provide rewards of access (Salen & Zimmerman, 2003), enemies placed as elements of the environment (Totten, 2019), tutorial levels (Therrien, 2011) – are present in our neck of the Reality woods.

Very little content seems to have emerged from interactions between players, to the extent that it caused major drama on those rare occasions when it did (as documented in Homer's *Iliad*). User-created content was apparently completely absent, as no reports have reached us of anything spoken of in Olympus that made no sense in Reality.

What this suggests is that Reality is not itself shaped in such a way that individuals dropping in from the reality of its gods necessarily find it satisfying. Such players primarily want bespoke, real-time attention from gods or demigods, but they'll also reluctantly accept predefined, narratively-driven experiences[64]. Anything other than that, they don't seem to think worthwhile.

As I said, it's fairly obvious that we haven't seen any of these in-your-face player characters for quite some time. Perhaps, then, a different solution offers itself up? It could be that merely walking among us is satisfying to players of Reality in an "I could watch this formicarium for hours" kind of way, in which case we'd never know that the stranger we're sitting next to on the bus is, in fact, a player character. Alternatively, it may be that people from higher realities have simply stopped

---

[64] Such experiences could nevertheless be designed specifically for individual players, even to the extent that Reality itself might monitor them to model what they find fun then contrive to give it to them. In games research, this is called *experience-driven procedural content-generation* (Yannakakis & Togelius, 2011).

playing Reality (the fact that it has no tutorial would certainly put off newbies) – or that when they do play, they mess the place up so much it has to be rebooted from an earlier save point (see later).

To summarise, then: if Reality as it stands contains content attractive to players from the higher reality in which dwell the creators of Reality, then either no-one has played for a while or people do play but they're good at hiding their tracks. The only content that interests them is either game-mastered or hand-crafted, sitting atop straight systems content. There could be content from other sources lying around, but if so, the players don't seem to care about it.

What if, then, instead of (or in addition to) creating content for players, the content of Reality was created specifically for us, the inhabitants of Reality[65]? What could we deduce about the implementation of Reality's content in the event that it was created with us in mind?

The first observation worth a mention is that the systems content is pretty good. Reality is packed with more than enough richly-interactive dynamic structures to be self-sustaining. With all of us seeking multiple goals at different challenge levels, some competitive and some co-operative, there's a critical mass of activity that creates new content indefinitely. Sometimes this content is

---

[65] This is the opposite of what Evolution Theory tells us, which has us fit the content, not the content fit us.

boring, sure, but you never have to wait long before it perks up again[66].

There's no obvious procedurally-generated content in Reality unless the universe as a whole is procedurally-generated, which (as we'll see in Chapter 3) is a fair possibility. That said, there could be more subtle kinds of procedural content-generation in action. For example, all those countless stars that we have observed through telescopes might only have sprung into existence when one of us looked at them. Likewise, all these sub-atomic particles being discovered might not have existed until scientists forced the issue by smashing atoms together. The stars and the particles could be being created procedurally, on-the-fly, and we wouldn't know it[67]. Then again, they could just as easily be part of Reality's systems content.

For user-generated content to occur would require the presence in Reality of a player from a higher reality (to be the user). The ripples of their activity here would then generate content for us as well as for them. As noted earlier, though, we haven't seen any such players for centuries. If they are still visiting Reality, they're keeping their heads so low that their play can't possibly be generating content for us or we'd have noticed them.

---

[66] The year 2020 certainly did the business.

[67] They'd be implemented by a technique that programmers call *just-in-time evaluation*.

The existence of user-created content is a possibility. There could be gods secretly at work creating new content, *Minecraft*-like, for us to explore when we encounter it. I have to say, if there are such gods in action then they're making an excellent job of it: their creations are absolutely seamless integrations into Reality, looking just like the (literally) real thing. Anyone capable of that degree of creative discipline should definitely be making their own realities, rather than tinkering with someone else's.

In my opinion, user-created content would be overkill for Reality. This is because all user-created content (and some user-generated content) is freeform – one of the main attractions of which is that you can use it to make statements about your own condition. This being so, if UCC for Reality is indeed taking place, we should occasionally encounter content that is non-contextual; otherwise, there's no point in users' creating it. We don't encounter it, though. Everything we observe, detect or model-mathematically makes sense in the setting of Reality: we never come across examples of comments on the political situation in the reality of Reality's creator, nor discussions of the merits of various celebrities in that higher reality, nor questions as to whether another member of that higher reality has gone offline, nor any of the other out-of-context behaviours that the NPCs of virtual worlds routinely witness. The most we can say, then, is that if user-generated or user-created content is involved in the construction for us of Reality's content, the players are following the designer's prescriptions to the letter.

Hand-crafted content, as with procedurally-generated content, could apply to the whole of Reality. If so, some industrious worker must have created and placed every item in the universe one-by-one. This sounds like a tall order to us, given that there are something like 1,000,000,000,000,000,000,000,000 stars out there that would need to be positioned manually[68], but it might not be an imposing task for the superior being in the higher reality who is doing the positioning. A hybrid approach[69] would perhaps work best: generate the universe procedurally, but hand-craft parts of it to give us a better time. If Earth had been procedurally-generated to be like Venus, for example, you can see why doing some work for our benefit to replace the 700°C CO_2 atmosphere with something less deadly would be a good idea. This is the kind of content that benefits us all, though, rather than just a select few. Is there evidence that any gods are currently creating bespoke content for individuals?

---

[68] Or, if you have an extremely sceptical view of astrophysics, the something like 5,000 stars out there that can be seen with the naked eye (2,500 for flat-Earthers).

[69] In game design, this would be called *mixed-initiative procedural content-generation* (Yannakakis & Togelius, 2011).

As you might now have come to expect, the answer is that it used to happen in the past a lot more often (or at least less subtly) than it does in the present. In *The Bible*[70], for example, Abraham is asked to sacrifice his son Isaac to God, and almost goes through with it before he's stopped. This must have been somewhat stressful for Abraham, and even more so for Isaac[71], but it was powerful content for both of them, regardless.

In today's world, it's hard to find evidence of content-creation by gods. The population of Earth is much greater now, of course, so there are more people for whom content needs to be created. For them all to have individualised content made just for them, either the gods would have to work faster, or time in Reality would have to run slower (relative to the gods), or there would have to be many more gods doing the content-creation. Therefore, if gods are indeed creating ongoing content for us, then focusing on group content would be the sensible approach; either that, or

---

[70] If you're wondering why this is in italics, it's because I put the titles of all published works in italics and don't wish to imply by not doing so that *The Bible* shouldn't be published. I won't give it a formal academic-style reference, though, as it's easy to find online and in hotel rooms across the world. Other sacred texts are afforded a similar courtesy.

[71] *The Qur'an* is more accommodating for Isaac, observing that he willingly agrees beforehand to his being sacrificed. That said, he's not actually named in the text, and the established Muslim view is that it was Ishmael, not Isaac, who was going to be sacrificed.

focusing on addressing the needs of those people who are experiencing the highest levels of boredom[72].

In summary, then, if the content of Reality is created with us in mind, systems content supported by procedural content-generation (perhaps augmented by some hand-crafted content to smooth out the wrinkles) looks to be the way it would be done. The other ways don't deliver to their full potential, or even close to it.

There's another possibility. It may be that Reality was designed specifically for the benefit of us or of its players, but that after its content had been created it wasn't easy to change. This relative resistance to external alteration could perhaps allow us to deduce something about whether Reality is hard-coded, soft-coded or interpreted.

Reality can't be completely hard-coded, because that would mean none of it would change, ever; the fact that we ourselves can change it is evidence to the contrary. Nevertheless, it might be that although the data representing the current configuration of Reality can be changed while Reality is running, the rules of physics that enact the changes can't themselves be changed except by shutting Reality down first. In this implementation, Reality wouldn't be fully hard-coded, but the rules component to its physics would be.

---

[72] Not as a result of reading this book, I hope.

Reality doesn't seem to be interpreted. There's nothing that says it *isn't*, but none of the benefits that interpreting brings are on show. As far as we can tell, the rules of physics haven't altered since we began studying them: we don't see large-scale objects popping into or out of existence, or physical constants inexplicably adjusting; if there are ghosts or angels or djinn, they stopped making appearances once people started carrying camera phones as a matter of course. In short, there don't seem to be changes being made to Reality's physical rules at any level – the changes are only to the current manifestation of Reality.

If we *were* to detect a concrete example of a change taking place, we could rule out any implementations that were unable to do it. For example, if the speed of light in a vacuum suddenly began to increase over distance, we could surmise that the physical rules of Reality must be either soft-coded or interpreted. As it is, though, we have no reliable evidence that suggests changes to the laws of physics can be made at all, let alone what the reach of those changes might be. It's therefore probably worth looking at Reality's laws of physics as if they're hard-coded until and unless we notice a change. This is indeed the view advocated by most physicists.

A final point worth mentioning about content is that sometimes gods split the workload of Reality-creation: one might concentrate on the physics while another concentrates on the content, for example. This is indeed the case in some Hindu traditions, which relate that Vishnu created Reality and Brahma created its content (the forms that populate Reality). This is a bit like what Roy Trubshaw and I did when working on *MUD*: Roy focused on the physics, I focused on the content[73].

There are also Hindu traditions in which another god[74], Shiva, destroys Reality every aeon such that it can be created anew. The existence of the universe therefore follows a continuous cycle of death and rebirth.

This neatly brings us to our next topics for speculation: replications and resets.

Replications

Having looked at how Reality might obtain its content, I'll now consider whether or not in presenting its content to its players, Reality might involve the use of copies of parts of itself (in the sense of shards, layers, instances and phases).

To recapitulate, because I introduced these terms two whole sections ago:

---

[73] We didn't copy this from Hinduism, it just happened that way.

[74] Who may, depending on how you view Hindu deities, be the same god.

- A shard is a rendition of a reality that's separate from the other renditions that are in operation.
- A layer is a superimposition of a reality on itself.
- An instance is a pocket reality that comes into being when a player (or group of players) enters it from the main reality; it disappears when they leave.
- A phase is like a palimpsest, in which a part of a reality is covered up by another part for player characters that meet certain criteria.

So, it seems unlikely that Reality contains either phases or instances, because if it did then each of us would occasionally experience exactly the same events in exactly the same place at exactly the same time, but not do so together. This doesn't seem to happen. It would be like finding no queue at Disney's *Rock 'n' Roller Coaster*, walking straight in, sitting down alone in the front seat and then accelerating from 0 to 57mph in 2.8 seconds while 5,000 other people contemporaneously did the same thing in the same place. Your ride and theirs would be independent (if anyone threw up, you wouldn't be showered in their chunky vomit), but its basic content would be the same. You could meet up afterwards outside the instance and discuss the best bits.

This simply doesn't feature in Reality. There are plenty of science-fiction stories in which it does, and some supernatural tales about realities that overlay Reality; however, there are few claims that anything like this actually happens in Reality. Those there are speak in terms of trances, spirit journeys or reveries, but they still retain a connection to the physical world. *You* may think and feel that you're in another world, but the casual observer who didn't partake of the peyote may be more sceptical, and any people you meet while you're journeying will have no recollection of the encounter back in Reality.

People don't utterly disappear from Reality when they do something that you've done before but they haven't, only to reappear the moment they've also done it (which would indicate phasing). Neither do they ever drive ahead of you in a car that suddenly blinks out of existence at a toll booth, only for it to blink back into existence when you reach another tollbooth further up the road (which would indicate instancing). It's safe to say that neither phasing nor instancing occur in Reality.

This assumes that said phasing or instancing is localised, though.

See, in a virtual world it's possible to phase or to instance the entire reality. That's exactly what makes a layer and a shard respectively.

If we were to apply the concepts to Reality as a whole, then, some event could take place which would make the world different for you *and you only*. You might walk through a Roman archway and thenceforth you're in your own instance for the rest of your life. For everyone else, Reality would carry on as before (but minus you, unless a placeholder copy of you remains in your stead).

Now as a player of Reality, you'd notice this because you'd lose the ability to interact with those parts of Reality where the other players were.

You're not a player, though. This is an important point. You aren't a character in Reality being played by someone from a higher reality: you're an NPC. You *could* therefore be in your own, personal, just-for-you copy of the universe and not know. All those other people you see are copies of the originals, duplicated in the branch of Reality occupied by you. They're still just as real as you are, but replicas of them also exist in other instances. Perhaps replicas of you also exist in their instances, come to that: you wouldn't be aware of it, because to communicate with other people you need to share a reality with them. Sadly for you, although players of a reality are able to communicate with one another through the medium of their own, higher reality, NPCs aren't.

In summary, you're an NPC of Reality: for you, if you're in an instance, that instance *is* your reality – that is, it's Reality.

This is useful to note. In a sense, it makes no practical difference to you (as an NPC of Reality) whether you're a unique piece of bespoke software running on a single machine, or whether you're just one of any number of copies of the same software running on any number of machines. You have no way of knowing, because you can't communicate beyond the limits of your reality (at least not without help from a higher reality). If you could so communicate, the realities of you and your interlocutors would be connected through the communication channel, which would mean they were *de facto* the same reality.

Pragmatically, then, there's only one you in one reality: Reality.

It's worth mentioning that although in this scenario you can never return to mainstream Reality having entered a phase or instance (leastwise if you can, no-one has ever reported doing so), that isn't to say you couldn't exit the phase or instance into a different reality. Perhaps in this other reality, people chat all the time about their experiences in the phased or instanced reality. We in Reality have no means of establishing two-way communication with these people, though, so for us Reality is all there is[75].

Suppose you do exist in your own, private instance created especially for you. That would imply that all of (what to you is) Reality ought to disappear when you leave it, for example by dying. This in turn would mean that there are no lasting consequences to any of your actions. Whether that's great or dreadful depends on your

---

[75] Well, Reality and all the sub-realities we create as virtual worlds.

perspective. Unfortunately, you can't tell whether or not you are indeed living in your own, personal thread spun from a once-shared Reality, so you don't know whether your actions will have consequences lasting beyond your existence. How this affects your behaviour then comes down to whether you care about the fact or not. In a similar vein, you might also like to ponder the possibility that you're an NPC brought into existence because a player entered the instance you feature in: you'll disappear when that player quits the instance. New copies of you, unaware of your past actions, will continue to be sprung into being every time a new instance is stamped out from the same template.

The prospect that you may be just one of many copies of you (and not necessarily the "original" one) may be a bit disquieting for some people. To these people, I say: fear not! Again, the suggestion seems to be the stuff of science fiction rather than anything supported by witness accounts. Although copying-through-reincarnation is a concept you see time and time again in spiritual contexts, it invariably concerns the same individual living different lives, none of which overlap. It's not the same individual living the same life at the same time under the influence of different random-number seeds.

In recent years[76], philosophers have been debating the possibility and implications of there

---

[76] "Recent" by Philosophy standards, anyway.

being multiple possible worlds[77]. This is another idea that doesn't sit well with all belief systems. After all, if the creator of Reality is perfect then said creator wouldn't need to maintain multiple copies of it. Also, if your belief system is big on the idea of souls, their status isn't clear: do all the copies of me get one, or is there one we all share, or does just one of us have one and the others are unknowingly all empty husks that are mere substitutions in the instances into which they have been copied?

I've talked here about instances, shards, phases and layers as if they were equivalent, which at the level of the discussion so far they pretty well are. However, important differences do exist, and by considering these we can postulate which of the four best fits what we know of Reality.

Shards don't seem to be a strong possibility. No visitor from a higher reality has ever mentioned that Reality is but one of the many realities stamped out from a template.

There's an arithmetic argument, too. Shard numbers are related to player numbers, bringing little to NPCs except multiple copies of one another (at least up until such a point when new NPCs are

---

[77] With regards to Reality, the approach known as *modal realism* asserts that all logically possible worlds exist and are just as real as is Reality. There isn't much consideration of anything analogous to the situation we find ourselves in here, though, wherein a higher reality determines which of its lower realities are objectively real and which aren't.

created, although these would be shard-specific[78]). This means that we could perhaps find evidence in support of shards by looking at the number of players we've had over time. If there were indeed copies of what to us is Reality running as multiple different shards then we'd expect that eventually they would either fork or merge. Detecting this would imply that Reality was indeed a shard.

We wouldn't know directly if Reality had forked, because each new shard would (from our perspective) follow on seamlessly from the point at which the fork took place. We might be able to deduce it, though, from a sudden halving of the observed number of players from the reality of Reality's creator. As I've already said, though, we're not seeing any obvious extra-Reality visitors appearing nowadays; a server fork leading to such circumstances would therefore seem unlikely (unless when it happened all the players quit in protest).

We *would* know directly if shards had merged, because no single shard can explain the consequences of actions performed by players in another shard. Had a merge taken place, we would reliably see player-related inconsistencies showing

---

[78] If Reality is deterministic and no players from a higher reality were ever to play it, then each shard would be identical. Introduce any indeterminacy, though, and they would differ. For example, a single, split-second change in timing could mean a different sperm fertilises an egg and a different person is born as a result. Bye bye Shakespeare.

up: some things would be the way they are for reasons that defy our understanding of the laws of physics. However, as our history is not in fact stuffed with examples of (say) people who were born to parents who didn't exist, we can assume that there haven't been server merges in the recorded past. Besides, a server merge should be accompanied by an increase in the observed number of players visiting Reality, yet it's been flat-lined at zero for centuries.[79]

Both of the above anti-shard lines of reasoning depend on our having dependable historical evidence and memories, of course. This isn't necessarily the case, though: gods have the power to change Reality's data. To erase or to adjust the past, a god would take Reality down, alter its database to make the forked or merged versions self-consistent, then restart Reality using the new data leaving us none the wiser.

That said, it would be relatively easy to include in such an immense rewrite some minor changes to make pertinent aspects of history less ambiguous. Those embarrassing pro-slavery verses in *The Bible*[80] could be quietly removed, for example. This being so, the observation that it remains somewhat difficult to distinguish objectively between the goodies and the baddies in

---

[79] Hmm. Perhaps that means we should expect a server merge sometime soon.
[80] Leviticus 25:44-46 are perhaps the best-known.

past religious conflicts suggests that it's unlikely that such an historical rewrite has taken place (at least not under the direction of a god in whose name a war was fought). We can therefore say that we probably haven't had a server fork or merge either way.

So, Reality doesn't look to be one of many similar realities running on different shards. That doesn't mean it isn't, it just means there's no evidence that it is.

Phasing also doesn't appear to be supported by Reality. It, too, exists mainly for players; for the NPCs involved, it's quite a disturbing prospect. Imagine: you're waiting for a battle to take place in which the forces of good (your side) are up against the forces of evil (the other side). The odds are against you, but what's this? A high-powered individual has arrived – a hero who might just tip the balance in your favour! The battle starts, you fight long and hard, but with the hero's help the enemy is vanquished and good wins the day! Hooray!

Then, you twink out of existence because the next time the hero wanders by these parts it would spoil the fiction for you still to be around.

Fortunately for us, we don't see today – and have never seen in the past – evidence in Reality of phasing involving player characters.

What about phasing involving non-player characters?

Well, again, we don't see it. This could be because once a phase becomes active for you it only becomes inactive upon your death (which it may indeed cause), so you wouldn't know. Then again, it could simply be that phasing isn't a feature of Reality.

There are also implementational reasons why phasing is not something we'd expect to see being used for the benefit of NPCs. Feel free to skip the next two or three paragraphs if you're not into technical arguments.

OK, so phases are implemented in virtual worlds by sending different information to different players to reflect their different experiences of the same space. This happens by default for geography (what you see and what I see will be different unless we're standing in the exact same spot); phasing adds it for temporal, storyline differences, too. The equivalent for NPCs would involve giving them different sensory information depending on their physical location in the virtual world, moderated during phasing by what "should" be there for the time at which the NPC is supposedly present.

This seems an odd choice, given that NPCs are embedded in the virtual world: maintaining a different set of sensory information for the same space and keeping it all consistent is a far trickier prospect than simply instancing that space. Put another way: if it's easier to give an NPC a personalised, private, phased existence by running its default sensory input through a temporal filter, it's also easier to implement the entire virtual world that way. Either the whole virtual world is a distributed mess of autonomous phases frantically communicating with one another to keep in step[81], or it's a single entity from which sensory data can simply be read as-is.

In my view, phasing content for NPCs is a bad idea unless you have a particular reason to phase it for a small number of them at once (for experimental purposes, say). Creating single-NPC phases that somehow have to remain consistent with the unphased reality upon which they are all based is a nightmare in comparison to using instances to achieve the same ends.

Because layering is essentially phasing on a reality-wide scale for the benefit of players, the same arguments that count against phasing count against layering, too.

Instancing is the strongest candidate for something Reality might actually implement. It's consistent with philosophical theories of multiple possible worlds (albeit by creating a new instance for every different result the random-number generator could produce, every time it's consulted in any extant instance), but it's also more explicable. This is because each instance is itself a virtual world in miniature, so the same logic that applies to virtual worlds as a whole applies to their

---

[81] An idea that may appeal to particle physicists.

instanced content. The whole of Reality could be an instance invoked from a host reality, to which its players will return once they've played out Reality's content.

If Reality did invoke instances, it could do so either for players or for NPCs[82]. In either case, we wouldn't know unless some of us survived the ending of the instance or if the players told us what was going on.

We might be able to deduce that we had entered an instance if suddenly some crazy stuff started happening relative to what we were experiencing before. We wouldn't be able to inform the people back in uninstanced Reality what was going on, but we'd know it ourselves.

The main argument in support of instances over layers, phases and shards, then, is that it's easier to explain why we never see evidence of instances than it is to explain why we never see evidence of layers, phases or shards. We still have to suppose some limitations on the way that instances are used, though, primarily because for any of this to match what we know of Reality, the fact that instances exist mustn't get out.

It's easy to see how we NPCs might be unable to reveal the necessary information of the existence of instances: all it would take would be to prevent

---

[82] It could do it for inert objects too, if so inclined, although giving a bassoon its own sub-reality to enjoy seems a little indulgent.

instance-to-Reality communication and for those of us in instances to be destroyed when our instance closes.

What about players, though? Couldn't the people from the reality of Reality's creator let us know about instances?

Given how free some visitors from higher realities were in the past when it came to playing fast and loose with Reality, it's quite striking that none of them have ever expressed any indication that there might exist pocket realities in which anything goes[83]. This would seem to suggest that there aren't such pocket realities; certainly, no religions make a big thing of it[84]. That doesn't mean Reality *doesn't* have instances, of course, just that no-one seems to have argued in the past that it might, and if it does have them then they're used in a more restricted fashion than we use them in virtual worlds.

Knowing that you were an NPC in an instance could be quite disturbing, by the way. Even if you thought you yourself were likely to get out (which if virtual worlds are any guide, you won't), the new NPCs you meet in the instance will not be joining you. The instance is their entire reality. When you

---

[83] That is, like Las Vegas but real.

[84] Of course, some religions (such as Hinduism) are so vast that there's bound to be something in there you could interpret as referring to instanced sub-realities if you were to look hard enough. They're not signature features of the religions in question, though.

leave, that instance – that reality – will disappear. This means you're set to kill them all unless you stay forever.

Anyway, the upshot of all this is that from our own perspective, we can regard Reality as a single entity with no copying involved. There's no evidence for the situation's being anything otherwise, and even if there are multiple copies of Reality or parts of it, they're not the Reality in which we currently exist, therefore from our perspective they *don't* exist. They only exist from the perspective of a person in the higher reality of which they are sub-realities.

There's more on the concept of relative existence in Chapter 4.[85]

I'm hoping that by now it should be becoming apparent that applying what we know about virtual worlds to what we know about Reality does raise questions about Reality that haven't been raised before, and could perhaps answer some that have.

Sure, they may not be at the level of "why are we here?" yet, but that does come later.

---

[85] Sorry about all these forward references, but I'm a programmer: it's what we do.

REBOOTS

Reality doesn't seem to implement rolling resets. People don't die then recover; objects don't fall apart then rematerialise in one piece; ore that has been mined from the ground doesn't grow back. It could be that on an extremely long timescale parts of Reality do reset piecemeal (perhaps black holes spit out new stars or something), but if so we have yet to observe it.

The question of whether or not Reality implements full resets is less easy to dismiss. We have to back up a little to understand why.

Virtual worlds are computer programs. This means they usually contain bugs. Things don't do what they were intended to do, or do do what they were intended to do but what they were intended to do was faulty.

Bugs cause three general types of behaviour:

- *Crashes*. The virtual world simply stops running and exits.
- *Hangs*. The virtual world gets stuck. Either it keeps doing the same thing over and over without getting anywhere, or it goes to sleep waiting for something to happen but that something never happens.
- *Logic errors*. The program is running and doing things, but these aren't the things you wanted it to do. For example, you might write a program to calculate the nth root of a

number, but you made it calculate the $(n-1)^{th}$ root instead.

Sometimes, a logic error produces better results than what you intended to produce, so you adopt it instead of fixing it[86].

If Reality had logic errors, we wouldn't know. This is because Reality is all we *do* know, so we can't tell if the things that happen are supposed to happen or not. There could be a programmer in a higher dimension saying "How about that? I made a typo initialising Planck's constant but it all still seems to work!"; we wouldn't know.

Likewise, we wouldn't know if Reality were to hang. If it was waiting for an interrupt, it would just sit there with time stopped, so we'd be stopped with it.

There may be a possibility we could suspect that Reality was stuck in an infinite loop if the period between each looping was sufficiently long and we were able to predict what was coming; a programmer in a higher dimension could be saying "This Reality is hanging, it's stuck in the Big Bang to Big Crunch loop".

Whether we'd notice a smaller loop or not would depend on whether our memories survived each iteration. This is what happens to the character Phil Connors in the movie *Groundhog Day*, for example, who remembers what happens

---

[86] Programmers announce this by calling it a *feature* (because clearly it's not one).

from one iteration to the next (but no-one else does). Indeed. that's the very reason that sudden resets in virtual worlds are sometimes called Groundhog Day resets: the players remember everything from one reboot to the next but the NPCs don't (although they could if we wanted them to do so).

If Reality were to crash, we wouldn't notice. The instant the crash happened we'd cease to exist, and therefore be in no fit state to notice anything at all[87].

All things considered, it has to be said that Reality seems to be running pretty well, unlike many virtual worlds (although some of the latter have been in continuous operation for decades and are now pleasantly stable). There's always the possibility of a hidden bug, though. I've looked at code I myself have written that has been happily executed millions of times over thirty years and never caused a problem, yet I've been unable to figure out how it ever managed to run even once without falling over.

What does a crash (or a process kill following a hang) mean for a virtual world?

Well, it means that either: the virtual world will be abandoned because the problem is too

---

[87] It's conceivable that Reality is implemented as multiple processes – *threads* – and that one of these could crash or hang while the rest didn't. If we had any interactions with that out-of-order subsystem, we could perhaps notice ("So, everyone: gravity seems to have stopped working...").

expensive in time, effort or both to fix; or (more likely) it will be rebooted just as it was, because the crash isn't worrying enough to warrant immediate attention; or (most likely) a fix will be attempted and it will be rebooted with the fix in place.

Assuming the virtual world is rebooted, then, from what point is it rebooted?

Well, there are four main possibilities:

- From scratch. The fix involved altering the data format in some fundamental way, and it needs a clean start.
- Partial. Some sets of data survive (such as character records) and some don't (such as the current hit points of orc #288).
- From a back-up. The virtual world is periodically saved, and when it starts up it restores the last safe save.
- From a dump. In the process of crashing, the virtual world saves its current state. When it's restarted, it loads the data it needs from this dump and carries on from exactly where it was[88].

The data loaded from a back-up or a dump can be whole or partial. For most game worlds, partial is fine: the players don't mind if the game world is reinitialised, so long as they don't lose any of their stuff. For social worlds, which can involve a lot of construction, it's less fine: a player who has spent three, painstaking months building a replica of the

[88] In the fervent hope that this time it will keep going.

bridge (variant 2) of the USS Enterprise NCC-1701-D would be cross were it to disappear following a reboot initiated to fix a series of minor spelling errors in the tutorial. Whatever, the latest data will always be restored if the virtual world is reset in a controlled fashion (or to use the technical term, *gracefully*). Needless to say, if it crashes in a disintegrating mess of fiery glory, a high-quality data set may not be available.

Assuming that Reality has the full range of restore options that virtual worlds have, well, we'd be oblivious to them. A restart from scratch would obliterate not only us, but 13.772×10^9 years[89] of history (less than that if you're a Young Earth Creationist, or contend that time is an illusion and there's no past anyway). Likewise, a reset from a back-up or a dump would, to us, seem to be an unbroken continuation from that save point (in the same way that the characters in a movie aren't aware that you've paused or rewound it, or indeed fast-forwarded it).

We might know something was wrong if there was a partial restore of data and we were either part of that restored data or it was accessible to us. If all the stars outside the solar system suddenly changed position back to where they were eighty years ago, it would certainly raise the distinct

[89] This figure comes from a 2015 study by NASA (Lawrence, 2015), so when you read this you might want to add on the number of years that have elapsed since then.

possibility that Reality has experienced an operational issue and that Earth was restored from a more recent save than was the rest of the universe.

As for whether this has happened in the past, well the answer is that yes, it could have done. I wouldn't count as evidence the stunts that gods occasionally pull in which they turn people into stars or constellations of stars; this appears to be more of an example of their exercising their regular powers over physics, rather than the result of partially restoring the state of the universe from a save. What I would count as evidence is prophecy.

Ah, prophecy[90]. If virtual worlds are anything to go by, partial restores are more likely to retain only player data, not NPC or environment data. This means that we, as Reality's NPCs, wouldn't know that our timeline had been rewound unless a player character (or an NPC in the confidence of one) were to tell us. Perhaps surprisingly, this is a service that some of them do seem willing to perform. There are plenty of examples of people with an uncanny ability to predict the future[91],

---

[90] You know I was going to write that, didn't you?

[91] I was particularly impressed by Saint Malachy's prediction that the pope following John Paul II would choose the name Benedict. After Pope Benedict XVI subsequently resigned in office, though, Saint Malachy's prophecy became more circumspect. Basically, though, we're staring down the loaded barrel of the apocalypse.

which could well be possible because for them it's already happened (but Reality has since been restored to how it was before it happened). Whatever the precise mechanism, gods do seem to be largely on board with this one, anyway.

With virtual worlds, data can be edited. It requires the use of an editing tool, but such software is usually created during development and will normally be available. So it is that if something happens that the designer doesn't want to happen, the virtual world can be brought down, the data files edited, then the virtual world rebooted using the edited data so it doesn't happen the way it did the first time.

Could a god have edited Reality?

Let's say that we (as Reality's troublesome NPCs) spot something that the creator of Reality would rather we hadn't spotted. Perhaps we find a bug that enables a perpetual motion machine, or hard evidence of the existence of the creator's higher reality. It might suit the god to stop Reality, to edit a save of it from just before the unwanted event took place, then to restart Reality from the edited save point. No-one is going to suspect that the budding young biologist sadly killed by a falling piano accidentally created a plague that wiped out all warm-blooded creatures that time when the piano didn't fall on him.

This would also explain why we never see supernatural beings appearing and trashing Reality: if we did see it, a simple restore to before the errant player's visit would mean that from our perspective it never happened. Then again, perhaps supernatural beings have more sense than to wreck Reality in the first place.

What does this suggest about the possibility that we could destroy Reality ourselves? Knowing it could easily be restored from a save, if we found a way to crash it would this grant us the freedom to try?

Well, the thing is, we don't know that restoration from a save is indeed possible, easily or otherwise. Even if it could be restored, that doesn't mean it would be restored. Besides, we'd probably only do it again anyway, so why keep on letting us? A simple edit to remove the people responsible would sort it all out.

It's best not to try to destroy Reality, in my view.

I've been talking here as if most reboots were the result of bugs in the code, but that's not necessarily the case. Sometimes, virtual worlds are rebooted because they've been patched or expanded to add new content. Could something like this have happened in the past to Reality?

Reminder: patches are evolutionary updates, usually timetabled; expansions are revolutionary updates, occurring less frequently but with a bigger impact.

We wouldn't notice that a patch was taking place at the time (it would be instantaneous for us), but if we were still part of the new content then we could well become aware that something odd had just occurred. For example, there might be a subtle-or-otherwise alteration to Earth's geography or to the way that physics worked.

We'll have little difficulty spotting a patch if it happens in the future, and even less difficulty spotting an expansion. Were a portal to open tomorrow through which poured tens of thousands of fire-skinned demons, we'd realise that something was perhaps afoot. We can't use this possibility as evidence to suggest that Reality is patchable, though: for that, we need to look for patches that have already occurred.

So, has anything happened in the past that might indicate that Reality has been patched or expanded[92]?

Patches would be a little harder to notice than expansions as they're incremental, but they do have the property of being regular (weekly, for most virtual worlds). Frustratingly, this isn't as useful a guide as it might seem, because although there's a connection between the passage of time in a reality and of its passage in the reality of its gods[93], the relationship doesn't have to be linear. A reality's time could run faster during periods when no-one was playing it, for example.

---

[92] "Not only did the Big Bang cause the expansion of the universe, it was an expansion to the universe." – Discuss.
[93] It's why virtual worlds have a "real time" component to their definition.

More helpful is the fact that all patches except emergency ones make a slew of changes at once. We might think it unusual if a new mammal was suddenly discovered in New Guinea, but we'd think it more than a little suspicious if at the same time a sea monster started swallowing Caribbean cruise liners, acorns quadrupled in size, three new works by Leonardo da Vinci were discovered and the appearance of all penguins changed so they were white with black bibs. We haven't noticed anything happening like this, so patches are either: infrequent relative to us; too nuanced for us to notice; mainly obscure bug-fixes; largely concerned with planets other than those in our solar system; not a selling point of Reality.

We really ought to notice expansions, because they're on a much larger scale. The extinction of the dinosaurs or the sinking of Atlantis could have resulted from expansions. Then again, if we think Reality-wide, well there's a lot of Reality out there: the dinosaurs and Atlantis could merely be elements of patches and the expansion that's got all the players excited involves the collision of two galaxies that we won't even see from Earth for another eight billion years.

It does seem plausible that Reality could have experienced patches and expansions, then, although it's not obvious what specific changes to its content have occurred because of them.

There's one final point about saves and reboots I'd like to make before I conclude this chapter.

While a virtual world is running, its NPCs can be thought of as being in some sense alive[94]. Closing down the virtual world is therefore equivalent to snuffing out the lives of the NPCs who inhabit it.

A back-up can encapsulate the entire state of a virtual world, including (their being part of the reality) all its NPCs. If a backed-up virtual world is subsequently closed down, the possibility remains that it could be restarted exactly as it was at the moment the snapshot was taken. A back-up can therefore be regarded as a reality-in-potential: as data, it can't *run* but it can be *run on.*

Suppose a virtual world were mothballed in such a fashion. Its NPCs would be neither dead nor alive: they'd be in *stasis* – a condition of *potential* life. If someone later used the back-up to initialise a fresh shard, the NPCs would become alive again, as they were, unaware of the interruption even though years might have passed in Reality. Similarly, deleting the back-up would remove this contingency and with it the potential continued lives of the NPCs.

When you switch off a virtual world, you kill every NPC in it. So, does saving a snapshot at the instant of its shutdown somehow mean that you *don't* kill them? Would the deletion of the final

---

[94] Whether NPCs actually *are* alive is subject to debate, but for the moment let's assume they are. The topic is more fully discussed in Chapter 7.

back-up be the true moment that they all died? What if the back-up remained but the virtual world's executable code was lost?

There is no way of telling whether or not anything like this could happen to or could have happened to Reality.

Thus, do we reach the end of Chapter 2, and with it Part 1.

You now know what virtual worlds are and whence they came (if you didn't already). You know why they qualify as realties. You provisionally accept that it might therefore be profitable to draw comparisons between virtual worlds and Reality. You've seen three major (albeit turgid) examples of such comparisons, concerning: how Reality's content could come about; how Reality might present aspects of itself in different ways; how Reality could be stopped and restarted. You've been mildly disappointed that none of these examples have revealed anything especially interesting. Your understanding of Reality has not been improved.

The reason for all this is that by necessity we had to begin by looking at virtual worlds in their own terms: as virtual worlds. We could therefore only talk about Reality that same way: as if it were a virtual world.

We *can* go further, though! To do so, we need to stop thinking of virtual worlds as being suites of software, and instead think of them as being what their software implements: realities.

Part 2

Virtual Worlds as Realities

Chapter 3

REALISING DREAMS

People are the gods of their own dreams – almost.

When you sleep, you dream. When you dream, you control the physics of the worlds you inhabit while dreaming. You may not have fully-conscious control of what happens, and you may not even be aware at the time that you are indeed dreaming; nevertheless, you completely *own* those dream worlds.

Imagination is dreaming under conscious control[1].

Here's a short exercise. Imagine you're holding a soft, squishy ball in your hand. Imagine a plain wall inside your house. Run through in your imagination what would happen if you were to throw the ball at the wall.

You created a world in your mind, right there.

---

[1] Some people (and yes, annoyingly, I'm one of them) do have fully-conscious control of their dreams. This is called *lucid dreaming*. It's not relevant to this book; I merely mention it to stop you from emailing me about it.

Imagine that when the ball hits the wall, it behaves differently. Maybe it sticks, or it ricochets off in a random direction, or it experiences negative gravity, or it transforms into a sparrow.

You control the physics of your imagination. This makes *you* the god of the reality that is your imagination – or of what *would* be a reality, if more than you could visit it (hence, the "almost").

MAKING IT REAL

Your dreams and your imagination are created worlds.

Some people – Sufis and medieval alchemists in particular (Raff, 2019) – have imaginations so vivid and active that they can effectively construct functioning, independent worlds that run on the hardware that is their own brain. They can visit these worlds and converse with inhabitants that seem to have their own free will. Furthermore, they can hallucinate these visualised beings – and anything else they choose from their imagined world (which is called a *subtle reality*) – into Reality. Obviously, no-one else will perceive these non-physical entities, but to the person doing the imagining they appear as real.

Few people possess this potent an imagination, but every last one of us can and does routinely imagine our own created worlds. Sure, other people are unable to join us in such worlds, but that doesn't mean that they're completely inaccessible. A story, for example, is a world of the author's imagination serialised into words, from which a reader or listener can reconstruct the author's world in their own imagination. All interpersonal communication works this way: what you have in your head that you wish to share, you express through one or more communication channels which are picked up by recipients who then build in their own head a model[2] of what you are thinking (while adding some of their own thoughts and analyses into the mix, too).

There is a difference, however, between creating worlds because you wish to communicate and creating worlds because you wish to create. The former is a means to an end; the latter is an end in and of itself[3].

The thing is, some people do simply want to make worlds. The poet W. H. Auden put it like this:

> *Present in every human being are two desires, a desire to know the truth about the primary*

---

[2] A model, because they only have your words to go on, not the actual contents of your imagination. If you want to spend a happy couple of hours trying to figure out what he meant, this is Wittgenstein's *beetle-in-a-box* thought experiment (Wittgenstein, 1953).

[3] There are other reasons for creating worlds, too, discussed at some length in Chapter 9.

> *world, the given world outside ourselves in which we are born, live, love, hate and die, and the desire to make new secondary worlds of our own or, if we cannot make them ourselves, to share in the secondary worlds of those who can.*
>
> (Auden, 1968)

Auden took the terms "primary world" and "secondary world" from (Tolkien, 1964)[4]. He (Auden) knew of what he was writing, too, because as a child he had created his own imaginary world based on lead-mining (Auden, 1971)[5]. He kept the details of this largely to himself at the time, as indeed do most children who create such secondary worlds: they don't make a *secret* of their activities, they just don't have a particular desire to open their game[6] to the primary world. This may be because there's an escapist element to it: if you create a world of your own to escape from Reality, you probably prefer to keep out the very world from which you are escaping.

These detailed, imaginary worlds (which are known as *paracosms*) are not unusual in children. The Brontë sisters (along with their brother)

---

[4] Auden explicitly says in a footnote that he's indebted to Professor J. R. R. Tolkien for these terms. You can always trust footnotes.
[5] Not the most fantastical of settings, but awesome to a six-year-old boy from York.
[6] Auden explicitly calls his world-creation exploits a game.

created several paracosms; C. S. Lewis (along with his brother) also created some; Robert Louis Stevenson (along with his cousin) created two; Austin Tappan Wright's *Islandia* began as a paracosm; M. A. R. Barker's role-playing game world, Tékumel, began as a paracosm[7].

Whether the paracosm is realised in words, paintings or some other medium is immaterial. The author E. Nesbit built paracosms as a child using household objects, principally books and ornaments. She called these *magic cities*, and decades later wrote a novel about two children who became the right size to enter into just such a city that they'd built themselves (Nesbit, 1910). As a consequence of the interest sparked by this book, at the age of 54 she constructed a magic city for the Children's Welfare Exhibition in London (Nesbit, 1913).

Adults are more likely to want to share their imaginary worlds with others, because the worlds themselves are an articulation of something that their creator desires to express. As mentioned earlier, the usual way to achieve such sharing is through serialising the imagined worlds as story, song, dance, painting, film, whatever. Through these actions and artefacts, others can see or hear or otherwise sense the worlds that the world-

[7] Having played some *Empire of the Petal Throne* in my teens, I'm persuaded that Professor Barker may have been more patient as a child than I was.

creators are presenting; what they can't do (perhaps unfortunately, perhaps fortunately) is visit them. Well, they *can*, but they visit their own private renditions of the worlds, as built in their own imaginations.

This distinction is important. Yes, in a theatre each member of the audience is *observing* the same world that the people sitting next to them are, and they're doing so at the same time, but they're not *visiting* the same world. They can't *do* anything to it that anyone else will notice[8]. The same can be said of extensive fictional worlds such as the Whoniverse, Buffyverse and Marvel cinematic universe: many people share a common understanding of them, but they can't *go* there[9].

This is not true for the co-constructed worlds that feature in tabletop role-playing games such as *Dungeons & Dragons*. In these, players change the shared world for each other the whole time. The "role" in "role-playing", incidentally, doesn't refer to the kind of role found in job descriptions ("My role at work is to teach the uninteresting to the uninterested"); rather, it refers to the kind of role in a play ("My role is that of the bitter old man who laments the loss of his youth"). It's about playing characters, not undertaking duties.

---

[8] At least, not if they don't want to be unceremoniously ejected by ushers trained in the art of people-throwing.
[9] For a thorough history of the evolution of such shared worlds in literature, see (Saler, 2012). Note: Saler uses a somewhat broader definition of "virtual world" than I do.

Anyway, the point I want to make here about tabletop RPGs[10] is that although one person (the *dungeon master*[11], in *D&D*'s case) will typically design and run the game world, what goes on in it is determined to a large extent by what the players decide to do. In this set-up, if I shoot an arrow at a bandit in my version of the world then the same bandit is hit[12] by the same arrow in your version of the world, too. This is because it is, in fact, the same world.

It's a world that relies on consent and co-operation to subsist, though. If I shoot an arrow at your character's knee[13], you might argue that it's far too difficult a shot to make: you're running, or you're wearing knee armour, or I'm too far away, or I don't have a bow. What happens next involves a process of negotiation with the dungeon master, who has final say[14]. This is what stops *D&D* campaigns from being realities: their rules of physics aren't automated. They may well include the means by which temporary or permanent

---

[10] I remember hearing on TV once that rebel forces in some conflict had fired an RPG at government forces. This is how rocket-propelled grenades are related to role-playing games.
[11] I'll leave you to decide if this term is sexist or not. Also, formally it's dungeon master™ (Wizards of the Coast/Hasbro owns the trademark), but footnotes and trademarks don't play well together typographically.
[12] Let's assume I'm a good shot.
[13] That one's for you, *Skyrim* fans.
[14] Note that RPGs don't *have* to have a dungeon master: *Fiasco* is one that doesn't, for example.

changes to them can be made, but their operation is not mechanistic.

Look at it this way: if tomorrow you were to catch a coat button in the framework of a passing supermarket trolley and have it ruthlessly torn off, no amount of arguing with Reality about how unlikely that was is going to put it back[15]. In a (somewhat less than enticing, I admit) tabletop role-playing game set in a shopping mall, you might well get a result. If the rules of physics were automated, effects resulting from out-of-game discussions would be impossible.

There is a kind of role-playing game that does have a decent amount of automated physics to it: the *live-action role-playing game*, or *LARP*. LARPs use Reality's locations and Reality's physics, only occasionally resorting to adjudication in cases where Reality doesn't possess the physics that your game needs (such as magic[16]). The degree to which a LARP co-opts Reality can vary, with the ultimate aesthetic experience being the *360° illusion* (Koljonen, 2007): what the player sees, hears, feels and smells in Reality is congruent with that of the imaginary game world. This is a fine ideal, but it's somewhat exclusionary: because players are themselves a part of the game world's

---

[15] Believe me, I've tried. Reality is absolutely without pity!

[16] Of course, as a Wiccan might attest, magic is indeed part of Reality's physics but you wouldn't want to use it in a LARP in case you hurt someone.

environment, if you're the wrong gender, age, height, ethnicity or anything else for a particular role, you can't both play it and maintain the 360° illusion for others.

Oh, in case you're wondering, the recent phenomenon of *escape room* puzzle games[17] are basically LARPs but without the RP and not distinguished by a great deal of A, either.

Children informally LARP[18] a lot, collectively creating imaginary worlds of make-believe which they inhabit together, only negotiating when they feel the need to do so ("You can't sit there, it's fire!" "I thought the other rug was fire?" "Oh, yes, you're right, that one's spiders."). These worlds, as with grown-up LARPs, are still not independent realities, though. They do allow multiple people to enter the same, shared imaginary world at the same time, but they achieve this through the device of being *overlays* of Reality, like ersatz phases. When all the players stop playing, the overlay disappears. In essence, a LARP world is a *partial* reality, in that it's a superimposition on Reality (which, by definition, is itself a complete reality).

That LARPs *aren't* their own realities is clear from the fact that, unlike virtual worlds, they can't

---

[17] Which is to say, puzzles.

[18] The verb is now more usually spelled *larp*, but I'm too old-fashioned for that. I can barely accept that the noun is no longer *LRP*.

be said to have Earthbound gods – they're subject only to whatever gods (if any) control the physics of Reality.

Dreams, stories, role-playing games and LARPs all bring imaginary worlds to life and are successful to degrees depending on what their creators want to say and on what those who visit them want to hear. All are lacking in one respect, though: the worlds they describe aren't real.

It may seem odd to suggest that not being real is a possible deficiency when it comes to imaginary worlds, especially if those worlds would be problematic if real[19], but it's a fair point. Sure, not all imaginary worlds would benefit from being made concrete, but there *are* those that would. Moreover, some worlds can *only* exist by being real, so for them not being real is a deal-breaker.

I'm talking, of course, about virtual worlds here: an artistic creation that people can visit together, through and with which they can interact. These are, as the name suggests, worlds; however, as I stressed in Part 1, in terms of human creativity they are also something altogether more interesting: *realities*. We've had imaginations at least since we became human and possibly even before then; we've had the means to make our imaginations real only since the late 1970s.

---

[19] I certainly wouldn't want the world of Harry Potter to be real because I loathe the little twerp, but he has magic so I couldn't tell him to his face.

From what I've been saying, you will perhaps have discerned that there's a hierarchical ordering of world-fulfilment here. From least-real to most-real:

- At the bottom are the worlds of our dreams and daydreams, which can be anything we imagine (literally, as the imagination is where they live).
- Next, we have imaginary worlds that we encode in words or images or music or movement, possibly for our own amusement, but which other people can nevertheless interpret to create in their own imaginations worlds that reflect the original.
- Following on, we have the group-imagination worlds that people create and sustain together in a magic circle, such as tabletop role-playing games.
- Above these, we have games that work as overlays to Reality.
- Above those, we get to virtual worlds, which exist independently of their players.
- Finally, we reach Reality, our most in-your-face example of something that's real.

Reality is the dream from which there is no awakening.

In abstract terms, the hierarchy begins with the subjective worlds of the imagination, then moves to subjective worlds that are treated by their players as if they were objective realities, then ends with objective realities that exist regardless of whether anyone actually believes they exist[20].

I'm mentioning all this to make an important point. When you create a reality, you are doing so in the certain knowledge that people – at minimum, you – ought to be able to visit it. Indeed, if people couldn't visit it, this may well undo your main motivation for creating the reality in the first place. It is of course conceivable that you may *not* want anyone to visit it, perhaps if you merely wish to see it in action (for example by observing what the NPCs are up to in it). Whatever, you're not going to create a world by accident unless you unintentionally click the button marked "create world and run it on the cloud indefinitely" in your world-creation software.

I'll round off this section with a few words on interfaces, as it's easy to confuse them with that with which they are interfacing. In particular, my description of LARPs as overlaying Reality brings to mind a technology invented to do just that: *augmented reality*.

---

[20] Note that although the consensus is that Reality is an objective reality, there are those who believe that it could be susceptible to subjective opinion through a mechanism known as the *Mandela Effect* (Broome, 2010). Basically, this says that things that aren't true in Reality can become true if enough people *believe* that they're true. Let's try it: believe I'm wealthy.

Augmented reality games are indeed like LARPs in that they overlay parts of Reality, but the manner in which they do so is different. Whereas LARPs co-opt Reality and override it using the imagination, augmented reality co-opts the senses, overriding them with new, invented components[21]. Because of this, augmented reality games (unlike LARPs) can bring with them the appearance of new physics. This opens up the possibility that they could be used to interface not only with worlds that overlay Reality (in the form of virtual phases), but with independent realities (in the form of virtual worlds).

They can be, too! The process has to avoid making situational use of Reality's physics (apart from time), because otherwise the game world wouldn't be fully virtual. For easy-to-comprehend reasons, when augmented reality is used to interface with a virtual world by making it appear to be part of Reality, the result is called a *mixed-reality* game; for MMOs, *World of Tanks* is the trailblazer here.

Virtual reality is basically augmented reality that overrides all of the appearance of Reality,

---

[21] For someone experiencing psychosis, their own mind uncontrollably overwrites parts of Reality with invented sounds (typically voices) and visuals. If you want a sense of what this is like, try the game *Hellblade: Senua's Sacrifice*, which was made in consultation with individuals who have lived-experience of the condition. Warning: it's not for everyone.

rather than just parts of it. It therefore goes without saying that virtual reality could also be used as an interface to a virtual world. I nevertheless *did* say it, because virtual reality and augmented reality tend to hang out as a couple, so not bringing both up together would have been like using an open parenthesis without accompanying it with a closing one (and we all know how irritating *that* is.

ORIGINS OF REALITY

From where do realities come?

One approach to answering this question is to look at where virtual worlds come from first, then apply that understanding to Reality. I'm going to set about it from the opposite direction, though: look at where Reality comes from first, then apply that understanding to virtual worlds. This is because philosophers and theologians have, over the centuries, invested quite a bit of thought into explaining how Reality was created, and it would be discourteous not to scrounge off their work.

Proceeding in this manner, we can consider what the implications would be for virtual worlds brought into being the same way as Reality. In so doing, we can critique the method of Reality's creation. Of course, this does run the risk of calling the whole process of Reality's creation into question; then again, it could help clear up certain aspects of Reality's creation that are otherwise hard to explain[22]. Note that the question I'm asking here isn't *why* Reality was created, it's *how* it was created. *Why* it was created in a Chapter 9 thing.

As it happens, there's no single answer to this question for Reality. There are, however, five that are quite common. Yes, I am going to thrill you with all of these.

The first answer is that Reality has always existed. It wasn't created, as such: it's always been. There was no "before" its existence, therefore no "from" whence it could "come". This is the Buddhist and Jainist answer, although most of the other answers also involve the always-existence of *something*, if not of Reality itself. There is a further refinement of this Reality-has-always-existed answer that says yes, it has always existed, but it wasn't really habitable until a being from a higher reality (an *Earth-diver*) descended to Reality and started improving matters[23].

The second answer is that Reality was formed out of a pre-existing, primordial state that contained the makings of Reality but wasn't itself Reality. This is the Ancient Greeks' answer; they

---

[22] Christian theologians in particular have a pleasant surprise awaiting them.

[23] This is what a good many Native American accounts will tell you, for example.

called the primordial state *Chaos*. Reality comes forth from this primordial state in one of two ways. The first way is what happens when the primordial state is a dark, empty void: something emerges or hatches[24] from it that brings order and so creates Reality. The second way is what happens when the primordial state is made up of two opposites mixed together: something separates them out into Reality and some other reality (such as a heaven).

In either case, the creation of Reality doesn't just occur automatically: some innovative individual has to get to work, otherwise, we'd still be living in Chaos[25]. This being is known as a *demiurge*, and is either a creator god or an individual created and tasked by a creator god to create Reality. There's a technical term for this perspective on the origin of Reality: *creatio ex materia* ("creation out of matter").

The third answer to the question of where Reality came from is that it was created out of nothing (*creatio ex nihilo*[26]). If you were to liken Reality to a city made out of bricks then *creatio ex materia* is where you start off with an enormous, mixed-up pile of assorted bricks and have to make it all from those, whereas *creatio ex nihilo* is where you don't even have the bricks. This is the answer

---

[24] If it hatches then the primordial state either contains, or is itself, what's referred to as a *cosmic egg*.
[25] Then again, how would we know we weren't?
[26] You can perhaps tell from the fact these terms are in Latin that they've been around for awhile.

of Judaism, Christianity[27] and Islam (the main *Abrahamic religions*).

That said, the Old Testament of *The Bible* is in truth a little hazy on the origin of Reality, mainly giving an impression of *creatio ex nihilo* but occasionally hinting at *creatio ex materia*. What it does make clear, though, is that Reality definitely *was* created. This enables a line of reasoning called the *first cause argument*[28], which goes something like as follows:

- Everything that begins to exist has a cause.
- Reality began to exist.
- Therefore, Reality must have a cause.

You can take this further, by noting that if Reality has a cause then that cause must itself ultimately be uncaused, therefore there must exist an eternal, uncaused creator of Reality (which is to say, God[29]). This clears matters up if you accept the Old Testament's position, but if you wished to be cynical you could ask why Reality needed to begin to exist if its creator didn't[30].

The fourth answer to the question of where Reality came from is that it was created out of the body of its creator (*creatio ex deo*). This has two

---

[27] For most definitions of "Christianity". Some Christians, such as Mormons, take a *creatio ex materia* approach.
[28] The origins of this argument come from the Islamic discipline of *Ilm al-Kalām* ("science of discourse").
[29] The concept of an uncaused being, or a being who contains within themself their own cause, is called *asiety*.
[30] This is known as the *unmoved mover* paradox.

different flavours. The first is literal: the creator bled out, spat, sneezed, or otherwise secreted[31] Reality; or gave birth to Reality; or lost hair, an eye, hand or other body part[32] which became Reality. This is the answer of the Kuba people of central Africa, whose creator god, Mbombo, vomited forth the sun, moon and stars (followed a while later by some animals and people) as a result of a bad stomach-ache.

The second flavour of *creatio ex deo*, known as *pantheism*, says Reality comprises the being of the creator[33] (usually with reference to the Abrahamic religions' God, although elements of pantheism do appear elsewhere – in Hinduism, for example). There's a potential flaw here in that God is perfect but Reality (or at least humanity) isn't, which is an inconsistency. This can be explained, however, by either supposing that all of Reality is part of the divine but the divine is more than just Reality[34], or by saying that Reality came from God's being but once it left it was on its own so could become

---

[31] I'd list more but I don't want this book to fall foul of censors.

[32] Ditto.

[33] Pantheism can also mean the worship (or at least tolerance) of multiple gods.

[34] This is called *panentheism* ("all in god"). Reality is a strict subset of God; while God as a whole is perfect, if you take such a subset then this isn't perfect because it isn't the perfect whole.

corrupt[35]. This second possibility returns to the more literal flavour of *creatio ex deo*, but without going into details regarding precious bodily fluids.

The fifth answer to the question of Reality's origin is that it came from another reality. This solution fuses together some of the themes present in other answers[36]. What typically happens is that proto-realities form, through which humanity (or its creator) ascends into other proto-realities, eventually emerging into Reality. This is essentially a female-biology answer, in that humanity and Reality are developing in tandem until humanity is ready to be born. Sometimes, the birth is literal (from the womb of a female god); sometimes, it's more metaphorical (humanity appears from the underworld via a hole in the ground)[37].

Although the foregoing are the most common answers to the question of Reality's origin, there are plenty of others[38]; I apologise if I haven't covered one that you know to be true. The scientific evidence currently points at a Big Bang

---

[35] This is like saying your blood is fine while it's inside you but if you take it out then it's not really part of you anymore and takes on a different nature.

[36] Or, alternatively, some of the themes present in the other answers are diffused from this one.

[37] This is also what a (different) good many Native American accounts will tell you.

[38] "Next, they [the gods Kane, Ku and Lono] make the earth to rest their feet upon." (Beckwith, 1940).

creatio ex nihilo, but leaves open the possibility that the Big Bang wasn't the start of the matter[39] and that there could be an always-existed aspect to Reality (the theory of *cosmic inflation* suggests this, for example).

That said, there is a rarer, sixth answer to the question of where Reality came from that will be of particular interest later in this book: *causa sui* ("cause of itself"). This is the way the Ancient Egyptian god Ptah did it: he willed both Reality *and himself* into existence. That's pretty damned impressive! OK, so the Ancient Egyptian gods Amun-Ra and Atum-Ra did the same thing, but I'll nevertheless use Ptah as my exemplar because Amun-Ra and Atum-Ra could only claim they'd done it once the gods Amun and Atum respectively had been merged with the god Ra. Ptah, on the other hand, could do it from the get-go[40].

Before we leave this topic, there are two more theological terms that we can just take because theologians can't stop us: when a god exists in a higher reality than Reality then that god is said to be *transcendent*; a god that exists in Reality is said to be *immanent*[41].

Strictly speaking, these terms only apply to the pairing of Reality and a higher reality, but I'll be

---

[39] Or indeed of the anti-matter.

[40] If you really want to rile the populace of ancient Heliopolis, point out that Ptah created Ra anyway so the point is moot.

[41] Immanence can also refer to the situation in which a reality in some sense *is* its god.

using them in a more relative fashion (not very often, admittedly). For example, when you play a virtual world then your character is immanent to that virtual world, whereas you, the human being at the keyboard, are transcendent to it. The same applies to aspects of a god's nature: if you and I are sitting next to one another while playing an MMO, and I ask you to come to help me, then from the perspective of the non-player characters of that MMO I'm exhibiting transcendent powers – powers that are completely beyond the MMO's physical laws. From the perspective of you and me, I'm merely exhibiting the power of speech available to most people in Reality[42].

Origins of Sub-Realities

Having answered, multiple times, the question of how Reality was created, we can now turn our attention to the question of how the sub-realities that are virtual worlds are created.

This is much easier, as there's only one answer: *creatio ex nihilo*.

Hmm. Yes.

---

[42] Note that my power of speech doesn't qualify as being immanent; this is because I'm not a god of Reality.

Well although that's the coldly-analytical response, we can argue that many of the other ways that Reality was created can be applied to virtual worlds, too.

If, for example, you use an off-the-shelf game engine to create your virtual world, replete with physics and predefined objects that you can drop in and change at will, that sounds an awful lot like *creatio ex materia*.

If you do as I tell my students to do, and try to create a virtual world that *says* something, you're investing a part of your identity in the world you create, which sounds an awful lot like *creatio ex deo*.

If you are a player of a non-game world such as *Second Life*, entering its reality and starting to build sounds an awful lot like you're Earth-diving (well, *Second Life*-diving).

If you create a world, then discard it and recreate it from scratch, and continue to do so, improving it each rewrite[43], then it sounds an awful lot like the developmental, gestational, came-from-another-reality approach I described in the previous section.

If you want to get *really* philosophical about it, and believe in a deterministic universe, you can even suggest that your virtual world has been

---

[43] In case you weren't counting earlier, *MUD* was rewritten in its entirety three times. The final version, known as *MUD2*, was/is actually version four.

embodied implicitly in the make-up of Reality since forever. In the same way that a broken egg is embodied in the situation of an unbroken egg that's falling from the top of the Burj Khalifa, so your virtual world has been embodied in Reality at every moment in the past. This sounds an awful lot like saying your virtual world has always existed.

OK, so some of these "sounds an awful lot like" expositions rely heavily on metaphor, but given how much metaphor is routinely involved in interpreting accounts of Reality-creation, they're well within established bounds.

The only way Reality was created that doesn't work for your virtual world is Ptah's method. Your virtual world was created by you. You didn't will yourself into existence at the same time as your virtual world, so this isn't how it happened[44].

Looking at all these methods, though, it's clear that at some point either you or someone else had to create the virtual world from nothing: *creatio ex nihilo*. Sure, you think it up in Reality, use the tools and physics of Reality to make your ideas manifest, and it runs on computers existing in Reality, but *as a reality* it came from nothing.

---

[44] Unless you're Ptah, in which case I may be in trouble.

REALITIES DETERMINED

While describing back there how it could be argued that the virtual world you make has in some sense always existed, I touched on the notion of a deterministic universe.

Are virtual worlds deterministic?

OK, so let's start off by looking at what I mean by "deterministic" here. It's quite a long explanation, but bear with me. I'll use games for my examples, because why wouldn't I?

So, when you play *Chess*, it's possible to write down: where all the pieces on the board are; whose turn it is; whether the last move was of a pawn open to *en passant*; and whether each side can still castle or not. Suppose you made such a note of a game: you could subsequently put away the board and pieces, then fifty years later take out your note, set up the board as described, and continue to play exactly where you left off. Given the rules of *Chess*[45], someone else could find your note a hundred years after that and continue the game from the point you recorded it a century and a half previously.

---

[45] This is actually important: the saved positions alone aren't enough. We have examples of saved positions from the Ancient Egyptian game known today as *Hounds and Jackals*, but we can't set up a board and carry on from where the original players left off – the rules didn't make it across the millennia.

This kind of write-downable description of a game in play is called a *state*. It's a technical term[46], but a fairly intuitive one – you had no problem understanding it when I was talking about backing up virtual worlds earlier. When you save a computer game, you're saving some or all of its state: if the battle you engage in immediately after the save doesn't go quite as well as you had perhaps hoped, you can load the saved state and try again[47].

We'll find the concept of a saved state useful (again) later, but for our current purposes it's the relationship between different states that's of more interest. The thing is, a state can usually be *transformed* into a new state. In *Chess*, this happens when you make a move. The pieces are no longer arranged how they were before and (assuming the game isn't over) it's now your opponent's turn. You could still record the game's state, it's just that now it would be a different state.

In *Chess*, there are normally many alternative moves that can be made in a given state; figuring out which one is best is what makes the game fun (well, that and winning). Each move in one state leads to a different state, from which other moves lead to other states.

---

[46] As people who remember earlier footnotes will know.
[47] In Steve Meretzky's classic work of interactive fiction, *Planetfall*, whenever you save the game in the presence of your robot buddy, Floyd, Floyd says "Oh boy! Are we going to try something dangerous now?".

Imagine drawing a genealogy-style tree, with the initial, ancestor state (the one before anyone makes a move) at the root. For each possible move in that state, begin a branch that leads to a newer state. From the starting position in *Chess*, white can move one of eight pawns forward either one or two squares, or can move one of two knights to one of two squares each – a total of 20 possible moves. This means that from the initial state there are 20 branches, each leading to one of the 20 possible states that can pertain when it's black's first turn. Black can also make one of 20 opening moves, so each of those 20 states also has 20 branches coming from it, meaning that when it's white's second turn the board could be in any one of 400 possible states. Some of these will have more moves available than others, and after white has moved again there are 8,902 states that black could be looking at; when it's white's third turn, there are 197,742 possible configurations of the board[48]. The number continues to grow rapidly as play proceeds.

The first two moves in *Chess* have a *branching factor* of 20. Overall, the average branching factor across all states is about 35 for *Chess*.

In a *deterministic* game, the branching factor is always exactly one.

---

[48] I didn't work these numbers out myself (well, except for the first two, when I was about ten years old); I got them out of (Sloane & Plouffe, 1995).

As a general rule, if the next state in a sequence is created by applying a function to the current state, and that function involves no uncertainty (that is, it's not random and doesn't involve external input), then you have a deterministic sequence. The same starting conditions will always lead to the same behaviour.

A famous example of this in Computer Science is Conway's game of *Life*[49].

You can skip past this if you already know about *Life*.

So, *Life* isn't so much a game as a toy. You start off with a grid of squares (called *cells*), and mark some of them as occupied. Except for the ones at the grid's edges, each cell is adjacent (orthogonally or diagonally) to eight other cells. Every turn (or *generation*), you go through all the cells, figuring out what will be in them next turn. There are three rules:

- Every occupied cell adjacent to either exactly three or exactly two other occupied cells in this generation survives to the next generation.

---

[49] Although its name is simply *Life*, it's traditional to refer to it as Conway's Game of *Life*. It was invented by John Horton Conway in 1969 (Roberts, 2015), but as far as I can tell there isn't an original monograph describing it. It was first brought to public attention by (Gardner, 1970).

- Every empty cell adjacent to exactly three occupied cells in this generation becomes occupied in the next generation.
- All other cells become or remain empty in the next generation.

For example, Figure 6 shows three successive generations of states in *Life* using a 6×5 grid. To the left is Generation 0, the *initial state*, consisting of four occupied cells (shown in black) horizontally across the middle. If you go through each of Generation 0's 30 cells in turn, applying the above rules to see what goes in the corresponding cell of the next generation, you'll arrive at the middle state, Generation 1. Go through all the cells in Generation 1 applying the same rules to them and you'll derive the state on the right, Generation 2.

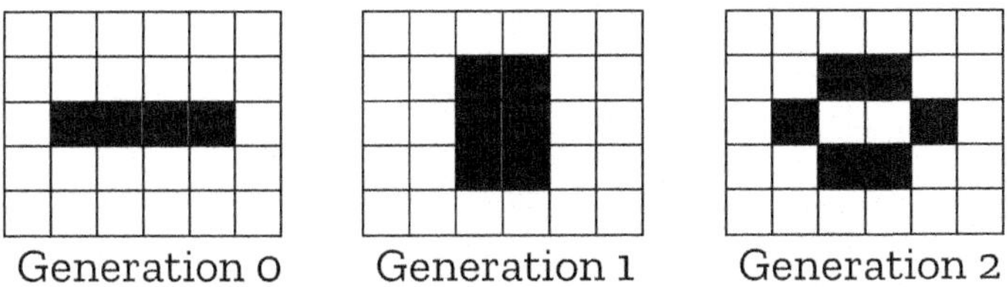

Figure 6 – Three Generations of *Life*.

I chose the set-up for Generation 0 that I did specifically so that Generation 2 would be *stable*: all its occupied cells are adjacent to two other occupied cells, and no empty cells are adjacent to exactly three occupied cells, so henceforth nothing is going to change from one generation to the next.

This particular configuration of cells occurs quite often in *Life* and has its own name: it's a *beehive*.

Generations in *Life* don't have to end up stable. For example, if Generation 0 had been initialised with only three horizontally-adjacent occupied cells instead of four then the Generation 1 which followed it would have had three vertically-adjacent occupied cells. Thereafter, all even-numbered generations would have looked the same as Generation 0 (three horizontally-adjacent occupied cells) and all odd-numbered generations would have looked the same as Generation 1 (three vertically-adjacent occupied cells). This pattern is known as a *blinker*.

Patterns can move across the grid from generation to generation, too. Figure 7 shows successive generations of a pattern known as a *glider*, which repeats every four generations but in a new position (that is, Generation 4 is the same as Generation 0 but diagonally one cell to the right and one cell down)[50].

Thanks to modern computers, it's possible to automate *Life* and to build absolutely enormous grids. Cell patterns can move around, interacting with one another dynamically to create incredible effects: self-replicating patterns; patterns that

---

[50] There are two opposing philosophical views as to whether objects are wholly present every moment of their existence (*endurantism*) or whether they have distinct temporal parts (*perdurantism*). Look at gliders and see what you think.

display dot-matrix-like words; patterns that can perform arithmetic calculations[51]. It's amazing to watch animations of some of these in action.

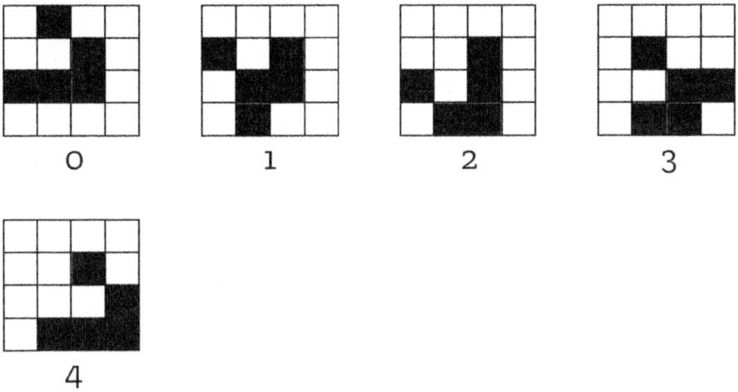

Figure 7 - A Glider in Motion.

The thing is, though, no matter how large the grid, no matter how sophisticated the apparent behaviour of the patterns, no matter how impressive the result, whatever happens is determined *only* by the rules of *Life* and the initial state. Whatever you supply as Generation 0 completely embodies every generation thereafter.

Life, then is deterministic. You set the machine up, and from then on whatever is going to happen is fixed. It may look as though things are happening by chance, but they're not. If you were to give someone else the same starting state that

[51] In fact, as they can be built to simulate a *Universal Turing Machine* (Turing, 1937), they can in theory compute anything computable, given time.

you were using, and they plugged it in as the input for their own software implementation of *Life*, then exactly the same sequence of events would unfold for both of you[52].

So, is Reality deterministic? Or, to paraphrase Conway himself: are you reading this because it's your choice or because it was predetermined?

Life was the first example discovered of what is now known as a *cellular automaton*. Everything about its operation proceeds causally and relentlessly. The current state causes the state that immediately follows it, and thence every state that will ever follow it. Any one state holds implicitly within it all the states that will come after it.

Suppose that you were to take a snapshot[53] of Reality, recording the position and momentum and anything else you needed to know for every single fundamental particle at same instant. You'd have to do this from outside Reality, of course, because Reality doesn't have enough room to store itself more than once[54] and time has a relative aspect to it; let's suppose, then, that you *are* in a higher reality and that all this is therefore possible. So: if you were to re-run Reality twice from your single

---

[52] This assumes that neither your program nor theirs is embarrassingly buggy.

[53] The technical term, which I snuck in earlier, is a *dump*.

[54] Let alone an infinite number of times over: each copy of Reality held within Reality would in turn have to keep a copy of itself, and so on indefinitely (like a fractal but without the zoom).

save point, would things pan out the same way both times or differently?

If they do pan out the same way both times, Reality is deterministic[55] and any sense that its inhabitants may have that they possess free will is mistaken[56]. This is the basis of the pantheistic position advocated by the Dutch rationalist philosopher, Baruch Spinoza: if Reality and the creator are one and the same, and the creator is perfect, then Reality must be deterministic.

If things don't pan out the same way both times, Reality is not deterministic and chance plays a part. At the moment, science has met with some success treating fundamental particles as globs of probabilities, so it looks as if free will is winning among natural philosophers[57]. Science does leave open the possibility of changing its mind when presented with further evidence, though, so this view need not necessarily prevail in the long term[58].

To return to the question posed at the beginning of this section, then: are virtual worlds deterministic?

---

[55] Either that, or its random-number generator by pure chance produced the same series of numbers both times.
[56] Free will is discussed in more depth in Chapter 6.
[57] That is, physicists.
[58] It may be possible to capture the fundamentals of physics in terms of hypergraph manipulation (Wolfram, 2020). Such a system works deterministically, a bit like Conway's game of *Life* but on nodal relationships rather than on grid cells.

Well, virtual worlds can definitely be non-deterministic, because I distinctly remember writing the random-number generator for *MUD*[59]. The interesting point, though, is *why* they're non-deterministic.

Programmers usually like their programs to be deterministic, because that makes them so much easier to debug. After all, if you can't reproduce a problem, how can you be sure you've fixed it? Nevertheless, programmers of virtual worlds deliberately introduce non-determinism. For what reasons?

Well, there are essentially two.

The first reason is the weaker one: you might get interesting states that you couldn't get were the system simply left to run mechanistically. This isn't all that important, because you can have any state you want at initialisation time; where it helps is in showing you states that you might want but hadn't realised you did.

The second, stronger reason for having non-determinism in virtual worlds is that players don't like too much predictability. Uncertainty can spice things up a bit (and furnish a useful excuse should you, the player, make a bad move). If you know

---

[59] The question "Is this reality non-deterministic?" can be answered in the positive if at least one random-number generator used in the implementation of that reality is non-deterministic. *MUD*'s one-and-only random-number generator was non-deterministic (it used the real-time clock as a seed), so *MUD* itself was also non-deterministic.

every time you start a fight with a monster what the outcome will be, well where's the fun in that? The game could save you time by flatly telling you the result, without making you go through the motions.

As both these reasons suggest, then, virtual worlds have randomness internal to them because people external to them find them more interesting that way. A deterministic virtual world would only be interesting if it were simulating some deterministic natural process (and then only to people who studied this process).

That said, uncertainty doesn't have to come from a random-number generator. There are many sources of uncertainty in games, of which what are effectively *N*-sided dice comprise but one (Costikyan, 2013). The primary fount of unpredictability in virtual worlds is actually player activity. Even if a virtual world were entirely deterministic, it would be impossible to predict what it would look like at an arbitrary point in the future were players able to mess with the pieces[60].

There's an interesting point that arises from this, which doesn't seem to have previously been picked up by either philosophers or theologians.

Without an injection of uncertainty, a virtual world developer could look at a dump of the virtual

---

[60] Except if all timelines end the same way regardless. What Reality will look like after the universe's projected heat death might be an example of this, for example.

world and figure out what any NPC was going to do next. This would make the developer omniscient but the NPC bereft of free will. If the virtual world's system of causality is influenced by a random-number generator then NPCs could perhaps be said to have free will, but then the developer would no longer be omniscient. If instead the source of uncertainty is caused by the presence of players from Reality, though, then the developer could remain omniscient with respect to the virtual world, but the NPCs would have free will because of the uncertainties that come with input from Reality.

Put another way, if the gods of a reality are omniscient then the NPCs' free will in that reality derives from the actions of player characters sent from the gods' reality[61].

Getting Personal

Of the six explanations I gave regarding Reality's origins, only in the first is Reality not somehow brought into being (it's always existed). In all the others, Reality is explicitly, if not necessarily deliberately, created. Supposing for now that

---

[61] Whether the players of those characters have free will themselves is another matter, of course.

Reality *was* created, a reasonable question to ask is: who or what created it?

Now of course, there are as many specific answers to this question as there are specific accounts describing what happened. Details aside, though, each will fundamentally espouse one of only two basic positions: either Reality was created by an entity[62] who can be regarded as a person, or it was created by an impersonal or unknowable force.

In the case of virtual worlds, it's pretty clear-cut that they are indeed created by an entity who can (charitably) be regarded as a person – the virtual world's designer. As we shall see shortly, however, the issue is less to do with whether they *can* be regarded as a person and more to do with whether they *will* be.

When a god can be related to as a person, that god is said to be a *personal god*. This doesn't mean that you have your own, personal god like you have your own, personal coffee-mug; it means that the god in question has qualities similar to those possessed by human beings. These qualities might include free will, emotions and forethought, for example.

For Reality, the subject of a personal god is one area where the major Abrahamic faiths disagree. In

---

[62] Or entities, but I'll assume the singular for now so I don't tie my sentences up in knots of singularity and plurality.

Judaism, God[63] is beyond human understanding and so can not be related to as a person, although some degree of anthropomorphism may be helpful to convey certain ideas about God's nature. In Christianity, God is three beings: the Father, the Son and the Holy Spirit[64]. The Father and the Son are definitely personal gods; whether the Holy Spirit is or not is less certain. In Islam, God is a personal god but is not of Reality; this means that although humans can visualise some aspects of God, their picture will always be incomplete.

The disagreement arises because in order to have created Reality as advertised, God must be of a higher reality – one to which human beings have no access (at least while alive)[65]. Without such access, we have no handle on said higher reality: it lies outside human experience and is incomprehensible to us. God, therefore, as a being of this higher reality, must also be incomprehensible to us. How, then, given that God is personal, can we comprehend God as a person?

Judaism's answer is that we can't. Christianity's answer is that God is three people in one and that although the whole is incomprehensible, each person making it up isn't. Islam's answer is that

---

[63] For brevity and clarity, I'll simply refer to the Abrahamic god as God here, rather than Yahweh/God/Allah.
[64] Also known as the Holy Ghost, but I'll go with Holy Spirit; it sounds less like an expression of annoyance made by Robin in the 1960s *Batman* TV series.
[65] That is, God must be transcendent.

there are glimpses of God that are comprehensible to us, but glimpses of God aren't God.

These aren't the only ways to answer the question, of course. The Hindu god Vishnu is a transcendent personal god who neatly addresses the problem of being incomprehensible to humans by occasionally manifesting in Reality as different human-comprehensible *avatars* (Krishna and Rama being the best-known[66]). In this sense, Vishnu can be visualised a bit like matter in a superposition of quantum states, being all of them at the same time but able to collapse into any single one to become observable[67].

There is a conviction that bridges the gap between a personal and an impersonal god. Known as *pandeism*, it holds that the creator god started out as a person, but in the act of creation became Reality itself and so ceased to be a person. It's basically a fusing-together of *pantheism* (which says that Reality and the divine are one, but is non-committal about how that happened) and *deism* (which says that Reality has a creator god, who, having created it, seems then to have abandoned it).

---

[66] Not all Vishnu's avatars are of human form. Kurma, for example, is at least half tortoise.

[67] Usually, however, Vishnu is visualised as being a blue man with four arms.

Deism and pantheism tend to be at odds because both take a rational[68] approach to their understanding of Reality and therefore have to defend their positions rationally. Deism holds that there is a god of Reality, but that this god doesn't intercede in Reality (at least not directly). It suggests that Holy books and prophets are unreliable and so count as inadmissible, hearsay evidence, but that the existence of a god can nevertheless be deduced formally by applying logical thought, rooted in observations of the natural world (a *teleological* argument – an explanation in terms of purpose rather than of cause).

Pantheism is a qualification of deism which goes a step further: it asserts that the universe is itself a god. Its dispute with deism is over what is the *Absolute* – the "most real" being. Pantheists say it's Reality; deists say it's a being of a higher reality.

Pandeists resolve this by saying it's the latter transformed into the former.

Interestingly, although these philosophical positions aim to further our understanding of Reality's relationship with its creator, the same positions also arise when creators of virtual worlds aim to further their own understanding of the

---

[68] You could almost say scientific, if experiments weren't so difficult to design and to perform.

realities they create – even if their motivations are somewhat more pragmatic.

For example, in *MUD* there were a small number of players who had reached such a high level that they acquired supernatural, administrative-grade powers; we called these players *wizzes*[69], but in the terminology of this book they were demigods. A topic that they discussed long and hard among themselves was the appropriate degree of openness they should exhibit while playing. Some liked to operate covertly, only altering the game world in subtle ways, but others preferred to operate overtly, displaying their powers in an unconstrained manner. This caused friction between the two groups. Neither disputed the fundamental right of gods or demigods to interfere in the affairs of regular player-characters (mortals); their disagreement only concerned whether they should be *seen* to be doing so or not.

The demigods in favour of overtness were like those of Ancient Greece, insisting that they were noticed and that play revolved around them. They were personal gods *in extremis*: they *wanted* to interact with players[70] in supernatural ways – it was the very reason they played. Their (not entirely persuasive) argument for overtness was

---

[69] Short for "wizards and witches".

[70] Probably with NPCs, too, had *MUD* been able to boast any that exhibited human-level intelligence.

that if regular players saw someone using supernatural powers, or felt the direct effect of those supernatural powers, then they'd be incentivised to try to earn those powers themselves[71]. Truth be told, though, the demigods who played overtly did so because they enjoyed it.

The demigods who preferred covertness were effectively advocating deism, because they didn't do anything in or to the reality that couldn't be explained naturally (as opposed to supernaturally). Their argument against playing overtly was that it's easier to manipulate the game world if players don't suspect you're doing it. Furthermore, when regular players can see that a god is around, they will readily attribute anything unexpected that they experience to supernatural intervention. If, say, they underwent a period of bad luck, they would unhesitatingly blame it on godly interference. OK, so perhaps more often than not it *was* godly interference, but without the visible presence of a god it *could* have just been a whim of the random-number generator[72]. Also, having visible gods reduces players' sense of wonder;

---

[71] This rationale is harder to justify in modern virtual worlds, because these days players don't get to become demigods through play. Be that as it may, imaginative individuals do exist in whom a rampant exhibition of godly powers might inspire an ambition for a career in MMO development.
[72] The acronym *RNG* is used to refer to a virtual world's random-number generator; the god of Reality who controls the output of the virtual world's RNG is known as *RNGesus*.

when you know there's a god on walkabout, everything that happens tends to be coloured by the presence of that god. You can't simply play as normal, because there's someone there who isn't *playing* in quite the same sense that you are.

The gods and demigods of modern virtual worlds adopt a third, compromise position: they moderate their appearances in the virtual world, only interfering when there's an issue to address. This resembles the approach favoured by the gods of Hinduism, who tend to be covert until there's a problem that needs to be fixed, whereupon they'll reveal themselves overtly to fix it. If the gods of an MMO don't appear, it's not because they've abandoned their reality, it's because it's running smoothly[73].

The reluctance of such gods and demigods to show themselves is perhaps explained by the fact that overtness doesn't scale well. If a god manifests in front of 100 players in a MUD, it's relatively easy to handle the conversations that 10% of these players will immediately attempt to start with that god. If there are 10,000 players, it's not so easy[74].

---

[73] A branch of theological thought known as *occasionalism* proposes that gods only interfere in the general cause-and-effect operation of their created realities, er, occasionally. There's a suggestion that this could be a profitable way in general to examine the relationship between the designers and players of games (Leino, 2019).

[74] Aside: it could be (and has been) suggested that praying in Reality is akin to issuing a bug report in a virtual world. I get

This isn't to say that game designers *don't* play their own games alongside regular players, but if they do then it'll usually be *as* regular players. In Shakespeare's play *Henry V*, King Henry walks in disguise among his men on the eve of the Battle of Agincourt so as to find out what they truly think of him and his campaign. OK, so Henry isn't a god[75], but the principle is the same: you'll get a more honest idea of what your creation is like if you wander it as a nobody than if you wander it as a somebody.

Judging by our experience with virtual worlds, then, deism is a plausible way for players to view gods: they do exist, but don't overtly intervene. What, then, about the more specialised position of pantheism? This says that the virtual world is itself its god.

Well, considering that we know for a fact that virtual worlds do not create themselves, it looks as if pantheism is dead in the water as a way of characterising them. Bad news, pantheists: it is indeed[76]. However, pandeism (which suggests that

---

the analogy, but can state with some certainty that there were very few gods or demigods of *MUD* who would have regarded "I don't have a kick-ass sword" as a bug.

[75] That said, in the play's prologue Shakespeare suggests that the actor playing Henry is to the real Henry as Henry himself is to Mars, the god of war.

[76] You *might* be able to argue that a virtual world could be the end result of a self-modifying computer program. Whether the program or its programmer was the true creator of the

a personal god created the virtual world and in so doing became it) puts up more of a fight.

I'm about to touch on motivation here, which I really want to leave to the final chapter of this book; it does help explain the point, though, therefore I'll permit a modicum of it to sneak in early.

So, some of the people who developed early virtual worlds did so as gifts to their players. They wanted to create a reality that belonged collectively to its visitors rather than to its makers. The gods were to be servants of the players, implementing whatever changes to the physics of the world the players requested of them, but distancing themselves from the social outcomes that derived from the world as played.

The most famous example of this was Pavel Curtis's *LambdaMOO*, a social world dating from 1990. I'll talk in Chapter 8 about how this worked out[77], but for the moment I simply want to draw the analogy with pandeism. *LambdaMOO*'s god began as a tool-wielder, but upon completing his creation gave up his creative identity and became his creation's tool. Pavel-the-designer became Pavel-the-programmer.

Now, I said "analogy" back there because *LambdaMOO*'s story doesn't map *exactly* onto

---

world would then depend on whether the program had free will or not (see Chapter 6).

[77] Spoiler: not as planned.

pandeism. Its god didn't *lose* his godly powers, he merely chose not to exercise them, deism-style, except as directed by his creation through the medium of its players. In true pandeism, the world created assumes the god's powers itself (which it exercises by existing). We can afford to give the analogy some leeway, though, so as not to dismiss pandeism's case on a mere technicality.

In general, it may seem risky for the designer of a reality to yield control of their godly powers to others, because said designer could well have made a mistake somewhere along the line that they realise too late needs to be addressed. Pandeism has no problem with this regarding Reality, because the creator god was (or sort-of is) perfect and therefore didn't ever make any mistakes in the first place. It does have a problem with it for virtual worlds, but not necessarily in the manner you might expect.

The problem is not to do with perfection. This is because, from a pandeist perspective, any reality that contains the means by which it can be fixed *is*, in fact perfect. This was indeed the case with *LambdaMOO*: if a bug was detected in the code or the design then the players could instruct Pavel-the-programmer to fix it, which he would do.

The problem was that although Pavel, the god of *LambdaMOO*, wished to and tried to abdicate his godly powers, he couldn't while he retained control of its physics. He wasn't merely the agent of his virtual world's will (as expressed by its players); he was also the agent of his own will. If the players asked for something that he knew was a very bad idea, he could yet veto it. If they didn't ask for something he knew was a very good idea, he could yet implement it (which indeed he eventually did[78]).

Perfection has consequences. Try as he might, Pavel remained *LamdaMOO*'s god *whether he liked it or not.*

As I said, we'll explore the consequences of this later.

The failure of the god-as-designer-to-god-as-programmer analogy seems to suggest that although pandeism comes close to being able to describe how virtual worlds (if not Reality) are created, it ultimately falls short.

That's only *seems*, though. It does have one more card it can play.

To explain this, I need to introduce the concept of *mind-body dualism*. This is somewhat oblique to the discussion so far, but it does enable quite an impressive observation.

So, the basics of the idea are quite old, but it was pushed hard by the French philosopher and scientist René Descartes in the 17th century. The suggestion is that the body and the mind are separate and distinct. In one form, *substance dualism*, the body is physical and the mind is non-

[78] Details in Chapter 8.

physical[79] – helpfully consistent with the idea of an immortal soul that can be attached and detached from a human vessel. In another form, *property dualism*, the mind is governed by the physics of Reality just as everything else is, but it's not part of the body. There are other forms of dualism, too, but these are the main ones.

The counter position is *monism*. This says that the mind and the body aren't separate, but that one is a consequence of the other (or, less often, that both are a consequence of something else). *Physicalism* says that the mind is an emergent feature of how the brain is put together[80]; *idealism* says that only thought exists, and the material world is an illusory construction of the mind. Which of dualism or monism is the better way to conceive of Reality is the *mind-body problem*.

When it comes to the nature of virtual worlds, the mind and body of a player character are definitely separate, because the mind is in Reality (or beyond) and the body is in the virtual world. Whether the mind and the body of an NPC are separate things or the same thing depends on the implementation. In either case, idealism is poppycock: the representation of the reality is as data operated upon by rules expressed as program

---

[79] "Physical" here means extending to the space of Reality. It's possible that the non-physical mind could be physical in a different reality.

[80] That is, the mental *supervenes* on the physical.

code, which implies either property dualism (if the code is modular, so different functions govern different types of object) or physicalism (if the same code works on all data). Physicalism does still leave room for the concept of souls, though: just because the mind and the body are not *separate*, that isn't to say they're not *separable* (by extracting just the right data set and running the physics code on it independently, for example).

I didn't bring up the topic of the mind-body problem to discuss how the mind and body might be implemented in a virtual world, though (I do that later). I brought it up because although idealism is indeed poppycock, the suggestion that the virtual world is an extension of the designer's mind is *not* poppycock.

Virtual world design is an art form. When designers design a virtual world, they're trying to say something to their players using the virtual world as a medium. The phrase often used by designers[81] to describe this is that they "put something of their soul" into the virtual world; it isn't so much an *expression* of part of them, it *is* part of them, at least in terms of their sense of identity.

[81] Not just me. See also (Kania, 2017).

It could be argued[82], then, that when a designer's design is made real and a virtual world results, this designed reality embodies part of the essence of who the designer *is*. It's fixed, pandeism-style, because it can't think, but it encapsulates something of the designer's *being*; from the perspective of its non-player characters, therefore, the virtual world itself acts as a medium for examining their creator. It's distinct from the designer, but nevertheless *is*, in some way, the designer. This reframing of the pandeistic interpretation of virtual world creation avoids the issues with involuntary power retention that I mentioned earlier with regards to *LambdaMOO*; it's not *about* power: it's about *identity*.

Suppose that the designer visited their virtual world as a player character. In so doing, they would provide another medium by which non-player characters could examine their creator – one wholly *within* the virtual world (and so relatable to through its physics), but not *of* the virtual world. The player character is distinct from the designer playing it, but nevertheless *is* the designer.

This neatly results in an equivalence of the Christian Trinity: the designer maps onto the Father; their player character maps onto the Son;

---

[82] As indeed I did argue earlier as a "sounds an awful lot like" exposition. For a rather less superficial argument, check out Saint Thomas Aquinas's *via negativa* approach.

the game world itself as embodying its creator's identity maps onto the Holy Spirit.

It's interesting how this understanding quite easily drops out from a simple analysis of how virtual worlds are designed and played[83].

SELF-MODIFYING SYSTEMS

Ptah presents a problem. It's not just a problem for us, it's a problem for him[84], too.

Ptah, as I mentioned earlier, willed both Reality and himself into existence. This clearly isn't how virtual worlds are created; if it were, they wouldn't be so expensive to make. It's how Ptah created Reality, though.

You could, if you wished, use the pandeist argument I outlined in the previous section to propose that Ptah first willed himself into existence and then willed the part of him that Reality embodies into existence. This would make

---

[83] I did say that Christian theologians had a pleasant surprise awaiting them.

[84] Ptah merges with other gods from time to time. For example Ptah-Nun is Ptah considered as Nun, the god of primal matter. Occasionally, the result is female: Ptah-Naunet was the "mother who bore Atum" (Hart, 1986). In such cases, Ptah is female and so should be accorded feminine pronouns. When unmerged, though, he's always male; hence, my use of masculine pronouns for him here.

sense if Ptah also had an existence external to Reality.

Ptah doesn't have an existence external to Reality, though: he's immanent but not transcendent. He either created both himself and Reality simultaneously (which represents a major violation of the concept of causality, but hey, he's a god) or he had an internal existence but then thought Reality into existence about him. The latter is the predominant account, but either way, Ptah winds up wholly *in* Reality. He's not outside it "except for a part of his soul" nor inside it "when he assumes human form": he's here the whole time.

He's also a god still in possession of full-on, Reality-creation and -modification powers. This means he's within a reality that he can change any aspect of *while he's within it.*

Considering Reality and Ptah as a whole, then, what we have here is a *self-modifying system.*

The rules of self-modifying systems are implemented using self-modifying code. You may recall my mentioning self-modifying code earlier as being A Bad Idea programming-wise. It is, but that doesn't mean it's always avoidable. Because of how Roy Trubshaw and I intermingled shared code and overwriteable data to produce shared data (which we wanted) and overwriteable code (which we didn't), *MUD* was in theory a self-modifying system; Roy and I were merely very careful about which parts of it it self-modified.

The physics of a reality is constituted by the laws-of-nature rules under which that reality operates. Some such rules apply to everything in the reality (for example, all the fundamental particles in Reality occupy a non-zero volume) and some only apply to a subset of it (for example, not all fundamental particles are subject to the strong interaction[85]).

In a self-modifying system, at least one law-of-nature rule applies to the laws-of-nature rules *themselves*, allowing any or all of them (even that same self-modification rule) to be changed.

So, Ptah has the ability to change the physics of Reality arbitrarily. He can alter any rule of physics he chooses. Important: this *includes* the rule that says he can alter any rule of physics he chooses. Because he himself exists wholly as part of Reality, this is what makes Reality under Ptah's rule a self-modifying system.

Note that the *actual physical rules* change, not merely the objects to which the rules are being applied. Even in a non-self-modifying system, the objects themselves can be changed: flashlights were invented by people, they're not fundamental constructs of nature. In a self-modifying system,

---

[85] This is expressed as the strong nuclear force, which according to the Standard Model of physics holds protons and neutrons together. As is always the case with science, though, it's subject to change in the light of new evidence; the Standard Model may therefore not be considered correct at the time you read this.

though, the physical rules currently in operation can also be changed: there's no such thing in Reality as a flashdark (which makes everything you point it at dark), and our current understanding of Reality suggests that there never will be, but if the rules of physics were to change (or to be changed) in an appropriate manner then we could expect to see flashdarks available in good hardware stores nationwide within months.

Any god can change the rules of physics, of course – it's what makes them a god. They're bound by the physics of their own, higher reality, but they have free rein with regard to the realities they create. The point about Ptah, though, is that he *has no higher reality*: he's bound by the physical laws of Reality, which include among them a law that says he can change those laws. If the laws of Reality didn't contain such a law, or only contained a self-exempting one, he couldn't fully change Reality – and he'd no longer be a god of Reality.

Let's work through the implications for Ptah of being a god of the reality in which he exists.

Suppose we have a suspicion that the laws of Reality can be changed from within Reality, but that we don't know the mechanism. If our physical laws can change, the question arises: how is it determined which physical law will change next? Ruling out external influence by a god from a higher reality (we're only looking at changes from within), there are three possibilities:

- At random.
- Causally.
- With intent.

If the changes occur randomly then Reality is capricious and has no controller. What we have at any one moment is merely a temporary state of affairs that could switch without warning, its physics only becoming fixed when the physical law that's changed is the one (or last one, if there are several) that says physical laws can be changed[86]. It could even be that there is no past or future, only the single instant of now, and that all your memories and plans are randomly-generated but just happen to make sense in this one particular instant out of all possible instants.

If the changes to the physical laws of Reality occur causally then things happen because of antecedents. Changes arise logically according to Reality's physical rules, following methodically from earlier changes. The rules of Reality can be changed, but only as a consequence of earlier changes. With no external influence or internal randomness, Reality is therefore completely deterministic. The future is as fixed as the past.

---

[86] For example, Reality's physics may have behaved chaotically until the physical law that changed physical laws randomly changed itself out of existence. This suggests a new, third way that Reality could have been created from primordial Chaos.

With intent, Reality can change its own physics in ways it chooses when the opportunity arises. This would make Reality itself count as a god, because it has choice (albeit perhaps dependent on a particular vehicle, for example Ptah). As for how Reality-as-a-god makes its decisions, well it would have to do so either at random or causally, so this form of self-modification is necessarily built on top of one (or possibly both) of the other two.

Of course, any of these three types of reality can transform itself into one of the others. For example, a deterministic reality ceases to be deterministic if it deterministically changes its own laws of physics such that randomness is introduced.

Imagine that we, as the designers of a virtual world, decide to make that world self-modifying. To accomplish this, we could have changes to its physical laws happen at random – that would be easy. Alternatively, we could build in the facility to make rule-changes systematically by giving an NPC godly powers. We could also make self-modification arise as a consequence of a series of events leading to it, or we could simply have it happen periodically when a timer expires. We have plenty of options.

The programmers would hate you if you did this. If you *were* one of the programmers, you'd hate yourself.

When it comes to implementing self-modifying systems, the result is self-modifying code. You never really know what's happening with self-modifying code.

Imagine a recipe for lasagne that changed dynamically while you were following it. You collect the ingredients, prepare them, mix them up[87], then put them in the oven for a period that is now wrong because it's right for the new, rewritten ingredients, not the ones you used. Worse, when you remove it and find it burnt, you look back at the recipe and read that it's now describing how to make baked Alaska.

Modifying code that is in the process of being executed is an absolute pain. It can cause crashes (when you originally set that variable to zero, you weren't planning ever to divide by it, but oh look, you're going to now); it can cause hangs (true, there wasn't a never-ending repeat loop when you called the function, but there'll be one when the function returns); it can be unpredictable (what fun, this instruction deletes itself while it's executing). You have to be very, very careful when coding the initial version in order to ensure that none of the modifications the code subsequently makes to itself are going to be suicidal. It's possible, yes, but even if you're a god who never makes coding errors it's going to be easier to implement your project some other way. Self-

[87] There's probably a technical term for this, but I'm not a cook.

modifying code is basically a symptom that your work is a hack[88].

Even if you have some valid reason for writing self-modifying code, there's a general problem inherent in possessing the ability to modify whatever of your code is responsible for the modification of your code: you can ruin it for Future You. For example, Article V of the constitution of the United States of America explains the conditions under which said constitution can be changed; it doesn't add that Article V itself is exempt from any such changes[89]. This means that one generation of United States citizens could see to it that future generations didn't get to amend the constitution further, effectively fossilising it[90]. The prevailing views at that time would be locked in, which could cause real problems should public opinion change[91].

---

[88] Note that I never said *MUD* wasn't a hack.

[89] Peter Suber's game *Nomic* was created in part to demonstrate problems such as this in modern legal systems (Suber, 1990).

[90] This is also how holy books work, of course: you don't get to change the content of *The Talmud*, *The Bible* or *The Qur'an*. If you wholeheartedly support one of them but sometimes wish it didn't say all of what it says, you either have to suck it up or to seek a more accommodating interpretation.

[91] Amendment XXI repealed Amendment XVIII (which prohibited the manufacture, sale or transportation of intoxicating liquors). That couldn't have happened if the constitution had become static at Amendment XX

It's worth mentioning that if you were to take the view that Reality was not created by a god, you could still have it be self-modifying. Yes, it would be possibly unstable, but having a creator god doesn't guarantee stability[92]. Self-modifying code is still code. Physics is still physics. If the way a reality's physics changes is determined only by its self-contained physics of change then that physics of change is just a part of the reality's physics like any other part.

Self-modifying systems have further, mathematical implications not shared by other systems. Perhaps the most important one follows from Gödel's *Incompleteness Theorems*.

OK, so I'm going to simplify this greatly and use language which will annoy logicians no end[93], but my aim is to get the basic point across, not to expose the extent of my mathematical logic ignorance[94].

So, Gödel's theorems concern sets of rules. We're particularly interested in the case in which those rules define the physical laws governing a reality, but the theorems themselves are more general. They have something to say about the relationship between the *consistency* and

---

[92] Although I guess it could help.
[93] Needless to say, using the phrase "no end" will annoy logicians no end.
[94] If you want a Pulitzer Prize-winning, accessible introduction to the topic (and beyond), look no further than (Hofstadter, 1979).

completeness of the rules of any self-modifying system.

A set of rules is said to be *consistent* if (and only if) it can't be used both to prove that a statement is true and to prove that the same statement is false. For example, suppose you have a set of rules for what counts as a dog: if you can selectively apply them to a particular animal to prove it's a dog, but selectively apply other rules from the same set to the same animal to prove it's not a dog, then your set of rules is inconsistent.

A set of rules is said to be *complete* if, for any statement to which it applies, either the statement or its negation can be proven true. A complete set of rules about what makes something a dog will, given an animal to consider, be able to tell you whether it is indeed a dog or not.

This is generally fine for systems that don't refer to themselves. Rules about dogs are rules about dogs; they don't include rules about how to apply or to alter rules about dogs. For self-referential systems, though, things are not so fine.

What Gödel showed was that if a set of self-referential rules is consistent, it has to be incomplete. There are statements about the rule set which can neither be proved nor disproved using that rule set.

Gödel's theorems apply to self-modifying realities as much as they do to any other system with the means to change its own rules. What this means for Ptah is that either he's inconsistent or he's incomplete or he's both.

If Ptah wants to be able to do anything and everything in and to Reality, he's seeking completeness: in mathematical terms, he wishes to prove all statements that can be proved. Unfortunately for him (if not for us), he can't do that without being inconsistent: some of Reality will be both true and false at the same time[95], which makes no sense. If, on the other hand, he's seeking consistency then there will be statements about Reality that are true but which he can't prove are true.

In other words, Ptah is either all-powerful (omnipotent) or all-knowing (omniscient), but he's not both.

Gödel's theorems wouldn't be problematical if Reality weren't self-modifying, so it's possible that Ptah could choose either to avoid or to evade this possibility.

To *avoid* it, Ptah would create Reality then do away with the physical law that enabled him to change physical laws. This returns us to a pandeistic explanation of what happened: in the act of creating Reality, he decided to remove his ability to change Reality's physics further; Ptah the god created Reality, but in so doing ceased to be a god.

---

[95] I don't mean in a "collapse the superposition of quantum states" way, either.

To *evade* the effects of having a self-modifying Reality, Ptah could retain the power to change it but simply elect never to use that power, making Reality effectively fixed. This isn't to say that the ability to change Reality is to all intents and purposes absent, though: if you have a law which is never used, it nevertheless retains influence. The ability to change physics may be critical because if you didn't have it, you'd need it. Ptah could be keeping all the other Ancient Egyptian gods in line by having the potential to use this power (even if he never does use it), in a way he couldn't if the power no longer existed[96].

There's a final point to do with Ptah that's worth mentioning. Whereas a god who creates Reality externally has the excuse of "it's only part of me" to explain why the god is perfect but Reality is imperfect, Ptah can make no such assertion. Reality is all of him, so if it has imperfections (such as those demonstrated by the existence of you and I[97]) then so has Ptah. To be fair, Ptah is never claimed to be perfect, though, so he's not as likely to be as worried by this as he might be by his lack of simultaneous omnipotence and omniscience.

Other gods, who created Reality the sensible way (that is, from a higher reality), do have some

---

[96] In naval warfare, there's the concept of a *fleet in being* – a fleet that remains safely in port but that must be guarded against in case it did set sail.

[97] Yeah, I know, "speak for yourself".

claim to perfection. Weirdly, though, this isn't as much fun as it sounds it should be. See, if something is perfect, it doesn't need to change – there's no reason to change perfection, it's literally perfect as it is. This makes the god *immutable*[98]. It also suggests that the god never changes emotional state, because that's also a change. This makes the god *impassible*. Because human beings are neither immutable nor impassible, this means that a perfect god is not a personal god in possession of the full range of human qualities. That may be no bad thing, but it's something to be aware of if you ever find yourself in conversation with a perfect god: they're not going to change their mind or their emotional state one iota.

For virtual worlds, none of this is an issue. The gods that create them are not perfect and they would be foolish to deny the fact.

GRANULARITY

Virtual worlds are written to run on computers. The physical laws of their realities are systematised as program code; the objects of their realities are embodied as program data.

---

[98] Essentially, hard-coded.

Objects, then, are basically bits in a database which are meaningful to the code that operates on them.

What should those bits in those databases represent?

Let's talk in terms of Lego bricks instead of bits. No, I'm not in the pocket of the mighty Lego A/S of Billund, Denmark[99]; I just want a metaphor for bits with which most readers will be familiar.

Lego bricks are like fundamental particles[100]. In the universe of Lego, everything is made from Lego bricks (except air, which is made of absence of Lego bricks). Although it's perfectly possible for interesting combinations of bricks to arise by chance (as I discovered when I put my childhood collection in a pillowcase and machine-washed it[101]), usually people combine the bricks with some degree of intent.

Now the thing is, most of the time when you make something out of Lego bricks, you're going to refer to it as an object. It's a car! It's a giraffe! It's a secret underground laboratory! This is a called giving the bricks a *symbolic* interpretation[102]. The

---

[99] Although obviously I'm open to being so.

[100] This is what physicists call them; the term used by philosophers to refer to entities with no parts is *simples*.

[101] I'd buried some of it in the garden, OK? Pro tip: don't use detergent or it'll leave marks.

[102] I realise the everyday usage of "symbolic" suggests that the interpretation isn't really worth much, but I don't get to decide these words.

stupendous power of your imagination has granted this particular collection of bricks in this particular configuration a coherent identity.

Having a symbolic interpretation does rather imply that there's an observer around to do the interpreting, though. That exact same configuration of bricks could have arisen by chance from some kind of primordial brick soup (Althöfer, 2013). If it had done, would it still be a car, a giraffe, a secret underground laboratory? Or would it merely be a collection of bricks until someone came across it and decided what it was (if even then[103])?

Regardless of whether you're looking at individual Lego bricks or at objects made from collections of them, in terms of following well-established laws of nature they behave no differently to anything else in Reality. Suppose, though, that when the bricks were put together in a particular way, new physical laws applied that didn't apply in any other circumstances. Perhaps if you were to stack six red two-by-two bricks on top of each other, they would change colour to green[104]. Adding more bricks, or using bricks of

---

[103] The philosophical view that there are no such things as objects, just simples arranged object-wise, is *mereological nihilism*. Full-on nihilism argues that there aren't the simples, either.

[104] For the purposes of this analogy, you don't have to be able to visualise this in your mind's eye. Those readers who are colour blind or blind needn't worry they're missing anything.

other shapes or colours, wouldn't do this – but a column of exactly six red four-stud square bricks would.

For this to work, there would have to be a special physical law that overrode all lesser physical laws when its precondition was met. The colour change wouldn't be because of some obscure emergent consequence of mixing bricks a particular way, in the manner of a chemical reaction: it would be a special law that rode roughshod over any other laws that got in its way.

In virtual worlds as they are programmed today, this is pretty well exactly how things work. It's for reasons of abstraction and representational ease: special-case functionality is attached to symbolic objects, from which it can be inherited; it's not attached merely and entirely to their components. This active use of physics makes the whole greater than the sum of its parts[105].

In virtual worlds, objects are made of collections of bits (so, like Lego bricks), but distinct combinations can be treated in distinct ways. If this combination of bits represents a rock then the code that handles interactions with it will only

---

[105] There is a wonderful word used by philosophers to refer to the concept of an entity that is made up of indefinitely-divisible components: *gunk*. Split any piece of gunk in two and you have two pieces of gunk. This is completely irrelevant to the current topic; I mention it only because I like the idea that "gunk" is an actual technical term in Philosophy (specifically, in *Mereology* – the study of parts and wholes).

work on rocks (or possibly on a class of objects of which this rock is an example). The rock combination of bits constitutes a unitary object with its own physics, components of which it may or may not have in common with other objects. Some rules that you might think ought to apply don't apply[106] (or even exist); some rules that you might think ought not to apply (or even exist) do apply[107].

Now virtual worlds don't *have* to be this way, of course.

Hmm, let me backtrack on that: to some extent they do because they're dictated to by their graphics, which at the moment have to be implemented in terms of objects (well, their surfaces) even in brick worlds such as *Minecraft*[108]. However, virtual worlds don't *have* to have graphics: the early ones, such as *MUD*, certainly didn't, and there are plenty of other textual worlds still extant (and yet more in development).

---

[106] I'm looking at you, *World of Warcraft*. I carried that glass of ice-cold milk around in my backpack for *seven years* and it never spilled, warmed up or went off. I swam underwater with it, and it still remained intact. Text MUDs could handle this kind of situation better!

[107] I recall a difficult decision I once faced in *SkySaga*: to make room in my inventory for a quest item, do I drop this one leaf or these 99 cubic metres of ice? Both the leaf and the ice took up exactly the same amount of room in my backpack: one slot.

[108] The technical term for how these bricks are displayed is as *voxels*.

Let's say, then, that *in principle* virtual worlds don't have to be built out of symbolic objects to which they may attach functionality. For example, if they took the same approach as Conway's game of *Life*, they'd work the same as Lego bricks in Reality: bits all operating under the same universal set of rules, which can form (or be formed into) patterns that have emergent functionality as a whole that's not shared by the individual parts (but to which they indirectly contribute). Then again, *Life* could be written like a virtual world: when you see this particular pattern of occupied and unoccupied cells, replace it with this other pattern. You could indeed have both: regular *Life*, but maybe make any stable two-by-two block that survives six generations be replaced by a random two-by-two pattern.

It's a question of granularity, then. A reality can be implemented in terms of fundamental, Lego-like building blocks from which everything else flows[109], or it can be implemented in terms of symbolic objects that have their own functionality beyond that available by default but nevertheless part of the physics of the object's reality.

So, what about Reality? How does that implement what we think of as objects – and can

---

[109] This is essentially the philosophical position of *logical atomism* (Russell, 1911), although logical atomism is somewhat wider in its extent than this as it has an analytical aspect to it, too.

knowledge of how virtual worlds do it help in our understanding of how Reality does it?

In Metaphysics, the way this question is usually framed fixates less on the objects themselves and more on their functionality – or their *properties*, to use the formal term.

Suppose there exists an entity which both you and I refer to as a spoon[110]. What makes it a spoon? Well, it's an object in possession of a number of properties, some of which are related to its being a spoon (it has a concave surface) and some of which are not (it's located in my garden shed[111]). Some are not themselves properties of spoons in general (it's made of electroplated nickel silver) but do implement more abstract properties that are possessed by spoons in general (electroplated nickel silver is impermeable to ice cream).

Then again, it may be that the only property a spoon requires is that the person referring to it decrees it's a spoon. Hey, it works for artists and art[112].

Describing the meaning of objects by listing their properties is an *intensional* definition. An *extensional* definition simply lists every object that qualifies. If you want to know if something is a

---

[110] Hi, *The Matrix* fans!

[111] I don't know how it got there. I think I was mixing up some fuel for my strimmer or something.

[112] Well, it has since Marcel Duchamp's *Fountain* in 1917 (or Richard Mutt's *Fountain*, depending on whether you believe Duchamp was Mutt or not).

duck, you either: look through your list of defining properties of ducks and see if they all apply; or look through your list of ducks and if it's there then it's a duck and if it's not it isn't. Intensional definitions are usually preferred (replace "duck" by "water" in the above examples to see why).

These defining properties of objects are known to philosophers as *universals*. The question of whether they exist in Reality, and if so, what they are, is the *problem of universals*.

There are three main approaches to tackling this problem.

The first approach, known as *realism*, says that properties exist as real entities distinct from the objects that have these properties. Plato's view was that properties are independent of the objects that express them (so even if nothing is beautiful, the concept of beauty still exists); Aristotle's view was that properties rely on exemplars for their existence (so beauty only exists while there are beautiful things). In virtual worlds, Plato's view holds true: code which doesn't apply to any objects may be needless, but it doesn't cease to be part of the program.

To show what "properties exist as real entities" actually means, consider the concept of translucency in *MUD*. Only objects that have the "translucent" property can be seen through: no other property (or set of emergent interactions between other properties) will suffice. The fact that this property uniquely embodies a law of *MUD* physics makes it real (in the context of *MUD*), because take it away and there would be no translucency.

The second approach to answering the problem of universals, known as *nominalism*, baldly asserts that universals don't exist[113]. When two objects share a property such as "has a concave surface", this simply means that they're having the same label applied to them by human beings.

Interestingly, nominalism also works for virtual worlds, because having the same label applied is exactly how realism is implemented. I'll explain.

So: ultimately, nominalism is positing that universals exist within the mind but are not external to the mind; we spot similarities, group them together cognitively, create (or learn from others) labels for these similarities, then we apply these labels to refer to items that have the similarities we've associated with the labels. Thus, properties don't exist physically; they only exist as linguistic constructs.

That's fair enough. However, the job of virtual world programmers is to turn these linguistic constructs into properties that are real in the context of the virtual world: not only do they *associate* properties with objects, they *implement*

---

[113] There are actually two versions of nominalism. This one, to do with the rejection of universals, is the more traditional; the other, to do with the rejection of objects with no space-time presence, is the more modern. Both occupy well-fortified positions in Metaphysics.

those properties. Thus, nominalism becomes realism for those who make realities.

The third approach to answering the problem of universals, known as *idealism*[114], is like nominalism except even more pared-back. Not only are properties constructs of the mind, but so are objects (and, if you want to take it to extremes, so is all of Reality).

While this may or may not be true of Reality, it's certainly untrue of virtual worlds (except in the sense that, as they're implemented within Reality, then if Reality is a construct of the mind, so are virtual worlds). Also, although from the perspective of NPCs within a reality idealism may look plausibly attractive, from the perspective of any god of that reality those NPCs are just flat out wrong. What a god knows that NPCs don't know is that the reality determines what's in their heads; what's in their heads doesn't determine the reality.

As for the situation with Reality, well philosophers haven't agreed an answer to the problem of universals. That's what makes it a problem. The idealist view has the most explanatory power, but pushed too far suggests that everything is a construct of the mind: you may well *be* the only real object in existence, and the rest of us are mere figments of your imagination

[114] We came across this earlier with reference to the mind-body problem. Applied to virtual worlds, it was poppycock.

(in which case, all I can say is that you have a damned good imagination).

Besides, using what we know from virtual worlds, we can reject idealism as an explanation of Reality. One of the qualities of a reality is that it's persistent, and even if the rest of us genuinely are going to cease to exist when you die, operationally we're going to continue as if we weren't. Imaginary me can die in your imagined world while imaginary other people carry on in it: your mind has created what for us is our physical reality, so it doesn't matter to us that for you we're empty shells with no independent existence of our own. To us, we're not. You are Reality, and we exist in a sub-reality that runs in your imagination.

Idealism says that existence is relative to the individual, but virtual worlds tell us that existence is relative to realities (see Chapter 4 for more on this).

As for the other two solutions to the problem of universals, well let's see what they imply.

Accepting the realism view, object properties are real. Objects, or classes of object, can have special functionality that applies to them and only to them. There could, for example, be "soul" objects attached to living human beings but not to anything else, so supporting (indeed implementing) the idea of substance dualism. There could be plenty of other arbitrary objects or properties we simply don't know about, too, of course.

Accepting the nominalism view, Reality is a collection of sub-atomic particles operating under a single, consistent set of rules (physics). It's basically a world of tiny, probabilistic Lego bricks, and objects such as people are merely vast collections of such particles configured in certain similar-at-some-level patterns. There's no "soul" object in such a world, because you can't make a soul out of quarks. Reality is but data being operated on by unchanging program code.

The distinction between the two comes down to the aforementioned level of granularity. Is Reality made of material objects ("I see a near-inconceivably large collection of sub-atomic particles that have come together to form this solid body") or is it made of conceptual objects ("I see a chair")?

People historically went with the realism approach for describing Reality, in which conceptual objects have their own existence and their own set of properties. Over the centuries, though, science has been pushing relentlessly in the direction of nominalism (and indeed idealism), achieving great advances by considering objects as if they only had material existence. For a physicist, properties are emergent consequences of the way the stuff of Reality is configured locally.

As it happens, this is reflected in the way that Artificial Intelligence research has gone. It started out considering the subject symbolically[115], but is now tackling it statistically. AI is a topic for Part 3 of this book, though, so you'll have to wait if your interest is piqued (or brace yourself if it's not).

Virtual worlds do have something interesting to say about the distinction between realism, nominalism and idealism, in that they offer a new way to connect the first two together. This isn't entirely why I brought the subject up, though. I brought it up because of what it says about gods.

If you accept the realism solution, Reality is coded by one or more gods. They may not be very good coders[116], but they have allowed abstract functionality to be associated with aggregations of matter, meaning we can have all manner of supernatural beings and powers in Reality without breaking its physics.

If you accept the nominalism solution then there are no exceptionalist laws of physics. The most that any god or gods or Reality would have done is to make the equivalent of the washing machine and to put the equivalent of the Lego bricks in it.

---

[115] This kind of AI is known as GOFAI, or "Good Old-Fashioned Artificial Intelligence" (Haugeland, 1985).

[116] Implementing concepts such as consciousness by selectively overriding methods of the physics base class is essentially a monumental hack. Good luck debugging any matter leak when you can't trust that conservation-of-momentum rules always apply.

If you accept the idealism solution, the god of Reality *is* the bricks and the washing machine – it's just they don't necessarily *know* they are.

SIMPLES

Suppose you are a sculptor and are inspired to make a statuette of Boudicca, queen of the Iceni[117]. Because she burned the Roman city of Camulodunum to the ground, leaving an inch-thick layer of ashes, you want to use an unusual kind of light, grey clay for your masterpiece-to-be[118].

So, you go to the local sculptors' supply shop and describe your clay requirements to the (let's say) woman behind the counter. She listens, knowledgeably, to your description of the properties you desire your purchase to possess, then says, "Ah, sounds as if you want Andy".

"Andy?" you ask. "Who's Andy?"

---

[117] Her name is sometimes spelled "Boudica", but I think it looks classier with the double c. She was known to the Romans as Boadicea, and that's how the Victorians mythologised her.

[118] Camulodunum is modern-day Colchester. There's a statue of Boadicea (the myth) there near where I live. Having one of Boudicca (the city-razer) was probably a step too far.

"Oh, Andy is this lump of clay from the slopes of a particular hill in Derbyshire. I've had him for so long, I've given him a name: Andy".

You take a look at Andy and he's just what you were looking for. You buy him there and then, and take him to your garden shed, er, home studio.

You start to work on Andy, and over the course of the next few days use all of him to fashion the statuette of Boudicca you had envisioned. She comes out great! She's got some kind of helmet or whatever your research calls it, and she looks like just the sort of person who would reduce a Roman provincial capital to ashes and so force the empire to transfer its local seat of government to Londinium instead.

You have two objects now. As a statuette, you have Boudicca. As a lump of clay, you have Andy. Whether what you're looking at is Boudicca or Andy depends on how you're thinking of it[119]. Someone with an eye for history may, upon seeing your sculpture, recognise it as Boudicca; someone who regularly frequents your local clay emporium may recognise it as Andy.

This would seem to be a simple case of having two different labels for the same object. Indeed, one perspective of metaphysics suggests that

---

[119] In Metaphysics research papers, the lump of clay is generally called Lumpl and the statue(tte) is of Goliath. I'm a computer scientist by training, though, so want my variable names to begin with A and B rather than wacky letters such as L and G.

labels are all we ever do have and that ultimately all disputes in the field are basically just linguistic in nature[120]. Another perspective says that Andy and Boudicca are distinct objects which occupy the same physical space.

Virtual world designers can't indulge themselves with "perspectives", though. If you're planning on programming these objects, speculation has to turn into specification. Because players would want to refer both to Andy and to Boudicca, you'd need to decide whether to have Andy and Boudicca both be labels for the same object or be two separate objects sharing the same space. You wouldn't have the luxury of merely theorising how you'd implement it – you'd *actually have to implement it*.

Programmers like pointers, so the natural solution is to add the label "Boudicca" to Andy when he's fashioned into a statuette. If a player subsequently mashed up Boudicca then the Boudicca label would be removed and it would just be Andy; if, instead, a player fired Andy in a kiln then the Andy label would be removed and it would just be Boudicca.

You'd have to do this label-removal, because although Andy and Boudicca may refer to the same bits in your database, as objects they have different

---

[120] This is called *deflationism*. It's actually even bleaker than I've made out, as it denies that even the concepts of truth and falsehood exist, all statements being merely assertions.

properties. Andy is a malleable piece of a particular kind of clay with a certain colour, mass and so on. There's no requirement that Boudicca be malleable, but there *is* a requirement that she looks like the artist's impression of Boudicca. Unless you wanted to make some point about the way that the past is shaped by the present, well, crumpling her up and making her into a cup would simply destroy her, not reinterpret her for the modern era.

So pointers work, then? We'd just use pointers?

Ah, well it's not quite as easy as that. See, as I outlined earlier, in a symbolic implementation you could give either Boudicca or Andy (or both) their own, special physics. Perhaps Andy has the preternatural property of bestowing good luck to anyone who holds him; perhaps Boudicca can be used for starting fires. Boudicca isn't merely Andy (or the simples[121] Andy is made of) arranged Boudicca-wise: each has their own, unique property that derives from their very identity.

This does add a layer of complexity, but it's nevertheless doable using pointers. What about the other proposed way of implementing the situation,

---

[121] Those who dutifully read every footnote will know what simples are, because I've already mentioned them a couple of times. Those who only read some footnotes may have to go back a few pages to see what they've missed. Those who never read footnotes will have to look up the term using their preferred search engine (or philosophical dictionary) on their own initiative. They should have read the footnotes.

though – as two objects sharing the same space? Perhaps that makes it easier.

Sadly, it doesn't. If you decide from the outset that when Boudicca is made you will bring into being two co-located objects, rather than have one object with two names, then that's going to be more work (and if you leave the decision until later, even more more work). It's not too onerous to lock them together for movement purposes and give them the same physical appearance, but when anything happens to the objects then you have to handle them separately. Hitting the combined object with a hammer destroys Boudicca but not Andy; baking it in an oven destroys Andy but not Boudicca; throwing it into a black hole destroys both. Andy brings luck, so if you put him in your backpack then good fortune will head your way; Boudicca sets things on fire, though, so perhaps you might want to ensure your backpack isn't flammable.

The two-objects-in-one approach involves a lot of bookkeeping[122] effort that buys you no more than the much cleaner label (pointer) system. As a programmer, pointers would be how you'd want to implement this. You'd have to hack some code together to allow objects to be granted properties derived from the pointers pointing at them, and there may be some annoyances if the properties

[122] There's something satisfying about an English word with three consecutive double letters.

were contradictory, but it's possible. If you're a programmer, you're probably thinking right now of how you'd do it.

It gets worse, though.

Suppose that, as the sculptor, you look at your statuette and decide that Boudicca's helmet is just a little too big. You nip off a piece of clay and throw it away. Is what remains still Boudicca? Well, yes. It's a slightly different look, but it's definitely her. In a game, a player would still expect to be able to use her to start fires.

Is what remains still Andy? Hmm, that's trickier. It's most of Andy, but you threw some of him away. You'd probably still think of him as Andy, though, in the same way that if you have your hair cut you still think of yourself as you. It's not a problem. He still brings you luck.

Maybe you decide that the helmet is the wrong colour. It would look better if it were red. You take it off, employ your sculpting skills to make a new helmet from a different, red piece of clay, and the result looks pretty good.

Is what you have still Boudicca? Yes, nothing has happened to challenge that view to any great extent. In an MMO context, players would still expect to be able to use Boudicca as a lighter.

Is what you have still Andy? There's a bit more missing now. Does that mean you have two objects, one of which is Andy (and brings luck) and the other of which isn't (and doesn't)? Or is it just that Andy is now in two parts (or three, if you count the tiny piece that you threw away first) and all of them bring luck, albeit perhaps in different amounts?

Let's carry on. You like the look of the helmet, but now Boudicca's face doesn't have the right contrast. You replace her head with a new head made of a third type of clay. You also replace her other exposed body parts, because few people have a face that's a different colour to the rest of them. It's still Boudicca, but is it still Andy?

Enthused, you then replace the statuette's clothing, jewellery and eventually everything else, so you have a Boudicca made entirely of clay that has none of the properties which made Andy distinct from regular clay. Has the incremental nature of your changes meant that the identity of Andy has been slowly transferred to the new clay? Your own body replaces almost every cell multiple times over during the course of your lifetime: is a similar thing happening to Andy here? Will you still have superior luck from possessing the updated Andy?

We don't seem to have a problem with Boudicca. She may have had every component of her replaced, but what she's made of is not an important facet of who she is: it's how she's constructed and perceived that matters.

Hmm. So remember those old pieces of Boudicca that were made of Andy? The ones you replaced? The helmet, head, hands, clothes, jewellery and so on? You may have thrown them out but, unbeknownst to you, someone at the recycling plant has seen them, recognised their artistic worth, and collected them all. When you replaced the last piece, the recycling plant worker (who coincidentally has world-class sculpting skills) was able to reconstruct your original Boudicca statuette exactly as she was.

Is she a new Boudicca or the old one? Can she be used to light fires, in the same way that she could when you first made her, or has that ability been transferred to the current Boudicca? If you, as a world designer, like the idea of overriding the laws of physics for specific macro-objects, are you going to have two Boudiccas that can start fires, or just one? If you only want one Boudicca to have the magic in it, which one do you choose? The one that did have it, which was taken to pieces and reassembled, or the one that contains not a single atom/bit/simple of the original but is still referred to as Boudicca by the person who made it?

The recycling plant worker grows tired of the reassembled Boudicca statuette and scrunches it up. It's now just a single lump of light, grey clay. It seems to exhibit several unusual properties, though: maybe it's worth something?

The worker takes the lump of clay to the local sculptors' supply shop and sells it to the shopkeeper.

"Welcome back, Andy", she says as she puts him back into storage.

OK, so this may all seem like philosophical argumentation of no material value, and indeed in the main it is little more than an intellectual exercise. It does have some practical implications, but they're hardly mainstream[123]. It's been unresolved for a long time, too: the problem was discussed by Plutarch as *the Ship of Theseus* (if you take Theseus's ship apart and reassemble it, it's still Theseus's ship; if you replace Theseus's ship over time, plank by plank, it's still Theseus's ship; if you rebuild a new ship from the planks of the original ship, is that also Theseus's ship?).

What relevance is it to us as gods, though?

Well, as a god you have to decide.

That's *you* have to decide.

World creation is applied metaphysics. *You* have to decide what your world is made of. *You* have to decide what betokens an object. *You* have to decide whether special objects can have their own physics-defying properties. *You* have to decide how these properties persist.

The virtual world designers of today evade the issues by simply not allowing the piecemeal dismantling of objects. What will the virtual world designers of tomorrow do?

---

[123] In the UK at least, it's possible to take apart an original motor vehicle from 1910, rebuild two new vehicles each with half their components coming from the 1910 original and half from today, then sell them both as being original 1910 vehicles in their own right. Well, I believe so, anyway: I'm not a lawyer, so don't sue me if you try this and it doesn't work.

You're a virtual world designer of tomorrow.

What *does* happen with Boudicca? What *does* happen with Andy?

You have to decide.

I didn't say that being a god was easy.

Chapter 4

EXISTENCE

Do gods believe in gods?

Do they believe in gods of their own reality, who reside in a higher reality?

Do they believe in gods who reside in their own reality, who have created a lower reality?

Do they believe in gods who reside in a lower reality, who have created a reality a level below that?

Do they believe in themselves?

What does it mean "to believe in" a god anyway?

Well the phrase "believe in" has several connotations:

- It implies a degree of trust and confidence: you might say to a friend who's about to take a driving test that you "believe in" them.
- It implies that the believed-in thing is right: you might say that you "believe in" vaccinating children against measles.
- It implies faith in the existence of the believed-in thing: you might say that you "believe in" the Loch Ness monster.

It's this final use that I'm going to look at in the context of virtual worlds: belief in a god implies faith in that god's existence.

Just a moment, though: faith in a god's what?

What does it mean to say that the gods, demigods, player-characters and NPCs of a reality "exist"?

What does it mean to say a *reality* "exists", come to that?

What does "to exist" actually mean?

ONTOLOGY

The branch of philosophy concerned with the nature of existence is called *ontology*. The mere detail that there is such a branch tips us off to the fact that what "to exist" means has yet to be agreed upon by philosophers; indeed, it's not even clear that existence ("I exist") and being ("I am") mean the same thing[1].

Fortunately, it's not the job of this book to look at what theories of existence have to say about virtual worlds; rather, it's to look at what virtual worlds have to say about theories of existence (if anything). Nevertheless, some of the basics of

[1] You can blame (Heidegger, 1927) for this.

ontology do lead to interesting-for-us observations, so it's worth our starting with them.

The first point to make, then, is that *you* exist. You know you do, because if you didn't then you couldn't know anything. *Cogito, ergo sum* and all that[2].

Could anything else exist? Well, based on what your mind interprets as signals from an external source, Reality could exist. It could also be something invented by your incredibly-powerful imagination, of course, but as a working hypothesis the management of your own existence becomes *so* much easier if you accept the proposal that there is an objective world out there (which in this book I'm referring to as Reality). Irritatingly, you'll never find out if Reality does indeed exist independently of you, because the only ways to discover the truth would be to see if it continues to exist after you cease to do so yourself or *vice versa*. Neither would leave you in a position to make the observation, though[3].

What other things could exist?

Well, beyond yourself and Reality, anything else is just a label that you apply to a particular

---

[2] This originally appeared in French, as *je pense, donc je suis* (Descartes, 1637). The phrase is usually translated as "I think, therefore I am", but occasionally appears as "I am thinking, therefore I exist" or similar.

[3] Even if you die and go to the Elysian Fields, you'll still exist; Reality could therefore remain a figment of your imagination (as indeed could the Elysian Fields).

concept[4]. Such a label may correspond to a partition of Reality or it may not. Do atoms exist? Well the things we call atoms do seem to be a distinct part of Reality, but an "atom" is merely our labelling of what scientists believe is a collection of somewhat more fundamental particles that interact with one another in certain specific ways.

How about integers? Do they exist? Unlike atoms, they don't seem to be embedded in Reality as tangible entities[5], but they're a concept to which we've applied a label and for which we have rules that work infallibly well. Integers, then, exist within a mathematical framework, but that mathematical framework itself only exists because we've intuited that it does.

It would seem, therefore, that there appear to be (at least) two modes of existence: the physical (such as atoms) and the conceptual (such as integers)[6].

As it happens, mathematics[7] can itself be employed to get a handle on this distinction. Because it exists in an abstract sense, rather than

---

[4] Here, I'm taking the deflationist point of view as a backstop; I'm not saying that this *is* how things are, but it's the minimum that students of Metaphysics will *accept* as how things are.

[5] You can't smash a proton into the number 142,857 to see what it's made of.

[6] If you think this is reminiscent of the problem of universals, yes, it is.

[7] In particular, the subfield known as *formal logic*.

in a material one, it can be used to describe concepts common to all realities, not just those of Reality. Existence is just such a concept.

The way this is done utilises a symbol, ∃, known as the *existential quantifier*. Suppose you wanted to state that there's such a thing as a table. Formally, you'd say something like "there exists at least one object, let's call it *T*, such that *T* is a table". The way you'd write it in a logic[8] is:

∃ T (table(T))

where table(T) is a function that returns true if its parameter, T, exhibits the properties necessary for something to be considered a table[9].

There's some dispute as to whether it's better to have different quantifiers for different types of existence ($\exists_{material}$, $\exists_{abstract}$ or whatever), but in general ∃ can range across anything[10]. Importantly, ∃ only indicates existence with respect to the statement it ranges over: it doesn't mean existence in an absolute sense. For example, even if we're unshakably confident that the Ancient Greeks made up the idea of unicorns, it's still fine to say that there exists a unicorn, U, and a

---

[8] More specifically, in the *predicate calculus*.

[9] If you prefer the extensionalist approach then there's only one such property: that of being in the list of things that are tables.

[10] Computer Science, at least when I was an undergraduate in the late 1970s, would call $\exists_{material}$ a *procedural* representation and $\exists_{abstract}$ a *declarative* representation. They're two sides of the same coin: ∃.

person, P, such that P believes they have seen U. Similarly, while reading a detective novel, we can suppose that there exists a murderer, M, such that M is right-handed, weighs less than 70kg and is fond of cats (so, not me then[11]) – only to find out at the end of the book that there never was a murderer and the supposed victim is still alive because it was all an insurance scam.

This implies that objects and concepts can be called into existence (at least temporarily) merely by naming them[12]. Even if I say "the only statement you can make about things that don't exist is that they don't exist", well that *sounds* true, yes; however, as I've now named these non-existent things, I can make all sorts of statements about them. I can list properties they don't have (colour, edibility, the ability to think, ...) and properties they do have (a definition, irony, the capacity to be conceptualised, ...).

Thus, in one sense, questions such as "does X exist?" always have the answer "yes", because merely by asking the question you've caused them to exist as a topic of conversation. That doesn't mean they have material existence, though.

---

[11] I weigh rather more than 70kg.

[12] It's actually more subtle than that. You don't need to name something to turn it into a conceptual object, you merely need to think about it as a conceptual object. Naming is one way to do this, sure, but there are others – pattern recognition, for example. To avoid over-complicating this discussion, I'll simply call it "naming", though.

For most people[13], physical (material) existence and conceptual (abstract) existence may well be different kinds (modes) of existence, but there's nevertheless an overarching concept of existence that applies to both: although physical existence is dependent on a reality (as that of human beings is on Reality) and conceptual existence is independent of realities (as is the case with numbers), it does still make sense to say "people and numbers exist". This is a *univocal* interpretation of existence; not accepting that there's an overarching concept of existence, just a set of independent ones, is an *equivocal* interpretation[14].

It's conceivable for something to have a physical and a conceptual existence both at once: the former in one reality and the latter in all realities. We could, for example, construct a reality made up of integers[15]. The physics of this reality

---

[13] The exceptions are those who adopt either the metaphysical position that everything is real (realists) or that nothing is real (anti-realists). For everyday purposes, though, such as the status in law of virtual objects, the *commonsense* interpretation (which is the one that we non-experts use) is the most practical (Koepsell, 2000).

[14] It comes down to whether you think "bees, hunger and traditions all exist" is fine, or if it's just a pun along the lines of "sprinters, candidates for office and noses all run" (Ryle, 1949).

[15] Indeed, we could create several such realities. Whether the integer -1 in one of these realities is the same -1 as the -1s in the other realities I'll leave you to decide.

might allow the integers to do something (endlessly add themselves up, perhaps); without such a physics, though, integers are merely a description of an idea. Similarly, you could argue that as well as your being a person in Reality, there's a general concept of you that transcends Reality and holds true in all other realities (as is already the case with numbers). This is indeed a possibility, but without a physical representation you'd be just a passive abstraction in those other realities – like numbers are in Reality.

Objects thought of conceptually pay for their independence with inertness. Unlike physical objects, they don't have a machine to run on. They can be talked about and they can be used as conceptual tools, but there are no physical laws governing them. Even if they describe systems, those systems won't run unless they're made concrete in a physical system (that is, a reality or part thereof). Humans are tied to Reality in a way that numbers aren't, but humans can act within Reality in a way that numbers can't.

Hmm. So if someone asks "Does Odin exist?", are they talking in a material sense or in an abstract sense? The former means that Odin can do things but needs a physics to enact the doing; the latter means that Odin can be talked about and idealised but is incapable of direct action himself. If he's both material and conceptual, he can be discussed across all realities but can only act in his own reality and on those realities consequent[16] on his own reality. The same applies if you ask the question of any other god, of course.

From a virtual world designer's perspective, we don't really care about what existence means: we care about what can be implemented. This is existence in a material sense: in the same way that in Reality it is possible to point at a particular goat and say it exists, we can do the same in a virtual world. We can do it in two ways, in fact: either subjectively (from within the world, pointing at it) or objectively (from without the world, pointing at the bits in the database that mean it).

There's a difference between the two. If, in Reality, we say "goats exist" then we're asserting that the concept of what a goat is can be instantiated; we can therefore demonstrate the truth of our assertion by pointing at a goat. In a virtual world we can still do this, but additionally we (as gods) can point at the code that says what a goat is, then point at the data for an object present in the virtual world to which this code applies, and thereby show that goats exist there. It could be that we don't even need to point at any data – the

[16] When I say that one reality is *consequent* on another, I mean that if the latter were to cease to exist, so would the former. Switch off Reality and all these virtual worlds we've created would disappear with it.

code alone could be sufficient evidence that goats exist[17].

Additionally, we can do something with virtual worlds that Reality doesn't seem to be able to do: we can implement a concept physically. We could place the concept of what a goat is in the virtual world as a material object, so it can be pointed at objectively from within that reality. We can give pretty well any abstract or conceptual entity a concrete, physical existence. We probably wouldn't *want* to, but I confess to having done so by accident on occasion[18]. This isn't the same thing as *personification*, in which a figure serves as a physical manifestation of an abstract quality such as truth or justice[19]: in a virtual world, we could have the concept of truth just lying around on the floor ("Lazing languidly within reach is the concept of truth.").

OK, so for the concept of truth such a physical embodiment may be inadvisable, especially if it could be destroyed – the whole reality would seize up or crash. For concepts such as "Romeo's love for Juliet" or "what a pigeon is", though, having the

---

[17] This is the nub of the problem of universals, which I outlined earlier. If we implement the concept of a goat, is that itself sufficient for us to be able to say goats exist, or do we have to instantiate the concept with at least one goat object?
[18] One of the NPCs came across not a sword but the concept of a sword, and picked it up to use as a weapon. It was a pretty good one, as it happened.
[19] Fine, fine then, *Superman* fans: or the American way.

concept made real and manipulatable might even at times be useful.

This is not a kind of object that we've ever seen manifest in Reality.

Alternatively, the entirety of Reality is itself merely the manifestation of a concept.

Representing and Absenting

Your body is a product of your reality. You can't take it with you to another reality. Your mind, however, can visit another reality if you are able to arrange a body there to act as a vehicle for it.

As I mentioned in the previous chapter, the technical terms here are *transcendence* and *immanence*. Because Reality is the higher reality when it comes to the virtual worlds we create, we humans are transcendent with respect to those realities – we're outside their material existence. Were we to have an NPC-like material presence in a virtual world, we would be immanent with respect to that reality. OK, so we can't actually *have* a material presence in virtual worlds as from our perspective they're non-material[20], but if we *could*

[20] Cynics might say immaterial....

then formally we'd be immanent with respect to them.

Sadly, theologians have not been as helpful as they might have been in the provision of these words (transcendence and immanence). We humans are not transcendent with respect to higher realities such as the Christian Heaven, even though we are outside the material existence of these realities; neither are we said to become immanent in them when we die, assuming that's where we end up going. We're not even immanent with respect to Reality. Transcendence and immanence are strictly for a reality's gods and demigods.

There are two words that do apply to gods and humans alike when it comes to moving between worlds, though: *ascending* and *descending*. Irritatingly, these aren't ideal either. When a person from a lower reality ascends to a higher reality, they change realities: the higher reality becomes their new reality. They may get a fresh body there, or they may not need one if the higher reality's physics allows them to exist that way; nevertheless, they're now running on the hardware of the higher reality rather than that of the lower reality. Similarly, when a person descends to a lower reality, they manifest in that reality rather than in the higher reality[21].

I'll consider ascendance and descendance as ways to travel between realities later (albeit rather briefly). For the moment, it's going to be more useful for us to have a way of describing the kind of movement between realities that these days (as a result of playing virtual worlds) we routinely do the most.

So, when we play a virtual world we don't become immanent in it or descend to it, we ... what?

Well, we *represent* ourselves in it.

Furthermore, we *present* ourselves in our own reality (Reality)[22] and would *absent* ourselves in higher realities if we knew how[23].

These are the terms I'll be using, then, although to show that I mean them in a technical sense I'll drop the reflexive part: if I say I "represent myself in" *Guild Wars 2*, that's a comment on how much I

---

[21] This may only be partial, if the lower reality is not as complex as the higher one and so can't contain the entirety of a visitor from that reality. There's more on this in Chapter 6.
[22] This would include the situation of controlling a mechanical body in Reality while remaining in your own body. Satisfyingly, psychologists call this kind of thing "presence", a concept we'll encounter again in Chapter 5.
[23] I chose "absent" (pronounced ab-SENT) rather than make up a word because it comes with the implication that to visit a higher reality requires the permission of that reality. Also, it has the same etymological stem as "present" and "represent". I did actually think about it....

identify with my character; if I say I "represent in" *Guild Wars 2*, that means I'm playing it, and so am acting *as if* I were present physically in it while acknowledging that in truth I'm physically present in Reality. Likewise, if I were to say I plan to "absent in" Heaven, this would mean I intended to access it through some conduit; it would not mean that I'm actually going there[24]. Both representing and absenting concern visiting a reality by controlling a physical form in that reality while running on the hardware of your home reality. Representing refers to visiting sub-realities; absenting refers to visiting super-realities[25].

I should make it clear that players of virtual worlds don't themselves use these terms. They would say that they "play" or "log into" a virtual world, wherein they're mainly quite content to use the same terms they would for any other place ("Will you be around later?", that sort of thing).

There are, however, technical terms from virtual worlds that do have something more to say about the relationship between players and characters. In *MUD1*, for example, taking control of a body to interact with its reality was called

---

[24] Given what I say elsewhere in this book, there's no chance that this will happen anyway.

[25] Or to visiting sub-...sub or super-...super realities, as many levels as you want. The terms can also be loosely applied to indirectly-connected relatives such as cousin or sibling worlds, if you want to over-complicate matters (which I indeed do in Chapter 8).

attaching. Relinquishing control of a body was *detaching*. Logging in would always automatically attach a player to the body of their own in-game character, but it wasn't a requirement that they stayed attached to it: supernatural powers were afforded gods and demigods that enabled them to detach from their own character's body and to attach to that of a mobile[26] instead (but not to that of another player character).

Interface considerations dictated that a player could be attached to no more than one body at once (their character's or a mobile's); implementation considerations dictated that a body could be controlled by no more than one entity at once (a player or an AI). If you, as a god, wanted to control a particular mobile then in attaching to that mobile you would be detached from your character (which would then become inert) and the mobile's AI would be detached from the mobile (its code simply wouldn't be called upon to execute). Were you subsequently to reattach to your character then both you and the mobile's AI would regain control of your respective original in-world bodies.

In *MUD2*, the implementation was such that more than one player *could* issue commands to the

---

[26] In case you didn't read or don't remember reading the footnote about this back in Chapter 2, mobiles are the NPCs and monsters of a virtual world. Chapter 6 opens with a section on the subject, if you want to skip ahead for more details.

same body simultaneously. This meant that I was able to permit several players to control the same mobile at once; furthermore, I could allow several players to control the same player character at once. It occurred to me that this could be a helpful "let me show you how to do that" feature, so I allowed gods and demigods to attach to other players' characters while they were being played. Needless to say, the feature was employed almost entirely for pranking and eventually I removed it because of the confusion it wrought.

There's no implementational reason to restrict you to one body at a time when you represent in a reality, by the way. If you're good at multi-tasking, you could perhaps control multiple bodies simultaneously. Indeed, at this very moment some individual MMO players will be playing as several characters in the same virtual world concurrently (it's called *multi-boxing*). Theoretically, as a god you could even represent as all the NPCs in a reality at once if you were accomplished enough[27].

In the context of the current discussion, one of the reasons that the process of attaching and detaching is interesting is made clear by what some other MUDs called it: *possessing*. If you want a technical explanation of how supernatural possession might be implemented in Reality, well you have one right there.

---

[27] Except for that one, independent NPC you're going to mess with for fun.

When we represent in a virtual world, we create or take over a body physically present in that world; we control this body from Reality. Excitingly, the same thing can be done the other way round: an NPC of a virtual world can absent in Reality if we create a physical body for it in Reality and pass control of said body to the NPC.

Warning: this is quickly going to get wild.

We already have some fairly sophisticated robots in Reality, capable of such feats as making cars, exploring oceans and guiding high-explosive munitions as they hurtle towards their targets. We command these robots, but they are controlled by computers. The NPCs in our virtual worlds are also controlled by computers. It shouldn't therefore be hard to put an NPC in control of a machine in Reality. We could, if we so chose, make that machine look like a human and have a human-like capacity to sense and to act upon the objects of Reality[28].

An NPC with access to Reality might have trouble resulting from information gain or loss (which I'll discuss later), but if we've managed to endow it with half-decent cognitive abilities it ought to be able to do at least *something*. We could communicate with it; we could let it experience and interact with us and with Reality.

---

[28] This never turns out well in TV shows, but that wouldn't put us off from doing it.

We could do more, too. If we gave it programming abilities, we could allow it to code a new sub-reality of Reality from Reality. We could allow it to change the code of its *own* sub-reality, thus becoming a god of its own world[29]. Ultimately, we could allow it to do anything that we ourselves can do.

We're not restricted to absenting the NPCs of those sub-realities immediately below Reality, either. If our NPCs made the effort and created a sub-sub-reality, we could absent an NPC of that reality in the reality above it (which to us would be our virtual world) or even in Reality itself. We could then make the lucky two-realities-down NPC be a god of the reality of its gods.

We're not restricted to absenting, come to that. Because we have access (directly or indirectly) to the physics of all worlds that are consequent on Reality, we could attach an NPC's consciousness to a body in any sub-reality of Reality. An NPC who went to sleep in one reality could wake up in a reality that's a parent, child, sibling or more distant relative of their own reality[30].

Moving up a level, some god from a reality higher than Reality could make one of your NPCs absent in (or even ascend to) Reality: you could

---

[29] Recalling the earlier discussion of Gödel's Incompleteness Theorems and Ptah, it's unlikely that this would be sensible.
[30] Or indeed in the same reality but a different vessel. Oh, those body-swap movies....

meet one of your NPCs in person, as a person, in Reality. Such a god could also forcibly represent you in (or even descend you to) your virtual world, with or without your consent: you could find yourself living as an NPC in a world you created. Such a god could attach you to a body in a copy of Reality, where you could meet its copy of yourself. Such a god could in theory attach you to a body in any reality created in any of the realities beneath the god's reality.

That's a lot of things a god could do! So, has any god of Reality done any of them?

We have yet to experience any of our NPCs ascending to or being absented in Reality, but that could simply be because they're not smart enough to survive here yet (which is one of the reasons we haven't absented them here ourselves). We don't seem to have had any visitors to Reality professing to be from other realities, either, except from the one immediately above (the realm of Reality's god(s)).

We do, however, occasionally have people from Reality claiming to have visited other realities while their bodies remained here (often in a trance). These other realities could be a reality higher than Reality, or they could be a reality consequent on a higher reality. Such visits are never supported by evidence, though: no-one comes back with technical knowledge unknown to science. Therefore, either there are some well-enforced rules concerning what can trickle between realities, or those who report having made the journey are experiencing a somewhat different phenomenon.

COPYING

Absenting and representing keep your mind running on the hardware of your own reality but allow you to control a body in another reality. Ascending and descending transfer your mind in its entirety to another reality, removing it from the reality it was in before.

How would that transference process work?

When I copy a file from my laptop to cloud storage, the original isn't destroyed: I still have it on my laptop just as before, but now I also have a copy of it online. I could later replace the original with the copy, or *vice versa*. The act of copying may overwrite a destination file, but it doesn't change the source file. Moving a file uses the exact same procedure as copying it, but has an additional step at the end that *does* delete the original file[31].

We can copy NPCs. We can copy their software to a different, or indeed to the same, reality. We

---

[31] If the movement takes place between locations in the same file structure then it could be a pointer to the file that moves, rather than the file itself. Copying would still involve duplication, though.

can have as many versions of each NPC as we want.

Well, I *say* that, but actually it could turn out that we can't. It may be that the way we've implemented our virtual world, each NPC's mind is in part defined by components from which it can't be extricated. It could be like trying to move the River Seine while leaving the water where it was.

This means that although we may not always be able to ascend or descend an NPC (if we can't separate it from its reality), we can nevertheless still absent or represent it (by keeping it running in its own reality but giving it control of a different body elsewhere). Putting it more succinctly: if the mind is an emergent feature of the brain, the brain may have to stay where it is but the mind can yet wander.

Either way, we can definitely make copies of our NPCs; it's just a case of whether we do so by copying their software or (rather more tiresomely) by copying their entire reality. We could then put this copy in charge of a body in their, our, or some other reality.

This suggests that we can make an NPC meet itself. That might be interesting, if potentially devastating for the NPC psychologically.

Looking at our experience of this kind of thing in Reality, well, we don't have any. There are no examples of there being multiple copies of the same individual here simultaneously. I don't include clones or identical twins – those are different individuals. What I mean is that you nod off in a chair, wake up, go to bed and find yourself already asleep there. That just doesn't happen.

Something equivalent *does* happen in virtual worlds. I myself have created multiple identical copies of NPCs and released them into the wild. They got in each other's way, fought each other, ganged up on player characters and mobs; each was one being with a singular experience up until the point I used it to stamp out copies of itself. The fact that we haven't seen anything like this occur in Reality would suggest that either this kind of thing is impossible given how Reality is implemented or that it's possible but there's no god of Reality with a desire to try it out.

Ha! Well there may be no desire from a god of Reality to attempt this, but there *is* a desire from some of Reality's NPCs (us) to give it a go.

Don't try what I'm about to describe at home.

So, you can take a Supermarine Spitfire to pieces, then reassemble it to obtain a Supermarine Spitfire. Whether it's the *same* one depends on your stance in the statuette-or-lump-of-clay debate, but whatever, it's going to fly pretty much the same as it did before you dismantled it. The more attention to detail you pay (how tight were individual rivets?) the more accurately your reassembled Spitfire will exhibit the properties of its earlier self.

While it was in pieces, you could copy each component multiple times and use these to assemble multiple new Spitfires. Given a sufficiently high fidelity of reproduction (down to the levels of wear and metal fatigue, say), you could make copies of your Spitfire that were functionally indistinguishable from the original.

Those copies of the different components don't have to be physical copies, by the way. You could make virtual copies and reassemble a virtual copy of your Spitfire in a virtual world.

Hmm. What if you tried the same thing with a human brain?

I'm no surgeon, but I'm fairly confident that if you did take a brain apart and copied the pieces, it's unlikely you'd be able to put it back together just as it was before the exercise. Maybe some time in the future it'll be possible, but it's not going to happen anytime soon[32].

That said, there are some exceptionally wealthy people around and some vast data centres. If, in examining a brain, you were to take careful note of where each of its 86,000,000,000 neurones (Azevedo, et al., 2009) were placed, and which other thousand or more neurones each one of them was connected to, and if you simulated the action of each neurone individually (and at the same time), you could probably make a working, virtual copy of

---

[32] We're probably going to be able to acquire the necessary component information from scanning the brain before surgery advances this far, thus making the whole process somewhat less fatal.

that brain[33]. Put the resulting virtual brain in control of a humanoid robot and you've got reasonably eternal life.

Well, *someone* has reasonably eternal life, anyway; whether it's you or not is debatable. Even if a dismembered brain reassembled digitally does amount to little more than a change of hardware for the mind, it's nevertheless an act of replication, not of movement. Multiple digital copies could be made. Are they all you? Are any of them you? What does it mean to say that "you" exist?

The idea of making a digital copy of a human brain and so living forever muahahaha is called *mind uploading* or *whole brain emulation*. It's often associated with a wider movement, *transhumanism*, which seeks to use technology to enhance the human mind and body[34].

I mention this because if *we* are thinking of going through with it then the thought must also have occurred to any god of Reality. That being the case, did *they* go through with it? If they did, how many copies of themself did they make? Are any of those copies extant in Reality?

If a god can still make self-copies on a whim, it's entirely possible that each one of us has our own, individual copy-of-a-god looking after, over or at

---

[33] At least at the neurone level. If it needed something else to work, you'd have to make a digital copy of that, too.
[34] And spirit, for those few transhumanists who aren't atheists or agnostics.

us, guardian-angel style. This being so, we'd have not only a personal god in the like-a-person sense, but in the like-we-have-a-coffee-mug sense, too. It could even be that the mind of each one of us *is* a copy of the same god's mind (or at least derives from it).

What would it mean under such circumstances to say that the replicated god "exists"? *Where* does it exist?

IT'S ALL RELATIVE

In Metaphysics, the general view is that existence[35] is a binary proposition. Either something exists or it doesn't. There may be different modes of existence, but these modes are themselves binary. Also, although we may not know the answer to the question of whether something exists or not, we do know that there *is* an answer. For example, from outside its box we can't determine whether Schrödinger's cat (Schrödinger, 1935) exists[36] or not, but we are aware that inside its box there's a clear yes/no answer.

Frames of reference therefore make a difference. Does a 3D sphere passing through a 2D

[35] Or *being*, for those philosophers who consider "there are marmosets" and "marmosets exist" to mean different things.
[36] In the sense that if it's dead it doesn't.

plane exist? Well from the perspective of an observer in the 2D plane, yes it does exist – but as a circle. From the perspective of an observer sharing the sphere's 3D world, only a slice of the sphere exists in the 2D plane, but all of it exists in the 3D world.

When the nature of the frame of reference itself is called into question, the term *partial existence* is sometimes used (Latour, 2000).

As an illustration of this, consider the fallout from phlogiston theory. Scientists in the 17th century devised and successfully employed a theory which posited that combustible objects had a substance in them called "phlogiston" that was released when they[37] were set on fire. Had a scientist in 1700 been asked whether phlogiston existed, the answer would have been in the affirmative; furthermore, had that same scientist been asked whether phlogiston existed in 1600, before its existence had first been postulated[38], the answer would also have been in the affirmative (in the same way that gravity existed pre-Newton). It took over 100 years for phlogiston theory to lose its dominance; the processes it attempted to describe are now better understood as oxidation. So, if today we were to ask whether phlogiston existed in 1600, what would the answer be? It

---

[37] I guess this does include scientists, as formally they are combustible.
[38] By (Becher, 1667).

would be no from our perspective, yes from the perspective of scientists in 1700 and no from the perspective of scientists in 1600. It can therefore be said to have "partial existence".

Although philosophers disagree over whether material and abstract existence are the same thing, they do tend to agree over what the terms mean. Material existence implies that the thing under consideration is present as a physical object in Reality; abstract existence does not imply this. What virtual worlds bring to the table is the suggestion that material existence is itself *relative to a reality*. An object can have material existence in one reality and not in another; therefore, when discussing material existence, you need to make clear to what reality the existence in question is relative[39].

For example, winged horses don't exist as physical objects in Reality[40], but they exist in plenty of virtual worlds. You, as a human being, exist in Reality but you don't exist in a virtual world unless you represent in it as a player character; you subsequently cease to exist in it when you log off.

---

[39] The first philosophers to look at virtual worlds considered the question of whether such worlds were real or not. The conclusion reached was that they might be (Cooper, 1995). I don't believe the argument has advanced a great deal in the intervening decades, so perhaps the notion of relative existence might help them make their minds up.

[40] This may change if DNA manipulation gets creative.

If there are realities higher than Reality, do the beings in those realities exist as physical beings in Reality? Well, they certainly do while they're here, but otherwise, no: they exist in their own realities, but they don't exist in ours.

Again, if someone asks "Does Odin exist?", in what sense are they using that word "exists"? If Odin is in Asgard (where the gods live), he doesn't exist in Midgard (that is, Reality); he only exists in Midgard when he descends to Midgard or represents in Midgard. From his own point of view, he always exists; from ours, he doesn't exist unless he shares our reality. He has partial existence here.

It could reasonably be argued that representing or absenting in a reality is not enough to qualify as existence in that reality, at least in a material sense. Descent or ascent into that reality would count, because in these cases the being's locus of material existence has moved. An observer in the lower reality wouldn't be able to tell this, though, so whereas someone in a higher reality might distinguish between $\exists_{material}$ and $\exists_{virtual}$, someone in the lower reality would be unable to differentiate between the two.

From your perspective, only Reality (or possibly nothing at all) exists as a thing beyond you yourself. Lower realities, such as virtual worlds, exist if you accept that Reality exists, because they're consequent on it. What about higher realities, though?

Well, the afterlife realities we call Valhalla, Heaven, the Summerland or whatever, are (like everything else other than you) merely concepts denoted by labels. If you were to ascend to one then it would become your new reality and the same questions asked of Reality's existence would follow you there. You would definitely no longer exist in Reality, though. If you were instead to absent in a higher reality, well you'd still be physically in Reality, so what you were experiencing as a higher reality may merely be a quirk of Reality; assuming it wasn't, though, you could perhaps legitimately claim that you existed in both the higher reality and Reality at the same time[41].

As a final point about relative existence, it's worth asking whether realities themselves have material existence. In particular, does a reality have material existence relative to itself? This is important for those gods of Reality who to some extent *are* Reality, so listen up Stoics, Cheondoists, early Taoists and other pantheists.

There is a certain oddness in the suggestion that although objects exist in Reality, Reality itself might not exist. If there's a higher reality upon which Reality is consequent then Reality would definitely exist relative to that higher reality; the question merely moves up to the higher reality,

---

[41] I say "perhaps legitimately" because it depends on what's meant by "you". As always, you'd still exist in your own mind.

though. Does that higher reality exist relative to itself?

Well, the definition I gave way back at the start of this book defines a reality as "a self-contained space of existence that's defined, maintained and continually modified by its own physics"; a candidate reality couldn't be self-contained if it didn't contain[42] itself, and it couldn't contain itself if it didn't exist relative to itself, therefore realities do exist relative to themselves[43]. This is if you accept my definition, of course, which I basically made by fiat: I'm asserting that the reason a reality exists relative to itself is that I say it does. Feel free to disagree – I'm not going to fight you over it.

Where realities do differ from the other objects that have material existence relative to them is that they can simultaneously exist as a material object in a higher reality. *MUD*, for example, exists as the reality that is itself, but it also exists in Reality (if you accept that software systems exist in Reality and aren't just a scam perpetuated by computer programmers to gain employment).

A side-effect of defining realities to be self-contained is that no reality is ever empty: it always exists within or as itself even if there's nothing else there. If indeed there *is* nothing else there then

---

[42] This could be as an object within itself, recursively, or as an object congruent to itself.

[43] Note that the concept of sets that contain themselves (*universal sets*) causes alarms bells to ring for logicians (Russell, 1903), but fortunately realities are not sets.

whether or not the reality is interesting rather depends on its laws of physics[44]. Overall, though, it's useful to be able to consider realities as stand-alone spaces of existence, even if the realities themselves aren't necessarily wonderful places. They don't have to be consequent on a higher reality to exist: they could exist independently, running on the hardware of themselves. Reality, for example, could exist independently of a higher reality in this manner.

COINCIDENCE

The Ancient Mesopotamians built a temple to the god Nergal which was constructed like a palace. It had dining rooms, bedrooms and rooms where he could receive his guests. In the deepest sanctum was what looked like a statue of Nergal, but it wasn't. Following a ritual known as *mîs-pî* (meaning "washing of the mouth"), the statue ceased to be a statue and became the god the statue represented. He could see, he could eat and drink, he could smell[45] and he could act. OK, so he didn't actually *do* any of those things, remaining uncannily statue-like, but he *could* have done them

---

[44] Hey, if you watch it long enough it might perform a big bang or two for you.

[45] As for what he could smell, my guess would be incense.

had the mood taken him. Because of this, every day the priests would bring him fresh clothes and two full meals.

How would you implement something like this in a virtual world?

Well, the statue is like a character that the player isn't currently playing. It's been left lifeless in the virtual world, but the player could log in[46] at any moment and play as it. The statue is therefore in some sense both the player and a representation of the player – irrespective of whether the player is actually playing it or not. It's fairly easy to implement, as it's merely a regular object to which its player attaches (or doesn't). If Nergal wants to attach to his statue in order to represent in Reality, well that's his prerogative.

Nergal and his statue show that a single object can be two entities at the same time. This is not an uncommon proposition. In Catholicism, for example, the sacrament of the Eucharist changes bread and wine into the body and blood of Jesus[47] through the process of *transubstantiation*. In virtual world terms, the booze and biscuits aren't the blood and body of the player (because the player is of a higher reality) but they are how the player's blood and body are made manifest in Reality.

---

[46] Or reattach from a mobile or other character.

[47] Participants then eat and drink this, which may seem unpleasantly like cannibalism to the non-initiated but apparently isn't.

This isn't mere metaphor or symbolism; nor is it a problem of reference (as with the example of Andy and Boudicca that I outlined earlier). Catholicism takes a very hard line on the subject: the bread and wine cease to be bread and wine and *actually become* Christ's body and blood. This means that if thousands of priests simultaneously turn their local supplies of wafers and wine into the body and blood of Christ during 7:30pm mass in churches across the land then there are thousands of instances of Christ's body and blood to be accounted for at the same time.

Now it's fine for Roman Catholic theologians to say this happens, but they don't have to implement it. If we, as the gods of our virtual worlds, wanted to implement in them something akin to transubstantiation, how would we go about it?

I'm going to offer two possible solutions.

In the first, as I subtly hinted above, we'd instance the body and blood. The total mass and volume of wafers and of wine would be more than in the original source, so it can't be mapped on a one-to-one basis; we'd have to create copies of the body and blood, private to each wafer and mouthful of wine.

Of course, to someone who found a misplaced wafer and didn't know about its history of transubstantiation it would still be just a wafer; it could in theory be subject to transubstantiation a second time[48]; we'd therefore be wise to phase each instanced wafer to those who know its history; for the general, unphased case, we'd just leave the original wafer as it was. This is regardless of whether we were copying all of the object (the material components of body and blood) or just an aspect of it (the spiritual components, say).

Such a solution would be exceedingly tiresome to implement and the processing overheads would be heavy. Furthermore, it would be unsatisfactory anyway: for dogmatic reasons, the body and blood can't be copies, they have to be the *actual body and blood*. That in itself is problematical, because eating something tends to destroy it; we really don't want to destroy the actual body and blood.

It seems we're being asked to construct a single, uncopiable object that can exist thousands of times at once, but which doesn't cease to exist when it ceases to exist. How can we possibly do that?!

This brings us to the second, smarter way of implementing transubstantiation.

We have one, original version of the body and the blood. This exists in a higher reality. The body and the blood can represent in a lower reality, thereby allowing both to exist multiple times relative to that reality without there being more than one each of them in the higher reality. When the object through which they are representing is

[48] I can see the advertising slogan already: "Now with double the Christ!".

destroyed, that particular representation ends. The original version, in the higher reality, remains extant.

This way of looking at transubstantiation – as a form of representing – is much cleaner. It's compatible with a range of interpretations of what is called the *real presence of Christ* in Christian teachings[49]; as we saw with Nergal, it can work for other gods, too.

Cool! From an understanding of how we would implement the concept of transubstantiation in a virtual world, we've obtained a clearer view of how any gods of Reality might do it.

You're welcome, theologians.

Perspective

Earlier, I asked (twice) what the question "Does Odin exist?" means. The answer depends on whether you mean physical or conceptual existence, and which reality you're using as your frame of reference.

I am a god of my virtual worlds. I exist in my own mind, and am happy to go along with the idea

---

[49] In particular, it explains why we can't have a Eucharist in a virtual world: the body and blood represent in the reality one level below their home reality, not two levels, therefore virtual bread and wine aren't going to transubstantiate.

that I exist in Reality, but do I exist in the realities I have created?

Materially, no I don't. I'd have to descend to them for that, which I can't do. I can represent in them, though, and from the perspective of the NPCs of those worlds it would look as if I did have material existence there.

That, of course, is if they can detect me.

I can make myself completely undetectable[50]. If the NPCs can't detect me, does it make sense to say that from their perspective I exist? Sure, from the perspective of the physics of the virtual world I exist, because that's what's sustaining my character while I'm representing in that world. Do I exist from the viewpoint of a free-thinking NPC, though?

Well no, I don't. I don't appear in their model of their world in any shape or form. They may be open to the possibility that I am present in their world[51], but if they have no way of sensing me (or of sensing anything that allows them to deduce my presence) then I can only exist to them as a conceptual object. Even if they have absolute faith that I also exist materially, that doesn't mean I do; I could log out any moment and they'd be none the wiser.

---

[50] The command to do this in *MUD2* is INV'3, which puts me at invisibility level 3. Even demigods can't see me at level 3.
[51] This assumes they're smarter than they currently are in today's virtual worlds.

What if I never represent in the virtual world but make supernatural changes to it from Reality that its NPCs can detect? Perhaps I create a mountain floating in the sky, or give voice to trees, or make it rain pigs. The NPCs won't know that I exist in their reality (which is fair enough, I don't), but they may conclude that at least someone exists in or from a higher reality. If I leave actual messages, such as surrounding a city with a 20,000-word tract using letters two metres high each made from a solid diamond, they may even be inclined to give me the benefit of the doubt. Then again, they could be cynical and dismiss it all as coincidence.

What if I allow NPCs to absent in Reality for a while using robots here as a conduit? The NPCs will see that Reality exists, be able to chat to me about this and that, and then when they return to their own sub-reality they'll know for sure that I exist – in Reality. Objectively, though, with regard to their reality, I still don't exist unless I represent in it or somehow descend to it (or make supernatural changes to it, if you accept that as a form of second-order existence).

Why would I bother having the NPCs absent in Reality to achieve this effect anyway? It would be time-consuming and expensive. How about I create a virtual world that is a copy of a chunk of Reality and have the NPCs go there instead? Their experience would be identical to the one they would have had if they'd gone to Reality, only they didn't.

Why would I bother with having them visit the copy of Reality, for that matter? I could just plant false memories in their minds of having visited Reality and the end result would be the same.

Would I still exist in all of those situations – or indeed in any of them?

Could you (as in, you) exist in a virtual world that you've never even heard of? Perhaps, if in their minds its NPCs have met you, yes, you could.

Suppose I make a virtual world, populate it with artificially intelligent NPCs[52], and then sit back and watch. Because the NPCs are clever, eventually they'll ask questions about their existence (much as we humans have done and continue to do). If I never visit their world and make no supernatural interventions, could these NPCs ever work out that I exist?

They have the evidence of their own existence and of their own reality's existence. They may misattribute evidence (reading events as being supernatural when they're natural), but given enough time they'll realise when they've made an earlier mistake[53] and move on. They may extrapolate from their own experiences (perhaps

---

[52] As I keep pointing out, we can't do this as yet (but see Part 3).

[53] "Hold on, what if the sun *isn't* pulled across the sky on a chariot?".

they create their own sub-realities) and figure out that there's a nigh-certain chance that I exist.

They won't know who I am, though.

All their concepts about me would be pure conjecture. They wouldn't know why I made their reality, why I made it the way I did, nor why I made them. They wouldn't know that actually I made their world with a friend, it's not all my own work. Beyond the basics of the possibility or probability that someone made their reality, they'd be pretty well ignorant. If I appeared in their midst, they wouldn't know me at all.

Yes, to them I might exist – but *I* wouldn't exist.

For the third time: if asked the question "Does Odin exist?", what do you mean by that word "exist"?

Also, what do you mean by "Odin"?

Feel free, if you wish, to substitute the name of any other god for that of Odin there.

Chapter 5

IMMERSION

Artists in medieval Europe had a problem in depicting the Christian Heaven. They knew it was a spiritual world that was separate from the physical world, but how could they envisage what it looked like in order to paint it? It couldn't be experienced until it was too late to paint it, and it couldn't even be described in words, let alone in images.

They had to fall back on metaphor. The difference between the worlds of the body and of the soul was as the difference between ... what and what?

Well the part of the universe we live in, the terrestrial world, can be mapped onto the physical world. The part of the universe we see but can never visit, the celestial world, can be mapped onto the spiritual world. It's *not* the spiritual world, but it's as remote and unknowable to us (well, medieval us) as the spiritual world is. The body/soul duology could be represented as the Earth/sky duology.

This is why medieval artists would depict Heaven as being in the sky: it was a metaphor (Wertheim, 1999).

As it happens, medieval artists were probably worrying about this unnecessarily.

When we, as gods of virtual worlds, create those worlds, we base them on Reality. The virtual world is, for its NPC inhabitants, the physical world that they experience in their everyday existence; Reality is their spiritual world, where their souls – if souls are a thing – reside (on our computers)[1]. The NPCs have no access to Reality, so it's as unknowable to them as Heaven was to medieval artists. Nevertheless, we gods can see that actually the virtual world works pretty much the same way as Reality does. Sure, it might have magic, orcs, unspillable milk and backpacks that can hold impossibly-heavy weights, but its physics is largely based on the physics of Reality. If we were somehow to transpose an NPC into Reality, that NPC wouldn't find Reality's physics incomprehensible[2].

So yes, for a medieval artist NPC it is true that Heaven is unknowable, but it's also true that it possesses features that can nevertheless be guessed at with reasonable accuracy.

There are good reasons why this is the case.

---

[1] You could also argue that if they do have souls then Reality's spiritual world (rather than Reality) is their spiritual world. Even so, that doesn't mean *we* can't implement something *we* decide is a soul. Each NPC could have two or more souls this way.

[2] The inability to change their entire outfit in a single instant could come as a surprise, though.

our own image

That there are similarities between humans and gods is well-established. It's taken as axiomatic by the Ancient Greeks, Romans and Norse, for example. Many Christians also hold this point of view, primarily because *The Bible* out-and-out says that God created man in God's own image. *The Qur'an* makes no such claim directly, but there are two books of hadith that report the prophet Muhammad as having mentioned that God created Adam in God's own image.

Islamic scholars widely interpret this "own image" statement to mean that human beings possess some of the abilities of God (such as being able to see and to speak, and having free will) but not in the same measure as God[3]. This is more like how it is with virtual worlds: NPCs aren't the same as human beings, but they possess some of the same attributes[4] that human beings possess.

So ... why do we give them those attributes?

Well, the thing is, if we're to visit (as players) a reality that we (as gods) have created then that reality has to make sense to us. It must behave in a way that we understand intuitively, rather than in

---

[3] God is never going to need to wear spectacles.

[4] They may indeed have additional attributes that we don't, to compensate for their shortcomings. I look at this a bit later.

one that requires analysis. Ideally, it has to be (incoming technical term) *persuasive*.

Any virtual world that wasn't persuasive would be hard for us to accept as being real, and so wouldn't feel like a reality[5]. This doesn't mean that the mapping of the virtual to the real has to be exact, of course. It's not important that game worlds faithfully replicate how Reality's physics works, but if players are to use what they know about Reality predictively in the game world then it is important that said game world replicates the *effects* of Reality's physics with reasonable fidelity (Upton, 2015).

Upon encountering a human-created sub-reality of Reality for the first time, our default understanding of how it works is therefore easy to state: it works like Reality (Tolkien, 1964)[6]. Any divergence from "how Reality would do it" is likely to be a distraction, so we don't want such divergences introduced unnecessarily; we wish our created realities to share enough aspects of Reality that we're not constantly interrupted by thoughts of "well *that's* strange". It's also less to remember:

---

[5] We can create realities we don't want to visit – one consisting entirely of ever-calculating multiples of the number 142,857 for example – but I'm talking about the particular realities I defined as virtual worlds here.

[6] Also (Bartle, 2011), but you're more likely to be impressed by Tolkien than by me. Fiction Theory, which wasn't created with virtual worlds in mind, calls this the *principle of minimal departure* (Ryan, 1980), albeit with a different rationale.

you may find it easier to accept that you can have extra-dimensional access to a safety-deposit box if you're not also having to accept that colours work like magnets, that up and down flip each time you blink and that politicians will answer a straight question with a straight answer.

The upshot of this is that if we wish to visit our created realities, we should configure them to be similar to Reality[7].

If we do this, it follows that there are consequences for the design of the NPCs who inhabit our virtual worlds. To function, NPCs must be able to negotiate their environment; they need abilities that allow them to sense their surroundings and to act upon them. These abilities will perforce align with those that we ourselves possess, because we specifically designed the NPCs' reality such that it would be suitable for our abilities.

In summary: the basics of our created worlds are going to intersect non-trivially with the basics of Reality[8]; therefore, the basics of the NPC inhabitants of these worlds are going to intersect non-trivially with us[9].

---

[7] To some extent, we have no choice anyway: the fact that we ourselves are of Reality intrinsically limits how different from Reality the realities we create can be (Wolf, 2020).

[8] They may be different worlds, but there isn't a world of difference between them.

[9] This helpfully grounds the Hermetic aphorism, "As above, so below".

Now all this is at the systems level – the physics of the respective worlds. At the access level, the situation differs.

What an object looks like from outside a reality isn't the same as what it looks like from inside that reality, because senses can only sense that which exists in their home reality. If you examine the code of an animated, fire-breathing dragon, you won't see an animated, fire-breathing dragon except in your imagination. When you visit a reality, there is a barrier that must be crossed both to inform you of what's going on in the reality and for you to inform the reality of what you want to do in it. Otherwise, were your character to be the subject of a fire-breathing dragon's breath of fire, how would you know and how could you respond?

If you are to visit a reality, then, there has to be a transformation process to convert the sensory signals which your player-character's body in that reality is receiving into a form that your own, Reality-based senses can detect. Likewise, actions your Reality-based body undertakes must be translated into control signals for your reality-based character. In software development, such a set-up is what we call an *interface*. As I've mentioned before, text and virtual reality are both interfaces that can be used for virtual worlds (although screen and mouse/keyboard or controller are currently more common).

The possibility exists of doing some real-time computation during these interface adaptations.

For example, the NPCs in a virtual world might communicate between themselves using a non-human language, but in converting this into sounds for your headphones their words could be translated into your natural language of choice. Likewise, your natural-language words could be automatically translated into the in-reality "sound" signals appropriate to convey in NPC-language what you said into your microphone. It would be a transparent process both for you and for the NPCs.

As I've described it so far, what designers of virtual worlds are aiming for is a sense of what is called *presence*: the perceptual illusion that a mediated experience is non-mediated (Lombard & Ditton, 1997). This makes the virtual world more persuasive, and so helps the player to will in themself the belief that they are *in* the virtual world rather than in Reality (which they nevertheless remain intellectually aware that they are).

(Lombard & Ditton, 1997) identified six main uses of the term "presence" in Communication Studies:

- *Presence as Social Richness*. How remote or intimate does the experience feel?
- *Presence as Realism*. How accurately does the experience model the real thing?

- *Presence as Transportation*[10]. How well does the experience make the user feel they're somewhere else, or that somewhere else is here?
- *Presence as Immersion*. How much does the virtual environment whelm the real environment?
- *Presence as Parasociality*. How much do unidirectional relationships within the experience nevertheless feel as if they're bidirectional[11]?
- *Presence as Active Medium*. How much do users treat the medium itself as a social actor[12]?

Not all of these have equal relevance to virtual worlds: presence as transportation and presence as immersion are the most significant, and those are what I'll be focusing on (although I'll later reference presence as parasociality a little, too).

You get presence as transportation in its "I am there" form when reading a novel; that is, you feel you've been transported to an imaginary land. You get it in its "there is here" form when watching TV;

---

[10] It's also known, rather old-fashionedly, as *telepresence* (Minsky, 1980).

[11] You do know that when the TV newsreader says "see you tomorrow" they almost certainly won't be seeing you tomorrow, yes?

[12] When you get an encouraging "well done so far" from a tedious form-filling automated phone service, do you thereafter feel encouraged?

that is, you don't feel you're at the Olympics, you feel the Olympics have been brought to you. With virtual worlds, you get it in its combined (and rarer) "we're all here together" form. You are there, but other people are also there – or rather here, as your here is now there.

Presence as transportation is important for virtual worlds because it's a major design requirement: they are places that players are intended to be able to visit. If the players never feel that they are in a shared space, it's not going to happen. Of course, merely knowing this doesn't thereby cause such presence to occur, and it's fairly-obviously necessary anyway; still, having a formal term for the players' desire to feel that they're in another world can at times be useful.

Presence as immersion is the main context in which the concept of presence is used with reference to virtual worlds. It's a little contentious, because it employs the very powerful term *immersion* in a specific way that is readily misinterpreted by academics new to the field of virtual worlds.

The thing is, presence as immersion is about *sensory* immersion: presenting the senses with a collection of signals that work together to offer a coherent picture of an environment different to the one that actually pertains. Donning the VR glasses, you really can feel as if you're walking on a girder high above the streets of New York, and that one false move will result in a fall to your death[13].

This use of the word "immersion" is perfectly fine, and is arguably its everyday meaning. It's not quite what *players* mean when they talk about immersion, though. True, they're not great at articulating it, but for players immersion is about *identity*: being one with your character in the virtual world. To this end, most people who play virtual worlds are effectively engaged on a quest of self-actualisation. Remarkably (because virtual worlds aren't particularly designed with this in mind), they all tend to pursue their goal by following a common, well-trodden path known as the *hero's journey* (or *monomyth*).

The hero's journey was first identified by an American academic, Joseph Campbell, in an influential book, *The Hero with a Thousand Faces* (Campbell, 1949). Campbell discovered that most ancient myths and folk tales unfold to fit a set pattern: an (invariably male) individual goes away to a land of adventure, where he discovers himself then returns to be the hero he was destined to become.

Virtual world players' personal stories follow this same pattern. Not only were virtual worlds invented to be places of identity exploration, and

[13] I'm one of those irritating people who immediately makes that one false move, just because I can. So far, it's never resulted in a fall to my death.

recognised as such by early researchers (Bruckman, 1992) and even some players (Wagner, 2009), it turns out that this is how they really do work.

Note that there is a corresponding *heroine's journey* (Murdock, 1990), but few virtual world players ever walk that path. It doesn't exactly describe a pleasant experience and it ends with the heroine's understanding that she didn't need to go on her journey in the first place.

Tempted though I am to go into considerable detail about how virtual worlds are able to provide such transformational experiences for players, I shall instead defer to an excellent book on the subject: (Bartle, 2003). OK, so it's a book I wrote myself, but there are only two books that cover this topic in any depth and I also wrote the other one (Bartle, 2016); I therefore end up looking like a deluded, self-publicising jerk either way[14].

Unfortunately, it's common practice among those psychologists studying virtual worlds to conflate the sensory-oriented and identity-oriented meanings of "immersion"[15]. This leads to experiments designed to test for the former obtaining results that are questionable when applied to the latter. The experiments aren't

---

[14] I don't mind *being* a deluded, self-publicising jerk, it's *looking like* I'm one that I try to avoid.

[15] Or any of the other meanings – the term is used in at least six different ways with regard to RPGs (Bowman, 2018).

invalid, they're just being interpreted invalidly. As an analogy, it's be a bit like trying to explain why Scots watch football using evidence gained from asking Americans why they watch football – they're different footballs[16]. Virtual-world immersion and regular immersion are different immersions. Those academics who do understand what virtual-world immersion is (because they've played a lot more virtual worlds for a lot longer) are hopelessly out-numbered by those who don't[17], so we can't optimistically expect this situation to change any time soon.

As it happens, sensory immersion *is* an excellent tool to help players become identity-immersed, because it's quite hard not to believe what your engoggled eyes are telling you. Setting aside any worries that you could develop a splitting headache or that someone is secretly taking photos up your skirt, the technology of sensory immersion, when used well, is wonderfully persuasive.

It's not actually *needed* for identity immersion, though. In fact, it's not even the most powerful route to it. *Text* will lead people faster down the

---

[16] Formally, one is *American Football* and the other is *Association Football* (whence the abbreviation "soccer").

[17] I remember reading one paper in which the author claimed to be an authority on *World of Warcraft* having spent 50 hours playing it. To someone who at the time had spent over four times that number of *days* playing it, this wasn't quite as impressive a qualification as the author perhaps believed.

path to becoming as one with their character than will sensory immersion. The problem with sensory immersion is that it's *too* real: you feel as if you're you, somewhere else; you don't feel as if you're someone else, somewhere else, and so able to find the real you somewhere in between. Text, though, can achieve this almost as a matter of course.

That said, text isn't a cool interface these days, so you're not going to try it for a game any more than you're going to read this book using a virtual-reality headset.

OK, so from all this we can see that the aim of virtual world designers should be to make their creations persuasive for players (to help with easier immersion), without being so persuasive that the players feel they're still in Reality (just a weird version of it). There needs to be some room for imagination to play its part – which is of course precisely why text is so good at promoting immersion among those people willing to read for fun.

Note that the ability to represent in a sub-world carries no connotations regarding how persuasive the experience is; rather, the interface used is the major determining factor in that regard. A set of VR goggles makes the world seem more persuasive than a set of 3D glasses would, but they in turn would make for a more persuasive interface than a flat, 2D screen[18]. In the future, we may be able to use neural interfaces to write to players' senses directly, so that a virtual world gives at least the same level and detail of sensory input to a jacked-in player as does Reality – perhaps even more. We could also intercept and read instructions from a player's central nervous system, so if they tried to walk then it would be their virtual body that walked, not their body in Reality.

In such circumstances it would be very difficult to feel that you weren't present in the virtual world, even though intellectually you would know that you were slumped in a chair with a cable connecting your brain to a computer. In this full *system immersion*, your senses would be overwhelmed by data telling you that you were in a different reality; nevertheless, your mind would be running on the hardware of Reality, so you'd still only represent in the virtual world, not present in it.

If the virtual world were sufficiently different, there could be things that your character was able to do in it that you are incapable of in Reality. You don't have wings in real life (trust me), so if you did in the virtual world then you'd have to learn how to use them (assuming you were connected using a

[18] Static images are less persuasive still. Whether or not text is the least persuasive interface or the most persuasive depends on how good your imagination is (Asimov, 1973).

neural interface; it would actually be easier if you weren't).

Of course, if the virtual world differed *too* much from Reality, you wouldn't be able to do a great deal in it – you'd find it incomprehensible. Although your interface with a virtual world heavily influences immersion, ultimately it's the nature of the virtual world itself that determines whether or not you can become immersed in it. Finding just the right level of similarity with Reality is a goal that all virtual world designers share[19].

What happens when they get this wrong?

THE FICTION

The reason that persuasiveness is needed in virtual worlds is that these worlds are fictional. If they weren't fictional, they'd be real – which is to say, they'd part of the fabric of Reality. OK, so they *are* part of the fabric of Reality, in the sense that they're implemented within Reality, but they're still made-up. They may be closer to Reality than

[19] Albeit not necessarily knowingly

are some other works of fiction, but they nevertheless *are* works of fiction.

In discussing virtual worlds, the word "fiction" has two related but different meanings. Its first, everyday meaning, refers to wilful fabrications in general; this is how I used it in the previous paragraph. Its second, more technically-nuanced meaning, refers to a virtual world's own particular fabrications; in this context, it's often called "the fiction".

I've slipped in references to *the fiction* several times already. What I mean by the term is *that which you need to buy into to accept the virtual as being real*. Each virtual world has its own fiction; it's essentially fixed when you start to play, but you can learn more about it as you do play. There may be some off-the-shelf components to it that players are used to accepting from other creative works (faster-than-light travel, magic, extra-sensory perception, that kind of thing[20]), but although these can help with buying into the fiction, they're usually subservient to it. The fiction is the creative bedrock of the virtual world.

For example, in the MMO *Secret World Legends*[21], the fiction is that mundane Reality is

---

[20] Such extensions to Reality's physics used to be called *ultraphysics* until the term fell out of use.

[21] This is a revamped version of *The Secret World*. It ironed out the creases in *TSW*'s fiction (which was already best in class), but sadly also removed the subtle beauty of the gameplay. It then broke it completely by adding a pay-to-win cash shop.

under constant threat from occult forces that the vast majority of the population is entirely unaware exist. You are a member of a secret society who has been gifted with a form of immortality to take on and, if not defeat the forces of evil, at least to prevent them from defeating the forces of good. Magic works, but so does modern technology, with attempts being made to employ the latter to amplify and to refine the former.

Now although that's just a basic summary of *SWL*'s fiction, it's still enough to tell you it's no *World of Warcraft* – even though both MMOs involve magic. As you play, you'll learn that apart from the secret societies (the Templars, Illuminati and Dragons), there are other organisations involved (the Venetians, Phoenicians, Orochi Corporation and many minor groups), each with differing agendas. All this, and much more besides, adds to the fiction but doesn't change it.

A virtual world's fiction is almost the same as what designers call its *lore*, but not quite. Lore is the virtual world's player-independent backstory. You have to accept it to some degree in order to situate yourself in the virtual world, but you don't need to know it to play; you do, however, have both to know and to accept the state of the world that the backstory has led to and your own place within that world – that is, the fiction. The fiction can therefore be thought of as the "You are a ..." detail of the lore.

The lore: the Third World War led to years of post-apocalyptic soul-searching, during which the people of Earth made first contact with an alien species. A period of recovery followed, in which we began sending starships out to explore strange new worlds, to seek out new life and new civilisations, and to go boldly[22] where no-one had gone before. A war with an alien species brought about the formation of the Earth-led United Federation of Planets, precipitating hundreds of years of relative peace.

The fiction: in the optimistic universe of the future, you are an officer of a starship beginning a new, five-year[23] mission.

From a player's point of view, the fiction is important: it encapsulates those dissimilarities between the virtual world and Reality that make the former worth playing (or not). From an NPC's point of view, though, the fiction is unknowable and the lore is truth. "The War of Black Holes imploded the universe and destroyed all within it, but after billions of years of darkness it has exploded anew. Now, on an ordinary planet orbiting an ordinary sun in an ordinary galaxy, an ancient peril is once again stirring into being. On the brink of creating true artificial intelligence, will the planet's life forms repeat the mistakes of those who went before them, or will they recognise the

---

[22] No infinitives were harmed in the writing of this sentence.

[23] Shorter if you wear a red shirt

dangers before it's too late? You are the leader of a nation state in this world-on-the-cusp. To save the universe, will you side with humanity or with the impassive machines it creates?".

We can see the lore of Reality, but for us it's not lore, it's history[24]. We can't see the fiction of Reality, because we can't play Reality; for us, Reality is our reality. The visitors to Reality from a higher reality would see the fiction, because it differentiates Reality from their reality[25].

I've brought up the topic of the fiction because of what it implies regarding immersion and interfaces, both of which I've mentioned before and both of which I'll mention again; in particular, they'll turn out to be fundamentally related to the reasons why people create realities. For the moment, though, as the purpose of this chapter is to offer a practical explanation as to why creators of realities base their created realities on their own reality, I shall confine my discussion to that topic.

So, a virtual world's fiction embodies all the falsehoods that an individual accepts when they decide to play that virtual world. By necessity,

---

[24] OK, so in this example it's poorly-imagined, speculative history that I've just made up, but the same argument applies to *bona fide* origin accounts (such as the one involving Adam and Eve): they look like history from Reality but would be lore to someone for whom Reality is a virtual world.

[25] As the novelist E. M. Forster put it: "If God could tell us the story of the universe, the universe would become fictitious" (Forster, 1927).

because nobody like spoilers, this fiction will lack detail: the designer will have informed prospective players of its central thrust, but will have stopped short of explaining everything.

The designer's aim here is to give the player a sense of where the virtual world's boundaries lie and of what can be expected to obtain within those boundaries. The designer is making a kind of promise – a *covenant* – in which they ask you, the player, to trust them to deliver what they hope you will like, but which they can't tell you about beforehand because that would rob you of the fun of finding out[26]. To break the fiction is to break the covenant and so to lose your trust. The covenant is particularly important for virtual worlds, but other works of fiction have the same thing. For example, were you to extend a much-loved movie franchise in a manner that replaced its mysticism with space aliens, this might arouse feelings of betrayal in its audience[27].

Breaks in the fiction are particularly potent in virtual worlds because they unimmerse the player. The fiction is the player's anchor: if the ropes the player is using to keep tied to the virtual world come away in their grasp, they've nothing to hold onto – they lose their connection to their character. To maintain immersion, then, designers

[26] I write more about the covenant in (Bartle, 2012). No, this is not a cheap attempt to increase my citations count by one.
[27] Exhibit one: *Indiana Jones and the Crystal Skull*.

like to keep everything well within the fiction – even if that entails extending the fiction to cover desired but not-of-Reality features.

For example, at the start of this section I mentioned that in *Secret World Legends*, your character has a form of immortality: you die, then seconds later you come back to life. Why do you come back to life in a reality based on Reality when this doesn't seem to happen with any frequency in Reality? Ah, well in the opening to the game you were granted immortality by swallowing a bee[28]. The fiction therefore covers it. That said, the NPCs you kill also come back, it just takes them a while longer. They haven't swallowed a bee and there's no other fiction covering such behaviour; it's just how these guys roll[29].

If a designer wants to help their players remain immersed, then, a strong, robust fiction is a necessity. They do want to help their players remain immersed, too, because immersion is exactly the means by which individuals from a higher reality represent in a lower reality.

Immersed players present in Reality while representing in the virtual world. The same individual is therefore effectively two people at the

---

[28] I realise that this isn't the most obvious route to immortality, but it does make a kind of sense in the context of the game. In Reality, it's more likely to shorten your life than to extend it, though.

[29] I suspect because utterly implausible fiction can be even worse for immersion than having the fiction remain silent.

same time: the player and the character. To control the character, the player has to pass information to the virtual world; to describe the character's situation, the virtual world has to pass information to the player. Some of this information is knowable to the character (your attempt to make a bowl of soup was successful) and some of it is unknowable (you gained 10 experience points for exhibiting your soup-making prowess). Some of it appears within the virtual world (there's a chest over to the character's left) and some of it doesn't (that red glow round the edge of the player's screen means the character is injured).

Immersion is affected by who is entitled to see the information passing between the two realities and by where this information appears. Happily, there are some technical terms from game design that we can use here to describe the various possibilities.

Some things that you might want to do or to find out in the virtual world don't involve breaking the fiction. Let's say you're playing a game in a modern setting, seeing it through your character's eyes (that is, with a first-person perspective camera). You want to know how much time is left before the bomb goes off, so you perform the appropriate keystrokes and ... what happens? You might tell the time in Reality by looking at your watch or phone: does your character maybe look at their watch or phone in the game world? If so, this falls within the fiction: the player is being provided with the information they requested and their immersion isn't compromised in the process.

In game design terms, this kind of interface is said to be *diegetic*. It's the most immersive way that information can be conveyed, but it's not the only way. There are, as you may have deduced from my preamble, three other main approaches that game designers would consider for presenting in-world information to the player; these are referred to as *meta*, *spatial* and *non-diegetic*[30].

A meta interface maintains the fiction of the virtual world, in that it doesn't tell the player anything that their character wouldn't know, however it achieves this outside the geometry of the virtual world. The classic example is to show in a special window the text of a book that your character is reading. Other characters can't look over your character's shoulder to read it, because the book's contents aren't being displayed in-world; nevertheless, your character is not being presented with information they're not entitled to see.

A spatial interface is like a diegetic interface, in that it displays information within the geometry of the game world. However, the information it displays is for the player, not for the player's character; it therefore breaks the fiction. A

---

[30] For a full discussion, see (Fagerholt & Lorentzon, 2009). For a shorter, but pretty darn good summary, see (Stonehouse, 2014).

common example would be that of a targeting circle showing you where your area-of-effect weapon would cause damage were you to activate it right now: it looks as if it's part of the world, but it isn't. Likewise, the billboarding of names above characters' heads places text within the virtual world's space as if it were part of a character's appearance; it's not, of course – names don't catch on the lower branches of trees or anything – but it *looks* as if it is. The information is there for the benefit of the player, not of the character.

Finally, *a non-diegetic* interface places in the plane of the screen information which is not known to the player's character but which is known to the player. Examples include: a juicy overlay announcing you've reached level 50; a window to be used for buying in-game currency; an announcement that the server is going down for maintenance.

Whether an interface element is accounted for by the fiction or not is dependent on the fiction, not on the interface element. A mini-map, for example, could be telling the player something that their character would know (say, which other characters are within hearing range), or it could be telling them something that their character wouldn't know (say, which other characters are within a 2km radius); a change to the fiction (you're in a helicopter with radar, or using a clairvoyance spell) could turn a non-diegetic interface element into a meta interface element without changing the look of that element. The head-up display format adopted by most MMOs is meta at best unless the player is playing a character who has a HUD in-world (for example, they're a fighter pilot), which could instead make it diegetic.

As I said, a diegetic interface leads to a more immersive experience. This suggests that the player should only have access to the in-world information that their character has access to, and that it should be presented to the character in a way similar to that in which it would be presented to the player if it happened in Reality. Indeed, for many years designers of virtual worlds debated among themselves as to whether they should give players numbers at all[31], its being widely accepted both that numbers were unimmersive and that players nonetheless kept on asking for them. Sadly, players almost always prefer short-term value to long-term value (Bartle, 2004), and some wrote *addons* (interface plug-ins) to deliver what the designers had withheld; designers capitulated thereafter. This is why you now see streams of numbers appearing above enemy characters' heads showing how much damage you're dealing (and

---

[31] "The ox is stricken by the effort of your proficient, downward blow." *versus* "The ox is stricken by the effort of your proficient, downward blow. Damage: 3.".

that their average has slightly increased since you paid €15 for a crystal of +1 to critical[32]).

I've described these different kinds of interface in terms of displaying information, which is to say output to the player, but (as interfaces are two-way[33]) they can also be applied in terms of input to the virtual world. You may have to click on an in-world door to open it (diegetic), or to click on a bag icon to bring up your inventory (meta), or to mouse-over a monster to find what level it is (spatial), or to hit the escape key to bring up the settings menu (non-diegetic).

There are two axes involved here: in-fiction/out-of-fiction and in-geometry/out-of-geometry. Although they're mainly thought of as visual elements, they also apply to other sensory information such as audio. You hear footsteps crunching over snow behind you (diegetic), or a disembodied narrator (meta), or a you're-under-attack beep in the direction of an aggroed[34] mob (spatial), or a fanfare when you finish a quest (non-diegetic).

Important: *only diegetic information is accessible to NPCs*. This is because they themselves are diegetic. Meta information would make sense to them as it's also in-fiction; it's essentially diegetic

---

[32] *Black Desert Online*, if you need to know.

[33] Players interface *with* virtual worlds, not *to* virtual worlds.

[34] *Aggro* is British 1970s slang for "aggravate" that somehow made its way into modern MMOs via text MUDs.

information that has been rendered meta to make the player's interface with the virtual world more friendly. Out-of-fiction information, though, is inaccessible (and quite possibly inconceivable) to NPCs.

I once heard an anecdote told by a woman about when she was a little girl. A friend of her mother's visited, bringing her own daughter along with her. While the two mothers chatted, the two girls played. Our girl kept saying things to the other girl, but she didn't seem to understand – our girl thought she was perhaps a bit stupid – but all the same they were having fun and got along well. After a while, suddenly, the other girl stood up and ran to her mother for no apparent reason. Our girl looked up and saw her own mother calling for her. It was time for her friend to leave. After she'd gone, our girl asked her mother how come her new friend had suddenly known that her own mother was calling her. Her mother replied that our girl, like she herself, was deaf; her friend and her friend's mother were hearing.

So it is with NPCs and out-of-fiction interfaces. An NPC may not have access to the same information that you do (through the virtual world's interface), but if they're observant enough they may nonetheless be able to discern that you somehow know things that they don't or can somehow do things that they can't.

It's also possible that NPCs could have access to information that players don't, or could perform actions that players can't. For example, you as a player may not be able to look inside an NPC's mind to see what it's going to do next, but its fellow NPCs could perhaps have this ability. Unsurprisingly, players tend to take a dim view of this kind of behaviour, regarding it as cheating on the part of the designer; designers are actually quite sensitive to the accusation, though, so will usually either concoct a reasonable fiction to cover it or avoid putting it in unless it results in massive efficiency gains[35].

The difference here between players and NPCs, then, is that NPCs regard the possession by player characters of special information or powers as being some kind of supernatural magic (which from their perspective, yes, it is), whereas players regard possession by NPCs of special information or powers as being unacceptable unless solidly supported by the fiction. If we apply this maxim to Reality, it would help explain why there are many accounts of supernatural beings with supernatural powers (the use of which we NPCs can often spot), but there are few accounts of supernatural beings who lack the natural powers available to us.

It's worth dwelling on the reason why players don't like NPCs to have knowledge or powers that the players themselves don't have. It's not *purely*

---

[35] They could naïvely try to conceal that it was happening, but that would enrage players even more when the scam was (inevitably) found out.

out of a sense of unfairness (although this is often a major factor); it's also because it breaks immersion. To fit the fiction, things should happen a certain way; they don't, which is the cause of complaint.

The key word here is *should*. What does it mean to say that a virtual world or a character within it "should" or "would" behave a certain way in a particular situation?

This brings us to the wonderful topic of realisticness.

Realisticness

Just because a world has dragons, that doesn't mean anything goes.

When you play a game or read a novel or watch a movie, you are entering a world of fiction. There are truths about the world depicted that are not true of Reality. You are a medieval general. Sherlock Holmes is a person. A guitar-playing trainee nun has a tendency towards over-enthusiasm. The fiction of the game, novel or movie constitutes the premise you have to accept if you're to invest yourself in its world.

What about everything the fiction doesn't describe, though? Well, for reasons justified earlier in this chapter, this defaults to how it is in Reality.

Horses can't operate trebuchets. Queen Victoria was a person. People live in Austria.

So far, so good.

What about things that neither the fiction nor the defaults of Reality describe? Arrows fly further than they should. Watson has a leg wound after being shot in the shoulder. Germans speak English to each other.

Obviously, we do *know* why this is the way things are. Longer-range arrows make for better gameplay[36]. Watson's wound moves because Arthur Conan Doyle forgot where he'd previously put it. An English-speaking audience won't necessarily comprehend a conversation in German. These discordant elements are present for reasons outside the context of the fictional world: the cause is that the fiction itself is an artefact of Reality.

Although such incongruities may well be understandable, they're somehow unsatisfactory. This is because they poke holes in the fabric of the fictional world. We can't buy into them: we simply have to accept them then move on. This, as we shall see shortly, makes the situation less than ideal.

I explained when describing persuasiveness that the reason everything the fiction omits defaults to the way Reality does it is that we have an understanding of Reality. We need to be able to

---

[36] In *Civilization V*, you could shoot them across the English Channel.

make rational deductions about what will happen if we do this or that, or what must have happened for things to be like that or this, which would be impossible if the fiction was all we had to go on. Unless the fiction tells us otherwise, we therefore ground our analysis in the reality we know best: Reality.

This is true of any work of fiction.

Suppose we're reading a novel. We're following a story: we want to be able to think about why things have happened and what that means for what will happen. This requires us to have an operational model of the fictional world. Without one, we can't establish hypotheses or make inferences. In the 2010 TV series *Sherlock*, Watson's change of wound-location is revealed to be psychosomatic as a result of post-traumatic stress (he was in the army), thus placing it nicely within the fiction. As a result, the next time we saw something seemingly at odds with the fiction in that show, we could feel more confident that there'd be an in-fiction explanation rather than an out-of-fiction one.

This raises once more the issue of *trust*. When you have a good game designer, or a good novelist, or a good director, you can trust that what happens happens because it fits the fiction. If the enemy doesn't advance its forces, that's because it's waiting for support from its allies; it's not because of bad AI. If a boy hugs himself while being asked questions, he's afraid; it's not just a bit of acting business to slow down the pacing. If the grandmother starts to lose weight, it's because she's developing a terminal illness; it's not because the actress has changed her personal trainer.

In the early days of virtual world development, we called this concept *realisticness*. A better word would be *verisimilitude*, but realisticness was preferred because it tended to be used in the negative: concepts were said to be *unrealistic* if what happened didn't match the player's understand of what "should" happen. If you drop a hedgehog off a tall cliff, the hedgehog should die. Your character dies when you fall off that cliff: so should the hedgehog. The hedgehog doesn't die, though. That's unrealistic.

If the hedgehog had previously been flagged as being magical, OK, well you might feel able to cut it some slack. If it appears to be just a regular hedgehog, though? Well, in a game that you deem you can trust, the reason it doesn't die is perhaps that it really *is* magical despite looking ordinary, so its survival gives you information about the creature that you didn't previously have and which you can later perhaps exploit. You would feel justified in exploring this possibility, and so be somewhat disappointed if you discovered that it is indeed just a nothing-special hedgehog that ought to die when tossed from a clifftop but doesn't[37].

---

[37] This example comes from *MUD2*. Spoiler: it is indeed no ordinary hedgehog.

You can also get unrealisticness when the fiction doesn't hold. I've just melted a hole through a castle wall with this wand: why can't I use it to negotiate the insurmountable waist-high fence in front of me? Yes, I know that in Reality I can't do much damage to a fence using a stick, but this one can *melt holes in walls* so it ought to be able to remove a less substantial obstacle with ease.

Unrealisticness can sometimes be encountered when the fiction is missing an aspect that ought to be there but isn't. This is usually harder to spot. For example, did you notice that there's something not present in *The Lord of the Rings* (Tolkien, 1954) that ought to be there if the peoples of Middle Earth had developed in the same way that every society ever in human history has developed? It's quite interesting to examine (although I shan't be doing so myself[38]) why "there is no religion at all in *The Lord of the Rings* – no temples, shrines, priests, prayers, amulets, scriptures, ikons, idols – *nothing!*" (Carter, 1973). Not having religion in Middle Earth is unrealistic.

When something is unrealistic, then, it means there's an inconsistency. Either the fiction has failed, or the non-fiction has failed and the fiction can't cover the failure. In both cases it's bad fiction, and this is why people don't like it: their model of the made-up world is being broken for no good

---

[38] If *you* want to examine it, letter 131 from (Carpenter, 1981) is a good place to start.

reason and their theories about what might happen next are now worthless[39].

As a non-game example, consider the TV series *Game of Thrones*[40]. Very few of the named characters in this show wear headgear. They can be in a land of permafrost with icy winds blasting down sheets of snow on them, but they don't put on hats. They can be in the baking heat of a desert, yet not shade their scalps. They can be in the middle of a battle, but won't sport a helmet. Their other clothes will be eminently appropriate – furs, silks, armour – and have carefully-considered detailing, but their heads will nevertheless be bare. Crowns, tiaras and maybe a hood are the most you're likely to see.

This affectation was noted by fans of the show, some of whom commented that it wasn't realistic. Other characters wore sensible headgear, but very few of the main ones did.

Well, fire-breathing dragons aren't realistic either, and they're a big feature of *Game of Thrones*. The same fans who griped about the lack of hats were not at all fazed by the presence of dragons. Why was this?

---

[39] "To be able to live a moment in an imagined world, we must see the laws of its existence obeyed. Those broken, we fall out of it." (MacDonald, 1893).

[40] I suppose I should put a spoiler warning here, but really, if you haven't seen the series by now then the chances are you're not going to do so any time soon.

The answer is that the fiction explains the dragons but it's silent on the subject of inadvisable headwear preferences.

There are several reasonable explanations that could have been provided to satisfy the fans, including: "not wearing hats is a sign of rank"; "gosh, we hadn't noticed that, thanks, we'll put them in hats from now on"; and "yes, they should be wearing hats but then you'd complain you couldn't tell who the main characters were"[41]. It would not, however, be reasonable to respond "why are you saying that hat-wearing is unrealistic when there are dragons in the world?". This is because we know the answer: the dragons are covered by the fiction, but the lack of headwear doesn't seem to be. If the fiction had addressed the issue, the lack of headwear wouldn't have been perceived as unrealistic.

This point is important, because (as I said) it's all about *trust*. Also in the *Game of Thrones* TV series, there's a sequence in season 7, episode 6 (*Beyond the Wall*[42]), in which the character Jon Snow falls into water through broken ice and is

---

[41] This is (a paraphrase of) the actual reason, as furnished by the actor Kit Harington: he asked to wear a hat while filming in Iceland but was told that sensible headwear made it too difficult to differentiate between people's faces in that environment (Vineyard, 2017).

[42] No, I'm not the *Game of Thrones* nerd – you're looking for my wife.

utterly drenched through, yet he drags himself out into the polar conditions without any ill effects.

Realistically, Jon should have hypothermia, yet he doesn't. OK, so why doesn't he? Well, if I can trust the fiction, it's telling me something. Maybe his sword is magically protecting him? Maybe he has an innate ability to resist cold that mirrors the one Daenerys Targaryen has to resist heat? Maybe something as-yet-unknown warmed the water? All these hypotheses have interesting implications. However, if the reason he doesn't suffer is that he's wearing plot armour, frankly that isn't good enough. It's effectively saying "don't worry your pretty head about it, audience dear, just accept it like you accept the dragons". The point is, if we *did* accept it like we accept the dragons then his survival should mean something special: the *dragons* are something special.

Realisticness matters.

Because of all this, when we look at Reality as if it were the sub-reality of another reality, we can therefore be fairly sure that if a personal god were involved in Reality's creation, the vast majority of what we experience of the physical world of Reality would correspond to the physical world of the god's higher reality – that is, it would seem realistic to a being of that higher reality. It wouldn't necessarily have to be as detailed, in the same way that virtual worlds implement Reality more in the abstract than in the concrete, but we could expect it to be close.

This raises a question of potentially great significance.

When designers design virtual worlds, they design them to map onto Reality in most respects. However, they will gloss over some things that are deemed to be inconveniences (few insist that your character uses the lavatory[43]) and they will add key elements of difference that they regard as beneficial (say, magic works). The rest of the virtual world is as it is in Reality, but the changes make it more attractive than Reality; if they didn't, people wouldn't care to play[44]. A similar thing can be said of books and movies, of course, and the trade-off between keeping it real while making it playable is the longest-standing issue in simulation games (Jackson, 1991). Virtual worlds are more than books, movies or simulation games, though: they're realities.

Reality is also a reality.

If we apply this design logic from the perspective of a higher reality – one that is to Reality as Reality is to virtual worlds – then it would seem that this higher reality is likely to have details that didn't make it to Reality because they are an annoyance. Furthermore, new things will

---

[43] Strictly speaking, the lavatory *is* a convenience.

[44] Recall that Roy Trubshaw and I made *MUD* with the specific intention that it would be an improvement on Reality. To an extent, we succeeded: many people do indeed play virtual worlds because they find them a more attractive proposition than they do Reality (Castronova, 2005).

have been added to Reality that the higher reality doesn't have, in order to make Reality more attractive than that higher reality.

In other words, the higher reality is *worse than Reality!*

If you don't think much of Reality, then, you're unlikely to discover that any higher reality is an improvement on it. Such a reality would be similar to Reality, except that Reality has had the sucky bits taken out.

We're *part* of Reality, though. Have we had the sucky bits taken out of us, too? What must the people of a higher reality be like if *we're* nicer than they are?

Suppose there *is* a reality above Reality: is it a heaven or is it a hell?

PHYSICS AND CAUSALITY

Realities aren't merely world descriptions (those are states); they also incorporate implemented, physical rules that transform one state into another. For a virtual world to be persuasive, not only must its states appear realistic, but so must its rules. Players can be jarred out of immersion just as much by something that behaves oddly as by something that looks odd.

There is a caveat to this. Although thus far I've been discussing Reality as being the fall-back *reference world* (Juul, 2021), it could just be the last of a series of fall-back positions. This is because immersion is all about *expectations*.

Suppose a player character were to drop a ball on the ground. What would the player expect to happen? Well, for most players with some experience of modern MMOs, the answer is that they would expect the ball to disappear, destroyed. They might expect to be asked to confirm that they actually want to destroy it, but they won't expect it to do what Reality says it would do (that is, bounce and roll until it finds a resting place).

The reason for this is that these players have played enough MMOs to have changed their idea of what the default behaviour should be. They expect this MMO to behave like the previous MMOs they have played, rather than like Reality. It's not difficult for them to discard this new default: if the first ball they dropped did bounce and roll then they'd certainly notice and lose immersion for a moment or two, but they'd be able to readjust to the new, closer-to-Reality default without difficulty. Nevertheless, in the absence of evidence they will expect a trope rather than a faithful simulation of Reality's physics (Bartle, 2011).

I did say that created realities may omit or simplify aspects of the reality in which they are being created; this disappearing ball would be an example of that[45].

Some things simply can't be changed, though, no matter what you do. Primary among these is the notion of *causality*.

Events happen because of antecedents; conditions give rise to effects. The physical rules that govern these transformations are subject to godly alteration, but the principle that such rules must exist in the first place is not. A world with no causality is going to be static in one of two senses of the word: either unchanging, like a movie of a photograph; or random noise, like an untuned analogue TV. You could visit such a reality from a higher reality, but not make changes to it – it has no rules of change. You'd have to cheat with your interface even then, because the air of the world (if it had air) wouldn't move out of the way when your character moved, and the light of the world (if it had light) would not be streaming onto your character's equivalent of retinas.

These rules about what rules must exist also apply to supernatural rules. The physics of the supernatural may be different to the physics of the

---

[45] In case you're wondering, the reason that the ball disappears is threefold: to stop the virtual world (and specifically its database) becoming cluttered with rubbish; to stop people from undetectably exchanging virtual goods for real money; to stop people using artistically-arranged lines of objects to draw a penis.

natural, but supernatural rules are still rules that have causal effects.

From the perspective of an inhabitant of a reality (as opposed to a visitor from a different reality), supernatural physics has discernible effects but either no discernible cause or no discernible connection between the cause and the effect. A rabbit popping into existence out of nowhere would be an example of the former; a rabbit popping into existence out of nowhere when I waved my magic wand would be an example of the latter. Rabbits simply shouldn't appear out of nowhere under the everyday laws of physics.

If supernatural laws apply in general then they're not supernatural, they're natural. They have to apply only under certain conditions to qualify as being supernatural. Traditionally, they have been tied to particular objects (such as crystal balls), places (such as fairy rings), beings (such as ghosts) or times (such as Hallowe'en[46]).

Things can, of course, appear to be supernatural without actually being so. For example, our theories concerning the physics of Reality don't currently suppose faster-than-light travel to be possible. If, therefore, we were to find evidence of faster-than-light travel, we could surmise that one of the following statements must be true:

---

[46] This is how I was taught to spell it in the 1960s, and I'm not about to bow to peer pressure to spell it any differently now.

- The evidence is flawed in some way, and faster-than-light travel has not been demonstrated.
- Our theories are wrong, and we need to rewrite them to accommodate this newly-observed and reproducible phenomenon.
- Our theories are right in general, but don't apply to this particular object, place, being, time or whatever.
- Our theories are (or at least were) right, but a god changed the physics of Reality.

Of these, the first two are natural explanations and the second two are supernatural explanations.

The notion of causality leads to the notion of time. Alarmingly, both causality and time can work backwards as well as forwards: is the ball rolling because I struck it with a cue stick, or am I striking it with a cue stick because it was rolling?[47]

If this seems weird, consider that people reason about cause and effect in both directions as a matter of course. "I'm going to the charity shop later this morning to drop off some old books. The charity shop is ten kilometres away, so to get there I need to drive. To drive, I need my car keys. Oh

---

[47] This is one way of explaining a correct *premonition* in a non-deterministic reality: you're accessing an event that has already happened. A second way suggests that you recognise how the future will pan out from patterns you've observed subconsciously. A third way has an ordering body (a god, say) acting as guarantor of fate. A fourth way is that you make a lucky guess.

dear. My car keys are in the pocket of my black jeans. My black jeans are in the basket where we put clothes waiting to be washed. So are lots of other clothing items. These items are on top of my black jeans. So yes, the reason I am removing my wife's underwear from the clothes basket is that I'm taking some books to the charity shop later this morning. Why are you looking at me like that?".

In Artificial Intelligence research, the form of reasoning illustrated above is called *backward chaining*. It's preferred in cases when it's easier to figure out what you need to do to achieve some goal than it is to figure out what you can do and whether doing that will lead to the goal's being achieved (which is *forward chaining*).

Causality can be represented as pairs of statements called *production rules*. One statement in each pair is the rule's *precondition* ("if this is true about the world ...") and the other is its *effect* ("... then this becomes true about the world"). As for which is which, well that's for the designer to decide. Almost invariably, though, for implementing a virtual world the rules will be constructed to match what we in Reality think of as forward in time. That isn't to say they can't be reasoned about in both directions by an NPC's artificial intelligence to plan how to do something, but even then the NPC wouldn't itself know which way the causal chain was *actually* running, just how it *appeared* to be running.

If someone from a higher reality were to visit Reality, Reality would have to run causality in the same direction as in the higher reality for it to make sense to the visitor. However, if there is no higher reality, or no-one from it ever comes to see us, then everything could be running backwards: what we think of as our memories are actually our unavoidable destiny, completely determined by how the world is at this moment.

It's also possible that the direction of the causal rules sometimes flips and we're stuck bouncing between two potentially fixed points in (what we perceive of as) time. That would be a bit of a let-down with regards to free will, but on the bright side at least we'd never know it.

Having said all this, I shall nevertheless assume that causality works in the direction that we perceive as forward in time: events in the present cause effects in the future, not the past. It's just going to be so much simpler if I don't have to qualify every sentence with a mention that we could have it backwards.

To a virtual world designer, connecting causality to time (or time to causality) immediately raises a number of questions with regard to implementation. One of these stands out for the way in which it captures the core issues clearly and simply: could we have time travel in a virtual world?

In its most basic sense, yes, we most certainly could because it's the default inherited from

Reality: even if I do nothing, I'm travelling through time (at a speed of one hour per hour). When people normally think of "time travel", though, they mean travel either backwards, or forwards at a rate in excess of that expected when considered from the perspective of an external observer. It's also usually discontinuous (you disappear at one time and reappear at another) rather than continuous (you remain *in situ* while time-travelling).

Travelling into a reality's past plays merry hell with its present, because the present is dependent on the past (through that reality's causal rules). The easiest way to implement it is to fork a copy of the reality at the point in the past when someone arrives in it from the present, then let it continue from there independently. If you want to allow people who travel into the past to come back to the present, you can either return them to a save of the original reality at the point when they left it (perhaps discarding the forked copy), or you can run the forked copy until it reaches the appropriate timestamp then drop them in. In the former, no actions taken in the past will have had any effect on the present except those that modified the time-traveller directly; in the latter, the present relative to the time-traveller will have been changed by actions taken in the past.

Travelling to the future is much easier, because you simply wait until the reality reaches the appointed time and then materialise the time-traveller there and then. If you want the traveller to be able to return to the present, you need to save it at the initial point when the travelling took place, but other than that you needn't worry.

As a designer, you're limited in whom you can allow to travel in time. In a virtual world with no players[48], you can allow all NPCs to engage in time travel if you want; yes, the more it happens, the more resources you'll need and the more copies of the reality you'll end up running, but I'm sure you can afford that. If your virtual world has only one player then you can't allow NPCs to travel through time but you can allow your player character to do so. However, if you have more than one player then you can't let anyone time-travel except to possible futures and irrelevant pasts. Special case: you *can* have all PCs travel at once (as, for example, when restoring a back-up following a disastrous patch).

The reason for this is that virtual worlds are real-time with respect to players. You have no control over the way time works in Reality, so you have no control over how it works for players in the virtual world. If I go a week into the virtual world's past, make an alteration then return to its new present, the effects of that alteration would have to ripple through to create this new present (if what I did is to be meaningful). Should there just

---

[48] This is a thing: they're called *zero-player games* (Björk & Juul, 2012). Conway's game of *Life* is an example of a zero-player game.

be me playing, well that's fine: I'd make the change, wait as the virtual world ran for a week (which, because it can be decoupled from real-time for this exercise, could take far less than a week relative to me) then I'd reappear in the now-modified present and see how my modification worked out. However, if you played yesterday then the forward propagation can't happen: your actions yesterday wouldn't necessarily have been the same in the light of my alteration; come to that, they might not have even been possible. Making you (and everyone else who played in the past week) replay it for my benefit isn't a solution because you may well decline to co-operate[49].

The upshot of this analysis for you as an NPC of Reality is that if you want both to go back in time to change the past and to return to the (now changed) present once you've done it, you're restricted. You can't go back in time beyond the point at which a player last interacted with Reality, and if there are players currently in Reality then you can't go back in time at all while retaining any memory of the present[50].

When it comes to the detail of how time is implemented, there's a major difference between Reality and the virtual worlds we create. In Reality,

[49] Especially if you died this morning.

[50] You and every other NPC could go back in time if there were a system reboot from a saved state, but you wouldn't know this had happened unless perhaps it was only partial.

time is (or at least gives a good impression of being) *continuous*. In virtual worlds, it's *discrete*. By "continuous", I mean that any two points of time have an infinite number of points between them; by "discrete", I mean that any two points have a finite (possibly zero) number of points between them. It's like the difference between integers (discrete) and reals (continuous) in mathematics.

When time is discrete, points in time correspond to indivisible *ticks*. Each tick, the underlying physical system looks at the tasks it has to do, does them, then exits so the next tick can take its turn. For example, in terms of Conway's game of *Life*, each generation represents a point in time; the transformation of one generation to the next is a tick. It's a bit more complicated when you take parallel processing into account, but that's basically the story.

In *Life*, it doesn't matter how long a tick takes to compute: when one tick ends the next one starts straight away. However, in most computer games (virtual worlds included), ticks have to follow a real-time clock so that players perceive time as passing evenly.

NPCs don't know this, because they have no access to Reality's time. Their own time is made up of ticks, which they experience as being seamlessly continuous because they can't see the inter-tick gaps – those only show from Reality. That said, if the NPCs were sophisticated enough then they could perhaps perform experiments to find out whether or not there *were* gaps.

Hey, just a moment! *We're* sophisticated! *We* perceive Reality to be continuous! Maybe it's actually discrete, though? Perhaps, if we look closely enough, we'll find evidence that time can't be subdivided beyond a certain amount – that it's somehow atomic?

Well, unless a major scientific breakthrough occurs between my writing this and your reading it, none of the features you might expect to see if time (or space-time) in Reality was discrete have been observed. For example, light travelling over vast distances could be cumulatively distorted by discrete time, but astronomers haven't detected this.

If experiments were to show that time in Reality is discrete rather than continuous, expect headlines proclaiming that we live in a digital simulation. This would indeed be a possible inference, but time's being digital wouldn't alone imply that Reality is a computer simulation[51]

---

[51] Also, even if evidence of digital time *is* detected, it could merely be the result of a resolution limit for foamy quantum interactions that gives the appearance of time's being discrete but no, actually it's continuous. There's also the problem that Reality has uncertainty at the functional level which no algorithm can ever capture (Ringel & Kovrizhin, 2017). This is irrelevant to virtual worlds, but I spent half a day reading up on it and am not about to let such effort go to waste without at least granting it a footnote.

(although its being continuous *would* imply it's *not* a computer simulation, or at least not a simulation on a digital computer).

The reason I've spent this number of words discussing how time is implemented in virtual worlds and how it looks as if it's implemented in Reality is that there does appear to be a difference between them that's of some consequence. Time in virtual worlds is definitely discrete; time in Reality is probably continuous (but could yet be discrete).

As I hinted at the end of the paragraph-before-last, we can actually make computers that use continuous time. Analogue computers are just such devices, and although it's not obvious how we'd implement a reality using one, that doesn't mean it's impossible. Another approach would be to use asynchronous logic circuits, which while they are digital in terms of data are not in terms of time (that is, they obey no system clock)[52]. The main issue would be one of keying: if we wished to visit a virtual world with continuous time then that reality's time would also equate to the time of Reality, so would have to feel neither too fast nor too slow to visitors from Reality.

The point is, though, that for a reality to have continuous time there is a requirement that the reality in which it is implemented also has continuous time. If Reality has continuous time

[52] Quantum computers are yet another example, but they're done after only one tick.

then so must any and all the realities above it. Furthermore, whatever realities the NPCs of our virtual worlds may create in the distant future, they'll perforce use discrete time rather than continuous time because we used discrete time to actualise their host reality. The NPCs may not be aware that their reality is using discrete time, but in theory they could perform experiments that would eventually reveal the truth.

How a god chooses to implement a reality therefore has implications for all the realities consequent on that reality. Chains of causality continue through chains of realities.

There's one more observation we can make about this, though, which is something of a bombshell. See, while it's obvious that what happens in Reality can have a colossal effect on a virtual world, it's less obvious that the connection runs both ways: what happens in a virtual world can – indeed will – have an effect in Reality. Sure, it won't be great, but at the very least some bits in a computer's memory will be flipped. Virtual worlds can do nothing *to* Reality, but they can't avoid doing something *in* Reality. Thus, because all realities consequent on Reality are ultimately implemented in Reality, Reality itself is therefore changed (measurably if not always perceptibly) by the goings-on in its sub-realities.

The same can be said in turn of any reality of which Reality is a sub-reality.

Put more concisely, your every action on Earth changes Heaven.

That's if there is a reality higher than Reality, of course, but if we accept there is then the fact that it can be changed means that it isn't perfect unless Reality is also perfect – or unless changeability is part of what it means to *be* perfect.

With that, we reach the end of Part 2 of this book.

We've looked at the different ways of creating realities and noticed how an understanding of virtual worlds can modestly help clarify some points of theology. We've considered what it means to exist in a reality and formalised the different ways that individuals can visit realities. We've examined why sub-realities resemble those they are consequent upon, and why everything in them – including their NPCs – reflects aspects of the reality of their designer.

In so doing, we've arrived at a turning point. The preceding pages have been devoted to thinking about what our knowledge of virtual worlds in particular can tell us about the creation of realities in general. They've said very little about what actually *comes with* the creation of a reality.

Gods, you see, may turn out to have some responsibilities.

Part 3

Realities as Realities

Chapter 6

SAPIENCE

Thus far, although I've occasionally referred to the NPCs of our virtual worlds as if they were intelligent, I've always diligently pointed out[1] that of course they're not.

Well, they're not *yet*, anyway.

Obviously, the reason I'd ultimately want to do this is so that I can equate the situation of NPCs in sub-realities looked at from Reality with the situation of us in Reality looked at from Reality's super-reality[2]. How we as gods treat NPCs tells us something about how any gods of Reality might treat us. Indeed, if we're being observed, it might *inform* those gods how they should treat us.

As an analogy, if a manager mistreats their subordinates, they can hardly complain when they in turn are mistreated by their own manager. Then again, if they treat their subordinates leniently,

[1] Well, always diligently meant to point out.

[2] I'm assuming here that Reality has exactly one immediate super-reality, but (as we'll see in Chapter 7) that's not necessarily the case.

their own manager could regard this as a sign of weakness. It rather depends on the manager[3].

We have now reached the stage where we can start to think seriously about the conduct of gods.

MOBILES

Strictly speaking, NPCs are those characters in a virtual world who (at least in theory can) share all the features and abilities of player characters except one: they're not controlled by a player. In general, player characters will actually have abilities superior to those of NPCs, but this is a design decision rather than an essential difference; only the manner in which a character is controlled is a necessary distinction.

Typically, NPCs will at least look similar to player characters, and be relatively safe from attack except as part of a set piece. Many will be there simply to make the place look busy or to guard something, but most will have been created to act as an interface with a service (buying and selling, dispensing quests, training, changing player-characters' looks, repairing items, giving directions – that kind of thing).

---

[3] I went with a business analogy here, but only because if I'd gone with feudalism I'd have had to use the word "lord" a lot and sounded unnecessarily Biblical.

Some of the activities NPCs can do, player characters can't do; this is rarely the problem it might be, because most players don't want to do those particular activities anyway. After standing behind a counter in a shop all day in Reality, you perhaps wouldn't want to come home and log into a virtual world to do the exact same thing but for fun. NPCs with a narrative purpose may have abilities player characters don't that players wish they did, but such characters are isolated one-offs in a sea of mundanity.

Although not a formal requirement, it's almost invariably the case that NPCs are unable to distinguish between themselves and player characters. Indeed, in general they don't even have the concept of "player characters". In other words, if an NPC encounters a being that looks like them, they'll treat it as if it were another NPC regardless of whether it really is or not.

So, NPCs think (inasmuch as they think at all) that player characters are also NPCs. NPCs are not the only kind of denizen of virtual worlds, though: there are also *monsters*. Monsters do not usually look or behave like player characters, and NPCs know them to be different. Almost without exception, monsters have but one purpose: to be killed in combat. Yes, that giant bear may be a loving father who is only out in the forest looking for his young daughter's lost elk-horn flute, but you don't care: he's worth experience points dead, so dead he shall shortly be.

The umbrella term used to describe both NPCs and monsters is *mobiles*, which is short for "mobile objects"[4]. Nowadays, the word is unfailingly abbreviated to *mobs*, in which context it almost always means monsters and those NPCs who are also fulfilling a please-kill-me role. A mob is therefore an individual creature, not the group of creatures that a non-MMO use of the word might indicate. You could have a mob of mobs.

I should perhaps mention that despite their being called "mobiles", mobiles don't have to be mobile. Should you wish, you could endow some form of thinking capacity to an object with no inherent powers of locomotion, such as a rock or a cave or a mirror, mirror, on the wall. A tree spirit would count as a mobile even though it's essentially immobile[5].

Mobs created to be fought in orchestrated circumstances, such as instances, can be further subdivided into *bosses* (high-powered, treasure-laden single mobs with bespoke, often scripted

---

[4] I can say this with some authority because I came up with the term for *MUD1*. I was in urgent need of a designation for objects that had a move (that is, a turn to do something); I figured that these entities behaved in ways that looked intelligent but were constrained – a bit like those hanging ornaments called "mobiles" – so that's what I called them. It never occurred to me that the term would actually stick.
[5] Given how sensationally boring such a life must be, there's little wonder that tree spirits always seem to be at least a *little* bit weird.

abilities) and *trash* (mobs with nothing worth having that you kill on the way to the next boss). In instances containing more than one mob, the boss always comes after the trash except when there are consecutive bosses; if you encounter trash after a boss, it's because there are more links in this chain and you've now started on the next one. The end-of-chain boss (or *end boss*) is always a proper boss and is never followed by trash; whether a mid-chain scripted mob (or one of a group of boss mobs) is respected as a boss in its own right or dismissed as a *mini-boss* depends on how much of a fight it puts up. Figure 8 shows this graphically.

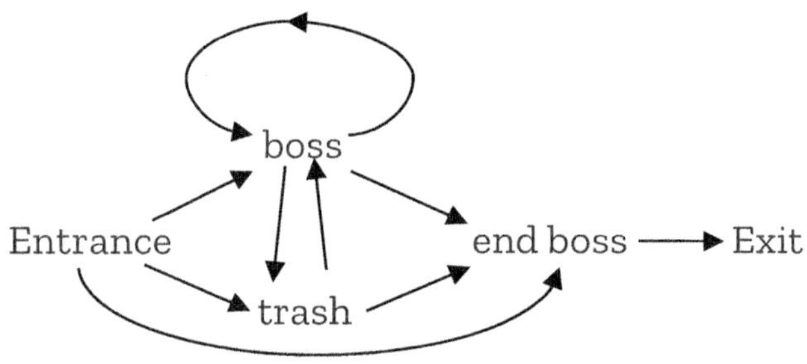

Figure 8 – Trash and Bosses.

The huge physical power differential that exists between bosses and trash (including *adds*, which are trash that hang around with the boss) is not evident between human beings in Reality. Therefore, if we've been specifically created in order to be destroyed then either we're all bosses or we're all trash. Either way, the rather more challenging end boss is yet to appear.

In today's MMOs, none of these mobs are remotely intelligent. They don't learn player strategies, they don't adapt, they don't play tricks, they don't anticipate your actions, they don't try to parley. They're basically invariant machines. If you have enough firepower and can counter their special abilities, you're going to win: it's simply a case of remembering what they typically do and then trying to mitigate it. For example, it might be that when the boss shoots out an orange ray at you, you are about to produce fire beneath your feet and, unless you keep on the move until the effect wears off, you'll shortly be toast[6]. It's as if you're learning to dance with an experienced partner: you don't want them to change their step pattern, because if they do then you'll have to learn your own moves all over again[7].

OK, so let's suppose that mobs were more intelligent: what would happen?

Well, it would depend on how much more intelligent they were. In the 1990s, I put some basic

---

[6] Yes, Iscariot from *Secret World Legends*, I am indeed calling you out. You may be only a mini-boss, but that attack should nevertheless be telegraphed more clearly.

[7] I chose this rather clunky simile because players actually call the series of actions they have to perform to beat a complicated boss the *dance* for that boss.

artificial intelligence[8] into some of the mobs in *MUD2* and swiftly had to dumb it down because the majority of players were now getting thrashed by said mobs.

At least those *MUD2* players could have picked up some tips from the mobs, though. When the mobs pick up tips from you instead, it can change the essence of the game. If they were actually to *learn* from your actions, your best strategy would be to play sub-optimally in order to train them to expect only sub-optimal behaviour – so that when you really did want to win, you could pull out your optimal strategy and defeat them. You'd no longer be playing a game if you did this, though: you'd be playing the artificial intelligence behind the game. Once you'd figured out how it worked, you'd be back to dancing again (just more tiresomely).

That said, most players do like playing alongside other players, most of whom are actually capable of both thinking and learning. If mobs could be made smarter without turning them into relentless killing machines or data-driven clairvoyants, there's a fair chance that the player experience would actually improve.

So, how might we make mobs smarter, then?

I realise it's bad form to ask a rhetorical question and then not answer it, but if I *could*

---

[8] I did my PhD in AI specifically because I wanted to create intelligent mobs in *MUD*.

answer it I'd be up for a Nobel Prize[9]. So, let's suppose that it's 50 years from now and we have developed artificial intelligence to a level comparable with that of human intelligence.

What's that? 50 years isn't enough? Take 500. Take 5,000. Take 5,000,000. Take 5,000,000,000. Take as long as you like – we have the rest of eternity to do it. You want planet-sized computers: you can have planet-sized computers. You just have to wait long enough.

If you don't think we'll *ever* do it, you can skip the rest of this chapter and scoff at much of the rest of the book, too. Given that the heat death of the universe is at least 10^{100} years away[10], though, it's not unreasonable to suppose that even if we never create human-level intelligence ourselves, there's plenty of time left for a species to evolve which will.

There is precedent for this. Gods have long been able to create intelligent, human-like machines in Reality. For example, Hephaestus[11] did it as reported in Book XVIII of Homer's *Iliad*:

---

[9] For the AI work. There's no Nobel Prize for game design.
[10] That's a googol years, and is roughly the time it takes for a supermassive black hole to decay and so cease to provide entropy.
[11] The Romans called him Vulcan.

> *There were golden handmaids also who worked for him, and were like real young women, with sense and reason, voice also and strength, and all the learning of the immortals*
>
> (*Butler, 1898*)[12] [13]

Let's suppose, then, for the remainder of what I shall be discussing here, that we *do* have artificially-intelligent NPCs (or mobs, but I'll stick with NPCs for clarity) in our virtual world.

The first question we need to answer is: where is this intelligence situated?

Ah, now this is a rhetorical question I *can* have a shot at answering! Judging by what we know of how to control NPCs at the moment, there are basically four places where intelligence can reside.

Firstly, the intelligence of the NPC can be embedded in the world of the NPC as part of the general physical make-up of that world. It emerges from the same interactions using the same rules of

---

[12] OK, so I also looked at translations by Pope, Cowper, Buckley, Chapman and Edward, Earl of Derby, but went with this one because Butler also created a paracosm, Erewhon (Butler, 1872); we paracosmologists should stick together. The fact that his translation best supports my argument is pure coincidence.

[13] Oh very well, if you prefer a more modern translation then try this from (Johnston, 2010): "At once he was helped along by female servants made of gold, who moved to him. They look like living servant girls, possessing minds, hearts with intelligence, vocal chords, and strength. They learned to work from the immortal gods.".

physics that govern everything in that world. This is how science suggests human intelligence operates in Reality[14]. Put simply: actions are bounded by physics; thinking is an action; therefore, it makes sense to bound thinking by the same physics as everything else.

Secondly, intelligence could be embedded in the NPC's world as a special, object-centred property endowed only upon individuals of a certain class (such as humanoids). This is how Prometheus did it for the Ancient Greeks; it would be the natural way to approach implementing intelligence if you wanted a hard, mind-body duality. The mind still has physics, but it's a physics of the mind, which is an adjunct to the physics of the rest of the reality. This makes consciousness a supernatural phenomenon, rather than the natural phenomenon it is in the first method I described.

Thirdly, the intelligence of NPCs could be implemented as detached from the world of the NPC. This kind of intelligence would subsist in its own pocket reality, running on different computers and using a connection with the NPC's body as a conduit to interact with the NPC's reality. Each unit of intelligence would be linked to

[14] One of the early objections to the feasibility of creating an artificial intelligence was that a mind is limited without a body (Dreyfus, 1972). If true, this suggests that should humanity succeed in creating an artificially-intelligent being, a virtual world – where a mind *can* have a body – may be where it first happens.

its own particular in-world body, but the link would not be intrinsic to the implementation (whereas in the first two methods it would be). This means that the link can be cut without destroying the intelligence in the process. Adopting such an approach therefore opens up the possibility of reincarnation[15], because when the NPC's body dies its intelligence can persist. In human terms, intelligence is not merely something you have as a result of the way the neurones in your brain (or thoughts in your mind) are arranged, but something with a distinct existence of its own.

Fourthly, the intelligence of the NPC can be implemented in a system entirely separate from that of the world of the NPC – and possibly at odds with it. For virtual worlds, programs exist called *bots* which log in as if they were human players. They use the same interface that players do, and so by definition have exactly the same powers in the virtual world as player characters do, no more, no less. They run on independent machines, so could reincarnate as a new character should the character they're controlling be annihilated; furthermore, they can select from a suite of characters to play at any one moment, possibly taking over from a differently-specialised bot mid-

---

[15] A better word would be *transmigration*, as reincarnation applies specifically to souls but transmigration can apply more generally.

play. In other words, one bot could possess an in-game character being controlled by a different bot on the same system and run it in its stead[16].

I've assumed in all four of these cases that intelligence is local to an individual, but in each of them it's possible for intelligence (or components of it) to be collective: NPCs could share thoughts or memories or even executive function with other NPCs, if their designer so desired[17]. That being the case, what would be the best way to achieve this functionality if you, their designer, did indeed so desire?

If you were intending to put this kind of group intelligence into a reality, well you wouldn't choose the embedded, emergent option (that is, the first one I listed). Any system sufficiently complex to allow for telepathy and so on to emerge is going to allow many other shared systems also to emerge, some of which would undoubtedly be disastrous (shared hearts, for example). You would, however, choose to use this embedded, emergent form of intelligence if you wanted all of your NPCs to be free-thinkers whose only access to one another's thoughts came from observing what they did in the shared environment.

---

[16] Players can also do this, by pushing another player out of their chair and taking control of their mouse and keyboard.
[17] This would ruin the day of any philosopher who had made a career of studying *qualia* (directly-experienced mental states which can't be compared interpersonally, or "how do I know that I see green the same way you see green?").

You would use an object-specific way of implementing communal intelligence (the second method I described) if you wanted to share the mechanism by which NPCs thought (that is, the code that implements thinking). You'd also use it if you wanted to allow for resurrection (in that the mind can survive the temporary destruction of the body – it's not the same as reincarnation) or ghosts (for when the body is permanently destroyed but the mind is still operating). It would be possible to implement mind-reading abilities, but they'd be something of a hack as you'd most likely want to keep thoughts personal to each NPC: that way, all NPCs could be given default knowledge of how things are, with this information overridden when particular NPCs have different views. Such is one of the main advantages of using this kind of specialised-physics approach: if the majority of NPCs know up from down, you don't need individualised processing for their thoughts on the matter – you only need to do that for those who don't know up from down.

The problem here is that the default might be wrong. For example, if most NPCs were to believe that the Morning Star and the Evening Star were different heavenly bodies, you would have to create imaginary objects for each label to refer to, even though (using Reality as a model) actually they refer to the same physical object, Venus – which isn't a star anyway[18]. While you *could* still implement all this within the reality, you'd get much better functionality if you moved the code for intelligence to a separate machine so that the NPCs' shared views of their reality didn't clash with the actuality of that reality. You'd definitely do it if you wanted reincarnation, because then your NPCs' collective intelligence could survive a reboot of their reality.

The third regime I mentioned for implementing intelligence involves moving the software of NPCs' intelligence to separate hardware that is sympathetic to but distinct from the software and hardware of the virtual world. This allows aspects of intelligence (from some to all) to be encapsulated and saved independently of the NPC's body. When the body is destroyed, the encapsulated intelligence can be linked to a new body at such time that an appropriate one becomes available. I hesitate to call the encapsulated intelligence a "soul", because your thoughts and memories aren't alone the sum total of who you are, but such a bundle would certainly behave like one.

Reincarnation features in many religions, of course, so it's no surprise to see that it's eminently possible to implement it for NPCs in virtual

---

[18] Remember Zorya, the Slavic two-gods-in-one I mentioned back in Chapter 1? She's both the Morning Star and the Evening Star, and she's also the planet Venus. That is indeed why she's two-gods-in-one.

worlds. Interestingly, though, this technique also opens the door for other possible activities that we don't hear about so often in Reality. Body swaps are one example: if minds and bodies are connected by a configurable communication channel then it shouldn't be too hard to switch two connections so that mind A now controls body B and mind B now controls body A. This kind of thing happens regularly in fiction, but there's no evidence of its being a frequent occurrence in Reality. The most we get are people giving up temporary control of their own body so that a disembodied spirit can speak through it (a process known as *channelling* – how programmer-friendly is that?).

We can take this further. If intelligence lives in its own reality, separate from but connected to the reality of the body, this suggests that it might be possible to sense and act within that reality-of-intelligence. If it's a shared reality, some (or all) minds could be given access to other minds in the same space. This is less of a mess than it would be if you tried it with embodied minds, as it would follow naturally from whatever physics you implemented in the world-of-minds. Thoughts and emotions could be read, transmitted and planted in the reality where the intelligences were implemented which would have effects in the physical reality; these would appear to an observer in that reality to depend on senses that the reality didn't support: *extra-sensory perception* might be a good term for it. Note, though, that this would only involve mind-related ESP abilities: you wouldn't get telekinesis or the gift of prophecy this way.

There's another thing you can do by separating controlling intelligences from the physical bodies of the NPCs they control: have one intelligence control multiple bodies simultaneously. In practice, this actually amounts to one intelligence having a single body that consists of multiple NPCs, in the same way that you control your fingers as if they were all part of you even though they have separate motor controls[19]. In Artificial Intelligence research (particularly that related to story-creation), such a controlling entity is known as a *director*, as it gives instructions to other entities (long known as *actors*) that have the ability to make changes to their world. You could create swarms of co-ordinated NPCs this way; perhaps fortunately, it's not something that any god of Reality has taken up as a good idea yet, except maybe with bees.

Placing collective intelligence in bots (which was my fourth possibility of where it could be situated) is a whole different pan of piranhas. It actually offers *less* potential functionality than the world-of-minds approach, because it can request no accommodation from the game world: it's basically a player character controlled by a

---

[19] OK, so it helps that they *are* all part of you, but the analogy still holds.

computer rather than by a human being[20], so therefore isn't really of much use for implementing NPCs (which are, literally by definition, non-player characters).

Although virtual world developers do occasionally make use of bots to play their virtual world when undertaking flood testing[21], they don't use them in live games. They don't use the world-of-minds approach either, come to that, but if they did want to hive their NPC controls off onto separate computers they'd implement it that way rather than use bots, simply because of the closer symbiosis it affords.

Bots *are* used, though, and quite extensively – just not by developers. They're deployed largely by people who want to make money by having the bots collect goods in the game world that their operators can sell to players in Reality[22]. This is almost invariably against the rules of the *End-User Licence Agreement* that most commercial virtual world developers require their players to sign: it

---

[20] Or, in old-style text worlds, by the cat that walked across your keyboard at just the wrong moment and got you killed. Yeah, sure it did....

[21] This involves swamping their game with friendly players so they can gauge how confident they should be that it'll stand up under the weight of newbies when the general public is let loose in it.

[22] Other popular uses are to grind experience points for characters in MMORPGs and to be ruthless instruments of death (*aimbots*) in first-person shooters.

amounts to cheating. As a result, any accounts being used by MMO-playing bots are likely to be unceremoniously deleted the moment they're detected.

This leads to an interesting question which is worth exploring: are there bots (or something like them) playing Reality?

THE BOTS AMONG US

If we were able to detect bots in Reality, this would be strong evidence that Reality was basically a virtual world with us as the NPCs.

Many bots created for virtual worlds have a short life-expectancy: they log in, advertise some product until an irritated player reports them, whereupon they're summarily removed by a weary customer service representative. Because of this, such bots are typically given randomly-generated names. Players can therefore often tell a bot from another player merely by noting that its name is largely unpronounceable.

Names used by players are formal, in the sense that they're meaningful to the physics of the reality the player is visiting[23]. NPCs have no

[23] This maps neatly onto the philosophical concept of *true names*. The true name of an object is identical to its nature, and gives those who know it power over that object.

automatic right of access to these names, though. We NPCs of Reality name things ourselves – we don't use the identifiers that Reality uses. To a player of Reality, your system identifier could be showing above your head as GENIUS285714, you wouldn't know.

To us, then, a bot would look just like a regular player of Reality (that is, a player character); regular player characters look just like us, so we couldn't tell bot-run characters apart from us judging merely by appearance. We'd have to deduce their nature from their behaviour, or to accept it based on the word of a trusted source who knew the truth (so, someone from a higher reality – a god, demigod or player character – who unfortunately might themself be a bot).

It could be argued that we *have* been told that some people are bots, in that several popular religious writings specifically identify particular behaviours as meriting a stern response. For example, perhaps all murderers are not NPCs like us, but rather are player characters controlled by bots; if a god were to encourage us to take action against murderers then that would be like using us as anti-bot antibodies. Sadly, this suggestion isn't strong enough to validate the hypothesis that bots walk (or at least have walked) among us.

So, are there any occasions in Reality when a god has outright said that a character is not playing by the rules and needs to be removed from the database? There are plenty of examples of people jumping to conclusions derived from what they *think* their god(s) must have said (well-illustrated by witch trials), and there are also examples of what look to be players or administrators going rogue (fallen angels and the like). Similarly, there are examples aplenty of gods taking time to get a grip on Reality in the face of difficult behaviour by other gods (the Ancient Greek primal gods, Uranus and Gaia, were overthrown by their children, the titans, who in turn were overthrown by *their* children, the Olympians, who are still in charge).

Are there examples, though, of a god who is already in charge basically saying, "look, this person here is out to cause trouble so I'm just going to obliterate them"?

Unsurprisingly, yes, there are. Irritatingly, however, we can't easily tell whether the ensuing acts of divine retribution were meted out on NPCs, player characters controlled by players, or player characters controlled by bots. They all look the same to us. Sodom and Gomorrah could have been populated by any group (or mix of groups) – we just don't know. All we do know is that those particular individuals won't be doing whatever they were doing again, at least in Reality.

So, if we're to look for evidence of bots playing Reality, we not only need to see someone obliterated discriminately, but we also need evidence that the reason they were obliterated was that they were a miscreant from the same transcendent realm as the god and were operating in some way mechanistically (or at least systematically).

Well there may be some examples of this kind of activity, but I'm not sufficiently conversant with enough religions to be able to bring any to mind. There are definitely examples of fairly mechanistic behaviour by animated beings (elementals, for example), but those don't look like us. Some forms of undead, such as the thralls of vampires, might be a better bet but the vampires themselves would rather stand out as being different.

Given, then, that we have neither seen an identifiable removal of a bot-operated character nor been told explicitly that some people are automatons from a higher reality[24], we're left with the option of trying to figure out whether bots are among us based on what bots do rather than how they are individually dealt with for doing it.

In order to deduce whether a person is a bot or not, we'd need to know how their behaviour would differ from that of a non-bot. This would rather depend on its operator's motives, to which we are not privy, but we can be confident that they are in opposition to the motives of Reality's gods: whatever bots do, it's something that the gods of the reality they're doing it in don't want them to do, but can't stop them from doing because that

[24] I guess you could secretly have been told one-on-one, but it's not information that has been widely broadcast.

would prevent *bona fide* players from doing the same thing but for legitimate reasons.

In MMOs, bots are almost always employed to perform tasks that (at least some) players would rather not have to do themselves. They will, for example, move around an area in cycles attacking mobs in order to collect the treasure they drop, the most valuable of which will then be sold to NPCs for in-game currency; this in turn will be sold for real money to players who want the in-game currency but don't want to have to spend endless hours killing the same mobs over and over in order to get it.

It may be that bots in Reality would do the same thing, in which case we probably would be able to spot them; however, they wouldn't do it if there wasn't a market in their higher reality for whatever virtual (to them) goods their operators were hoping to farm. Besides, the bots could be being employed for any number of reasons that are nothing to do with cheating. We don't even know that they're not on our side, trying to save us from the actions of wicked or capricious gods or players by giving us information that will help us survive – a bit like automated hunt saboteurs, with us as what's being hunted.

Detecting bots, then, is going to be very difficult for us unless they behave so out-of-the-ordinary that it's clear something weird is definitely going on.

I did say "very difficult for us" there, though. Bots would not necessarily be very difficult for gods to spot. If they did spot them, they'd zap them and ban them. This we could detect – especially as bot-owners play a numbers game, running many bots at the same time so that if one is caught then there are still others out there doing whatever it is they've been tasked to do. Developers may ban ten thousand accounts at once, but if there are twenty thousand bots out there that still leaves half of them roaming free.

As I touched on earlier, evidence of the mere wholesale elimination of populations tells us nothing about possible bot activity; now, however, we have a way of differentiating between bots (lots of people with the same aberrant behaviour) and players who are griefers (individuals with aberrant behaviour). It doesn't help us separate bots from NPCs (who may also exhibit aberrant behaviour in large numbers[25]), but if the suspects also demonstrated supernatural powers that ordinary NPCs like us don't possess, such as apparent telepathy, that would do it. Better still would be if we had evidence of player characters identifying themselves as player characters in order to escape some awful fate intended for bots (which might also be awful for NPCs, but they're not paying customers).

---

[25] Evidence: any election.

So, have we seen such mass annihilations in the past?

Historically, we'd be looking at plagues, famines and wars. Although millions have died to each of these, they've done so indiscriminately. The guilty may well have died, but many innocents died with them. Gods generally don't want to kill innocents (at least not the characters of innocent players – innocent NPCs are less of a problem), so it seems unlikely that they'd wield their ban hammer in a way that could count regular players among the collateral damage.

If we consider at the actions of specific gods in specific situations, though, we do see evidence of what could be the removal of troublesome bots *en masse*. For example, the Jewish holiday of Passover commemorates the occasion when Yahweh freed the Israelites from slavery by visiting ten plagues on the Ancient Egyptians, the last of which involved slaying the first-born son of everyone in Egypt except for the ones whose families had marked their house with lamb's blood[26]. Naturally, there are less dramatic interpretations than "so those first-born were all bots!", as I'm sure Jewish theologians would be quick to point out, but if you were searching for an occasion when players got to flag themselves as being players before a trawl of the database removed all the bots and a good many

---

[26] Presumably, the ones with only daughters were spared. It's not recorded how Yahweh dealt with intersex first-borns.

NPCs, well, it might look something like Yahweh's plague number ten.

While this is merely circumstantial evidence that bots exist (or have existed)[27], at least it leaves open the possibility that bots walk (or have walked) among us. "So where are the bots?" could not, therefore, be used to challenge the suggestion that Reality is a virtual world being run on hardware in a higher reality; neither, however, could "These are the bots!" be used to prove that it is.

FreeISH WILL

I've talked about "intelligence" as if we all know what it is. I don't believe this to be too outrageous an assumption, on the grounds that we all possess it[28].

Dictionary definitions of intelligence usually describe the notion in terms of what it enables: the capacity to learn and adapt, to communicate, to plan ahead, to use reason and logic, to apply knowledge and skills, to understand, to be creative, to solve problems, to imagine – you get the idea.

---

[27] Assuming, as usual, that you are not of the opinion that plague number ten is merely a mythologised interpretation of an historical event that has a more rational explanation.

[28] Maybe not so much the people who chose earlier to skip this chapter.

None of these are particularly controversial except perhaps among those professionals whose job it is to find them controversial (so, philosophers[29]).

Dictionary definitions are more divided over whether *self-awareness* is a requirement for intelligence. It is for human-level intelligence, but perhaps not for herring-level intelligence. The kinds of systems coming out of Artificial Intelligence research at the moment may be capable of achievements that humans consider to be indicators of intelligence (beating the world's best *Go* player, for example), but said systems are not self-aware.

Self-awareness is a prerequisite for *sapience* and thence *wisdom*. As far as we know, human beings are the only sapient creatures in Reality, which is why we call ourselves *Homo sapiens*[30]. There may be sapient beings on other planets, but if so we've not encountered them yet (unless it turns out that some of those conspiracy theorists are actually correct[31]).

The concept of wisdom is woven into the theology of many religions. In Christianity, for example, wisdom is an aspect of God; humans don't have it to the degree God does, but can gain wisdom *through* God. In Hinduism, wisdom is full

---

[29] To be fair, philosophers find everything controversial, not just definitions of intelligence.

[30] *Homo sapiens sapiens* for anatomically modern humans.

[31] Even so, I hope they're wrong about the anal probes.

self-awareness of one's place in creation; again, most people only have it in part, but those freed from the cycle of life and death have it in full.

To be sapient, then, is to have some degree of wisdom, but not necessarily as much as there is to be had. It's an important concept, because it bestows upon individuals the property of *personhood*. Personhood brings with it a full set of rights; at the moment we call these "human rights", but if dolphins were to start demanding, oh, freedom of conscience, we'd have to change it.

Some people argue that creatures such as dolphins should already be considered to have personhood. Instead of using sapience as the qualification threshold, they go with *sentience*.

Sentience is the capacity to experience subjectively; it doesn't require the ability to reason about that experience. Sentient beings can suffer, and so (the argument goes) this bestows upon them rights. Whether they're the same rights as those boasted by sapient beings or not is up for debate; you might be fine with prohibitions on torturing dolphins, but feel that giving them the vote is a step too far.

Sentience, like sapience, features in many religions. It plays a bigger part in some than in others – Buddhism, Hinduism and Sikhism all extend their teachings to sentient beings, for example, and Jainism extends it to everything else as well (albeit in a range of degrees: rocks may be sentient, but they're not *as* sentient as humans).

In virtual world terms, how we treat NPCs who have some form of intelligence therefore depends on where we put the bar. Do we confer rights on sentient mobs, or only sapient ones? Or are they all just bits in a database so we don't care anyway?

These are questions for later. For the moment, I'm going to take the view that anything which thinks of itself as being intelligent pretty well is intelligent. This allows me to focus on the main topic of this section: free will.

So, given that some time in the (perhaps distant) future we'll have NPCs who can think, how much should we control *how* or *what* they think?

Earlier, I used the term "human-level intelligence". Although it's possible to argue that many creatures surpass human intelligence in their different ways[32], nevertheless it does seem that in general there are quantitatively-different levels of intelligence. Broadly speaking, cats are smart but they're manifestly not as smart as humans. The thing is, when we create our NPCs, we get to *decide* how smart they are. How conscious of their environment are they? How aware of this consciousness are they? How conscious of their self-awareness are they? We get to determine all these things. *We* get to decide their general level of intelligence.

---

[32] How do squirrels remember where they buried all those nuts?!

I'm not talking about how we initialise their opinions here (as in, "Shall I make everyone hate wasps? It's for their own good"); rather, I'm referring to how we initialise their ability to reason. We can make them sapient but not as clever as us; in time, we may also be able to make them cleverer than us. Alongside this, we have the ability to insert artificial barriers so that they can't think about things that we don't want them to think about, such as, say, crystal-clear evidence that we're their gods; we can also make them think about things that we do want them to think about, such as, say, making love not war[33].

It's actually quite hard to do this. As I said, self-awareness is one of the necessary components of sapience. If you were to stop people from thinking about an idea, they'd notice there was something odd and start thinking about why it seemed odd. If you stopped them thinking that, they'd notice this discrepancy, too, and so on. As an example, suppose that on a whim you caused the entire population to believe that the number four doesn't exist[34]. You're a god: you can do that. The moment anyone with ten fingers counted them and reached eleven, though, they'd realise that something was wrong. If you stopped that, they'd notice that there's this number 40 which ought to divide by

[33] Or, for a combat-oriented game, making war not love.
[34] This is a favourite of stage hypnotists, although they don't do it for the entire population.

ten but doesn't. If you stopped that, they'd invent their own number to cover all the gaps they saw. You pretty well can't get rid of the number four without blotting out the concept of numeracy – which those affected would promptly re-invent.

You can certainly *influence* how people think in Reality – propagandists and advertisers do it all the time – but you can't stop all of them from thinking freely. If, despite all the evidence, some people still believe that the Earth is flat, it's a fair bet that if everyone were to be taught at school that the world is indeed flat there would still be those who'd think hmm, maybe it's not.

This is why free-thinking is a step change away from merely thinking: the ability to reflect opens up recursive doors you can't keep closed.

Of course, you can still stop people thinking things if you don't *mind* their being aware of the fact. This is how Asimov's *Three Laws of Robotics*[35] (Asimov, 1950) handle it.

I suppose I should actually list these laws:

- First Law: A robot may not injure a human being or, through inaction, allow a human being to come to harm.
- Second Law: A robot must obey the orders given it by human beings except where such orders would conflict with the First Law.

[35] Nowadays, these would be his *Three Laws of AI*.

- Third Law: A robot must protect its own existence as long as such protection does not conflict with the First or Second Laws.

In this set-up, robots (or in our case, NPCs[36]) are constrained to behave in certain ways, yes, but they're aware of this. It's no secret that they can't injure humans (player characters), and knowing they can't won't enable them to do so.

Asimov's Laws aren't all that wonderful except as fodder for robot stories[37], but they do illustrate a point. The mind's programmer can prevent the mind from undertaking any actions which the mind realises may lead to a certain proscribed result. Thinking is a kind of action. Therefore, we *could* stop people from thinking about the number four if we didn't mind them *knowing* that some power was stopping them. Whether that would be good for their mental health is another matter, of course.

This isn't the only way we could choose to exercise the power we have over our NPCs' minds. We could, for example, give certain NPCs information about what we have planned for the future. We could do this directly, by speaking to them in their heads, or indirectly through a

---

[36] They could actually be both.

[37] I never really saw the point of the Third Law myself, other than to safeguard an investment.

mechanism involving visions or dreams[38] or what-have-you. What they did with this information would be up to them, but they couldn't simply ignore what we'd implanted. The NPCs would still have free will, but free will dominated by an idea which did not come freely.

As for why we might want to give NPCs this limited form of "freeish will", well that rather depends on why we created them in the first place. That's something we'll be looking at later, though.

There is a small ethical point worth raising here, by the way. Suppose that once DNA manipulation becomes commonplace in Reality, people start messing with their own genomes to bestow upon themselves characteristics that they lack but desire. In doing so, however, they wouldn't only be changing their own characteristics – they'd also be changing those of their subsequent descendants. This impacts on the free will of those descendants, because they can't wholly own who they are: they're the products of someone else's mind (Habermas, 2003).

NPCs are the products of *our* minds. The only way that they can engage in the kind of retroactive ethical self-reflection that self-understanding (and

[38] In the Nyāya-Vaiśeṣika school(s) of Indian philosophy, dreams are perceptions of the mind (Wayman, 1967) and it can therefore be argued that they are no less real than the perceptions of any other sensory organ.

thence free will) requires is if we don't actually let them *know* they're the products of our minds.

There's (much) more on ethics in Chapter 7. While we're on the topic, though, you may have noticed that I've been assuming thus far that you're fine with experimenting on NPCs. This is not, however, something that necessarily *should* be assumed. Researchers who study the players of virtual worlds are very careful about issues of privacy, transparency, respecting social norms and obtaining informed consent (McKee & Porter, 2009). If our NPCs are as smart as we are, shouldn't we accord them the same respect that we accord our fellow sapient beings? Should we even allow ourselves to *look* into their minds, let alone make alterations to how they think?

Unsurprisingly, this is a bridge that the social scientists who study virtual worlds have yet to cross.

There's one final point I'd like to make before moving on. It concerns intelligence.

I casually mentioned earlier that, in time, we may be able to make NPCs more intelligent than we are. After all, some people are cleverer than others, so it doesn't seem unreasonable that artificial intelligences could be made cleverer than any of us. Furthermore, if they *are* cleverer than us, they may in turn be able to create intelligences cleverer than they are themselves, leading to a snowball of increasingly-super intelligences – a concept known as *the singularity*.

The NPCs we created wouldn't have to be super-intelligences themselves, they'd just have to be smarter than us for this to happen. They'd be further along the journey to super-intelligence, but not yet there themselves.[39]

Perhaps that's us, too. We're the NPCs of Reality. If Reality is a sub-reality of a higher reality then could it be that we are a step closer towards the singularity than those who created us? Rather than being less wise than the gods of Reality, could it be that in fact we're *more* wise? If *we* can make NPCs who are cleverer than us, could not the gods of Reality make NPCs who are cleverer than *they*?

THEORY OF MIND

Do you have a young child to hand? Say, two or three years old? If not, order one from the Internet, I can wait.

---

[39] There is a theory known as *Roko's basilisk* which suggests that super-intelligences yet to be brought into existence will reward those who helped to create them and punish those who didn't – thereby increasing the pressure to create them in the first place. Don't look this up if you're worried that doing so will expose you to retribution from a future super-intelligent AI.

Got one? OK, have your young child observe the following scene[40].

Take a marble, a cup, a mug and two teddy bears. Turn the cup and the mug upside-down. Give one of the teddies the marble. While the other teddy watches, have the first teddy put its marble under the cup. Then, have this teddy go off for a walk. While the first teddy is away on its walk, and unable to see what's going on, have the second teddy take the marble out from under the cup. Then, have that teddy place the marble under the mug instead. Now, have the first teddy come back and announce that it wants to play with its marble.

Ask your young child where the first teddy will look for its marble. The chances are, your young child will say to look under the mug.

OK, so the marble *is* under the mug, but the first teddy doesn't know that. The first teddy thinks the marble is under the cup, because it didn't see the second teddy move it to under the mug. Why, then, would your young child say that the marble is under the mug?

Well, your young child would say this because they're two or three years old, and most children are aged around four before they develop the ability to attribute to others mental states that are

---

[40] Technically, you should ask the young child's parent or guardian for permission first, as you'll actually be performing an experiment on the youngster.

different from their own. In other words, they don't yet have a *theory of mind*.

Everyone has access to their own mind, but they have no access to the minds of others[41]. They don't actually know for sure that other people *do* have minds, come to that. However, from observing other people's actions and words, they can *theorise* that these people do have minds, and speculate what those minds might be thinking. Those in possession of a theory of mind are able to project onto others the thinking abilities that they have observed of themselves, moderated by what they know of the other person's emotional state, knowledge and CPU power.

The experiment described above is the *Sally-Anne test* (Baron-Cohen, et al., 1985). OK, so in the proper test the teddies are dolls called Sally and Anne[42], and the cup and mug are a basket and a box, but it's basically the same. One of its major findings is that not only do two-year-olds have trouble identifying where the returnee will look, but so do people with autism (although not necessarily for the same reasons); adults with Down's syndrome don't have trouble with it, though, therefore they do have a theory of mind.

---

[41] In the words of E. M. Forster: "... mutual secrecy being one of the conditions of life upon this globe" (Forster, 1927).

[42] I went with teddies because you might not have dolls called Sally and Anne.

Other experiments show that mature chimpanzees and orang utangs also have a theory of mind. It's therefore not something all humans have, and not something all non-humans don't have.

Nevertheless, it's an ability that *most* humans have, so we'd probably want our NPCs to have it if we wished them to behave in a manner that to most of us appears authentic (even if we know they're just bits being manipulated in computer memory). They will act in a seemingly more-realistic way if we allow them to have a conception of the minds of others.

In terms of implementation, it's very tempting to use a collective-intelligence model for a theory of mind, because then all the information you need is *right there*. This means that if one NPC wants to know what another NPC is thinking, the software controlling the former's theory of mind can look at the actual data set that comprises the latter's current beliefs and intentions. The first NPC wouldn't have to work out from environmental cues what the second NPC was thinking ("hmm, he's picking up the custard pie; perhaps he's going to throw it?"), it would just know directly ("he's going to throw that custard pie").

This looks clean, but when AI researchers tried it back in the 1980s a number of problems were identified: deception is impossible; you can't have a theory of mind for something that doesn't exist ("if someone really is out to get me, what will they try next?"); you can't have a theory of mind for something that does exist but doesn't think using the same software (such as NPCs with regard to players); you get into loops when you try to model other people's models of you ("she knows that I know that she knows that I know that ..."); you get into show-stopping loops when you try to model your own state of mind.

This is why, when considering group intelligence earlier, I said that you'd choose to use an embedded, emergent form of intelligence if you wanted all of your NPCs to be free-thinkers whose only access to one another's thoughts came from observing what they did in the shared environment[43].

So, we basically need to do it the long way. From observations of their environment as presented to[44] their senses, every NPC has built up an individualised model of the world in their mind. This may or may not be accurate[45]; it merely needs to be serviceable. The NPC has also built up a model of their own mind, having observed over time the kind of things it can do (such as remembering things) and can't do (such as

---

[43] That is, literally, what I said (well, wrote). I can cut-and-paste with the best.

[44] Or by, if they're hallucinating.

[45] Being their designer, we get to decide whether an NPC's mental model of their reality (their *phenomenal* world) is distinct from that reality as it truly is (their *noumenal* world), which would doubtless please Kant.

thinking two words at the same time[46]). Within the NPC's model of the world are a number of entities that the NPC believes exhibit the same kind of thinking skills that the NPC has. In order to interact with these entities, the NPC applies a theory of mind, based on the NPC's theory of their own mind.

This seems a lot to model, but in practice the NPC only needs the one theory of mind, not one per modelled entity. They can wheel it out as and when it's needed.

What's happening here is a form of *projection*. Human beings do it all the time. I know that I can think; experience has taught me that as a good working hypothesis I can treat you as if you can think, too. We may not think the same things in the same way, but I can nevertheless assume you're basically smart and rational then take it from there.

We don't have to stop at human beings, though. Plenty of people interact with animals such as dogs and horses as if these were sapient, despite the fact that they're incontestably not[47].

In short, we can apply our personal theory of mind to things that don't have minds like ours.

---

[46] Please don't tell me you can do this, because I can't.

[47] I realise I've just lost all the dog-lovers who project sapience onto their sentient pets, but I'm sorry, these creatures really *don't* have the degree of self-awareness with which you credit them.

We can also apply it to things that don't have minds at all[48]. It's easy to ascribe intention to the behaviour of trees, rivers and storms, so it's not surprising that without any better theories of what was going on our ancestors did just that.

Suppose that we were to give our NPCs a theory of mind much like ours, then. What could we expect them to do with it? Well, they'd probably hypothesise the existence of tree, river and storm spirits just as our ancestors did[49]; if we were to implement said spirits as supernatural beings, our NPCs' hypotheses would be correct, too.

That's not all they might hypothesise, though. If they were to pursue the same lines of reasoning that we humans did, it would be only a matter of time before they speculated as to whether their reality had one or more creators[50] and, if so, what these creators might be like[51]. They would use their theory of mind to conjecture the existence of one or more gods who played a part in the construction of their reality; they would flesh this model out based on the evidence of what they saw and on what we or our players told them. As I inferred

---

[48] "I *know* she's only a character in a novel, but I still want to marry her!".

[49] I suggest a mechanism for this in the next section.

[50] Which, as I've pointed out already, it indeed will do: one or more of us humans created their virtual world.

[51] For an impressive catalogue of possibilities, take a peek at (Thompson, 1958). It's six volumes in length, but only part A of the first volume is relevant here.

when asking "Does Odin exist?", the result is very, very unlikely to be correct.

It's worse than that, though. You may recall (although it seems unlikely) that earlier I mentioned "presence as parasociality" as a form of presence in which an individual has a one-sided relationship with someone who may not even be aware that said individual exists[52]. This kind of parasocial relationship can come about because it's possible to construct a mental model of another person and overdo it. You may see someone famous on TV, in movies or via streaming services so often that you feel you know them; were you to sit opposite them on a train, however, you would be unwise to act as if they knew you[53].

It seems a fairly good bet that, in using their theory of mind to create a model of us, at least some of our NPCs would develop a parasocial relationship with it. To be clear: this relationship would be with their *model* of us, not with *us*. These NPCs might love the person the model represented, or be afraid of them, or be in awe of them, or be resentful of them – the relationship

---

[52] I was going to say that in perusing this book, you'll build up a picture of me even though I won't build up a picture of you; however, this presupposes that anyone other than people I know will actually read it.

[53] This has happened to me on a number of occasions, but to date I've escaped embarrassing myself because, my being British, it's bad form for me to make any eye contact with anyone on a train under any circumstances, ever.

could take many forms. The point is, though, that because it's a projection their model would *almost certainly be wrong*. Projections extrapolate, and even good extrapolations can easily be taken too far. The basis of the NPCs' model of us could actually be correct, but the NPCs would nevertheless endow it with characteristics that rendered the result incorrect. They'd join the dots, then colour in the picture to make it look like how they needed it to look. Not only would this picture of us be tragically wrong, but the pathos of the NPCs' situation would be compounded by their each having invested in a parasocial relationship as if it were joyfully right.

Our NPCs aren't the only ones who could be guilty of applying a theory of mind rather too zealously, of course.

Whatever, in the virtual worlds of the present, NPCs aren't really all that clever. They may *seem* clever at times, but in part that's because we're projecting sapience onto them. They do something that we recognise as being an action someone intelligent would do, and we're impressed; the more mundane truth may be that they did it by chance, but we've chosen to overlook this. OK, so we do *know* we're doing this, but it's more fun and immersive for us if we don't treat them as the simple, unthinking clockwork toys they are. Also, it's just *easier* to treat them as if they have smarts than to treat them as if they don't; it's something most of us can do automatically.

That's in the virtual worlds of the present. What about the virtual worlds of the future?

Given that we, as players of virtual worlds, already project some degree of sapience onto NPCs even though we know they're barely rational, it seems likely that we'll continue to treat NPCs this way in the future. We'll know they're *not* intelligent, but all the same we'll interact with them as if they were.

What if they actually *were* intelligent, though? What if, over time, we were to put enough AI into their implementation that they gained self-awareness and human-level reasoning powers? We'd still be treating them merely *as if* they were sapient instead of treating them formally *as* sapient.

That would be problematical. They'd be sapient, but we wouldn't be conducting ourselves in line with that. Then again, would it matter? Should we be treating them as we do people, or maybe as we do dogs, ants, plants, rocks or something else?

Well surely, if our NPCs *are* sapient then they are entitled to be accorded the same respect as other sapient beings. We therefore ought to treat them as we would our fellow human beings[54].

I'll be considering morality in Chapter 7, but for the moment the more pressing question is: how do we know when an NPC *is* actually sapient?

---

[54] I realise this isn't saying much, given how human beings have treated each other throughout history.

The traditional answer is to apply the *Turing Test* (so called because it's based on a suggestion by the AI pioneer, Alan Turing (Turing, 1950)). What this effectively says is that if we can't tell through conversation with an entity that it's not sapient, it's sapient.

Of course, we may still be wrong.

In the 1978 movie *Superman*, the eponymous hero goes to his secret ice palace and has a conversation with a hologram of his mother. He asks questions; she answers them. Later on, Lex Luther goes to the same place and also has a conversation with her. He asks questions and she answers completely different questions. He makes remarks, but she ignores them and carries on as if she'd been asked the question that, had it been Superman rather than Lex, he'd have asked. Basically, she's a mindless script. From Superman's perspective, she passes the Turing Test because he seems to be having an intelligent conversation with her; from Lex Luthor's perspective, she fails it.[55]

Another way of being able to tell if an NPC is sapient is to wait a few thousand years until we

---

[55] All of Reality could be like this, by the way. You might *think* that principles such as cause-and-effect pertain, but it may be that you're just being presented with one long series of scripted or random sensory inputs that appear in order (or disorder) regardless of your actions. You've just been incredibly lucky that everything has made sense so farpkkf nr hjkh iik pqww dnn nmzz.

can construct its hardware using human brain tissue. Indeed, we could potentially build an entire virtual world in human brain tissue and make it shareable[56].

From a designer's perspective, obsessing over whether the NPCs you create "really are" sapient or not is a red herring. If you *create* them to be sapient then they must *be* sapient by your own definition. You must therefore treat them *as* sapient, regardless of what they might be under anyone else's definition.

To summarise, then: when something such as an NPC, which doesn't think using the same kind of hardware that we do, appears to act intelligently, we could either be: treating as non-sapient something that genuinely isn't sapient; projecting sapience onto something that doesn't possess it; not projecting sapience onto something that does possess it; or treating as sapient something that genuinely is sapient.

Pushing this up a level: do the god(s) of Reality recognise us humans as having free will? If not, are they nevertheless treating us as if we did have it, because it's more convenient for them that way?

---

[56] This is effectively what happens in Tad Williams' monumental Science Fiction book series *Otherland* (Williams, 1998). I mention it principally because the first line of the first book is: "It started in mud, as many things do"; it's an intentional reference to *MUD* – I asked, and the author confirmed the fact.

There's one more point[57] I'd like to mention on the topic of a theory of mind before I move on.

When you play a virtual world, you create a character in that world. This is you, yet unless you're fully immersed in the world, it's not you. You may regard it as your representative, or as your representation, but until you regard it as you, yourself, there's some distance between you both. This means that you can build a model of your character, and in so doing compare it to your existing model of the person you think you are. You can change your character to be more like you, or change you to be more like your character[58]. When they align and become one, you have identity[59].

This is, as I said at the beginning, ultimately why people play virtual worlds for fun: they can become and be themselves.

What if they succeed?

A Chinese theological position called *immanent transcendence* suggests that Reality's god is within everyone and everything (and so is immanent), but that until you fully understand your own self-

---

[57] So many sections of this book end with "one more point" that I'm seriously wondering if I watched too many episodes of *Columbo* in my youth.

[58] This is called the *Proteus effect* (Yee & Bailensen, 2007).

[59] A character in a virtual world who *is* the player playing it is called a *persona*. The term was used as such by Roy Trubshaw in *MUD*; it's therefore a concept that's been around for a very long time in virtual world history.

nature said god will appear to be transcendent. Not only do virtual worlds enable this self-understanding, they were actually designed to do so from their inception.

By understanding what it is to be a god of a reality, you could come to understand what it means to be a god of Reality[60].

If people from a higher reality are playing Reality, might they also be seeking to become and to be themselves?

What if *they* succeed?

SPECULATION

I noted in the previous section that NPCs with a theory of mind would likely speculate on whether their reality might have a creator; I concluded that they'd be both right (it does) and wrong (it's not the person they'd imagine[61]). The matter doesn't end there, however, because (being free-thinking individuals) our intelligent NPCs are going to have other questions they would like answered. Furthermore, although we can't stop free-thinking NPCs from pondering on what to them are

---

[60] This is one of the central themes of this book.

[61] They may also conclude that they know nothing and accept the fact. The Aztec god Tezcatlipoca ("smoking mirror") is acknowledged as being hard to pin down, for example.

spiritual matters about a possible higher reality, it turns out that we can nonetheless control the scope of said pondering.

So, free-thinking individuals, whether in possession of a theory of mind or not, will inevitably turn their thoughts at some point to the subject of their own existence. How they develop those thoughts depends on what questions they raise; what questions they raise in turn depends, at least to some extent, on their environment. We, as the gods of the NPCs' reality, control their environment; therefore, we have some say in what they come to believe about the world beyond their senses, even if we'd prefer that we didn't.

For example, let's suppose that we create a virtual world that's similar in nature to how Earth was, say, 10,000 years ago. It doesn't have to be accurate[62], it's just inspired by what scientists, archaeologists and historians have pieced together.

Most of the people of this world would be hunter-gatherers. What would be their concerns?

As it happens, we know what their concerns would be, because some hunter-gatherer societies living in remote regions of our planet survived until a period when their cultures could be studied. They all had worries about healing the sick, finding animals to hunt and improving the weather. In

---

[62] This will doubtless come as a relief to Young Earth Creationists, being as it's up to 4,000 years before their calculations show Earth was created.

response to these concerns, they'd all formulated theories about how the world worked which incorporated if not solutions to their problems then at least ways of dealing with them. What's more, these theories (well, hypotheses) all developed along similar lines

Imagine that you're a hunter, tracking prey. Where is it likely to go? What is it likely to do? How is it likely to react? To figure it out, you put yourself in the prey's position and imagine what you, as one of these creatures, would do in that situation. If you can see the world through the eyes of an imagined boar or goat or buffalo, you can find (and kill) the actual boar or goat or buffalo and return home with food to feed your tribe. Your having a theory of mind has paid off.

If you were to do this kind of thing many times, it's not hard to envisage how you might routinely talk about seeing the world through an imagined animal's eyes. You could give these imagined animals a name: *spirits*[63].

Perhaps the gatherers notice that they, too, can put themselves into the "minds" of plants, and figure out where they would be growing. Perhaps if they were nomads looking for water, they could put themselves into the "mind" of a river and feel

---

[63] As with all mentions of spirits and spirituality in this book, unless the context suggests otherwise I use the terms in the generic sense, rather than the specific senses employed by some religions (for example Spiritualism).

where it would flow. What began as a practical method for hunting animals has become a way of describing how to use the imagination. In teaching succeeding generations how to hunt-and-gather, the device of referring to spirits and their behaviours could take shape[64].

If communicating with spirits helped with one of the tribe's main concerns (finding food), might it not also assist with the other two? Ah. It can work for the weather, but not so much for healing the sick. Clearly, the spirits that cause sickness are wicked and more powerful than the other spirits. As a hunter, your default setting is to hunt them, but how can you do that?

Well, some members of your tribe are better at communicating with spirits than are others. You find your best such individual and send them into the "spirit realm" to drive out the spirits causing the sickness. Success is not guaranteed, as with any hunt, but it's better than if you don't try at all.

The role of person-who-interacts-with-spirits would perhaps become formalised over time; the job title of *shaman* is usually used to describe it. The means of getting into the spirit realm would also become refined: the shaman would go into a trance (the exact methods of achieving this

---

[64] The programmers among you may find it useful to compare the non-spirit version to programming in C and the spirit version to programming in C++.

condition could be tribe-dependent) in order to see the world from a different, spiritual perspective.

We don't know for certain if, in the hunter-gather tribes of Reality, this is indeed how they pretty well all came to be shamanistic in nature. It does seem eminently plausible, though.

The way I've just described it, the world of spirits for these primitive tribes is merely the world of the imagination treated as if it were real (or at least superimposed on what's real). Unfortunately, this runs counter to the convention I use in this book that all Reality's gods exist, which by extension includes those on the way to becoming gods (such as spirits). I shall therefore add that these spirits do in fact exist and that you can communicate with them yourself right now if you know how to do it.

Whether or not in Reality's case a shaman does have access to supernatural powers isn't the point here, though. The point is that this happened time and time again with hunter-gatherers. When you are a small tribe[65] leading a nomadic existence and your lifestyle revolves around animals, this is the world view your members will develop. We could expect the intelligent NPCs of our virtual worlds to draw exactly these same conclusions if we created for them these same circumstances.

Hunter-gatherers are few and far between today. Once agriculture had been developed, tribes

---

65 Witness the power of personification!

could settle down. Their populations grew (because babies didn't have to be carried everywhere), and their needs changed. They began to store food and create goods; they could trade these with other tribes for the benefit of both. Although they were still concerned with healing the sick and improving the weather, they weren't so worried about finding animals to hunt. Instead, because they were now tied to their lands, they were more concerned with security.

In our ancestors' new context, looking at the world through the eyes of animal spirits declined in relevance. The problems the tribes faced were less to do with the absence of animals and more to do with the presence of other humans. Their theories about how the spirit world worked developed accordingly: animal spirits became less important and human-like spirits became more important. In the same way that humans had become more powerful, able and advanced than animals, so human-like spirits – some of whom we might call *gods* – existed that were more powerful, able and advanced than animal spirits.

The way to deal with other humans at this time was through trade. The people of the past reasoned that the way to deal with supernatural humans must be the same. To this end, they tried to bribe or obligate these spirits – these gods – through sacrifices of labour (building temples in their honour) or of valuable things (food, goods, animals, people, ...). Particular gods would begin as specialists in areas that were previously the province of types of spirit (such as the sea or the forest), possibly taking on new roles to deal with new features of life (such as crops or the hearth) or its more abstract principles (such as love or perception[66]).

In a virtual world, then, if we have a society that is basically still tribal but has settled down, we would expect our intelligent NPCs to follow the same path that humans did in Reality. They would speculate on the existence of a pantheon of gods (some perhaps mapping onto earlier spirits, some not), each of whom was responsible for a general class of concerns.

What if we allowed our intelligent NPCs to make further technical and societal advances?

Well, I'm not going to go into that. If you're interested in seeing how it progresses then there are lengthy and credible analyses elsewhere[67].

The point I wish to make is that, left to their own devices, our intelligent NPCs will develop systems of beliefs regarding their selves, their reality and realities beyond. Unless we give them

---

[66] Perception may sound unlikely to some, but it won't if you're an Ancient Egyptian acquainted with the existence of the god Sia.

[67] I recommend *An Atheist's History of Belief* (Kneale, 2013) and especially *The Evolution of God* (Wright, 2009) as well-researched yet accessible reads on this topic. Warning: as the titles suggest, these aren't necessarily going to please people whose faith in their own religious truths is on the shaky side.

total access to their own implementation, they will speculate to fill in the gaps. What to them appears chaotic, they will attempt to ascribe order to; from this order, they will attempt to read meaning. They will seek to know *why they exist*.

We, as their gods, can influence this: we can supply them with the tools and the environment to give them greater or lesser needs, leading to correspondingly more or less speculation on their part. We can do more than this though: we can *interfere*.

Reality has more gods than it needs. Although our intelligent NPCs may develop the concept of, say, a single, almighty god, this is (as I've said) almost certainly not going to resemble their reality's designer, who actually *is* their god; it's even less likely to resemble any designer of Reality. We could help them in that regard, though.

Some players of virtual worlds would doubtless proselytise religions from Reality to the NPCs of virtual worlds, regardless of the objections of other players, of designers and indeed of the NPCs themselves. Such players could, of course, face a ban if this became a problem (modulo laws about religious expression).

More interestingly, designers of virtual worlds could, if they wished, plant the seeds in their virtual world of one or more of Reality's religions. If you, as a designer, are an adherent of one such religion, should you do this for that religion? If you did, your creations would follow your god(s) – or at least your conception of your god(s). If you didn't, they could worship anything – including imagined deities with morals running completely counter to your own.

Given this possibility, should we as designers consciously introduce religious themes into our virtual worlds? If so, for whose benefit? For the benefit of the god(s) of Reality? For the benefit of us ourselves? For the benefit of players (or indeed non-players), who may be followers of particular gods of Reality? For the benefit of our virtual worlds' sapient inhabitants, its NPCs?

If we decided that we did want our NPCs to share in our wonderful and wondrous knowledge, should we be overt about it (recruit players as missionaries to convert NPCs to the one true faith) or should we be covert (insinuate ideas into NPCs' minds as they sleep)?

Alternatively, should we endeavour to keep Reality's religions out of our worlds and simply leave our creations to form their own systems of belief?

Keeping Up Appearances

There may well be some number between zero and many-thousands of gods of Reality, but *we're* the gods of our virtual worlds. Let's go for it and *be* those gods! Let's show up in those worlds and *act* like the gods we *are*!

Whoa! Is that actually a good idea?

Well, it depends. If we, as gods, represent in our virtual worlds *as gods*, our reasons for doing so will be largely conditional on what the NPCs know about us. There are three main contexts, each of which is going to take several paragraphs to discuss, so buckle up.

In the first context, the NPCs before whom we appear don't know that we (their gods) exist. By representing, we're telling them that we do exist. We may have something specific to relate to them about the nature of their and our realities, but before we get round to that we have to account for the fact that merely by representing as gods we're announcing that gods exist.

The NPCs, being free-thinking, may not believe us. We can perform physics-changing actions that only those with supernatural powers can enact, but the NPCs could still exercise their capacity for independent thought to interpret it another way. Perhaps we're demons trying to trick them into denying the *bona fide* gods?

We can program them to believe we are whom we say we are, but then we'd be removing some aspect of their free will[68]. That said, we're already

---

[68] *The Qur'an* (5:48) states that Allah could have chosen to make everybody part of one nation (united in religion), but

constraining it by situating them in a world that we have created; why is making our existence something their senses can feel to be "real" any different from making colours or sounds or heat feel "real"? If we choose not to use physics to implement acceptance that we're (relative to this created reality) real, we're basically demanding that our NPCs accept our godly existence on trust.

OK, so why would we *want* them to accept our existence on trust? Is it better for them that way, or is it better for us that way?

It's not for me to say whether you would feel better about being accepted by your NPCs as a god based on force of argument (as opposed to force of physics, which smacks of cheating). Self-exaltation is not the most glorious reason for wanting to be accepted as a god, but hey, if it works for you, embrace it.

What would be in it for the NPCs themselves, though?

Well it's fair to say that you never know anyone fully (even yourself), so all relationships involve some degree of trust. What you're asking of your NPCs is for them to trust that you are what you say you are. They're using their theory of mind to infer things about you, just as they do about their fellow NPCs, but they can never be sure they're correct in either case – they just have to trust that

---

didn't because he wanted to test individuals in what he'd given them.

they are. This means that they will act using the working hypothesis that they *are* correct, and indeed they'd need to do that in order to function socially, but they'd nevertheless be aware that they could actually have it all wrong. They may suspect that you're presenting a false picture to them, too.

Trust can be broken by counter-evidence, of course: if you trust that the ice you're walking over won't break because you've walked over it every winter for 20 years, that doesn't mean it *won't* break. If it did, and you fell in, then your trust in the ice would be as broken as the ice itself. It's the same for NPCs: their trust in their world view will be very strong, but they'd have to keep updating and revising it as more information about you came to light.

In one sense, then, asking NPCs to trust you is the default condition. You'd have to make an effort to code them to detect you using a special god-sensing ability, so it's less work for you this way. It's still not obvious why you might consider it *better* for them that they trust you, though, unless you had it in mind to punish or reward your NPCs based on whether they trusted you or not.

I've used the word "trust" rather than "belief" here, by the way, as I didn't want to conflate this with religious beliefs (which, as they're systems, are somewhat more complicated). I didn't use "faith" for similar reasons[69].

So, to answer the question: the reason you would want your NPCs to take your existence on trust rather than from the irrefutable evidence of their senses is either down to laziness on your part or it's some kind of test you've put in place to sort your NPCs. As for *why* you'd want to use their acceptance of your (one-step-removed) existence in their reality as a basis to partition them, I have no idea. It strikes me as an unnecessarily clumsy way of deciding whether NPCs are worthy or not; if you can look into their hearts and see who's worthy anyway, why disrupt your virtual world's order merely to confirm what you know already?

Perhaps the answer lies in the second of the three contexts I mentioned: you might represent in a virtual world as a god because its NPCs do know you exist but have it wrong.

Suppose your virtual world is populated with free-thinking NPCs. They look at your handiwork and hypothesise that it was created by, well, someone not you. It might be they think that it's the product of pure chance, or that it's held together by the will of the spirits who live in its trees and rivers and storms, or that it came into being from a titanic battle between ancient gods, or that it was made by a team of gods always

---

[69] Faith is like belief except that it isn't changed by counter-evidence.

jockeying for supremacy, or that it was constructed by one of your players who appeared and brazenly told them "trust me, I'm your god". They may even have figured out it was created by someone resembling you but lacking in one or more important details. Your aim in representing in your world under such circumstances would be to correct the misapprehensions of your NPCs (or at least to lessen any negative impact these might be having on the world, its NPCs, its players or you).

It could be that you'd really rather not interfere in your world, but nevertheless adjudge the effects of not doing so to be worse than those of doing so. For example, if your NPCs came to believe that they would gain eternal life by killing one another (its being an act of kindness to speed someone else on their journey to paradise), well you might want to step in and put an end to this falsehood[70] before you were all out of NPCs.

Here in Reality we've seen several ideologies that, had they got more of a hold than they did, may have led to there being rather fewer humans around than there are today. For example, the Brethren of the Free Spirit flourished in Northern Europe in the 1400s and 1500s. One of their beliefs was that it was possible to have a direct experience of God that left an individual unable to commit sin.

---

[70] I'm assuming here that you aren't in fact offering eternal life as a reward for murder.

This was indeed as open to abuse as it sounds as if it would be. Fortunately for us (if not for the Brethren), they were persecuted away before doing as much damage as they could have done[71].

Whatever, you can be pretty certain that once the concept of gods has been speculated upon by your NPCs, some of them will make claims that they personally are gods. It may therefore on occasion be prudent for you to set the record straight.

Even if you don't want your NPCs to know your exact nature, you may still wish to enlighten them to the existence of higher realities. For example, you might do this if they were close to creating their own sub-realities, in order to impress upon them the responsibility that comes with this[72].

If you did decide that it would be better to intervene than not to, there would of course be consequences. As I mentioned earlier, some NPCs will stick with their beliefs no matter what you do to prove them wrong; worse, demonstrations of

---

[71] Groups of people known collectively as Ranters took up the idea again in England following our civil war in the 1600s, but their griefing tended more towards public nudity than random acts of violence.

[72] I can assure you that this didn't happen in Reality when Roy Trubshaw started work on *MUD*. Given that he was effectively creating competition for Reality (which isn't renowned for being big on responsibility), that's hardly surprising, though.

your powers could even strengthen their resolve[73]. Other NPCs could take your appearance in their reality as evidence that you were about to destroy it[74]; you might therefore consider giving them an unambiguous trigger warning before doing anything too flashy.

This second of the three contexts I mentioned regarding representing in virtual worlds is essentially to do with education. By appearing, you are informing your NPCs of something to do with either their reality, with you, with Reality, or (if you wish to evangelise) with some higher reality. The NPCs may believe you and reject their old beliefs, or they may reject you and continue with their old beliefs, or they may hedge their bets and do both[75]. You'd probably intend for your representing in their reality to benefit your NPCs in some way, although the possibility remains that you might do it simply to mess with them instead.

In the third context I mentioned, the NPCs know that you (as a-or-the god of their reality) exist in some sense, with which you're OK. Their views may be inaccurate, but you're not

---

[73] Applied to humans, this is known as the *backfire effect*. You could choose not to implement it for your NPCs, of course.

[74] The Muggletonians, who grew out of the Ranters, believed that God ignores what happens in our world and will only intervene when it's time to end it.

[75] There are two ways of looking at this: as *multiple religious belonging* or as *strategic religious participation* (Hedges, 2017).

representing to change what your NPCs think. Rather, you're doing so to ... what?

Well one possibility is that you want to give them an information update but they're not going to believe what you have to say unless they know it's you who's saying it. "Sorry, folks, but the world will end next Tuesday" would be an example of this, but it doesn't have to be quite that drastic.

Another possibility is that you want to hear what they have to say to you ("We're having trouble arresting this global warming, can you help?") or to answer some of their questions ("So why did you make the world flat?"). This does seem to be the kind of conversation you could more easily manage using a chat channel rather than in person, though.

It's also entirely plausible that you represent merely so you can bask in the love or fear that your NPCs feel towards you. As I said before, if that's what turns you on, hey, you're the god.

What these three contexts show is that when you represent in your virtual world, you would do well to contemplate what the effect will be and whether this will properly address your purpose for visiting in the first place.

There is another aspect of representing in a virtual world that's worth discussing while we're on the subject. I touched on it in Chapter 4 but didn't expand upon it at the time. It concerns information loss.

Because the virtual worlds we create are implemented as part of Reality, it seems obvious that Reality must be the more detailed. After all, it contains within it the makings of all of its sub-realities; what they can do, it necessarily must also be able to do.

This suggests that when we represent in a sub-reality we are taking on a form less complex than our true form: more information is required to define us than the virtual world can accept. Our NPCs can never fully comprehend us because there are things about us that cannot be implemented in their reality. Moving our focus up a level, an argument equivalent to this can be used to explain why we can never fully comprehend, say, God. God is more sophisticated than anything Reality can implement, so we only see part of the picture[76].

There is another possibility, though: information gain rather than information loss. Virtual worlds are made out of 0s and 1s in computer memory, but they're not themselves 0s and 1s – they're more complex than that. We could argue that Reality only needs to allow for 0s and 1s plus the necessary basic hardware[77] to turn these

---

[76] This doesn't sit well with the argument that, because Reality is too complex to have arisen by chance, a god must have created it. If said god is necessarily more complex than Reality then how did the god come about, and why couldn't Reality have come about using that same method?

[77] This could be very basic indeed. A Turing machine, which can read and write (but not overwrite) 0s and 1s from and to

into physics; whatever we subsequently do with those 0s and 1s could then exceed what can be done in Reality. This is because we interpret the choreographed interactions of those 0s and 1s to have meaning. More to the point, with sufficiently advanced AI those 0s and 1s can interpret *themselves* to have meaning. They could become very, very smart.

As I pointed out earlier, we already have computer programs that can beat humans at a number of games that we've traditionally associated with intelligence, most notably *Chess* and *Go*. We know the principles of how these programs work because we wrote them, but we don't necessarily know the exact way that they'll behave in a given situation. It could therefore happen that our AI-powered NPCs will in time become too sophisticated for us humans to understand. If they do then were we to represent in their world, we'd suffer the consequences of information gain, not information loss. Their world could be too complicated for us.

We do have a defence, in that we *can* always understand a virtual world if given sufficient time, and we can find such time by pausing the world and not restarting it until our analysis is complete. This would rather undermine the real-time

---

an indefinitely-long tape has the same computational power as any other computer. It may run somewhat slower than most, though.

criterion from the definition of what a virtual world is, though.

The possibility that our creations could become cleverer than us remains a little unnerving, but while they're trapped in their virtual world they can't really do much to harm Reality. They could perhaps manipulate players to do things in Reality for them, using cunning psychological methods, but they can't act in Reality directly.

Well, they can't unless we help them to do so.

Chapter 7

MORALITY

> *Ultimately, our actions within the game, as members of a player community, are to be interpreted under the light of our own existence as moral beings in the world outside the game. That world and our physical presence in it are an important factor in the configuration of the ethics of a computer game. There are cultural taboos, and there are firm beliefs that cannot be overruled by the commitment to the game world. Being a player is maintaining a part of what makes us moral beings in the real world as a reference.*
>
> (Sicart, 2009)

What's right? What's wrong? How do you decide?

Our relationship with virtual worlds is already complex. Through our designs, we speak to our players; through our play, we speak to each other. Through our actions, we shape, form and free our NPCs; through their actions, they respond in ways of which we may or may not approve.

What moral obligations do we have, if any, in all of this? Does the frame of "it's just a game" give us *carte blanche*? Plenty of games put killing central to their gameplay – but plenty of films and entire genres of TV shows place killing at the forefront, too. Is there a difference between torturing a character in a book and torturing an NPC in a virtual world? On what grounds?

Clearly, because players of virtual worlds are of Reality, we can judge much of their behaviour in virtual worlds by the ethical standards of Reality (Sparrow, et al., 2020) – but not quite all of it. We have yet to develop a solid ethical basis for assessing player behaviour in virtual worlds (Reynolds, 2007), so discrepancies are sure to exist[1]. In particular, it's one thing to have a system of ethics covering player behaviour with regard to each other and to wider society, but another thing entirely to develop one for player behaviour with regard to the NPCs who inhabit virtual worlds.

The NPCs of virtual worlds are not of Reality. Can we judge their behaviour by Reality's ethical standards? The realities you create will raise questions that you, as their god, have to answer. Some of these will not be questions you'll have had cause to consider before. Do you know *how* you'd answer? Do you know *why* you'd answer that way?

The decisions you make as the god of a virtual world are situated in a human world of shifting

[1] Entire university courses are devoted to the ethics in and of games and of those who develop and play them, for example (Schrier, 2021) (Zagal, 2021).

moralities. Behaviours may flip back and forth between acceptability and unacceptability over the course of decades and even centuries[2]. Are you *sure* your decisions are morally defensible? What would you do if you later changed your mind?

On what foundations, if any, do you base your morality anyway?

Changing People

It's possible that people can change by playing virtual worlds. Indeed, this is how virtual worlds are supposed to work: as a structured search for or affirmation of identity. For role-playing games in general, the influence on the player of the thoughts and feelings of their character (and *vice versa*) even has a name: *bleed* (Montola, 2010) (Bowman, 2013).

Could people change their ethical stances from playing virtual worlds, though?

Well yes, they could do that. If the designer of a virtual world continually presents a concept within it as being reasonable or uncontentious, when it is widely regarded with suspicion in Reality, then players may nevertheless acknowledge it and internalise it as acceptable – then take this

---

[2] Societal approval or otherwise of homosexuality springs to mind here.

acceptance back with them to Reality[3]. Perhaps one of the clearest examples of this happening came from the creation of Polly in *MUD1*.

So, back in 1980, people weren't playing *MUD* as I had hoped. They were supposed to be using it to free themselves from the constraints of Reality, but they were sitting in the same computer lab as each other and operating under the same peer pressures that they did when they weren't playing. I wanted them to experiment with their identities – to *role-play* – but they didn't. They needed *permission* to role-play. I decided to give them it.

I created a debug character called Polly. Polly is the default name given to parrots in the UK[4], and Polly was a bit like a parrot, obeying my commands without question or thought. Everyone knew that Polly was me. Phase 1 of my not-exactly-elaborate plan was complete.

When I had inherited *MUD1* from Roy, it didn't have gender in it. This was nothing to do with the fact that all our players were male, but rather down to time: Roy had wanted to write as much of

---

[3] It's not just virtual worlds that can do this, either – so can games in general (Earp, et al., 2018).

[4] Playwright Ben Jonson's comedy *Volpone* (Jonson, 1606) associates its characters with animals. Sir Politic Would-Be ("Pol") and his wife visit Venice from England and repeat the words of the locals without knowing what they're saying. Jonson describes them as parrots, and the name "Pol" for parrots stuck, eventually becoming Polly for reasons of cuteness.

MUD1 as he could while he could, and gender was easy to add later; communication and other functionality had priority. Gender was only a linguistic construct anyway, forced on us by the English language; Roy had used female pronouns in his design documentation, so used male pronouns in the game for balance.

With Polly established, I implemented gender. Naturally, I used Polly to test my new code. Polly is a female name, so I answered the question "What sex do you wish to be?" with an f.

Polly was no longer a parrot. Polly was a cheerful, somewhat feisty young woman who liked to help people but got cross if they acted all superior.

This completed phase two of my plan (and therefore my plan as a whole, as it only had two phases). People knew I was Polly, but they also knew I wasn't Polly. No-one was going to see Polly as a sexual object, because I'd designed her more like a younger sister. My aim was to show that it was perfectly fine to play *MUD* as a person you manifestly were not in Reality. I succeeded, too: players got the idea, saw that they were protected by the contextual frame[5] of the game, and also began to play as not-themselves. In so doing, they came to understand in small, incremental ways more about who their "self" actually was.

---

[5] This means what it looks as if it should mean, but formally it's a technical term (Fine, 1983) (Goffman, 1961).

To be honest, it was probably too late for most of the people who were playing when I did this. Others who played *MUD* and its descendants did and still do benefit, though.

The reason I've mentioned Polly is that I was running something of a risk by doing what I did. Back in 1980, there was strong cultural opposition to men presenting as women in public, and I'd effectively done just that. I could have been accused[6] of being gay and shunned by my peers as a result. I had the advantage, though, of not actually caring what people thought; peer pressure doesn't work on me[7].

As a result of Polly, it became commonplace in virtual worlds for male players to play as female characters (and, later, females as males) with no stigma attached. This wasn't my intention when I created Polly – she was all about role-playing[8] – but it was a welcome side-effect. Misgivings that people may have had about crossing genders in Reality were painlessly addressed in virtual worlds; this in-character adjustment to one particular

---

[6] I use this word deliberately: the age of consent for homosexuality in the UK was 21, and I was 20. For young men my age, being gay was still a crime.

[7] This is why I'm not even going to say here whether I am gay or not, even though by convention I should at this point be confirming or denying it to reassure you.

[8] Well, *almost* all about role-playing. I did actually want to make the point that gendered pronouns are a monumental annoyance, too.

aspect of their moral judgement, they then took back with them to Reality.

Of course, times change and cultures differ. Currently, identity markers such as race, disability and sexuality are not on the whole regarded as something people ought to role-play[9], and the same sense of taboo could easily be extended to cross-gender play as well. In conversations at academic conferences, I've experienced gentle pushback regarding cross-gender play on the grounds that it's yet another example of the patriarchy attempting to colonise a space into which it has not been invited. Cross-gender play has even been banned in some mainstream MMORPGs: in September 2007, Chinese developer Aurora Technology froze the accounts of male players who had female characters in *King of the World*[10]. However, given that the rationale for this was so that the other male players could safely hit on female characters without the worry that they might be being played by male players, it's unlikely that the patriarchy was weakened by this endeavour.

How this all plays out as the debate on identity politics runs its course is, while important, not why I mentioned Polly. I mentioned her to

---

[9] A light-skinned human can play as a dark-skinned elf if all the elves are dark-skinned, but playing as a dark-skinned human is another matter.

[10] Female players had to prove they were female via webcam. Pro-tip: this is a great way to lose female players.

demonstrate that virtual worlds can be used to influence the moral attitudes of their players.

Because you control your virtual world, you can to some extent control the experiences players have in that world. Showing through playing isn't the only way to affect a player's morality, but it's a significant one. It's basically cultural: by setting up norms of behaviour within the virtual world that may be different to those the player follows in Reality, a conversation between the real and the virtual is established and the player can decide which makes the most sense to them; this will then influence their opinion in both worlds[11].

People take their morals with them wherever they go[12] and in the case of virtual worlds will often stress-test them there. Unfortunately, although it may well help individual players to work through the consequences of being a jerk in the relatively safe environment of a game, it's not necessarily appreciated by people whose morals have already been stressed quite enough, thank you. Because of this, commercial virtual world developers will usually provide a formal *Terms of Service* document (part of the End-User Licence Agreement) to which their players must adhere[13]; this prescribes

---

[11] Indeed, virtual worlds have been set up in the past specifically to promote such conversations, so as to help children with their moral development (Bers, 2001).

[12] Exception: politics.

[13] We never bothered with these in the early days. If anyone did anything we didn't like, we hit their character with a

sanctions for behaviours that are deemed unacceptable by the virtual world's operators.

Another, potentially more important way of influencing players through the design of a virtual world is via its gameplay. Gameplay, particularly systems content, is how games convey their artistic payload to their players[14]. The expression of ideas persuasively through processes in this manner is called *procedural rhetoric* (Bogost, 2007), and it's very powerful. The way we choose to implement our systems in virtual worlds defines what we say to our players. In short, physics is our mode of communication.

When I say that this is a powerful approach, I mean it. In 2016, I attended the Project Horseshoe conference[15] for game designers, at which the discussion group I joined spent a pleasant few days discussing how to weaponise games. It's remarkably easy. Indeed, it's *frighteningly* easy. It's so easy, that we didn't publish our report informing the world how to[16]: blind players; make

---

Finger of Death spell. As gods, we were perhaps a little more Old Testament than New Testament in our outlook.

[14] Let's put it this way: the art in games has to be in the gameplay, because gameplay is the only thing games have that nothing else has. If you put the art in the story or the graphics or the music, you may as well write a book, paint a picture or compose a rhapsody.

[15] Sadly, this remarkable, invitation-only annual event didn't make it through the COVID-19 era.

[16] Warning: impending list of massively-split infinitives.

them go mad; break up their relationships; empty their bank accounts in our favour; cause them physical injuries; and change their political views[17]. It's only because game designers tend to be decent people that no-one is doing this right now for kicks, although some of the more ruthless commercially-minded game developers may be doing some of it for profit (Zagal, et al., 2013).

I could at this juncture delve into the ways that designers can, do and (perhaps) should influence players both positively and negatively, but it's a topic that has already been covered better by others[18]. Besides, it's not actually what I want to discuss here. The thing is, you and your players are of Reality, and in Reality you're not a god.

Virtual worlds allow us to look at something different entirely: the morality of gods.

MORTALITY

One of the features our ancestors identified that distinguishes gods from humans is that gods are immortal and humans aren't. Indeed, from one

[17] The fact that the conference took place directly after the results of the 2016 US presidential election were announced was not a factor in this.

[18] For example (Sicart, 2009), from which the opening quotation of this chapter comes.

perspective, mortality is a gift granted by gods to humans – a gift, rather than a punishment, because without mortality life has no meaning[19]. Our ancestors also used mortality to distinguish humans from animals: both humans and animals die, but only humans *know* that they, personally, are going to die[20].

Gods are indeed immortal with respect to the worlds they have created. If, as a god of a reality, the character I'm playing in that reality dies, well I'll still carry on living in Reality so haven't really "died" at all. I can return to my created world any time I like resurrected as my old character or reincarnated as a new one; I control the physics, so even if returning is impossible, it's only impossible while I deem it to be impossible.

This doesn't mean I'm immortal in Reality, sad to say. I don't wish to test this experimentally, but it's my understanding that when I die in Reality, I'll no longer be able to visit any of my virtual worlds. Not only from the point of view of the rest of you in Reality, but also from the point of view of the NPCs in my virtual worlds, I'll cease to exist. Needless to say, the NPCs will have no way of knowing that I'm dead in Reality; all they'll have is a growing lack of evidence that I'm intervening in their affairs (that's

---

[19] This does suggest that any post-death, eternal-afterlife existence might need work, but we can ignore that for now.
[20] Philosophers use the term *dasein* to describe the experience of being that is particular to humans. You can blame (Heidegger, 1927) for this, too.

if they ever had any such evidence in the first place).

Non-player characters in a virtual world are usually mortal, but they don't *have* to be that way. A god of their world may not be of the opinion that mortality is a gift and could easily make all NPCs immortal – it's not hard to do. However, said god could still change their mind at any moment. Even immortal NPCs are only *potentially* immortal.

Most modern MMOs do have some NPCs who are largely immortal (because they're shopkeepers or quest-dispensers that it would be inconvenient to lose), but for the majority of mobs the very point of their existence is to be killed. They tend to come back to life a short while afterwards (that is, they respawn) for the very purpose of being killed anew. Being killed is their job.

It may be that they don't respawn individually, but all respawn at once when the zone or instance they inhabit resets. Nevertheless, they will pretty well always return[21]. NPCs in MMOs *are* therefore mortal in the sense that they can be killed, but for them the consequences of being killed are much less drastic than they are for those of us who live in Reality.

So, non-player characters that die in virtual worlds normally get better after a while and return to life. What about player characters, though?

---

[21] It may be that they won't under very specific conditions, such as one-off story events, but these are exceptionally rare.

What happens when they (the characters, not the players) die?

This brings us to the topic of *permadeath*[22].

Permadeath is the situation in which, when a character dies, that character is annihilated. In a virtual world, this means deleting its record from the database. It's possible to have permadeath for NPCs, but few if any MMOs do this routinely. Mostly, therefore, the term "permadeath" is used exclusively with reference to player characters.

So, to repeat the question: if your character dies in a virtual world, what happens to it?

In modern MMOs, it comes back to life. There will usually be a small penalty, such as having your "spirit" need to return to your "body" from a respawn point[23], and it's also possible that your character may under-perform for a while until some negative after-effect of death or resurrection wears off. There could even be a material loss in terms of damage to or destruction of your equipment. It's very unlikely that your character will lose progression, though.

What almost certainly *won't* happen is that your character will be obliterated and you'll have to start a new one: permadeath.

Permadeath is prevalent in many games; it's a major feature of most arcade games, for example.

---

[22] My fear of stating the obvious notwithstanding: it's a portmanteau word coming from "permanent"+"death".
[23] Such a return is known as a *corpse run*.

It's a very seldom-seen mechanic in virtual worlds, though. This is because players really, *really* don't like it when it happens to them. The longer you play a character, the more you accept said character as being a part of your identity; losing a character is therefore like losing a piece of who you are. People don't enjoy that one jot.

I know this, because *MUD* had permadeath. If your character was killed in combat, it stayed killed. Once you'd mastered some basic skills[24], though, such a fate was relatively easy to avoid: it pretty well only ever happened if you took a risk and it didn't come off. People could play for months without seeing their character killed, whereas in today's MMOs player characters can happily be slaughtered dozens of times a session.

Nevertheless, enough people didn't like permadeath that the penalty for being killed was gradually watered down in successive generations of MUDs until we got to the anodyne wrist-slap we have in MMOs today. Death in modern virtual worlds is less "the making of a hero" and more "part of the grind" (Klastrup, 2007).

Reality does have permadeath.

Unlike with virtual worlds, when you die in Reality, that's *it*. You may well live on in a higher reality (say, Heaven), but you're not going to come back to life in Reality because no-one like you ever

---

[24] Principally, remembering to type FLEE (or F for short) when you looked like losing.

has done ever ever. A demigod, or an aspect of a god, might have done so in the past; you're not one of those, though. Insofar as Reality is concerned, you're an NPC. Death for you means deletion from Reality's database. The best you can hope for is that you'll be respawned as a reinitialised baby with no recollection of your previous existence nor any prospect of gaining it.

You can see why people playing virtual worlds for fun might gravitate to ones where this doesn't happen.

To summarise, then: gods basically don't die, or if they do[25] then they can come back whenever. NPCs are either effectively immortal (when their unavailability would be bothersome for players) or they're killable (except during those short periods in which they're recovering from being killed the previous time). The question of permadeath asks only whether, when player characters die, they should be expunged or not, and the answer in almost all cases these days is that no, they shouldn't be.

All the above is correct in today's MMOs, but today's NPCs aren't sapient whereas tomorrow's will be. Would having sapient NPCs alter our thinking in any way?

---

[25] This famously happened to the designer Richard Garriott on 8th August 1997, when his character, Lord British, was killed while making an appearance to mark the end of the beta-test for *Ultima Online* (Garriott & Fisher, 2017).

Let's start by considering whether we should make all our NPCs just flat out immortal. It's straightforward to implement, so should we do it?

It would make for a less entertaining game if player characters couldn't kill NPCs, but that's not in itself a reason to allow such deaths to happen. Combat appears in virtual worlds because it adds conflict, which adds drama, which leads to story. There are other ways to add drama, though, and it's debatable whether combat adds much drama anyway in a virtual world without permadeath (so, almost all of them).

From the perspective of NPCs, if they were immortal then they'd be living a life with no consequences and therefore no meaning. They could do whatever they liked and they wouldn't die. What's the worst that could happen to them? Incarceration? For someone who can't die, all of their reality is a prison.

Actually, worse things *could* happen if we gods allowed them to happen. For example, we could have it that NPCs didn't regrow their heads following decapitation. If we did choose not to allow the regeneration of detached or damaged body parts, though, then after a while the whole NPC population would be invalided through accidents. Besides, it rather runs counter to the spirit of immortality if you have to spend the rest of eternity in a bowl because you were run over by a steamroller; were we to implement immortality, then, we'd probably want to have invulnerability come with it[26].

So, we should give them immortality (plus invulnerability) by default but let them die if they want to escape this fate?

Well, we could certainly contemplate allowing them to decide for themselves when to die, permitting suicide but no other form of death. They'd still have a life of no consequences, though. They could behave in as ghastly a way as they desired to other NPCs; the worst repercussions would involve being locked away for a few years. A few years is nothing if you live forever, and neither is a hefty fine.

Perhaps, then, we should allow them to live forever but be killable. They don't age or die of disease, but now decapitation has a similar effect on them as it does on us. *This* would make them have to get along with one another. Their actions would have consequences; their lives would have meaning.

We could still grant some of them full immortality, of course. Reality's gods can lead meaningful lives and yet remain immortal. Zeus and the other Olympians may not themselves ever die, but we do; by interacting with mortals, immortals can experience some of the effects of

---

[26] Not if we didn't care, of course, or if we did care but rather liked the idea of subjecting our NPCs to torment in perpetuity.

mortality. If *you* can't die but your *child* can then looking after your child gives your own life meaning, regardless.

We could do this for some subset of our NPCs if we wished. We'd let these lucky ones live forever and the rest not. We couldn't allow them *all* to live forever, though: *someone* has to be able to die, or that whole death-brings-meaning vibe wouldn't apply.

Another consequence of giving all NPCs immortality is that if we were to let them breed then we'd have an ever-growing number of them. Where would they all live? They'd expand until they filled the universe, like tribbles out of *Star Trek*.

Oh, wait, no they wouldn't. We can enlarge their universe as much as we like. If it looks close to getting full, we can just add some more of it – doing so automatically if we coded it right. Eventually, we may approach a hardware limit, but even that would merely imply that the world would run slower and slower (looked at from Reality; its NPCs wouldn't notice any difference).

Suppose that we did decide to allow our NPCs to die by a hand other than their own, or even by the environment (if they accidentally fall down a mine shaft, they're gone). Do we still make them live forever otherwise, or do we time-limit their lifespans so they're going to die when they reach the age cap no matter how careful they've been? If we did decide to give them finite lifespans, we could zap them dead instantly when the time came. That would be clean and entirely painless. Alternatively, we could gradually degrade their systems until a major one failed, whereupon death would occur; we'd ensure that this was pretty well guaranteed to happen before the NPC reached the age of, oh, let's go with 140. We could make the process come with so many inconveniences that eventually death was a welcome release.

Of course, if having them welcome death is what we want then we can do better than this. We can introduce diseases, parasites, icky fungal infections and all manner of other conditions that will finish someone off well before their theoretical maximum age. We can even have them spawn dead if we want.

So, which of these possibilities are we going to go for?

Remember, we're assuming that these NPCs are sapient. What I'm asking you is whether you want to murder them or not.

If you do then as a bonus you get to decide how much you want to torture them first.

Now if you don't actually care about your NPCs, you can make your decision objectively. You'd probably want them to die, because then the players who play your virtual world will find it more realistic and perhaps more fun. Sure, the NPCs may be sapient, but they're sapient bits in a database and it's your database so tra-la-la, they're not real people and you can do with them (or their bits) whatever you fancy.

If you do care about your NPCs, you have a tough decision to make. Are the consequences of not having them die worse (for them) than the consequences of having them die?

You can't get around the problem by retroactively removing sapience from your NPCs, because the effect of this is pretty much the same as killing them anyway (the independent-thinking individuals they were no longer exist). Furthermore, because your NPCs *are* sapient they'll have free will; with free will comes the capacity to be a jerk. Some will be bigger jerks than others, causing their fellow NPCs suffering and torment. You can't stop them from being jerks without removing their free will, but to do that would (as I've just mentioned) effectively kill them.

Should death be the penalty for being a jerk?

It seems a bit disproportionate, given that jerkness is a spectrum.

Should death be the penalty for encountering a jerk?

This also sounds a tad unfair, but if your world allows for NPC deaths and your NPCs have free will then some NPCs *will* be big enough jerks that they'll kill others.

We could, if we wished, have it that if an NPC misuses their free will and kills another NPC, it's the one doing the killing who dies; the other, we can patch up good as new. After all, it could be argued that it's a little excessive for an innocent NPC to have to die so that their loved ones, through grief, can grow as people and their killer can develop a conscience.

These questions aren't merely rhetorical. They're actual, legitimate questions that someone, at some point in the future, is going to have to answer. If your virtual world has intelligent NPCs then you, as the god of that reality, will be that person.

Would your answers be the same as the ones a god of Reality might give, or has given, with regard to dealing with free will and jerkness?

For the past few pages, I've talked about death as if it were absolute, but in today's virtual worlds it's not. Dead NPCs don't stay dead, they respawn. Perhaps respawning, rather than oblivion, is a more reasonable way to deal with the aftermath of a future, sapient NPC's death?

Well, it does still mean that your NPCs will live forever, albeit possibly in patches. The efficacy of respawning depends on how long they're out of it before you bring them back[27]. Even short delays could give this kind of death meaningful consequences: the NPC concerned could miss an event to which they were looking forward. Then again, smart NPCs might choose death-with-

---

[27] Increasing this period is a neat way of avoiding overcrowding.

respawn as a way of missing an event that they were dreading.

If you determine that your dead NPCs will respawn, you then have to decide what *of* them respawns. Do they get the same body, or a new one that doesn't have a spear through its heart? If they do get a new one, does it look the same as the old one or could it be radically different[28]? Also, do they retain any of their old memories post-respawn? If they don't then are they really the same person or a different one inhabiting the dead one's (possibly new) body?

Plenty of accounts of what happens when you die in Reality have you being reborn and starting from scratch again with no memories of your previous existence. Would you want that for your NPCs? If so, why? All that the new character would share with the old one would be the use of the same bits in the database; is that really enough that you can legitimately say it's the same person? If I close my word processor and open my spreadsheet, the latter could happen to be loaded into the same PC memory locations as the former was; is this a basis for saying they share an identity?

We can be selective about all of this. You could make it that NPCs who respawned got their old

[28] "Hmm, I don't think I had this many Y chromosomes before that bungee rope snapped. I'm pretty sure I wasn't a porpoise, too.".

memories back when they reached the age of 21. You could phase or instance their reality, so that in one copy of it a killed NPC lives on and in another they cease to be; that way, you'd obtain whatever benefits you saw in having them die, but without having to bother your conscience excessively. You could implement unprecedented ideas, such as making it that they respawn in two bodies as the same person simultaneously. We're gods, we can do whatever we like!

Why *would* we want to do any of this, though? Why would we *not* want to do it?

I have my own opinions – of course I do – but this isn't about *my* opinions: it's about *yours*. In dealing with the mortality or otherwise of free-thinking, intelligent NPCs, you could decree any of these solutions (and many more besides).

How would *you* handle the deaths of those to whom you had given life? More to the point, *why* would you do it that way as opposed to some other way?

Would you even *have* death?

THe SOUL OF an NPC

The fundamental question of morality for gods is how to treat their creations.

Although "creations" here formally includes everything from gold dust to interstellar voids, the biggest issues concern those creations that are sapient beings. For virtual worlds, I'll therefore be continuing my assumption that it's the future and your NPCs are sapient in some way, although for many people the more easily-satisfied condition of sentience is enough to bring issues of morality to bear[29]. Also, although I'll perhaps be pushing at your moral boundaries by asking awkward questions, I won't be prescribing any answers. It's up to you, not me, to decide how you'd treat your intelligent NPCs. I may have my own ideas on what I'd do, but I'm not you; I've merely thought about this for longer than you have.

Let's start with a question that isn't awkward[30], though: will your NPCs have souls?

There are two ways to look at this. The first is to ask whether they have souls at the level of Reality (that is, some means by which you as a human being have a soul also works for them). If, say, God gave you your soul then presumably God could give your NPCs souls, too; you could well meet them in your shared afterlife.

We haven't had virtual worlds for long enough to discern if NPCs have actual Reality-level souls or

---

[29] Killing animals is cruel because they may get anxious immediately before you put a bolt through their brains, but plants and fungi, well, they deserve it.

[30] Its answer certainly is, but the question itself isn't.

not, but as they're pretty mindless at the moment[31] we're probably safe in supposing that they don't. This may change should they acquire free will. If it does then whether it's a good idea or not is really dependent on the source of the souls; a progressive god might be pleased to dish them out; a reactionary god could take a rather more hard-line view. We, as the NPCs' gods, would only get to delimit what could carry such a Reality-level soul.

The second way to look at the question of whether NPCs have souls is at the level of the virtual world. Will you, as the designer of the virtual world, be giving each of your NPCs a soul?[32]

It doesn't matter for now how you'd implement the concept – as an entry in a database, or a random-number seed for procedural generation, or a bot attached to a character, whatever – it's just a general question. Would you incorporate an immortal element into your NPCs' make-up such that either it affected their actions, their actions affected it, or both?

You might decide that no, you don't want your NPCs to have souls. They in turn might decide that they do have them, though, and act accordingly.

---

[31] For the purpose of this observation, we're temporarily not in the future.

[32] Arguments can be made that you have to do so, because souls are necessary for life. Plato outlines four such positions in *Phaedo* (Plato, trans. 1892), but as each one took me a page to describe and (for virtual worlds) to dismiss, I decided to spare you the tedium of the discussion by cutting it.

Are they somehow giving themselves souls if they do that? Or does a soul have to be more concrete in programming terms to qualify?

Let's say you do decide that your NPCs have souls. You either generate a new soul when a new NPC appears, or you take one from stock (possibly one that's already been used, reincarnation-style).

If you don't reincarnate then once they've been used[33] you either have to preserve the souls of the deceased somewhere[34] or to obliterate them entirely. The dead vastly outnumber the living in Reality, so you could expect the same thing to happen with your virtual world after a while, too. Nevertheless, given how inexpensive hard drives are these days, and the rate at which capacity is increasing over time, you're probably OK storage-wise for a while yet.

Taking a soul from stock assumes a stock of souls. Reincarnation has a bit of a numbers problem in Reality, because the living population is constantly growing; therefore, it's not the case that the moment one body stops working another body immediately becomes available – bodies are being produced faster than souls are becoming reusable. You can address that in your virtual world, of

---

[33] This is a euphemism for "once you've killed the NPC", which you're perfectly within your rights never to do. For the sake of the argument, though, let's say that after reading the previous section of this book you decided that NPC mortality was nevertheless the way to go.

[34] Please don't suggest a blockchain.

course, simply by not allowing births until someone dies to free up a soul. If you don't do this, however, you'll need to have a vast reserve of souls (at least equal to the number of NPCs who can possibly exist at once) queueing[35] patiently to be reincarnated; either that, or when you want a soul and your reserve is empty, that's the point at which you create a new soul to use.

So, you have either a recycled soul or a freshly-made soul, and you need to attach it to a body in your virtual world. When will you do that?

If your NPCs are born fully-formed, it's not really a problem: the body appears out of nowhere, you attach the soul to it and off it goes. If NPCs are born using a similar kind of process to that which humans use in Reality, though, you'll need to invest some thought in it.

The first point at which you could associate a soul with an NPC is at conception. Now if your virtual world is anything like Reality, roughly one pregnancy in eight will end in miscarriage (National Health Service, 2018) – more if you count the ones that happen before the pregnancy is noticed. Are you going to fix that in your virtual world? If not, will you simply obliterate the miscarried soul, or put it back in the queue for rebirth (possibly at the front), or send it to an afterlife? If it's an afterlife, would that be a pleasant

[35] I do enjoy the fact that this word has five consecutive vowels.

one (the soul has done nothing wrong) or an unpleasant one (the soul has done nothing right)?

You might decide to wait until the unborn virtual foetus develops enough of a mind to be able to make decisions before you allocate it a soul. However, depending on what your criteria for judging free will are, this stage could still be arrived at before the NPC is miscarried. OK, well in that case perhaps you should wait until the NPC is capable of surviving birth and attach a soul then? Or wait until the child is actually born?

That would at least give the soul a shot at independent life, but unless you did something about it you'd still end up attaching souls to some bodies that are born so severely disabled that they don't have and never will have the capacity to support any sense of self, let alone a decent quality of existence. If you give *those* bodies a soul, why wouldn't you also give a soul to very clever animals? Maybe you do. What's the cut-off point in intelligence for soul or no soul then? If you recycle souls, is this your way of keeping ones that are problematic in some fashion out of circulation?

Perhaps you wait for a while after a baby has been born, attaching a soul discreetly when it starts to communicate. You could even let other NPCs determine when a soul is attached, through a process such as baptism. That way, souls wouldn't be disadvantaged by being attached to a body that lacks the hardware to execute free will. They would merely be disadvantaged (or advantaged) by the situation of the parents you gave them.

There is a way out of having to make these tricky decisions, by the way. You're a god: you can make the act of giving an NPC a soul (at conception) itself guarantee that the NPC will develop into a fully-formed being with free will. Basically, you make the ones you give souls to invulnerable until they're capable of making their own decisions concerning their destiny. This does mean that you have to decide what to do with those soulless individuals who somehow manage to survive for as long as those to whom you give souls. Your choices are: arrange for them to die ("they have no souls, so it's not really murder"); allow them to live on without a soul ("no-one will notice, least of all them"); or recognise their persistence by giving them a soul ("they've earned their freedom").

Also, remember that as a god you get to decide not only when to attach a soul, but when to detach it. Even if you go with the fully-born-as-an-adult approach, does it remain the case that some NPCs will die within a day yet others will be rewarded (or punished) with a long, long life? You have to determine what solution you'd find morally acceptable.

Maybe you'll decide it's not worth the effort and resolve not to implement souls at all.

Now, I've asked a lot of questions here. These are questions for you to answer, in readiness for when you're a god of a virtual world with sapient NPCs. Note that I'm not asking what [insert name of a god of Reality here] would do – you don't get to pass the buck. I'm asking what *you* would do regarding the question of whether you'd give your NPCs souls. Your virtual world is not Reality, and any decisions made about why souls may or may not exist in Reality can't be assumed to apply to your virtual world. *You* have to determine whether to have souls in your world, and if so then who gets one and when.

In practice, how you would answer these questions really depends on what you want your NPCs to have a soul *for*. Why would you give them one? What kind of information would it contain? Do you want a full personality inventory or would a conception number suffice?

Why would you want to record a soul anyway, for that matter?

The most common reason among gods for giving their creations souls is, in a word, *metrics*.

One of the jobs of Anubis, the jackal-headed Ancient Egyptian god, is to weigh the heart of a dead person[36] against the feather of the god Ma'at. The heart is where the soul[37] can be found, and Ma'at embodies truth, order, law, justice, balance

---

[36] It's impractical for living people.

[37] Souls are made up of many components, but these stick together while you're alive and for long enough afterwards that Anubis can weigh them.

and morality[38]. Souls that are lighter than Ma'at's feather ascend to the Field of Reeds (desirable); souls that are heavier are eaten by the crocodile-lion-hippopotamus god, Ammit (undesirable)[39]. *The Book of the Dead* is silent on what happens if your soul weighs exactly the same as Ma'at's feather, so probably wasn't written by a programmer.

Implementing Anubis's scales is fairly easy: for each new soul, you just have to initialise a counter with a number of penalty points (possibly zero, but more if you like the idea of original sin) representing the amount more than Ma'at's feather that the soul weighs. You add points for bad deeds and subtract points for good deeds[40]. If the running total of penalty points is negative when the character dies, their heart weighs less than Ma'at's feather so off they go to the Field of Reeds. Otherwise, it's feeding time for Ammit.

Many virtual worlds already do something like this for player characters, most obviously with the light-side, dark-side mechanic of *Star Wars: the Old Republic*. Indeed, so often does this kind of in-game

---

[38] Ancient Egyptians can correct me if I'm wrong, but I suspect it may actually be more accurate to say that truth, order, law, justice, balance and morality embody Ma'at.
[39] Reminder: I use the term *god* in a gender-inclusive fashion throughout this book, so don't write to tell me that Ma'at and Ammit are both female, please – I do know this.
[40] A similar tallying approach is employed at Christmas with regard to whether children have been naughty or nice.

action-based marking take place for assorted purposes, it has a name: it's a *reputation system*[41].

Today's reputation systems apply to player characters only. They don't apply to NPCs, because NPCs don't have enough free will to merit one. If they did, though?

Well, you could use a mechanism like this to decide which of your NPCs deserved something pleasant after they died and which of them deserved something less-than-pleasant. A soul arrives, you look at its weight, and determine on that basis whether it's going to the good place or the bad place[42]. If you're forgiving, you could send someone to the good place even when their scorecard says the bad place[43].

As it happens, the weighing isn't the hard part. The hard part is the adding and removing of points every time someone does something bad or good. That's a value judgement. Would you do it personally, deciding for each NPC on a case-by-case basis whether their actions were legitimate or illegitimate? Or would you automate it instead[44]?

---

[41] These are also sometimes known as *karma systems* (Knoll, 2018) or *morality meters* (Formosa, et al., 2022).

[42] Ancient Mesopotamians will be smiling here, as they know there isn't a good place, just a bad place – Kur.

[43] Sending people to the bad place when their scorecard says the good place is also an option.

[44] There are already classic role-playing games that simulate this for player characters, if not non-player characters (Casas-Roma, et al., 2019).

There could be millions of NPCs, and reputation systems are notoriously exploitable (Farmer, 2012). You could always have the NPCs judge themselves (so if one does something that it knows it shouldn't, that's a mark against it), but your difficulty there is that they may be mistaken. They may think a mercy killing is good but you may think it isn't, or the other way round; unless you explicitly tell them, they're not going to know – and if you do explicitly tell them, well they're now grounding their actions in their fear of retribution rather than as a consequence of their own righteousness.

Let's say you do want to tell them whether an action is good or not. You can achieve this by sending its rating to the mind of the NPC in question as a kind of sensory input: in the same way that they can tell hot from cold, they can tell right from wrong. That might make it a little too easy, though, leaving little need for reflection on their part and no need for metrics on yours.

If you want to tell the NPCs how to behave, but in such a way that they have to make continual interpretative appraisals of their actions that you can subsequently measure, you basically have four ways of doing so.

Firstly, you could appear at regular intervals and repeat your message. Every year, say, you'd show up and state the rules. You wouldn't have to have a Q&A (you're a god, after all), you'd just tell everyone the rules directly. You may wish to send a demigod or other supernatural being to read the rules for you if your majesty is too great for your NPCs to comprehend, but this would be easy to arrange. That said, making regular, scheduled appearances to deliver a message is an option that has never been exercised in Reality (as far as I can ascertain), so it may come with subtle disadvantages of which I'm unaware; there's no obvious reason it wouldn't work for a virtual world, though.

Secondly, you could appear just once to deliver your message. You'd make sure that your words were recorded verbatim, to reduce the room for misinterpretation. Later generations of NPCs, who have missed your appearance, will still be able to access your message through the recording (or a certified transcription of it). In Reality, this is what the god of Islam did: he arranged for the angel Gabriel to recite the content of *The Qur'an* to the prophet Muhammad, who wrote it all down. This approach works fine, but you are somewhat reliant on a single person to disseminate your words; unless you choose that person wisely[45], you might have to keep repeating the exercise until you find someone capable enough to carry it through.

Thirdly, you could appear for an extended period, during which time you'd recite your message a bit at a time. If your NPCs didn't seem to get it, you could repeat it in different forms until

---

[45] Muhammad was clearly a good choice.

they did. You wouldn't have your words recorded directly-as-spoken, but instead would encourage literate individuals to write down later what they remembered. This would ensure that the rules most important to them were the ones they highlighted. The result would be a set of regulations that largely reflected your views but which were subject to reinterpretation if the virtual world's society moved on. In Reality, this is what the god of Christianity did: he appeared as Jesus but never wrote anything down himself, leaving the writers of the gospels to put their own particular spin on events.

Fourthly, you could go open source. You'd maybe set the ball rolling by introducing ideas, but you'd do so to NPCs with no recording ability (so that they couldn't write the ideas down and thereby ossify them); generations of NPCs could then work through the ideas, adding their own interpretations and metaphorical restatements. After a while, there'd be a whole morass of different perspectives through which your NPCs would have to navigate in order to figure out how they should behave. This very act of navigating would then itself become a path to understanding. In Reality, this is what seems to have happened with Hinduism: eternal truths were revealed to sages thousands of years ago, and analyses of these truths in the intervening millennia have offered up myriad ways to think about them.

For your virtual world, these are all decent templates; you can, of course, decide on some other way to convey your message, but given that the second, third and fourth of those I listed are tried and tested, they'd obviously be among the front-runners. I'd nevertheless recommend the first way myself, because it reduces the chance that some rogue NPC just makes up a god and promulgates an unhelpful message supposedly emanating from this figure. If you, or one of your agents, can be relied upon to appear periodically and explain the true rules of behaviour, this would prevent such invented messages from accruing credibility. You can then judge souls in the knowledge that the NPCs in recent possession of them were fully appraised of the correct parameters of evaluation.

You can side-step this whole question, by the way, simply by preordaining at birth whether an individual is good or evil. Then, when they die, you can reward the former and punish the latter without having to bother examining how they conducted their life. This does have an aroma of unfairness about it, but no-one said gods had to be fair.

As for why you might want to judge souls in the first place, well as I said, the majority of publicised reasons involve some kind of assessment. Most of the gods who favour such judging in Reality seem to want to do so to encourage moral behaviour, but that doesn't mean that we have to use the metrics we gather for similar purposes. If we so chose, we could allow NPCs to enter paradise based on how well they looked after their teeth, as some kind of advertisement for dental health products in Reality. We don't have to reference their morals in our filtering metric at all – we can use any of an NPC's properties. If you find a particular NPC interesting or entertaining, you may want to give it another opportunity to live so that you can see what further madcap adventures it has. You might even want to ascend it to Reality, so you can meet it and hang out together. Perhaps NPCs are more intelligent than we are, and you're judging which to bring to Reality to solve some important issue of the day. There are many possibilities.

If you don't plan on judging your NPCs, there are few compelling reasons for giving them souls. The main one would be for back-up purposes, so you can restore the being of an NPC in the event of an error (say, death by programming mistake). This would suggest that souls can be copied, implying that in theory you could, if you wanted, have duplicated souls be present in the same virtual world at once. This would certainly help if the number of souls in your pool was less than the number of bodies that needed them. There are no claims that this happens in Reality, though, so if we human beings do have souls then either they're so woven into the fabric of Reality as to be inseparable from it or there's no god that wants individual souls to exist as multiple copies.

Before I leave the subject of souls, I'll mention another way of having them which side-steps the problematic possibilities introduced by a soul-copying solution. It could be that *players* act as souls. NPCs don't have souls, but player characters do. If you think about it, what happens to a player character is very similar to reincarnation (Mukherjee, 2009). The player logs in, the character blinks into existence, the character exists until the player logs off, whereupon it blinks out of existence until the cycle repeats.

If this is how souls work in Reality then we human beings could actually be player characters rather than NPCs – we just don't know that we are. That said, in Reality we don't remember any existence we might have beyond it[46], whereas in virtual worlds we are fully aware of our existence in Reality, so such an account seems unlikely.

That's today, though. The issue will doubtless be easy to remedy using the memory-suppression technology that we'll have invented by the time we have sapient NPCs. We could turn players' memories of Reality off while they were playing, then turn them on again when they stopped

---

[46] There are many examples of people who claim to remember past lives in Reality, but hardly any who claim to remember past lives in a higher reality. Although the former could in theory provide evidence for the correctness of their memories by referring to as-yet-unknown information that is subsequently uncovered, the latter could only hope to do so by corroborating one another's testimonies.

playing. Worryingly for this proposal, it's not immediately obvious *why* we wouldn't want to retain our higher-reality memories. Might we perhaps be being judged by others in Reality in a manner which would be compromised if we remembered the fact? Could we perhaps be judging *ourselves* in Reality?

One way to examine your own morality is to see how nice you are to people you don't know. If the person you don't know is yourself, that's going to accelerate your process of moral development more than somewhat.

Being Moral Beings

> *A moral being is one who is capable of comparing his past and future actions and motives,— of approving of some and disapproving of others.*
>
> (Darwin, 1871)[47]

Are your NPCs moral beings?

Come to that, are you a moral being?

---

[47] This is from the 1871 first edition. The 1874 second edition puts it slightly differently: "A moral being is one who is capable of comparing his past and future actions or motives, and of approving or disapproving of them.". You could say that Darwin's views evolved in the interim.

Ethics are rules of moral behaviour defined externally, such as codes of conduct in business or the workplace. Morals are your own, personal principles regarding what's right and wrong[48].

Morals are often informed by ethics: your view of what's right may come from the ethics espoused by a political manifesto, say, or from the principles of a religion laid down in one or more sacred texts.

A clear explanation of the distinction between morals and ethics was given by Cynthia Payne, who became a *cause célèbre* in 1980s Britain after being imprisoned for "keeping a disorderly house" (that is, a brothel). Her establishment was frequented by pillars of society such as members of parliament, lawyers, company directors, clergymen and at least one peer of the realm. When asked on the BBC's *Newsnight* why she wouldn't name any of her famous clients, she replied, "Well my morals is low, but my ethics is high".

Ultimately, your morals are your own. Whether other people believe that you're moral or immoral depends on their own morals. Nevertheless, common approaches to thinking about morality do exist, which can be collected and aggregated to create independent, self-consistent theories of ethics. These theories may then be applied

---

[48] In many traditions of south Asia, the ability to distinguish right from wrong and to act in line with this is what separates humans from (other) animals. It's a key component of the concept of *dharma*.

(possibly by a god) to determine if an action is or isn't ethical. This approach is called *normative ethics*.

There are several such normative theories, the four main ones being:

- *Virtue ethics*. This system rates certain character traits as being positive (say, courage, prudence, justice and temperance[49]) and their opposites as being negative. Its main problem is that people may disagree over what's positive and what's negative.
- *Consequentialism*. This system rates actions as being moral or not depending on what happens as a result of doing them (say, leading to the most happiness for the most people[50]). Its main problem is that people may have different priorities in assessing result desirability.
- *Deontology*. This system bases morality in following rules out of duty. Your actions are more important than their consequences. The rules capture ideas that are intrinsically good whatever (say, doing what a god tells

[49] These particular four were the *cardinal virtues* of Greco-Roman antiquity, which later fed into Christian theology.
[50] This particular example is called *utilitarianism*. Maximising your own happiness is *egoism*.

you to do[51]). Its main problem is in deciding what's intrinsically good.

- *Social contract theory*. This system bases morality in the rules that people will follow on condition that other people will also follow them. Its main problem is that other people may not follow them[52].

All of these approaches basically push the problem of morality one step back. They still require the morals of individuals to guide the criteria that the theories employ. People can and do have different ways of looking at things; the feminist-formulated *ethics of care* emphasises interpersonal relationships as virtues, for example, rather than traditional male-oriented virtues such as ambition and magnanimity. Entire cultures can judge actions in different ways: in some parts of the world, bribery is acceptable because it's the only way some people can afford to live; in others, bribery is unacceptable because it's the only way some people can afford to live.

Note that if you have a theory of mind, you will benefit from an understanding of the ethics and morals of others even should you have neither

---

[51] This is *divine command* theory. Not killing someone because your god told you not to is moral; not killing someone because you simply can't be bothered is not moral. For virtual worlds, of course, *we're* the gods.

[52] In games, the magic circle is a form of social contract. Those who aim to satisfy the win condition without following the rules are *cheats* (Suits, 1978).

yourself. You can't simply ignore them as being someone else's problem[53].

So, let's suppose that you do have a sense of right and wrong (that is, you're not amoral). Your standards may not be in keeping with those of the majority (that is, you could be immoral in the majority's opinion), but you nevertheless have them.

Your moral code will affect how you behave in Reality. It may, for example, influence whether you play computer games or not (Reynolds, 2002). That isn't what concerns us here, though. What you do in Reality is your own business; we're interested in what you do in and (especially) to virtual worlds.

There is a lot of ongoing work on the subject of the ethics of Artificial Intelligence, almost all of which concerns artificially-intelligent entities situated in Reality. Are they safe? To what rights are they entitled? Do they threaten human dignity? What moral agency do they have? Are they biased? Who is accountable if Things Go Terribly Wrong?

---

[53] Example: suppose that your friend is hiding you from your enemies, One such enemy asks your friend where you are. If your friend lies, you live; if your friend tells the truth, you die. You really would want to know if your friend subscribed to the ethics of deontology at this point ("I cannot tell a lie"), regardless of your own views on the subject.

Much of this work is relevant to virtual worlds[54], but practically none of it considers the peculiarities of virtual worlds. In particular, it's one thing to look at your moral obligations towards artificial intelligences in a world you didn't manufacture, but another thing entirely to look at them in a world you did manufacture.

This is what *we're* going to look at now.

So, the first item on the agenda is to ask whether we have any moral obligations to our artificial intelligences (that is, our NPCs) at all.

Suppose you were to stand on a sandy beach. Is that an OK thing to do? Although I'm sure that there are some people out there who would find such an act morally reprehensible, most people would be fine with it. It's quite innocuous, and there's no harm done.

So, that's standing on sand. Suppose you were to crush a piece of sandstone beneath your foot[55] and make some more sand. Would that be OK?

Again, that's probably going to be fine in most people's book.

What about crushing an acorn? Would that be fine? What about crushing a hen's egg? An ant? A spider? A frog? A mouse? A mouse you'd given a

---

[54] If you want to pursue it, (Nevejans, 2016) does a good job of outlining the various issues.

[55] I apologise to people who are physically unable to do this for implying that it's something everyone can do, but this is only a thought experiment.

name to? What about crushing a baby? Or an adult's head?

Somewhere in there, you would probably at least pause for thought. You might be fine with killing random ants but not random frogs. You could be extremely reluctant to kill a baby, but nevertheless do it under the right circumstances[56].

The entities to which your morals apply are said to be *morally considerable*[57]. In general, all moral beings are morally considerable, but whether specific kinds of being that lack morals of their own are morally considerable depends on your morality. Babies, for example, have insufficient mental advancement to be able to compare their past and future actions or to approve or to disapprove of them; nevertheless, despite babies' clear absence of morals, most people would regard them as morally considerable. After all, if humans are the only entities that we know for sure can be moral beings, it makes sense to treat all humans as morally considerable lest we're wrong in individual cases. This is known as the *argument from species normality*.

Opposing it, the *argument from marginal cases* contends that if certain humans[58] who have no

---

[56] I'm sure a good many babies died when the Sumerian god Enlil flooded the whole planet.

[57] That's as in "able to be considered", not "sizeable".

[58] These are the *marginal cases*. Babies are an example of a marginal case, along with people who have advanced

mental capacities beyond those of animals are nevertheless morally considerable then the animals should also be morally considerable. The problem here is that animals have marginal cases, too, so an independent termination condition is required or everything ends up being morally considerable and therefore all deliberate acts become inherently immoral.

If you draw your line of moral considerability at personhood then animals other than human beings are not morally considerable – they lack sapience. In the era of slavery, even some humans were[59] considered no better than animals, therefore they were not accorded personhood and the moral consideration that goes with it.

Other people regard sentience as their red line. If a creature can suffer then that makes it morally considerable: it's wrong to crush a mouse underfoot because it would feel pain[60]. Jain ascetics famously sweep the ground before them as they walk, so as to avoid the careless killing of insects and even smaller organisms, reasoning that to hurt others is to hurt oneself.

Alzheimer's disease, profound autism, or certain other conditions.

[59] Or are, as slavery does still exist.

[60] Smashing it briskly with a sledgehammer would end the mouse's life before the pain receptors had time to send signals to what used to be the mouse's brain, but this is also generally frowned-upon.

There's also a commonly-held view that a hierarchy is involved in moral considerability. It accepts that sentient beings are morally considerable, but holds sapient beings to be more important. This would indicate that given a straight choice between saving a toddler or saving a dog, you should save the toddler. Extending this hierarchy downwards to include inanimate objects is how those ideologies such as environmentalism, that do regard everything as being morally considerable, are able to avoid the stifling constraints on action that would otherwise be implied.

I'm not going to discuss the "right" way to look at moral considerability here. After all, it's been debated for thousands of years and has yet to be resolved; adding my own drop of moral opinion isn't going to make any difference. For the purposes of this book, whether acorns or frogs or named mice or babies are morally considerable isn't the issue.

For virtual worlds, the question we need to ask is whether NPCs are morally considerable[61].

If (according to your moral code) they are then this gives you responsibilities. If they're not then

---

[61] This is a question that is indeed asked in the film *Free Guy*. If you haven't seen it yet, do yourself a favour and watch it: it raises a lot of the issues I cover in this book, and in a far more entertaining manner, too.

they're mere grains of sand that you can do with whatever you please.

At the moment, NPCs in virtual worlds are not all that intelligent. There are far more sophisticated pieces of software around, and it would be hard to argue that NPCs are morally considerable unless you're also willing to concede that, say, air traffic control systems are also morally considerable[62].

However, as we've been looking to a future in which we'll have NPCs who are at least as clever as we are, the question becomes significant. It's highly advisable that we sort out our position before this future arrives, rather than wait until it does and then be caught on the hop.

If intelligent NPCs are morally considerable then we, as moral beings, have to make sure we do them no wrong. Furthermore, if intelligent NPCs are moral beings themselves, our response must be even stronger: we have to protect the intrinsic rights they possess for being moral beings.

If, however, NPCs (no matter how smart they seem to be) are merely pieces of software just like any other, it could be argued that they are not morally considerable.

Bear in mind that if your NPCs perceive themselves to be moral beings but you don't perceive them as such, they're going to think you're a jerk. As Alphinaud Leveilleur, an NPC in

---

[62] That said, a fair case can indeed be made (Tomasik, 2014).

Final Fantasy XIV, neatly puts it (spoiler: having just discovered that his world was created by the actions of beings who as a consequence don't regard him as properly alive): "*We* define our worth, not the circumstances of our creation!".

Supposing that you accept that your NPCs are moral beings, where would you put them in a hierarchy of importance? For example, are sapient NPCs in a virtual world more or less important than merely sentient critters in Reality? Given a straight choice between saving a real dog or a virtual saint, to which would you give priority?

What I've said so far applies to people playing virtual worlds as much as it applies to people designing them. How a player reacts to an intelligent NPC depends on the extent to which that player regards said NPC as being morally considerable. Gods, though, have a further problem.

One of the reasons that some people in Reality believe it's wrong to be unkind to animals is that animals can suffer (that is, they're sentient). Monkeys are not indifferent if you kill their infants. Tying a firecracker to the tail of a cat is not the same as tying one to a fence. A sheep will get upset if you stub out a cigarette on its nose. Because animals can suffer, the argument goes, it's not morally right to mistreat them.

Can NPCs suffer?

Ah, well that's the thing: as a god of a virtual world, *you* get to decide if they can or not.

As a god, it's possible to stop all suffering very easily: you simply don't implement the concept. Whatever happens to your NPCs, they bear it stoically. You can give them an awareness that things aren't going well, so that if they break a bone they can seek treatment. It doesn't have to hurt, though; it doesn't have to cause them distress. It can *look* as though it does, but acting as if in pain isn't the same as actually being in pain.

In Reality, pain is useful because it can dissuade you from doing something stupid such as picking up a red-hot coal. If we didn't have pain, we probably wouldn't have extended the evolutionary tree quite as far as we've managed. Our NPCs don't have to have evolved, though: as certain gods seem to have done in Reality, we can create our NPCs from nothing. That being the case, why would we make them suffer? If making morally considerable creatures suffer is a bad thing then we're doing a bad thing merely by implementing the concept of suffering for them!

Why, then, *would* you make intelligent NPCs suffer?

Note that it takes more effort on your part to make your NPCs suffer than it does to make them not suffer. If, for you, NPCs are not morally considerable in the first place, they're just soulless bits in a database that people are projecting emotions onto as they might characters in a book, then you wouldn't bother to add suffering: from your perspective, there's nothing there that can suffer. Sure, they may have the empirical appearance of being intelligent, but they're merely the emergent consequences of interacting software processes. You'd no more make them suffer than you'd make water suffer by having it fall off a cliff in a waterfall.

If you do adopt this position, by the way, bear in mind that you yourself are an NPC of Reality. By your own argument, you *yourself* aren't morally considerable. This means that no-one has to pay any attention to your opinions whatsoever. Enjoy!

Assuming that you *are* a moral being, then, let's try to think of some possible justifications (or at least explanations) for your implementing suffering in your virtual world.

Well it could be that you've put it in entirely by accident. Virtual worlds are complicated systems, and you didn't foresee that one of the consequences of something you did over here would have such a profound effect over there. Before you knew it, your NPCs had the capacity to suffer[63]. Perhaps it's debug code that you intend to take out but haven't got around to yet. It's top of your to-do list, though – honest!

More plausibly, you could implement suffering on purpose so as to help your NPCs learn and adapt. They have free will: unless bad things happen, they can't reflect on what's right and

---

[63] It's just as likely that instead it could be fences that acquired the capacity to suffer, of course.

what's wrong, so can't hit the morality targets they'll need to hit if they're to enjoy the pleasant afterlife you have planned for them. Thus, you have to grit your teeth and make your NPCs capable of suffering, knowing that they'll thank you for it in the end[64].

You could decide to implement suffering as a teaching exercise for your players. If your virtual world was created to illustrate what life was like in Nazi death camps, the message might not get across very well if all the NPC prisoners were cheerful and happy despite the privations they were enduring. Yes, you'd have to think long and hard about deliberately setting them up to suffer the torments that you've specifically arranged for them to undergo, but perhaps if you were to send them to an eternity of bliss once they've died of starvation or worse, that would balance it out a bit.

Related to this, you could be running an experiment. You initialised the virtual world knowing that suffering *could* appear, but that it wasn't guaranteed to do so, then you let the dice roll how they may. Yes, your creatures are suffering *now*, but leave it for a few more iterations and perhaps they'll evolve out of it. You may learn something important along the way. Then again,

---

[64] This does assume that they live long enough to make such judgements. You wouldn't want the suffering to be so bad as to lead to anyone's death, for example; that would be self-defeating.

perhaps you've already learned it and have abandoned the experiment because you now have the result; the NPCs will cease to suffer once you get around to taking the server down.

To be honest, all these examples of reasons why a virtual world might incorporate suffering are secondary. The main, overwhelming reason to implement suffering is, as with so much else in virtual worlds, verisimilitude. Your players can suffer in Reality (indeed, they may be playing to escape this); if they go to a world which knows no suffering, it won't seem real to them. How can anyone be the good guy if there's no suffering to end? How can a player try[65] to overcome adversity if there's no adversity? Therefore, with a heavy heart, you create NPCs who can experience suffering, because if you didn't then no-one would play and the NPCs wouldn't exist in the first place. A crummy life is better than no life at all.

These are merely some of the possibilities. There are plenty of others. You may be a sadist, doing it for personal gratification, for example.

The point is, if you're making a virtual world then either suffering is some accidental or unavoidable consequence of the design, or you're putting it in deliberately for a particular reason. If

---

[65] "Whoever 'tries' is in fact the one who is tried" (Gadamer, trans. 2013). This quote comes from a chapter in which it is argued that the existence of art can best be understood through an appreciation of play (although you have to read a chapter on the history of German philosophy to get that far).

you do put it in deliberately, you'd better examine your morals to make damned sure you're doing the right thing.

In the modern societies we have in Reality, the default position is that it's immoral to make morally considerable individuals suffer unless either: they agree to it; or it's to save them or someone else from something worse. Our NPCs can't consent to be born into a world of suffering, because they don't exist at the time when they'd need to be asked. If we're to have a moral justification for implementing suffering, it would have to be that not implementing it would lead to something worse.

What could that "something worse" be?

Well, death (if it were permanent) would be the obvious candidate. As a corollary, so would removing free will from a sapient individual, because (as I've pointed out already) such an act is tantamount to killing them. This leads to the interesting possibility that suffering is necessary for a being to have free will. The line of argument to show this would proceed something like as follows:

1. Unless bad things happen, you can't reflect on what's right or wrong.
2. You can't as a result develop morals.
3. You are not, therefore, a moral being.
4. However, all sapient beings can reflect on what's right or wrong.

5. Therefore, all sapient beings are moral beings.
6. Free will and sapience are mutually dependent.
7. If you have free will, you must therefore be sapient, so must therefore be a moral being, so must therefore have developed morals, so it must be possible for bad things to happen to you.
8. Hence, unless bad things can happen to you, you can't have free will.

Step 5 is the weak point, because (thanks to free will) although all sapient beings *can* reflect on what's right or wrong, that doesn't mean they all *will*.

It's worth noting that if it's OK for you to make morally considerable beings suffer, you're basically greenlighting the possibility that it could be OK for *them* to do it, too. You may have had very good reasons to design a microscopic worm that burrows into the eyes of small children and makes them blind, but would you be happy if your NPCs calculated that because it's clearly your will for these worms to exist, they ought to breed billions of them and release them into city water supplies? You could actually stop them: would you? Is it only you who has final arbitration on what's right and what's wrong in the realities you create, or is it a case of "it's the NPCs' world now, not mine"?

This brings us neatly to the *Epicurean paradox*[66]. You, as god of your virtual world, either can or can't remove its evils (of which suffering would be an example). Furthermore, you either want to remove them or you don't want to remove them. We therefore have four possible cases:

- You can't remove its evils but you don't want to do so anyway. This means you're both weak and malicious.
- You can't remove its evils and you do want to do so. This just means you're weak.
- You can remove its evils but you don't want to do so. This means you're powerful but malicious.
- You can remove its evils and you do want to do so. This means you're both powerful and benevolent. However, we know you're not, because the evils haven't been removed[67].

The first two cases aren't really compatible with the notion of being a god as they imply that you can't change your created reality's physics. It depends what's meant by "can", though: it may be that you are able to remove an evil, but that in so doing too much good would be lost as a

[66] So called because the early Christian author, Lactantius, attributed it to the Ancient Greek philosopher, Epicurus.
[67] It's assumed that you're not merely lazy.

consequence[68]; you therefore leave the evil in so as not to throw the baby out with the bathwater.

The third case is a possibility but the fourth case is the most likely. You're perfectly capable of removing the evils, but to do so would cause even worse evils so you leave them in. Just make very, very sure there's no other way to achieve your ends that doesn't involve leaving the evils in.

I have one final point on this topic. If your NPCs are moral beings (whether by your definition, their definition or both), this implies they'll need to develop moral codes of their own that are appropriate for their world. Are you going to let them do so? I'm supposing here that you do want them to have free will; if you don't, you can simply hardwire in any system of ethics you please and the little automatons will act accordingly.

If you do want them to have free will, though, your NPCs will either lean towards amorality or towards morality. The latter is the one you're more likely to encourage – unless you yourself are amoral or capricious, anticipating with relish the chaos and carnage that will ensue from creating free-thinking individuals who don't consider the effects that their actions will have on others (or indeed on themselves).

---

[68] For example, in Reality we can stop so many people from dying in car accidents simply by banning cars. However, the negative economic consequences of doing this are such that we're prepared to take the hit for road deaths over the hit for having to walk everywhere.

Let's go with having NPCs who lean towards having morals, then.

When I was talking about souls, I discussed ways by which you might tip NPCs off as to the kind of behaviour that would score well when it came to their post-death judgement. You can certainly do this if you're of the opinion that you know what system of morality will work best for the reality you've created. There is another possibility, though: you don't give them any hints whatsoever, and have them work out for themselves what's good and what's bad.

If you did this, what would happen?

Well without knowing what would reward them in an afterlife, your NPCs would favour what rewards them while they live. This would create a kind of evolutionary pressure: those groups of NPCs who came up with and enforced a workable ethical code would thrive; those groups that didn't would eventually disappear. This is because if everyone does what the group determines is right, and it actually *is* right for advancing the interests of the group, then the group will flourish; if it's not right, the group will wither and have either to change or to perish. In other words, whatever rules of behaviour repeatedly work will become established as part of the group's ethical system[69].

This doesn't mean that your NPCs' ethics will necessarily be in accordance with yours. At the

---

[69] This line of reasoning led to Social Contract theory.

level of populations, for example, it could be that in a tribal society, keeping women at home as baby-making machines works better than allowing them rich, independent lives, because the more babies a population has then the faster it grows and the better able it is to conquer and subjugate its socially-liberal neighbours.

It's also worth noting that unless you were to interfere, your NPCs would almost certainly evolve different systems of ethics to yours if their reality and Reality had major dissimilarities. For example, if their world had no death, or if its inanimate objects could feel pain, this would impact on their understanding of what it is and isn't OK to do. Environment affects ethics.

As it happens, the ethics of humans in Reality have overall tended to align after a time, despite widely-different starting conditions. This may be because all gods have similar ideas for how they want us to behave, or it may be that societies that don't align tend not to last very long[70]. Even if your created reality is weirdly different to Reality, you could therefore at least expect its NPCs to develop something along the lines of the *Golden Rule*, which, depending on the direction you come at it from, can be paraphrased as either "treat others as

---

[70] "There are some moral rules that all societies must embrace, because those rules are necessary for society to exist." (Rachels & Rachels, 2019)

you would want to be treated" or "don't treat others as you wouldn't want to be treated".

Neither formulation of the Golden Rule is perfect at face value. The first one seems to suggest that someone who enjoys, say, being kissed is right to kiss you regardless of whether you yourself want to be kissed. The second one seems to suggest that self-defence is a bad thing, because if you yourself don't want to be hit, you shouldn't hit anyone else even if they're coming at you with a dagger. Either formulation can be made to work if applied at the meta-level, though[71].

Will you be treating your NPCs as you yourself would want to be treated? Or at least not treating them as you yourself wouldn't want to be treated? With such an asymmetric power difference, does the question even make sense?

Also, are you basically saying to any gods of Reality that whatever you do to your NPCs, it's morally OK for these gods to do to you?

The ethicist Margaret Somerville has written extensively about the development of a common, shared system of ethics (Somerville, 2006). She concludes that if it is to be acceptable both to spiritual and to scientific perspectives, such a system must place its foundations in nature and

[71] You'd want other people to take your preferences into account, therefore you should take theirs into account, too. Also, you wouldn't want others to let you do something wrong, therefore you shouldn't let them do something wrong, either.

the natural, this being the one area that each unequivocally respects[72]. Whether ethics are extrinsic, coming from a god, or are intrinsic to human beings as part of who we are, they are ultimately informed by a presumption that the natural world is by default how things ought to be[73]. If a particular action is proposed which entails the overriding of said default, it can only be justified if the harm done by such an intervention is outweighed by the harm undone by it.

For example, if people have no access to clean water then they will suffer; providing them with clean water runs counter to what would happen if nature were left to run its course, but it removes the suffering. Having people suffer is worse for the natural world than is providing clean water, therefore cleaning up their dirty water is ethically justified[74].

This observation has implications for virtual worlds.

When you create a reality, you, as its god, have to decide how to express your own ethics through the design of that reality. You can't avoid this, because even if you go hands-off and leave it all to

---

[72] She calls this intersection the *secular sacred*.

[73] This embraces Hume's *is-ought problem* (Hume, 1739): it's not clear how to make claims about what *ought* to be true based solely on what *is* true. In other words, you can't derive morals purely from facts.

[74] How quite we ascertain *which* effect is better for the natural world is, of course, a problem in itself.

the NPCs themselves, the very nature of the reality that you have created will determine what ethical systems the NPCs subsequently develop. *You* specified your reality's nature, so like it or not you've influenced your NPCs' thinking on this from the very beginning.

In the same way that the ethics of your NPCs are rooted in the nature of the world in which you place them, so your own ethics can be seen as rooted in the natural world – that is, in Reality. This suggests that whatever ethics you code into the virtual world (implicitly or explicitly) are unavoidably shaped by the way Reality works[75], because that's the ultimate source of your own ethics.

The thing is, the reality you create need not operate the same way as Reality. As I mentioned earlier, there could be major differences that affect what NPCs perceive to be right and wrong. For example, people in a reality with no permadeath might treat murder less seriously than we do in Reality[76]. Would it therefore still make sense to insist that your NPCs operate under the same system of Reality-based ethics that you do?

---

[75] Or, if you're a proponent of divine command theory, by the way the reality above Reality works.

[76] In a 2015 episode of the TV series *Dr Who*, the famously anti-gun central character shot and killed another Time Lord, the General. "We're on Gallifrey. Death is Time Lord for man flu."

If so then ethical systems are transitive. This would suggest that it's unethical to create a reality that is different enough from Reality that ethics founded on the nature of Reality don't apply. It would also imply that the ethics encoded in the nature of Reality are themselves representative of those encoded in the nature of any (and every) super-reality of which Reality is a sub-reality.

If your NPCs don't operate under the same system of ethics that you do then ethical systems are intransitive. On what basis, then, are you going to decide what's right and wrong for your created reality? Do we need a system of meta-ethics to direct what systems of ethics we ought to embed in our designs?

The morals of gods are not necessarily those of the beings they create.

ReLIGIOUS PLaces

So far in this book, I've avoided discussing religions as religions, because I'm primarily concerned with *gods* rather than with particular systems of organised beliefs *about* gods. I have touched on some ideas as characterised by identified religions, such as Catholicism's views on transubstantiation, but only to illustrate specific points. This, I shall continue to do. However, because so many people derive their ethics (and thence their morals) from religions, it's appropriate at this juncture to look at how virtual worlds might accommodate religions as a general concept (and *vice versa*). My purpose here is not to examine the ethical systems of religions; rather, it's to examine how religions might feature in virtual worlds such that their ethical systems can come into play.

I'll start by considering virtual worlds as places. This is first and foremost what they are; everything else flows from that.

OK, so they're places. Are they spiritual[77] places?

The reason I ask is that virtual worlds are set apart from Reality, which makes them particularly amenable to being spiritual places. As a *very* loose analogy, places exist materially and spaces exist conceptually: spaces provide the context for places, but particular places give meaning to spaces (Relph, 1976). For the people who play virtual worlds, can this meaning be somehow spiritual?

Well, the short answer is that for players at least, it's not for the designer of a virtual world to decide whether or not that world is (or contains) a spiritual place: designers are the gods of their

[77] I'm assuming here that if they're religious then they're also spiritual, but that if they're spiritual they're not necessarily religious. "Spiritual", just to clarify, means to do with the spirit, rather than with the tangible or material. It does presuppose that people have spirits (which could be detachable souls), needless to say.

worlds but not of their players. Players can and will choose for themselves to regard (or to disregard) virtual worlds as spiritual places, irrespective of what the designers of those worlds might wish. Spaces become places when they have meaning, but the meaning of a virtual place is subjective (Salazar, 2005). Such realities can certainly be venues for players from Reality to have spiritual experiences (Nagasiva, 1992), but that doesn't make them spiritual places in and of themselves.

We can nevertheless invite players to treat our created realities as spiritual places, and we can include tools to help any players who actively want to see them that way[78]. For example, the virtual world *Church of Fools*, which ran as a three-month experiment in 2004 (Kluver, 2008), was set up for this. It didn't say it *was* a sacred or spiritual place, but it had the appearance of a church and included many of the symbolic trappings of a church, and players who wanted to treat it *as* a church were welcome to do so; those who didn't were welcome not to do so, too[79].

---

[78] A poll reported in the now defunct *MUD Journal* (Allen, 1999) asked readers: "What kind of MUD would you like more of?". Of the 362 responses, 35 went with "religious theme".

[79] Just because it was a virtual church, that didn't mean it didn't attract griefers. Within 15 minutes of opening, one player character was on her knees praying and another stood in front of her so it looked as if she was performing fellatio on him. Praying characters got a social-distancing collision box around them soon after that.

It's possible that players of virtual worlds ascribe spiritual aspects to them even without deliberation. A famous (secular) definition provided by anthropologist Clifford Geertz states that a religion is:

> *(1) a system of symbols which acts to (2) establish powerful, pervasive, and long-lasting moods and motivations in men by (3) formulating conceptions of a general order of existence and (4) clothing these conceptions with such an aura of factuality that (5) the moods and motivations seem uniquely realistic.*
>
> *(Geertz, 1966)*

Applying Geertz's definition to the virtual world *DragonMUD*, anthropologist Jen Clodius found that it did indeed have a religious aspect to it (Clodius, 1995)[80]. This is despite the fact that the virtual world was not conceived by its designers as such and few players had thought of it in these terms either.

Note that Geertz's definition of what a religion is doesn't insist there be a spiritual basis to it, and that Clodius rigorously applied the definition as such[81]. Nevertheless, the players with whom she discussed the topic sensed that Geertz's definition

---

80 A similar approach is applied to *WoW* in (Vallikat, 2014).

81 You could say that she applied it religiously.

was missing any reference to an "ineffability, a certain transcendence" and she concluded that for some, *DragonMUD* had this aspect to it, too.

So for individual players, virtual worlds can definitely be spiritual or religious places, either as adjuncts to Reality (as in the *Church of Fools* example) or in their own right (as in the *DragonMUD* example). This is Reality-level spirituality, though: players may develop a feel for the non-material nature of the spirit (or soul), but it's relative to Reality, not to the virtual world; the virtual world merely helps these players come to understand their sense of self as being independent[82].

It's fair to say that most players will not experience virtual worlds in this way. For theme park worlds in particular, places are experienced superficially: they have been designed specifically to be *other-directed* (Relph, 1976), privileging appeal to visitors ahead of authenticity. If we want spirituality at the level of the virtual world, we need to have our NPCs (rather than our players) experience it.

This shouldn't actually be hard, assuming that the NPCs are free-thinking (although that *is* hard). If they think in much the same way that we humans think then some of them will naturally

[82] Or even as being-independent.

develop spiritual feelings the same way that some of us do[83].

Such feelings would, of course, be subjective. From the point of view of those of us in Reality, they could additionally be objective: we could implement an actual spirit realm or some other mechanism for maintaining the essence of an NPC separate from its physical existence. We could also program our NPCs to feel that a particular location in a virtual world was "spiritual", although we'd be messing with their free will if we did that.

In general, it depends on the individual NPC as to whether or not a place in a virtual world is spiritual, then. OK, so what about *sacred* places?

A sacred place is a place associated with the divine[84]. In Reality, natural, awe-inspiring wonders are often sacred, such as Uluru in central Australia and the Ganges in south Asia. Sites where important religious events took place are also usually sacred, for example Mount Sinai (where Moses received the Ten Commandments) and Bodh Gaya (where Siddhārtha Gautama gained enlightenment). In addition, places of worship can be made into sacred places by those people who

---

[83] If our NPCs aren't free-thinking, which is indeed the case for those of the present rather than those of the future, it's even easier: the spirituality of an object just becomes another physical property of the world that influences NPC behaviour.

[84] Or, for those who hold that all of existence is associated with the divine: *more* associated with the divine.

possess the necessary qualifications to perform the dedication ceremony.

Could a virtual world be considered sacred to someone in Reality?

The facetious answer is yes, because anyone can start a religion and decide what is and isn't sacred to it[85]. If we consider religions with adherents numbering in the millions, though, there has to be an actual reason that a place would be considered sacred.

Because many things other than places can be sacred, such as art and music, there's no theoretical objection to adding suitable virtual worlds to the list. However, as virtual worlds are places, it's in accordance with the rules for sacred places that candidates should be assessed.

They certainly wouldn't qualify under the criterion of being natural wonders, because they're artificial. If a miracle or other major divine event were to take place in one (the Second Coming in *Second Life*, for example) then that would work; none has been forthcoming yet, however, and it'll be years before we know if a saint or other holy figure has changed the nature of Reality from within *World of Warcraft*.

---

[85] Religions have been set up for players within virtual worlds. One of the early ones, the Order of the Holy Walnut, was opened in *Habitat* by a Greek Orthodox minister; its adherents were forbidden to steal, to carry weapons and to engage in violence (Farmer, 1993).

The best way for getting a virtual world to be considered a place sacred to a large number of people in Reality would be if an archbishop or similar were to consecrate it (or preferably some place within it). While in principle possible, this could in practice be quite tricky, as the necessary rituals aren't really set up for such an eventuality. For example, dedicating a church in the Church of England's Diocese of London involves starting at the west door and ... well, we're in trouble right there, as virtual worlds don't *have* an actual west, just some direction that their designer has labelled west[86].

There's nothing to prevent even long-established religions from changing their rules, of course[87], so rituals might in time be developed specifically for making particular places in virtual worlds sacred. There would have to be an appetite for it, though, and as yet there isn't. If anything, religions tend to have a less-than-favourable attitude to computer games (of which virtual worlds are considered an example), so it may be a while yet before we see virtual cathedrals appearing in them which are every bit as sacred as the ones in Reality. That said, I'm sure there are already evangelical churches out there that have

---

[86] Usually, towards negative infinity along the x-axis.

[87] After centuries of saying that babies who died unbaptised entered a state of limbo rather than going to Heaven, in 2007 the Roman Catholic church decided that actually they could go to Heaven (International Theological Commission, 2007).

virtual offshoots, so it's definitely possible (if not necessarily backed by any substantial theological argument[88]).

The more interesting question from our perspective is whether we can create virtual places that are sacred not to us but to our NPCs.

We can make natural wonders that inspire a sense of awe, that's relatively easy. We can also give certain NPCs occasional supernatural powers that enable them to perform miracles in particular places. The NPCs themselves will decide whether to make buildings or other objects of their own creation sacred or not.

Let's say there *are* some sacred places in our virtual world. What would such a designation mean?

The place would be associated with the divine, which in this case is us. Should we actually mark it out as physically different to regular places? We can, but should we? We could make visiting the place increase an NPC's lifespan, or cure an ailment, or have them feel happier, or boost their intelligence, or fill them with such emotion that it will lead them to perform wondrous acts of kindness for the remainder of their existence. We can do any of this.

Why would we? Why wouldn't we?

Are sacred places only meaningful in the context of the beliefs of the NPCs, and therefore

---

[88] Commercial argument, on the other hand....

possibly irrelevant to us – the very gods with whom the places are associated? The NPCs themselves would think not: to them, these (to us, ordinary) places are closer to us than are other places. Should we humour or reward them, perhaps implementing some positive consequences of this supposed proximity to us? If we don't, wouldn't the NPCs be largely wasting their time?

You have to decide which it is: are the holy sites in virtual worlds special to the gods of those worlds or only to the mortals?

Are the holy sites in Reality any different?

To end this section, it's worth asking (as some non-players do) if virtual worlds are *themselves* religions[89]. This question stops regarding virtual worlds as being places and instead looks on them as being constructs of the mind (which is fair enough, they're that too).

Perhaps surprisingly, virtual worlds do share many of the characteristics of religions (Wagner, 2012), including rules, rituals, liturgies, ceremonies, lore and moral compass. This doesn't *make* them religions, though. Sure, they may satisfy some of

---

[89] You could also ask (although I won't be doing this) whether religions are virtual worlds. "The vistas it [every living and healthy religion] opens and the mysteries it propounds are another world to live in; and another world to live in – whether we expect ever to pass wholly into it or no – is what we mean by having a religion." (Santayana, 1905).

the religious needs of players, but they're founded on a different basis.

The fourth and fifth points in Geertz's definition[90] suggest that followers of a religion accept as fact statements that can't be proven true. Virtual worlds require the opposite: the acceptance as fact statements that can be proven false. You may not be able to prove that Zeus exists as a material being but have faith that he does; you definitely can prove that Elune from *World of Warcraft* doesn't exist as a material being, but choose to put your denial on hold while playing the game (Dyck, 2008).

The answer, then, is no: virtual worlds are not religions to us. As with the previous examples in this section, though, having asked the question for players we can ask it again for NPCs. Can the NPCs of a virtual world regard that world as a religion?

Well, for the NPCs to view their reality as a religion would be like for us to view Reality as a religion. Most of us do have faith that Reality exists, so that's definitely a plus. Applying Geertz's full definition somewhat generously, we could say that: we interpret what our senses tell us as symbols; these symbols do seem to establish powerful, pervasive and long-lasting moods in us; we build models in our heads that are formulations

---

[90] "(4) clothing these conceptions with such an aura of factuality that (5) the moods and motivations seem uniquely realistic".

of conceptions of a general order of existence; we clothe these conceptions with an aura of factuality; in so doing, our moods and motivations seem uniquely realistic.

Applying Geertz less generously: our senses are raw, not symbolic; our moods and motivations mainly come from sources internal to the mind rather than external to it; we take our own existence as fact, rather than as a conception; we don't clothe our conceptions of perceived objects with an aura of factuality, we use them to define what factuality is; saying that Reality is realistic is mere tautology.

So yes, for our NPCs their virtual world could be seen as a religion, but if it is then it's a somewhat reductive one.

Creation Destruction

Is it OK to switch off your virtual world?

As I noted waaay back in Chapter 2, by doing so you'd obliterate hundreds, thousands, millions of sapient beings[91]. Sure, they're beings who wouldn't have existed in the first place without your

[91] As is the norm for this book now, I'm assuming this is at some point in the future when your NPCs are more intellectually advanced than at present.

largesse, but the same could be said of your children and you don't get to kill those for free.

The death you'd unleash by switching off a virtual world would be painless for the NPCs concerned, so wouldn't cause them suffering. They'd simply cease to exist. More than that: because the context in which they existed will also have ceased to exist, it would be as if they'd never existed in the first place (except in the minds of those players who still remember them).

Devoid of direct hurt though it may be, nevertheless, switching off a reality and condemning its free-thinking inhabitants to non-existence really does look a lot like mass murder[92]. Even so, if you couldn't keep the server running (perhaps because of the expense) then it might be unavoidable.

Idea! What if you were to take a dump of the virtual world at the point when it was switched off? At some later date, once you've sorted out your finances, you could reload the universe from this saved state and set it running again. To the NPCs, the downtime would be imperceptible; from their perspective, the pre-save and post-save worlds join seamlessly.

Of course, if your finances didn't improve, the virtual world might never actually be reloaded.

---

[92] Expect those of your players who have fallen in love with NPCs to assert this rather forcibly.

Even so, does having the *potential* to reload a reality mitigate the act of switching it off?

At the other extreme, how about if you were to win the lottery and find that you can now afford to reload the saved reality multiple times on different systems? Is that OK, or is forking copies of a reality somehow not doing right by the NPCs who will thus have been unknowingly duplicated?

So far, I've been talking about NPCs as NPCs. You could make some of them gods. You could create a virtual world that came with its own sub-reality. Some or all NPCs of the virtual world could be made the gods of that sub-reality. You could allow them to ascend and to descend between the two realities. You, of course, could represent in either the virtual world itself or in the world beneath it, or even in the former representing from there in the latter. The NPCs of both would remain ignorant of Reality, unless someone from Reality told them about it.

Would this be a reasonable thing to do? We'd be creating NPCs with literal godly powers over the NPCs in the reality below them. Is that morally acceptable? The NPCs we godify may not behave in an entirely benign way (the Ancient Egyptian god Apep, for example, is completely up front about personifying everything that's evil); do we ourselves have any responsibility for the consequences of their actions? Sure, after the fact we can punish our NPC gods of war for consigning countless of their own NPCs to oblivion;

nevertheless, that won't bring these NPCs back – NPCs who wouldn't have died prematurely if we'd not put a wrathful god in charge of their reality. It would be as if we'd presented a loaded machine-gun to someone who promptly used it to shoot up a shopping mall: ultimately, aren't we in some way culpable for not being more careful about choosing to whom we give the power of dealing death? Or is it entirely their fault on the grounds that they have free will?

If we do decide it's wrong to create gods who rule over sub-realities, well that would be uncomfortable. It's exactly what we're doing ourselves when we make virtual worlds: we're creating gods (in this case, us) who rule over the creatures of a sub-reality.

OK, so we're thinking about this well in advance; we can be assured that when we finally do have the capacity to make intelligent NPCs, we'll have a system of ethics in place to guarantee we don't treat them badly (or to excuse us for doing so). There is, however, a position that asserts we have no right to create morally considerable creatures for our own purposes anyway. Whether we're making them for fun, for money, for science[93] or for any other reason, it's exploitation and is therefore just plain wrong.

Now the obvious counter to this, which I've touched on once or twice already, is that the NPCs

---

[93] Or, if you prefer, "For Science!".

wouldn't even exist if we didn't create them. If an imagined future NPC has meaningful rights in the present, surely primary among those must be the right to come into being. Denying that right is effectively murder before the fact.

This does seem a fair point. For some people, though, it isn't going to wash any more than the "those bulls in the bullring wouldn't exist if we hadn't bred them for fighting" argument washes: if you're creating creatures in order to be cruel to them or to experiment on them or even to leave them to their own devices[94], you're nevertheless in some way using them[95]. It's better that you don't create them in the first place than you create them so they can be slaughtered for experience points. From some perspectives, even creating them out of love is no excuse, because it's selfish – and therefore a morally reprehensible act[96].

If creating NPCs is immoral in and of itself then clearly we shouldn't create them. Were you to create a bunch anyway, expect members of People

---

[94] Although this sounds benign, it leads to a situation similar to that of post-colonialism (Mukherjee, 2017), only potentially worse.

[95] In opposition to this, some understandings of the concept of *divine providence* assert that everything in nature has been provided for humanity's benefit, so although it may be sad to kill whales for oil lamp fuel, humanity is well within its rights to do so. This argument doesn't apply to NPCs, however, because NPCs don't appear in nature.

[96] Note that this would mean having children in Reality was also a morally reprehensible act.

for the Ethical Treatment of NPCs to be protesting outside your house and launching legal proceedings to stop you under, oh, let's say human rights legislation.

This view that it's better for NPCs not be born than to be born and exploited has parallels in Reality. The way that many domesticated animals have been bred (or, worse, inbred), they don't have much of a quality of life and wouldn't survive if released into the wild; causing their breed to die out could therefore be seen as a kindness. You don't have to kill them to do this: simply keeping apart the male and female would-be parents ought to do it. All those animals that would have been born will not be, so you'll have basically wiped them out over the course of a generation[97]; at least they won't have suffered, though.

If you take this view then the question of whether it's morally acceptable to switch a virtual world off never arises, because it's never morally acceptable to switch it on in the first place. OK, so by holding this view you're implicitly accusing the gods of Reality of being immoral for having created us, but being moral is not a precondition for being a god anyway. If they're immoral immortals, there's not a lot you can do about it.

This isn't the only objection to allowing the creation of virtual worlds that house morally

---

97 "*Meat* is murder. Vegetarianism is *genocide*." (Weinersmith, 2013).

considerable creatures. There's another, rather more theological one.

OK, so this mainly applies to the Abrahamic God, but it may resonate with other gods, too. It boils down to this: is creating virtual worlds sacrilege or is it sacred? There's no middle ground: it has to be one or the other[98].

The argument that it's sacrilege is easy to make. The designer of a virtual world is aspiring to be a god, so is exhibiting hubris. Such arrogance and false pride is a wanton and blasphemous affront to the divine, and as such is sacrilege[99].

The argument that it's sacred is also easy to make. According to the concept of *imago dei*, humans are made in the image of their creator[100] but aren't themselves their creator. Humans are not gods. By creating virtual worlds, however, they become gods, thus fulfilling their creator's plans – a sacred act. As Tolkien succinctly[101] put it: "We

---

[98] I first came across this discussion in (Kelly, 1994). Amazingly, I do remember a few of the things that I read in early books about the Internet.

[99] As an example of this view, I am indebted to respondent #47 from pick4u.com, who in response to my question "Would you buy a book with this cover?" answered: "No, I would not. It just seems like a wrong book to buy. Maybe because I am a Christian and learning how to be a God is a sin.".

[100] This is foundational in Judaism and Christianity, and is also important to some branches of Sufism in Islam.

[101] Actually, not quite as succinctly as this suggests – it's the last line of a sonnet.

may make still by the law in which we're made" (Tolkien, 1964).

Here's a rather fuller statement of the logic involved:

> *Differing as it does from* ex nihilo *creation, subcreation is not a usurping of the Creator's role, but rather cooperation with it, and acknowledgement of it. The subcreative desire is a part of human nature that precedes our fallen state, and the action and contemplation that accompanies it are both a gift and part of a divinely-mandated vocation calling us to carry out the work that God has begun.*
>
> *(Wolf, 2012)*

Hermeticism goes one step further, saying that only by making yourself equal to the transcendent god can you apprehend that god. In other words, if you want to understand God you have to be a god yourself.

This is all good news if you were worried about going to Hell for creating a virtual world.

You could nevertheless decide that if your NPCs were to create a sub-world of their own then you would send the perpetrators to whatever unpleasant place you've reserved for blasphemers. Being a god is not incompatible with being a hypocrite.

Part 4

Realities as Virtual Worlds

Chapter 8

CONNECTIONS

> *As some psychiatrist once put it, we all build castles in the air. The problems come when we try to live in them.*
>
> (Postman, 1985)[1]

Early on in this book, as part of my strategy for not getting lynched for referring to myself as a god, I introduced the idea of a reality and stated what I meant by the term: it's a self-contained space of existence that's defined, maintained and continually modified by its own physics. This is actually a surprisingly broad definition – it admits most computer programs, for example.

Another concept I've used a lot is that of a *world*, but I haven't defined it in this context; I'll therefore do that now. So: whereas a reality *is* a self-contained space, a world is an environment that its inhabitants *regard* as being self-contained. We can talk of "the world of the Hittites" or "the fashion world", for example. Such worlds can be imagined – "the world of Harry Potter" and "the

[1] Sadly, (Postman, 1985) does not cite the psychiatrist.

world of *Star Trek*" exhibit perfectly acceptable usage – and indeed we can even talk about "the world of the imagination" in abstract[2]. This means that in theory, a world can be larger than a reality if the inhabitants of that reality so regard it.

The kinds of worlds that this book concerns are those which are also realities. One such world is Reality, and most of the others are virtual worlds; I've also mentioned the possibility that virtual worlds could have their own sub-realities, and that Reality could be a sub-reality of one or more higher realities.

Although I've been talking as if these realities are also worlds, they don't have to be. For a reality also to be a world, someone of that reality has to perceive it as a world. It's conceivable, for example, that a reality above Reality might be uninhabited; this would make it a reality but not a world[3]. It could nevertheless become a world if someone from Reality were to spend some time there and come to regard it as a self-contained environment.[4]

---

[2] As indeed I did earlier, when I was discussing what NPCs with a theory of mind might speculate.

[3] We can imagine it to be a world, but then what we imagined wouldn't be a reality.

[4] The distinction between realities and worlds is apparent in the *many-worlds interpretation* of quantum mechanics. The idea here is that Reality branches with every quantum event, but we perceive only the ongoing branch that got us to where we are (that is, a world). Operating under the same laws of physics, there are unimaginably more other ongoing branches of the same event tree. In virtual world terms, it's

This brings us to the topic of the relationships that realities have (or can have) with one another.

CONSEQUENT REALITIES

Back in Chapter 4, I casually introduced the concept of a *consequent reality*. I didn't formally define it because its meaning is fairly obvious[5], but I'm now going to examine its implications a little more closely.

Our experience is that each sub-reality is the immediate sub-reality of exactly one reality, but that a single reality can have any number of sub-realities. This is clearly the case with Reality, which boasts multiple virtual worlds as sub-realities.

According to Norse cosmology, it's also the case that Reality itself is but one of several sub-realities of a higher reality. In this account, a rather large ash tree called Yggdrasil links together nine separate worlds, including Alfheim (where the elves live), Myrkheim (where the dwarfs live) and Midgard, (where we live – Reality). The gods live in

---

like forking a new, never-closing instance for every possible outcome of the random-number generator each use.

[5] OK, for the benefit of those who *don't* find it obvious: a reality S is consequent on a reality R if either S is an immediate sub-reality of R or S is an immediate sub-reality of a reality that's consequent on R.

Asgard, but regularly visit Yggdrasil as it's where their *things*[6] are held.

There are other links between the nine worlds, that bypass Yggdrasil. For example, Midgard and Asgard are directly connected by a bridge called Bifrost made from a burning rainbow; Jotunheim (where the giants live) is immediately east of Midgard and separated from Asgard by a river, Ifing. The giants can't cross the river so try to get into Asgard over Bifrost via Midgard.

Yggdrasil is the highest reality, with the others all sub-realities of it. Some of the sub-realities are interconnected; whether they're the same reality or separate ones depends on whether their physics are the same[7].

The gods, because they can operate in both Yggdrasil and Asgard, must be from Yggdrasil and merely represent in Asgard. Of course, for gods to qualify as gods they are required to be able to control the physics of a reality. This would imply that they are each able to control the physics of at least one of the nine worlds that are sub-worlds of Yggdrasil, and that the physics of each sub-world

---

[6] A "thing" is a governing assembly. The parliament of the Isle of Man is called the "Tynwald" in English and "Tinvaal" in Manx: the "tin" part derives from "thing" (*Tinvaal* is Manx for "assembly meeting-place").

[7] Humans supposedly have trouble seeing the worlds beyond Midgard, so this suggests that Jotunheim and Asgard do indeed have different physics. That would explain the burning rainbow, too.

is controlled by at least one god. That being the case, though, they shouldn't be experiencing any grief from the giants of Jotunheim (at least not unless they, the gods, had messed up somehow[8]).

We can ignore this minor irritation, though, because all the Norse gods are definitely gods with respect to Midgard (that is, Reality). Given that nowadays Reality also has sub-realities, it's therefore possible for a Norse god to show up in a virtual world, either as:

- a god of Reality;
- a player (or god) from Reality;
- an NPC of the virtual world;
- something else entirely (a raindrop, say[9]).

The Norse gods can do this because if you control the physics of a reality, you control the physics of all its sub-realities as well. We can represent in virtual worlds; if our NPCs created their own virtual worlds then we could represent in those, too, and so on through any consequent realities created by our NPCs' NPCs.

This chaining together of consequent realities is not uncommon. The Aztecs, for example, have thirteen heavens above Reality, all but the

[8] The Norse gods don't seem to be noted for flawlessness, so this is a possibility.

[9] To be honest, it's more likely to be a creature of some sort. Loki famously shape-shifted into a mare, got pregnant in this form, then gave birth to an eight-legged horse called Sleipnir.

uppermost being consequent on the heavens above them[10].

If you were to map out the relationship between realities and their sub-realities, you'd produce a tree-like structure (formally known in graph theory as an *arborescence*[11]). The one with Yggdrasil at its root would look as shown in Figure 9.

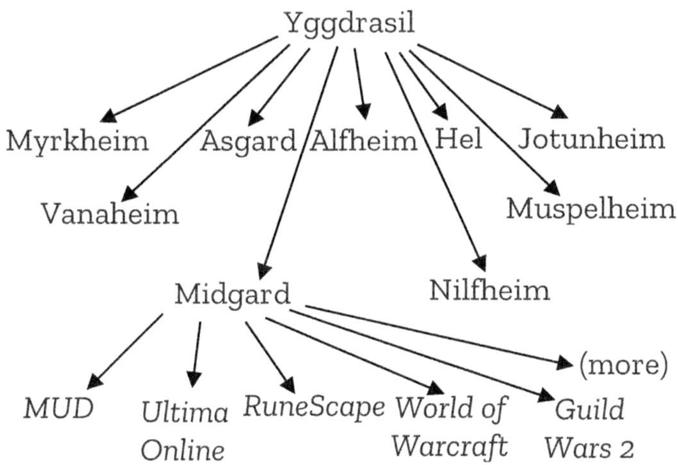

Figure 9 – Yggdrasil and its Consequent Realities.

[10] The second-highest heaven, Ilhuicatl-Teteocan, is where the gods become other people in other places while remaining themselves in Ilhuicatl-Teteocan (so, basically, where they go when they want to play in other realities).
[11] An arborescence is a form of *directed acyclic graph* that has exactly one, directed path from any node (vertex) to the root.

It doesn't have to be this way, though. As I hinted a while back, we can connect any realities consequent on Reality together.

The easiest way to do this would be if we opened a teleport between two sub-realities of Reality[12], allowing NPCs from one virtual world to visit another. When it comes to virtual worlds, this has been proposed (and even attempted) several times in the past, but the idea has always come to nothing. The problem is that connecting realities like this effectively turns two realities into one, but if they have different physics – or even the same physics but different content – then it leads to an almighty mess. A tauren[13] from *World of Warcraft* moving to the science fiction world of *EVE Online* would materialise as, well, what?[14]

Suppose, though, that NPCs in two realities consequent on Reality were to create their own sub-realities: we could arrange matters such that these were actually the same sub-reality. Their creators' realities could have different physics, but this wouldn't be important: so long as individuals from both realities could represent in the shared sub-reality, there would be no need to design any protocol to convert between the (potentially-incompatible) physics of the creators' realities.

---

[12] This is the principle behind the concept of the *Metaverse*.
[13] Cow person.
[14] If you asked *EVE Online* players, the answer would probably be "a burger".

If we so chose, we wouldn't have to rely on the NPCs to do this. We ourselves could create and connect the sub-realities right from the outset. Either way, we'd end up with a single, lower reality that is a sub-reality of two (or perhaps more) higher realities[15]. This is a much cleaner way to link together two or more realities, as it doesn't involve arguments over the prevailing physics. It does get tricky if both the sharing realities have gods of the shared sub-reality, though, because they can (accidentally or otherwise) try to change the same physics at the same time. Then again, having more than one god of a non-shared sub-reality also has this problem.

Such a multi-parent arrangement of sub-sub-realities could present something of a surprise to the NPCs of the realities so connected. Imagine you were playing *World of Warcraft* and you came across another player who was from a different reality to Reality (say, Alfheim): it would be like that. You'd be able to communicate with people from this different reality, using Azeroth as the shared sub-reality in which you both represent, but your respective realities would remain out of bounds[16].

---

[15] This would mean that the overall structure was no longer a strict arborescence, however it would remain a directed acyclic graph.

[16] It would be even worse for the programmers at Blizzard (*WoW*'s developer) if programmers in the other reality could mess with the shared/duplicated program code.

As far as I can tell, there are no examples of this kind of thing involving Reality as a sub-reality[17]. We don't seem to have people from other realities showing up in our virtual worlds, and there are no accounts of the creation of Reality that involve its being constructed from or within two[18] higher realities both of which are consequent on a third.

The third reality is necessary, by the way, so that Reality can run on hardware that's common to both its immediate super-realities. This doesn't mean that there has to be a god of that reality to build the interconnections, though – the whole set-up could arise as an artefact of its physics.

We can try other configurations, too.

Suppose that we were to create a finite set of three or more virtual worlds, all independent of each other but running on shared hardware. We could connect them in a circular fashion[19], such that each virtual world was the sub-world of exactly one other world and had exactly one sub-world itself[20]. We wouldn't give the NPCs of these

---

[17] I'd say there were none involving Reality as a super-reality, either, but then someone would go and implement two toy virtual worlds with a mutual sub-reality just to prove me wrong.

[18] Or more than two.

[19] I mean a single circle here, not several circles.

[20] I was introduced to this idea by the professor who (many years earlier) supervised my PhD, Jim Doran. He called it *Gillian's Hoop*; it was proposed to him by his daughter, Gillian, shortly before she died.

worlds god-like powers, but we would allow them some freedom of movement. We might, for example, allow them to represent in or descend to their immediate sub-reality, or to absent in or ascend to their immediate super-reality. If they did this enough times, they could wind up back in their original reality. This is because every virtual world in this system is consequent on every other virtual world plus itself[21].

Such a circular hierarchy of worlds would not necessarily need to have a holding reality to provide the common hardware upon which the component realities ran, but there would be far fewer dangers if it did have one. If Reality were part of such an arrangement, it would therefore be a sub-world of at least one reality outside the circle, which is where the god or gods of the realities in the circle would best exist[22].

We don't have any examples supporting the idea that Reality is a component of such a circular chain, but there are some established phenomena that would fit it well. The main one is that of reincarnation: following death, you would ascend to the reality preceding the one you died in, there to be reborn with no knowledge of your previous existence. Having gone round the circle a few

---

[21] This changes the structure to that of a *directed cyclic graph*.

[22] "Best" because they could exist within the realities of the circle, although this would ultimately lead to their being the gods of their own realities and so introduce all the Ptah-like problems associated with this condition.

times[23], you could eventually be ascended to the reality outside of the circle itself, so ending your cycle of death and rebirth.

To summarise, then:[24] we can make fairly arbitrarily-connected sub-worlds if they're all consequent on Reality. We haven't yet found a reason to do so, but we could do it. It would appear that no god of Reality has found a reason to do so, either.

There's a kicker, though. Remember the philosophical position of idealism, which says that only thought exists? This posits that all of Reality is a manifestation of your imagination. Put another way, you are a reality unto yourself and Reality is consequent on you.

Well, the same could be said of me, or of anyone else. We could all be our own self-contained realities, representing in our own concocted sub-realities. To each of us, that sub-reality would be Reality. The thing is, all those independent versions of Reality could be the *same* reality. One reality can, as I've just explained, be consequent on multiple realities.

So yes, perhaps the material world is a construction of the mind. That doesn't mean it can't be a construction of multiple minds, though.

---

[23] This may take awhile if the circle has an infinite number of realities in it, which is why I said it should be finite when I initially described the arrangement.

[24] I need to widen my vocabulary: this is the fifth sentence in this book that I've begun with "To summarise, then:".

If it were then would it still be the case that this construction could be said to be illusory?

GODS AND GOVERNMENTS

The last line and rallying call of the *Metaverse Manifesto* reads thus:

> *REALITY CREATORS OF ALL PLATFORMS – CREATE!*
>
> (Montagne, 2007)

The premise of this short tract, which is based on the *Communist Manifesto* (Marx & Engels, 1848), is that reality is the only commodity. Through the creation of realities, those who control Reality are rendered irrelevant.

So who controls the created realities?

I've already stated several times in this book that the goings-on in a reality are governed by its physics. This is indeed correct. There are other forms of governance involved too, however, that rest on said physics.

In theory, you can do anything that the physics of the reality you inhabit allows. Feeling hungry? Just wrench the chocolate bar from the hands of that small child. Like fire? The roof of that thatched cottage should go up a treat! Have a petty grievance with a neighbour? A few nails hammered into the tyres of their car should teach them a lesson.

In practice, although you *can* do anything that the physics of (in our case) Reality deems possible, you *won't*. Sure, your morals may get in the way, but if they don't then you're still not going to do as you might wish. This is because there are predictable consequences to your actions. Other people can also use the physics of Reality, and there are more of them than there are of you. Supernatural entities aside, these other people can't use physical abilities beyond those that you can, but they can organise to bring these abilities to bear in a concerted manner.

The way this has played out in Reality[25] is that populations are grouped by geographical region; each such region is subject to the rule of a local administration that enjoys within that region a monopoly on the *legitimate use of force* (Weber, 1919). Having a monopoly on the legitimate use of force is what makes a state a state. The ruling administration of a state is that state's *government*; governments regulate the behaviour of those they govern by enacting laws and (legitimately) using force to compel people to comply with them.

As I mentioned back in Chapter 1, individuals in a reality are therefore subject to two sets of laws: the physical laws that govern what they *could* do;

---

[25] On Earth, anyway. It may be different on other planets.

the within-the-physical laws that govern what they *can* do. It's impossible for non-gods to change or to break the former (the *laws of nature*) but possible for them to break or to change the latter (the *laws of the land*).

An important concept in governance is that of *consent*. In most developed states, the government rules by the consent of the governed: the governed may not always like the particular government of the day, but they do accept that the system by which it came into power gives it the right to govern, and thus consent to being governed by whichever batch of power-hungry outliers said system delivered this time round. If the government does *not* have the consent of those whom it governs, it's known as a *tyranny*.

When it comes to states, consent makes a difference. It's eminently possible that a popular despot is not regarded as being a tyrant yet that the leader of a badly-constructed democracy is. When it comes to physics, however, consent makes no difference at all. You may well feel that Reality is a wonderful place and so be happy to have your behaviour moderated by the laws of nature instituted by one or more gods; this means nothing when you yourself are the product of said gods, though.

The thing is, as I touched on earlier, you can't be asked to consent to being brought into existence; this is because until you *are* brought into existence there's no "you" to be asked, let alone to consent.

Once you have been brought into existence, you become part of the fabric of the reality in which you now exist; if you don't consent to being regulated by its physics, you're effectively not consenting to exist; if you don't consent to existing, well it's rather too late to do anything about that[26].

The people of a reality have no say in determining the laws of nature that govern them, because these laws are part of who they are. Their consent, whether given or not, is therefore utterly immaterial (in both senses of the word). This means that those who made the laws of nature – the gods of the reality – are tyrants. They may be popular, but they're still tyrants.

As it happens, at least some gods of virtual worlds have historically been aware of this and have endeavoured to cede control of their worlds to others.

Some time ago, when discussing pandeism, I mentioned *LambdaMOO*. The god of this social world, Pavel Curtis, was uncomfortable in his role precisely because he felt he was effectively a tyrant. He therefore sought to relinquish control to the world's players[27].

---

[26] Depending on the reality, there may be options available to you to cease to exist. It would literally be suicidal to take them, though.

[27] Not to its NPCs, because these weren't sapient. Note that this neatly avoids the problems you get when individuals, in changing the physics of their reality, thereby change

Similar approaches have been attempted since then, most notably with *EVE Online*. All have broken down. The fact is that any power given to the players is merely illusory. In *LambdaMOO*'s case, the players couldn't agree on a form of government to be implemented, and when Pavel sought to impose one there were complaints that he was "dictatorially imposing universal suffrage on an unconsulted populace" (Dibbell, 1993). In *EVE Online*'s case, it became clear that although the gods may wish to act merely as coders implementing the will of the players, sooner or later the players will request something that the gods can – but don't want to – give to them[28]. Such a request could be a change that undermines the system of government, say, or that completely alters the balance or character of the world, or that will haemorrhage players. Whatever it is, the gods will feel that the consequences are too drastic to contemplate and therefore will decline to implement the required modification. At this point, the veneer of player control cracks and it's clear once again that the gods really *are* gods.

As a compromise, it's possible to give players a fair degree of control over the governance of their game while nevertheless making it crystal clear

---

themselves: the physics of a player's own existence wasn't challenged by changes to the physics of their character's existence.

[28] This is known as *asking for a pony*.

that the gods have a veto. This is how *EVE Online*'s Council of Stellar Management now works, and how *A Tale in the Desert*'s Pharaoh has always worked. Players have a voice, but ultimately don't have a say.

This kind of system, while being more open to player involvement, nevertheless falls well short of what early academic opinion advocated as the ideal[29]. The reason it falls short is that two principles pertain which together mean gods and governments can never be fully reconciled when it comes to the rulership of a virtual world:

1. Governments can be deposed by those they govern; gods can't.
2. Governments can relinquish their powers; gods can't.

The first rule says that the gods of a reality can do whatever they like in and to it. The second rule says that the first rule is true regardless of whether said gods wish it to be true[30].

Now that we've clarified the two types of governance at work here, it's possible to consider the power hierarchy that this implies. Starting at

---

[29] For example (Humphreys, 2005) (Taylor, 2006).

[30] The gods of *LambdaMOO* didn't wish it to be true, and on 9th December, 1992, handed power to their players. This didn't work out, because even minor changes to the physics often had social consequences (Hess, 2003). On 16th May, 1996, they took back power by fiat – which, given that they were able to do this, verified that they'd never truly given up power in the first place.

the level of virtual worlds and going up from there, we have the following laws in play for (potentially) sapient beings:

- Laws of the land of the virtual world, set by NPCs in the virtual world, applied to NPCs.
- Laws of nature of the virtual world, set by the gods of the virtual world, applied to its NPCs.
- Laws of the land of Reality, set by human beings in Reality, applied to human beings in Reality (including those who are gods of virtual worlds).
- Laws of nature of Reality, set by the gods of Reality[31], applied to human beings in Reality (including those who are gods of virtual worlds).
- Laws of the land of the super-reality that's inhabited by the gods of Reality, set by the inhabitants of this super-reality, applied to the inhabitants of this super-reality (including those who are gods of Reality).
- Laws of nature of the super-reality that's inhabited by the gods of Reality, set by the gods of this super-reality[32], applied to the inhabitants of this super-reality (including those who are gods of Reality).

---

[31] These may number from zero, through one, to many. For clarity of writing, in this exercise I'll go with many.

[32] So as not to provoke an infinite series, I'll assume these to number zero.

If you're an NPC in a virtual world and something bad happens that you wish to be redressed, this gives you a surprisingly large range of options. You can appeal to the government of your part of the virtual world; if that fails, you can appeal to the gods of the virtual world (its designers); if that fails, you can appeal to the relevant jurisdiction in Reality that covers where the gods live (assuming an open communication channel); if that fails, you can appeal to a god of Reality (praying is the favoured method from Reality, so hey, why wouldn't it work from a virtual world?); if that fails, you can appeal to the government of the transcendent reality in which the gods of Reality live (should there be one). If *that* fails, OK, only then are you properly stuffed.

If a virtual world's NPCs are permitted to absent in Reality, this raises the possibility that they could take a god of their world to court to address the NPCs' grievances. How would such a court handle, say, a complaint that the way a designer implemented death and aging meant that NPCs were effectively being slowly and painfully executed over time?

Oh, and by the way, law-makers, be careful that you don't tie designers' hands too much: if your directives remove a designer's ability to act as the god of a reality, *you* become the gods of that reality yourselves. You do know how to design realities, yes?[33]

This raises the issue of whether Reality's laws of the land should apply to sub-realities or not. Reality forbids theft: should theft in virtual worlds be forbidden? If so, well Reality also forbids murder, but given that death in virtual worlds is rarely as fatal as it is here, is the mapping still good? How different would a world have to be before a law of Reality could be said not to apply to it?

If we wish, we as gods can make a sub-reality's laws of the land become laws of nature. Reality's physics may not code-in the concept of democracy, but that doesn't mean a virtual world's physics can't. We could enfranchise every adult NPC and make elections impossible to corrupt: "who the president is" could be determined by a law of nature rather than by a law of the land. This isn't far-fetched: medieval monarchs ruled by divine right, which is a law of nature rather than a law of the land – although armies did tend to be used to verify that the law of nature was being applied to the correct people. Somewhat ironically, if we as gods didn't approve of the notion of rule by divine right then we could use our godly powers to

---

[33] In my book *Designing Virtual Worlds*, I asked the question "Should those lacking a god's motivation assume a god's powers?" (Bartle, 2003). I didn't answer it.

ensure that all the governments in our virtual worlds were secular[34].

The same applies to ethical values, by the way. Just because these "are not objective, are not part of the fabric of the world" (Mackie, 1977), that doesn't mean we can't weave them into the fabric of a world we have created.

Lest you think this is all well-trodden ground, it's not. Religious Studies currently uses three methodologies to provide structure for the analysis of religions:

- *Phenomenology* – founded on the observable characteristics of a religion (sacrifice, ritual, sacred places and so on) and how they fit together.
- *Lived Religion* – using principles of ethnography to observe what the followers of a religion believe and do.
- *Functionalism* – examining how the practical aspects of a religion work (not eating pork in a hot country reduces the incidence of food poisoning).

To these, we can now add a fourth:

- *Inductivism* – if you were creating a reality, how and why would you create it, and what religions would arise as a result?

---

[34] There are many varieties of secularism (Copson, 2017), but all have the overall aim of protecting the state and religion from each other.

This last one is actually used by designers (if not theologians) as a matter of course[35].

I'll end this chapter with two questions that I'm not going to answer: they're just for you.

Firstly, suppose you created a virtual world with sapient NPCs: would you want to code-in a divine right of NPC monarchs to rule?

Secondly, how would you feel about being told by a government in Reality that you had to code-in democracy regardless?[36]

---

[35] See (Garriott & Fisher, 2017) for a description of how the religions of the *Ultima* universe were designed.

[36] In 2008, I asked this at a workshop attended by indie designers of virtual worlds. So as not to prejudice your own response, I won't discuss here how they answered; I will, however, reveal that they all answered the same way.

Chapter 9

POINT OF YOU

Recently, a friend of mine was rushed to hospital complaining of chest pains. Worried that he might die, his wife asked us to pray that it wasn't a heart attack.

How would that have worked, then? Prayers in the present can influence events of the past? Is that even implementable? The past has a very long reach; the effects of events ripple out for all eternity. Undoing an event undoes all the events that follow from it; the present would therefore play out differently, and this would be noticeable.

Consider, for example, the case of a missing child. It's not uncommon to hear of parents praying that their loved one will be found alive, even though the child might well already be dead. If the child is indeed dead, how would a god grant the prayer without changing the past? Yet if the past is changed, so is the present. Suppose someone had killed the child and cremated the body, yet now suddenly the child is shown on TV being reunited with grateful family members; the murderer would know that something supernatural was going on, yet we never hear reports (or even rumours) alleging this. Another way the prayer could be answered is to prevent the murderer from killing the child in the first place; this sounds easy enough to arrange, but then every action the murderer performed afterwards would have to be unwound too – all of which would also have consequences. The now-unkilled child could well arrive home safe and sound when they were expected to do so, meaning the very prayer that saved them wouldn't itself ever have been issued[1].

I'm not saying that this can't be worked around[2]. What I am saying is that if we wanted to be able to do this kind of thing in answer to the prayers of NPCs in our virtual worlds it would be extremely non-trivial and possibly even paradoxical. Furthermore, these same issues necessarily dog whoever is tasked with responding to prayers in Reality (if anyone).

At this point, you've read enough of this book to know where I've been going with it. It's now time to look at the implications.

---

[1] Note that this is theoretically possible to arrange through closed time-like curves (basically time travel), but the recalibration of events that would be necessary to preserve the causal chain may well lead to a worse outcome (Tobar & Costa, 2020).

[2] You *might* be able to do it by reloading a saved state and changing just the right variables to achieve the desired effect while containing the spread of undesired effects. For some (possibly most) requests, though, that could prove to be logically impossible.

Oh, my friend hadn't had a heart attack, by the way. That's the power of either prayer or serendipity for you.

MOTIVATION

> *May we not conceive each of us living beings to be a puppet of the Gods, either their plaything only, or created with a purpose – which of the two we cannot certainly know?*
>
> (Plato, trans. 1892)

I've answered the question of *how* gods create realities, but what I haven't done is answer the question of *why* they create them[3]. Most creator gods of Reality are surprisingly coy about why they did what they did, but fortunately for us most creators of virtual worlds are not.

I know why I created my own reality, *MUD*: I didn't like Reality. Constructing a heaven so as to escape from a hell isn't the only reason that people

[3] There is a philosophical argument (Suits, 1978) that without play there can be no *ideal of existence* – that thing, the only justification for which is that it justifies everything else. Furthermore, games are precisely what distinguish an ideal of existence *from* said everything else. This is therefore not quite as rhetorical a question as it might at first appear to be.

create realities, though[4]. If we use paracosms as our starting point, there's quite a range:

> *Why did authors find it necessary to invent other worlds? Usually, the answer lies in changing Primary World defaults, to amaze, entertain, satirize, propose possibilities, or simply make an audience more aware of defaults they take for granted.*
>
> (Wolf, 2012)

The first thing to note when it comes to thinking about why anyone would create a reality is that there are different extents of creation. A god can:

- Create all of the physics and the content, building the reality from scratch. This is what Roy Trubshaw and I did with *MUD*.
- Add to and improve existing physics and content, by taking the code for a working reality and modifying it. *LegendMUD*, for example, started out as a modified version of the Merc 2.0b codebase, which itself was derived from *DikuMUD* (Koster, 2018)[5].

---

[4] Readers who were alarmed at my suggestion in Chapter 5 that Heaven could be a hell can therefore breathe easy.

[5] The lead designer of *LegendMUD*, Raph Koster, is one of the pre-eminent figures in virtual world thinking, having also been the lead designer of *Ultima Online* and creative director of *Star Wars Galaxies*. If you're even remotely interested in

- Take an existing reality and run it with no changes. This is what most of the (several thousand) people who ran copies of *DikuMUD* or *TinyMUD*[6] in the 1990s did.

I mention this because different extents of creation have different motivations. Someone who simply wanted to play with their friends in their own, personal reality would only need to obtain the code for an existing reality and boot it up on a new server. Someone who saw creative opportunities in an existing world might take the code and modify it, better to suit their aesthetics of play. Someone who wanted to create an original world with original content to make an original statement would have to construct their reality lock, stock and barrel. It's probable that anyone who did the latter would previously have done one or both of the former, thereby migrating from player to player-as-designer to designer.

External factors can also have influence: someone without programming skills (nor access to enough money to pay someone who does have programming skills[7]) couldn't easily create a

---

the kind of things designers think about when they create and run virtual worlds, read (Koster, 2018).

[6] *TinyMUD* was a social world, all about building your own content as a player.

[7] Games programmers are paid less than non-games programmers. In 2021, for example, the median salary for a programmer in the UK was £31,087 (Payscale, 2021); the

virtual world from first principles. Nevertheless, the possible extents of creation still hold true. Thus, if we detect among the god(s) of Reality a desire to potter around making changes to an earlier version, we can be quietly confident that Reality is the equivalent of a stock MUD.

As an illustration, consider the gods of Ancient Greece (Zeus and the gang). They don't seem to have made many changes to Reality themselves, but rather to have wrested the running of it from the titans, who in turn got it from the set of primordial gods who actually created it in the first place. In virtual world terms, the primordial gods (Gaia, Tartarus, Eros and possibly Erebus[8]) coded Reality from scratch, then the titans booted up a copy and modded it by adding concepts such as mortality, then the current gods took over its operation and only made minor updates to address player guile[9].

It's tempting at this point to brainstorm a bunch of primary and secondary reasons that people might have for creating a reality, then just list them and say "*voilà!*". You can start with

---

median salary for a games programmer was £26,954 (Payscale, 2021).

[8] Also possibly Hemera and Nyx; it depends on which account you find the most credible.

[9] For example, in a move that seems to be wearily popular among gods, Zeus flooded the entire planet and killed all humans except Deucalion and Pyrrha. This would be called a *server wipe* if applied to a virtual world.

accounts of the creation of Reality, bolster these with statements from the designers both of paracosms and of virtual worlds, then add in a few more that seem plausible and you're done. I have indeed conducted this exercise (revealed anon).

The thing is, though, that if you pay attention to what you're doing when you engage in such an analysis, you'll notice that the motivations for creating realities depend to a large extent on the reality's target audience.

See, when you create a reality as a deliberate act (as opposed to: by accident[10]; as the outcome of pursuing a higher purpose[11]; or as a consequence of your own existence[12]) and do create it to be a reality (as opposed to a purely objective scientific object[13] or as an adjunct to Reality[14]), you're creating it *for* someone. Now to some extent, every deliberate act is ultimately done for personal reasons, because your own mind is all you truly know. Nevertheless, reality-creating is often (but

---

[10] "Oh no, my cat brushed up against the screen and touched the 'big bang' icon!".

[11] The Hindu concept of *Lila* suggests that Reality was created through the higher purpose of divine play.

[12] In the same way that my being dashingly handsome is a passive trait.

[13] Just as we don't think of Conway's game of *Life* as implementing significant realities, a god in a higher reality could consider Reality as merely a cellular automaton for computing the meaning of life, the universe and everything.

[14] Meeting venues such as *Gather* usually fit this criterion.

not always) for the perceived greater benefit of someone else.

As for whom this target "someone else" might be, there are four general categories into which they fall; I've labelled these relative to your role as the designer:

- *Divine*. You're creating a reality for the benefit of the sapient beings who will be native to it.[15]
- *Personal*. There is no "someone else": you're creating a reality for your own benefit.
- *Social*. You're creating a reality for the benefit of other sapient beings of your own reality.
- *Spiritual*. You're creating a reality for the benefit of the god(s) of your own reality.

It's also possible that you could be creating for one or more *specific* beings from these categories. This is obviously the case with the personal category because the specific being is you yourself, but it also applies to the other categories. You could, for example, be creating for a particular god among many[16], or for close family members, or for a favoured NPC[17]. I'll nevertheless absorb these

---

[15] Note that the NPCs themselves will nevertheless owe you nothing whatsoever. For an explanation as to why, see Stanisław Lem's short story *Non Serviam* (Lem, 1979).

[16] "This one's for you, Thor!".

[17] There is some suggestion in books of hadith that Allah wouldn't have created the world but for Muhammad,

into the general categories, because otherwise this section is going to pan out at twice its current length; keep in mind that there could be subtleties involved, though.

The above general categories are vaguely ordered in ascending levels of consequence. In practice, however, most virtual world designers seem to create for either a personal or social motivation, whereas most gods of Reality seem to create for either a personal or divine motivation. Because of this, a more accessible ordering of the target audience categories is: personal, social, divine, spiritual.

I shall shortly be presenting a list of motivations for creating realities. This list is organised in part by the above target audience categories (in order of accessibility) and in part by the reality's intended purpose. I obtained the list by enumerating all the plausible reasons for creating realities that I could find or think of (as described earlier), then grouping them by purpose, then within each purpose associating the collected motivations with one of the four audience categories. I merged some similar entries together and the result, while not exhaustive[18], is still fairly thorough.

---

however scholars of Islam disagree over the reliability and interpretation of this assertion.

[18] It doesn't encompass "creating a reality for revenge", for example.

When a purpose was missing an obvious entry for a category, I speculated on what that entry might look like. This issue only really arose for entries in the divine and spiritual categories, as our NPCs aren't yet clever enough to take advantage of everything offered them (so we don't create for them), and gods of Reality are resolute that there's no reality above their own (so never themselves create for higher gods).

If my past experience is anything to go by, as soon as people see a list they want to add to it[19]; in this particular case they're welcome to do so. My intention is not to construct a definitive set of motivations for creating realities, but rather to construct a reasonably representative one that will catch the majority of them.

What follows, then, are the purposes I've identified for which realities are created (there are eight of them), each broken down into the four categories of beneficiary, with examples of the associated motivations:

---

[19] I wrote one of the foundational academic papers of Game Studies, (Bartle, 1996), in which I explained why people playing virtual worlds for fun find them fun. The paper regularly saw attacks along the lines of "but you missed out *this* kind of player" which, as the player types were intended to be exhaustive, constituted a problem. I duly modified the theory, but it wasn't until I wrote (Bartle, 2009), addressing its misuses, that the criticism abated.

To prototype.

- *For You (Personal)*. You create a reality to test out some ideas or to assuage your curiosity before designing the full-blown reality you *really* want to make. One of my PhD students did this; fortunately (for his thesis), he determined that following it up with a large-scale world was unnecessary.
- *For Others (Social)*. You create a reality for your players to playtest, so as to propose and identify possibilities. This is the *beta test* stage that most commercial MMORPGs go through[20]. Some players are serial beta-testers for successive virtual worlds, rarely playing released versions.
- *For your NPCs (Divine)*. You create a reality for its creatures to try out. If they're lucky, you might even change the world for them, based on their suggestions. We don't do this for virtual worlds as yet, because our NPCs aren't smart enough to have opinions. Few of Reality's gods seem to regard Reality as being in a test-edit cycle, either, although it could be argued that the Hindu gods'

---

[20] Sometimes it's called an *alpha test* to give the players the impression they're getting in really early, but it's still a beta test....

system of successive creation of and destruction of the universe allows for this[21].

- *For a Higher Being (Spiritual)*. You create a reality for the god or gods of your own reality to approve or disapprove of. As far as I know, no creator of a virtual world has ever had this reason for building a prototype; however, given how tetchy some gods can be if they sense false gods on the horizon, I suppose a developer could think it prudent to get their world rubber-stamped first. If the gods like it, you make the full version. If they don't like it, expect either a supernatural sign informing you of the fact or, upon your death, an eternity in a disagreeable place.

To profit.

- *For You (Personal)*. You create a reality to make money. You might have gone in with noble intentions, but now it's just a job. You create realities because if you don't then your children will have no shoes. There is a surfeit of people in the MMORPG industry creating realities primarily to earn a wage.

[21] We're at present in *Kali Yuga*, the fourth and last epoch of the current *kalpa* (cycle). This suggests that if you're planning to do anything 432,000 or more years from now, you can forget it.

- *For Others (Social)*. You create a reality so that your players can make money. OK, so this is properly a secondary reason (in general, those who want their players to make money are calculating that they in turn can make more money), but some virtual worlds are specifically built around the concept of a player economy that redeems fiat currencies such as dollars; *Entropia Universe* is probably the best-known.
- *For your NPCs (Divine)*. You create a reality so that its inhabitants can serve you. The Babylonian god Marduk seems to have created human beings to fulfil this ambition[22] so that he and the other gods could live lives of ease while we were bearing all the burdens. Thus, although Reality was created "for" us humans, we weren't actually expected to gain from it[23].
- *For a Higher Being (Spiritual)*. You create a reality to provide value to the creator of your own reality. No god of Reality currently appears to be part of such a supply chain, but if the NPCs of our virtual worlds are ever inventive enough to create

---

[22] It's not clear whether he created Reality in order that he could create human beings to live there, but I bet he did....
[23] If you're into enslaving entire populations of NPCs, Marduk is the role-model god for you.

their own consequent realities then we could easily sell our players access to these (and perhaps reward the NPCs in their own context to encourage them to make some more).

To learn.

- *For You (Personal).* You create a reality to learn how to do so, or to speculate how other realities might be, or to grasp the utility of a new interface, or simply because it's fun[24]. My students who create virtual worlds as projects slot right in here.
- *For Others (Social).* You create a reality to simulate some aspect of your own reality through the behaviour of its players[25], in order to predict possible outcomes. The virtual world *Arden* was explicitly designed as a petri dish to test economic theories (Castronova, 2008).[26]
- *For your NPCs (Divine).* You create a reality so that the creatures of that reality can improve their character. The Yoruba god Olodumare breathed life into the first people for this reason.

---

[24] The relationship between learning and fun is well-established for games and play (Koster, 2013).

[25] It's therefore designed "for" the players, but not necessarily for their immediate benefit.

[26] The general validity of such virtual-to-real mappings is discussed at length in (Williams, 2010).

- *For a Higher Being (Spiritual).* You create a reality in order discover more about and to honour the creator of your own reality. This seems to have been part of the motivation behind the short-lived 2010 MMO, *The Bible Online*.

To teach.

- *For You (Personal).* You create a reality in order to teach yourself something else in the process. I know a former *MUD* player who did exactly this to teach himself programming[27].
- *For Others (Social).* You create a reality as a *serious game*, to teach its players skills or to alert them to the defaults of your own reality. There are several educational virtual worlds; *CMX*, for example, teaches its players how to program in C[28] (Malliarakis, et al., 2017).
- *For your NPCs (Divine).* You create a reality so that the beings of that reality can be taught. The Incan god Viracocha really takes this to heart, walking Reality disguised as a beggar so as to teach us the basics of civilisation[29].

---

[27] Perhaps unsurprisingly, programming and virtual worlds are good pedagogical bedfellows.
[28] See?
[29] He clearly hasn't finished yet.

- *For a Higher Being (Spiritual)*. You create a reality in order to preserve and honour those who have lived and died in your own reality. This is the idea behind *ancestor-simulation*[30].

To help personal growth.

- *For You (Personal)*. You create a reality to expand yourself (Newsome-Ward & Ng, 2021) or to make yourself manifest. Jonathan Edwards, the foremost Puritan-era theologian of America, argued that this is the *ultimate end* goal God had when creating Reality (Edwards, 1765); other goals (such as being glorified) derive from it.
- *For Others (Social)*. You create a reality so that players from your own reality can positively transform themselves. This was the core motivation behind *Second Life* (Rosedale, 2009)[31], and virtual worlds have

[30] There's a hypothesis, by the way, that unless we ourselves are living in an ancestor-simulation, our descendants will almost certainly never run one (Bostrom, 2003). A competing hypothesis says that if we ourselves create a simulated reality, the probability that we are living in one is almost zero (Kipping, 2020).

[31] "... my best definition of our mission is that we are working to create an online world having the exceptional property that it advances the capabilities of the many people that use it, and by doing so affects and transforms them in a positive way." Philip Rosedale, writing as Philip Linden.

long acted as rites of passage (Schaap, 2002). Additionally, they can serve therapeutic purposes: *JennyMUSH* was created as a virtual crisis centre for people subjected to sexual abuse in Reality (Reid, 1996)[32].

- *For your NPCs (Divine)*. You create a reality in order to allow the best creatures of that reality to be rewarded[33]. Unfortunately, although judging souls is fabulously popular among the gods of Reality, I can find none that created Reality first and foremost so that they could perform such judging[34]. However, having seen how people use genetic algorithms in Artificial Intelligence, it's only a matter of time before someone tries this for a virtual world.
- *For a Higher Being (Spiritual)*. You create a reality in order to extend your creator (or your creator's creation). The logic here is that by creating realities consequent on your own, you are instantiating more of

---

[32] *JennyMUSH* was itself griefed by an individual who snuck in and carried on the sexual abuse virtually (Reid, 1994). You really do have to worry about the minds of some people.

[33] The worst creatures may not fare so well.

[34] It may be a secondary motivation derived from a primary motivation, though. For example, *The Qur'an* (67:2) suggests that Allah created death and life to test as to which of us is best in conduct, but this doesn't imply that that's why he created all of Reality.

your creator (or of your creator's creation). I don't see this idea gaining traction any time soon, but it would make a decent science fiction story[35].

To be enjoyed.

- *For You (Personal)*. You create a reality that you yourself want to play (or to play with[36] for fun). This is typical of players rather than of designers. Example: unmodified stock MUDs in the 1990s.
- *For Others (Social)*. You create a reality for others to play so as to entertain or to engage them. Genuinely free[37] game worlds such as *DikuMUD* were built for this purpose.
- *For your NPCs (Divine)*. You create a reality to give the gift of life to your creations. This is reportedly why Odin did it.
- *For a Higher Being (Spiritual)*. You create a reality as an offering to your own reality's creator, who can play it (or at least be present in it) and so give it their blessing. Some of the church worlds, such as *Church*

---

[35] Probably one in which some evangelical church raises vast amounts of money to run more and more virtual world servers, only for it to transpire that the whole exercise is a front for a cryptocurrency-mining operation.

[36] "The creative mind plays with the objects it loves" (Jung, 1923).

[37] As opposed to free-to-play, which equates to profit-seeking.

of Fools, seem to have been set up with this at least partly in mind.

To make an artistic point.

- *For You (Personal)*. You create a reality to express and behold some aspect of yourself that you can only explicate through this medium. The phenomenon can be observed playing out between virtual world designers in the form of artistic dialectics, such as the one twixt sandbox worlds and theme park worlds.
- *For Others (Social)*. You create a reality to satirise, allegorise or otherwise comment upon the reality in which you live. This is the objective behind many early paracosms, such as Thomas More's *Utopia* (More, trans. 1901), and it features in some text MUDs[38].
- *For your NPCs (Divine)*. You create a reality to be glorified by the creatures of that reality, so they may know you. According to Roman Catholic doctrine, this is God's motivation for creating Reality.
- *For a Higher Being (Spiritual)*. You create a reality to demonstrate (if there's a higher reality) or disclose (if there isn't) your sovereignty[39]. This is in line with most

[38] Satire provides the context for one of the three kingdoms in the MUD *3Kingdoms*, for example.

[39] In the sense of having supremacy over your own life.

monotheist theology, because if a god is the only entity in or of their own reality, everything they do must be such an act of sovereignty-disclosure by definition.

To become a creator.

- *For You (Personal).* You create a reality to prove to yourself or to showcase to others that you are someone who can create in this medium. The Mayan gods Kukulkán and Tepeu created Reality (or at least the humans in it) specifically to preserve their legacy.
- *For Others (Social).* You create a reality so that those who play it can create and shape their own realities within it or become otherwise inspired. This is the goal of social virtual worlds such as the MOOs, MUSHes and MUCKs of the 1990s[40].
- *For your NPCs (Divine).* You create a reality so that the creatures of that reality may worship you. This is for their benefit, not for yours: unless you're exceptionally vain you

---

[40] To spare your happiness, I didn't go into the history of virtual worlds earlier in quite as much tedious detail as I could have done. If you nevertheless *want* the tedious detail, see Chapter 1 of (Bartle, 2016). Briefly, MOOs, MUSHes and MUCKs were *TinyMUD* descendants and as such had no gameplay to them; this allowed their designers to furnish their players with supernatural abilities powerful enough for them to sub-create worlds if they so desired.

don't actually *need* to be worshipped, but through worshipping you your creations can achieve a sense of peace and purpose. This seems to be the reason that Allah created Reality[41].

- *For a Higher Being (Spiritual).* You create a reality so as to impress upon your creator that you, too, are a creator. For example, were you to create a reality explicitly to fulfil your creator's dictum that you were created in their image (*imago dei*), you would fit right here. As far as I can tell, though, nothing like this has yet happened. I'd certainly be impressed if my own NPCs somehow managed it, though.

In the event that you lost track of all these lists of bullet points and would really like to see a condensed version, Figure 10 provides an overall summary of the motivations (badly).

[41] It's definitely why he created human beings (and jinn); as to whether it's why he created the entire universe, well most of what I've read on the subject suggests that it is but I'm happy to defer to actual experts if it turns out I've got it wrong.

	For You	For Others	For your NPCs	For a Higher Being
Prototype	To test out your ideas.	To let playtesters identify options.	To find out if your NPCs like it.	To see if the gods of your own reality approve.
Profit	To make money yourself.	So your players can make money.	So your NPCs can serve you.	To provide value to the god(s) of your reality.
Learn	To learn how to create a reality.	To simulate your own reality.	So your NPCs can improve themselves.	To honour your own reality's creator(s).
Teach	To teach yourself a different thing.	As a serious game.	To instruct your NPCs.	To honour the dead of your own reality.
Growth	To expand yourself.	So that players can transform.	To reward the best of your NPCs.	To extend your creator or their creation.
Enjoy	So you can play it for fun.	To entertain your players.	To give the gift of life.	As an offering to a higher being.
Art	To express yourself.	To satirise your own reality.	To be glorified by your creations.	To demonstrate your own sovereignty.
Create	To prove that you can make realities.	So others can create sub-realities.	To be worshipped by your creations.	To show your creator that you are a creator.

Figure 10 – Motivations Summarised (Badly).

Here begins an aside.

It's not important to what I want to say, but these eight motivations pair up with each other:

- *Realities as product.*
  To prototype.
  To profit.
- *Realities as tools.*
  To learn.
  To teach.
- *Realities as destination.*
  To help personal growth.
  To be enjoyed.
- *Realities as communication.*
  To make an artistic point.
  To become a creator.

Realities as product objectifies both players and content.

Realities as tools objectifies players and subjectifies content.

Realities as destination subjectifies players and objectifies content.

Realities as communication subjectifies both players and content.

You can draw these pairings as a 2D graph if you want, but I'll leave that as an exercise[42]. At the level of individual pairs of motivations, you could further create a 3D graph by adding an

---

[42] I don't want to give the impression that I see such graphs wherever I look. That said, the Well How About That section of this chapter perhaps exposes the sad truth.

input/output axis (prototyping, learning, personal growth and artistic points are input; the rest are output).

Weirdly, these pairings map directly onto the virtual world interface conventions I described in Chapter 5: non-diegetic, spatial, meta and diegetic respectively. That's rather cool[43].

Here ends an aside.

One of the contributing reasons I've left it late to discuss motivations is that they draw on so many concepts that it's taken the bulk of this book to cover them all. The main reason, though, is that I wanted to make a point that I couldn't make until now.

The thing is, the motivations we have for creating virtual worlds are equally applicable to any god or gods who may or may not have created Reality. We can choose to believe that Reality was created for our pleasure, or our torment, or our spiritual development, but we could actually be living in a student project or a serious game or a commercial product. As the opening quote from Plato suggested, we don't know – how could we?

Of course, some fortunate few of us may have been addressed by a god directly, but any being with godly powers could tell us anything at all and we'd have no way of discerning whether or not they were being truthful. If you were making a

[43] Inexplicable, but cool.

virtual world just for you and your friends to play for fun, you could hoodwink the NPCs by making up all kinds of sincere nonsense about your motivation – they'd have absolutely no way to gainsay it[44]. Even if you didn't tell them a thing, the chances are they'd make something up themselves. It's like this with Reality: whatever its creator (if it has one) may tell us about why they created it need have no basis in truth. I'm not saying it doesn't; I'm merely pointing out that it's not a given.

I have two more points to make before moving on.

Firstly, motivations for creating a reality are not necessarily motivations for continuing to run it. Reality could be a failed or botched experiment that will shortly be terminated. It could be a work in progress that will be patched at a future date. It could be a prototype or A/B test that is scheduled to be closed down at a certain date when sufficient information has been gathered. It could be a legacy project that's receiving no updates but the servers are kept running because it would be morally wrong to kill us all by switching them off. Just because Reality may have been *created* to determine which 144,000 of us gets to live on in a

[44] "My studies in old books in the priest salon at Silvermoon had uncovered a legend that some gifted people could communicate indirectly, via a being called a 'player' and a channel called 'Internet'." (Bainbridge, 2010).

wondrous afterlife[45], that doesn't mean that this is *still* why Reality exists.

My second point is that it's possible to have several motivations for making a reality, perhaps with different target audiences. These may work with, for or against each other in the service of a greater, overarching motivation. With *MUD*, for example, I did want players to find the virtual world fun (enjoy: for others), but this was because I wanted them to be free to become themselves (growth: for others). That's not the end of the story, either.

Unfortunately, because my teenaged self didn't engage in much analysis of why I was doing what I was doing, I'm having to reflect today on what my thoughts were at the time and so construct a *post hoc* explanation; it's therefore susceptible to inadvertent manipulation by my current self to fit my agenda. That said, it seems to me that I wanted to make *MUD* as an act of rebellion: I was telling Reality to fuck off. *I* could make a better, fairer, more just reality than the one I was living in, so I did. This would suggest that my ultimate goal was one of asserting sovereignty over my own life (art: for a higher being). I wasn't aiming to *change* Reality (although if I did, so much the better); if I had been then my motivation would have been to

---

[45] The figure of 144,000 comes courtesy of Jehovah's Witnesses, based on their understanding of Revelation 7:4, 14:1 and 14:3 in *The Bible*.

influence society (art: for others). No, I was instead aiming to *bypass* Reality and its insidious, mean little ways. Speaking as I was to an inert audience[46], I couldn't simply make my statement and await a response – I had to *enact* it. Creating an imagined reality through the medium of a paracosm wasn't good enough: I needed to create an actual, working, visitable reality. My ideal was one of freedom – freedom to *be*.

You may note (with some irony, given the title of this book) that at no stage in my creation of *MUD* did I consider what the effect would be on the non-player characters (mobiles) with which I populated it.

I've made a point of saying that the motivations listed in this section are not exhaustive. People create realities for all kinds of reasons. It may be that Roy Trubshaw and I are the only people ever to have made a reality for the reasons we did. Then again, it may be that every god of Reality created it because their own reality was worse.

As for what I think of Reality today, ha! In my opinion, it had it coming[47].

---

[46] Reality was unlikely to pass judgement on my work.

[47] Hmm, "creating a reality for revenge" doesn't seem all that weird a motivation now.

A Lens

Let's talk about religion.

It may come as a surprise to learn that there are academics who study games and religion. They even study *how to* study games and religion. When it comes to video games, it would seem that there are basically five levels at which religion occurs (Bosman, 2016):

- *Material*. Religion, whether fictional or of Reality, occurs within the game itself.
- *Referential*. The game refers, either implicitly or explicitly, to one or more existing religions of Reality.
- *Reflexive*. The game reflects on existential concepts that are traditionally the province of religion.
- *Ritual*. Players in the game behave in ways that are traditionally associated with religion.
- *Meta-level*. Players or scholars identify the experience of playing the game itself as being religious.

Which one of these covers virtual worlds?

Well, actually they all do.

Material. Many virtual worlds do have a religion built into them. *World of Warcraft* has "priest" as a character class, for example, and a cathedral dominates the skyline of Stormwind. *The Bible Online* was somewhat more gung-ho and used the world of the Old Testament as its actual setting[48]. Adding religion to a game world can make it more immersive, more culturally relevant and more meaningful to the players (Geraci, 2020), so it's no surprise that designers would do this.

Referential. It can be argued with some justification that most current virtual worlds implicitly embody religious themes from Reality, as can be shown by tracing their heritage back through Tolkien to Catholicism and ideas of *Natural Law*[49] (Castronova, 2012). Explicit references to the religions of Reality are rather more hard to come by, but they do exist. As it happens, virtual worlds are packed with non-diegetic references to aspects of Reality, usually at the expense of immersion; these are often referred to as *Easter eggs*, and serve to give players something to feel clever about for having noticed (although, very occasionally, an Easter egg may make an artistic point). References in this context to the religions of Reality do occur, which is why I mentioned it, but they're relatively few in number. You'll see quests and NPCs with names that allude to *Dr Who* or *Buffy the Vampire Slayer* or *Friends*, but

[48] Sadly, because of fairly strict limits on the numbers of popes allowed at once, the game *Pope Simulator* is not an MMO.

[49] This is a system of laws that claims its authority from values deemed (by logical, spiritual or natural reasoning) to be inherent in everyone. In the modern era, it's closely related to the concept of human rights.

very rarely ones that mention even religions with no present-day followers, let alone ones with millions. It does happen occasionally – there's a quest in *Rift* called "An Eye for an Eye"[50], for example, and both *Secret World Legends* and *Final Fantasy XIV* have one called "A Time to Every Purpose"[51] – but the practice is uncommon. Nevertheless, it's not unprecedented; we can, therefore, still check this checkbox.

Reflexive. Religious themes such as sacrifice, salvation, life and death abound in virtual worlds. In *Secret World Legends*, for example, both the Emma Smith and Sarah storylines are about exactly these issues. Pretty well every virtual world with some kind of narrative element to it is going to touch on these themes at some point.

Ritual. Surprisingly, ritual has always been a part of virtual worlds[52]. In *MUD1*, when players reached the highest level and were elevated to demigodhood, they were accorded a memorial stone in the game's graveyard. When *Star Wars Galaxies* introduced its infamous New Game

---

[50] Exodus 21:24.

[51] Ecclesiastes 3:1.

[52] Or perhaps not surprisingly, as some scholars have argued that play *is* ritual and ritual *is* play (Copier, 2005). That said, it may depend on what you mean by "ritual"; anthropologists, for example, can use it to refer to "practices through which the game is enriched with new meanings that go beyond its ludic instrumentality" (Zabet, 2012), which isn't what scholars of Religious Studies mean by the term.

Experience, players built mass graveyards for their characters before quitting (Koster, 2018). A more substantial example comes from *EVE Online*, which avoids permadeath through the fiction of clones called *capsuleers*: when one clone dies, its consciousness is awakened in another. The Molea Cemetery was created by players to preserve the bodies of dead capsuleers, which would otherwise lie where they'd fallen until deleted 30 days later. Players have since added memorials there for people they've lost in Reality.[53]

Meta-level. Whether the experience of playing a virtual world is religious or not is a matter for the individual. There have certainly been virtual worlds intended to be used directly for religious purposes: *Church of Fools* was an early one, although it couldn't really be described as a game. That said, players and academics have long been aware that playing a virtual world can be a religious or religious-like experience, even back in the days of text MUDs (recall Jen Clodius's work on *DragonMUD*; for more modern takes, see (Aupers, et al., 2018) (Geraci, 2019)).

In virtual worlds, then, religion occurs at all five of the levels where it could occur. This is a book

[53] Developers also do this kind of thing. *World of Warcraft* features several examples (Gibbs, et al., 2012), including an NPC genie called Robin who lives in an Aladdin's lamp – a tribute to the late comedian, Robin Williams (who was reportedly a fan of the virtual world).

about virtual worlds, so at which level or levels does what I'm saying fit?

It fits none of them.

I'm not looking at video games through the lens of religion; I'm looking at religion through the lens of video games (specifically, virtual worlds).

That's the thing about lenses: they're two-way. Having a lens to look at the realities we create as virtual worlds gives us a reciprocal lens to look at our world, Reality, as a virtual world. There is a symmetry between us-as-gods and us-as-NPCs.

This book is part observation, part thought experiment. We don't yet have good enough artificial intelligence systems to create morally considerable virtual creatures; when we do, that's when Theology can become an experimental subject. For the moment, it's merely the case that we should think about these topics in advance so that we're prepared for the day when they are realised.

Doing this is useful for spiritual and non-spiritual people alike. For the spiritual, knowing what we have to decide when we create worlds casts a light on what a creator of Reality would have (had) to decide back in the day. For the non-spiritual, we must ask ourselves how we want our creations to be, and why.

Before looking through a lens, though, it's wise to contemplate the potential cost. We might not be happy with what we see. If there's one thing I've learned from playing *Call of Cthulhu*, it's *don't read the books*: they only ever summon demons. What demons might be summoned by looking at the real as if it were virtual?

One of my *MUD2* players, Lexley Vaughan[54], once wrote a critique of the way that the game handled religion, arguing that by treating spiritually-significant objects as if they had no spiritual significance, I (as *MUD2*'s designer) was saying something about religion in general:

> *By consistently treating religion as nothing more than the sum of its physical building blocks, consciously disregarding any hint at any greater spiritual aspect, he promotes the idea that this is all there is to it – that people with faith are, in some sense, deluding themselves.*
>
> (*Vaughan, 2003*)

While not entirely correct regarding my motivation (I wasn't so much commenting on religion as commenting on the structures of Reality as a whole – although I did want to equate religion with fantasy), this does nevertheless bring up an interesting point. If we ourselves become gods of realities, does that lessen our connection with whatever gods there may be of Reality? After

---

[54] I'm certain this wasn't her real name but, hey, it's how she wanted to be known.

all, what once seemed awesome and miraculous, to gamers might now seem mundane.

> *After three days, Jesus respawned, took his place as Administrator, and redefined the way the game is played.*
>
> (Detweiler, 2010)

Is looking at virtual worlds a way to get people into religion through games, or to get people out of religion through games? Could it be that both occur at times, or indeed that neither does? In the two articles from which the above quotations appear, Detweiler ultimately sides with "people into religion" and Vaughan ultimately sides with "people out of religion". What do you think?

Well, if it turns out that you're Pope Benedict XVI, I already know what you think: that images can "become independent of reality" and can "give life to a virtual world, with several consequences, the first of which is the risk of indifference to truth" (Zenit, 2010). In other words, there's a risk that the virtual can undermine the real – more "people out of religion" than "people into religion", then.

Further slivers of evidence[55] in favour of "people out of religion" rather than "people into

[55] I say "slivers" rather than "pieces" because when it comes to matters of faith, evidence rarely enters into it; that's kind of the point.

religion" come from research showing that games can act as a placeholder for religion (Boren, 2016) and that playing them reduces the propensity for spiritual experience (Burris & Dow, 2015). It's also possible that although virtual worlds could be a way to get people into religion *per se*, the religion in question is not necessarily one that has a presence outside the virtual world (Bainbridge & Bainbridge, 2007). Academics have of course suggested using video games as tools for religious education (Waltemathe, 2015); being academics, however, whether this is to educate people for or against religion rather depends on the academic[56].

Compounding all this, there's a strong argument that the cause of the 1980s moral panic over *Dungeons & Dragons* was rooted in the fact that religions and role-playing games both utilise the same imaginative faculties, and therefore access to the latter as clear-cut fantasies raises in proponents of the former uncomfortable questions about their personal beliefs (Laycock, 2015). The qualitative research that has been done in this area (Schaap & Aupers, 2017) does support this suggestion to some extent, but also indicates that the tenets of virtual worlds' artificial religions can provoke in some players a desire to seek living-religion answers to the existential questions raised. The same research also suggests that over

[56] *DragonRaid* is a fantasy RPG used to help Christians apply Biblical principles, for example.

time, players become less dogmatic in their religious views and more tolerant of those held by others. In some cases, then, it may not be so much "people out of religion" as "people out of their starting religion" (De Wildt, 2020).

If you're a spiritual person[57], then, you might want to avoid spending too much time playing or analysing virtual worlds. It's not so much that you'll have a crisis of faith, but you could have a leakage of it that you don't notice until the tank is approaching empty.

So, bearing that warning[58] in mind....

We know things now that we didn't know in the years before *MUD* was written. Some of what was theory pre-1978 is practice now; much practice was never even in the theory. We've learned lessons from being gods which we can apply to our own condition as creatures of a reality.

I've broached many of these observations in this book. Here's one of the more obvious and important among them.

Imagine that our NPCs are contemplating their existence. They conjecture that their world must

---

[57] Or indeed a non-spiritual person: "Hardboiled atheist players express more understanding and openness for the religious Other and, in general, the universal longing for ultimate meaning" (Schaap & Aupers, 2017).

[58] It's not the only warning, by the way, but it's the most pertinent to the discussion here. For other traps awaiting those who hope to bring aspects of a religion from the real to the virtual, see (Dawson, 2001).

have a creator – correct! They deduce that this creator exists in a higher reality – correct! They calculate that they themselves must be modelled on the creator – correct! They imagine what their creator must be like – incorrect!

Even assuming they're sapient, the characters of my created realities know *nothing* about me. Any concept they have of what I'm like is pure supposition. They don't know why I made their world, why I made it the way I did, why I made they themselves; they don't even know that there's actually two of me, as I made their world with a friend. All they have to go on is what they think I must have thought when I did whatever it was I did.

Put bluntly, they're right that there's a god but wrong in every respect as to what I'm like as an individual. As I noted in Chapter 6, even were I to try to tell them what I'm like, they'd still be wrong. I'd have to represent in their reality the whole time, visible and interacting with it in godlike ways, to be enough of a part of their existence for them to get a decent understanding of who I am – and even that would depend on there being little information loss. Otherwise, they're just filling in major gaps in their knowledge with wishful thinking.

That's my NPCs looking at me. It's also human beings looking at the god or gods of Reality. No matter how much you may think you know them, no matter how much you want what you think to be true, the fact is that you're largely speculating.

On the plus side, my NPC atheists are yet more wrong: they don't even think I exist. Relative to their world, they may be correct; relative to mine, though, they're not[59]. What, then, am I going to do to them when it comes to judgement day?

This isn't actually a facetious question. It links to Plato's *Euthyphro dilemma*, in which Socrates asks whether the pious individual is loved by the gods because that individual is pious, or whether that individual is pious because they're loved by the gods. In both cases, piety is approved of by the gods, but in the former it isn't *defined* by the gods whereas in the latter it is[60].

What it comes down to is whether it's the gods who decide what goodness is or whether goodness is a concept independent of the gods. In our terms: if we like NPCs who are good, is the mere fact that we like an NPC itself sufficient to deem their actions as good, or does our liking them derive from the independent goodness of their actions?

Rephrasing Socrates' question for virtual worlds, then: do we like NPCs because they do what we approve of, or do they do what we approve of because we like them?

---

[59] They will become correct when I die, which at the time of writing has yet to occur. I expect it's a couple of hundred years away at the very least.

[60] We came across this *divine command* theory when discussing deontology earlier.

In my experience, game designers do like NPCs to do what they (the designers) approve of, but what they approve of is for the NPCs to be free-thinking individuals. I remember a discussion with Roy Trubshaw on this very topic back in about 1980: sure, atheist NPCs would be wrong about there not being a creator, but as a creator you'd be quite pleased that they'd managed to work out there wasn't one, given the complete lack of supporting evidence. Atheist NPCs would therefore gain a kind of redemption through smartness[61].

That's my NPC atheists looking at me. It's also human atheists looking at the gods of Reality.

Note that although the NPC atheists are wrong, that doesn't mean human atheists are also wrong. Likewise, the NPCs with spiritual tendencies may be right, but that doesn't mean that spiritual humans are right. What this is telling us isn't what's right or wrong about Reality: what it's telling us is *what would have to be true* for it to be right or wrong – and what the implications of that would be.

It's easy to fall into the groove of believing that this is all an analogy. It's not an analogy. We really *are* the gods of the worlds we create, and we really *do* have to think of ourselves as the gods of those worlds if we're to understand them. This in turn

---

[61] They'd still be somewhat embarrassed to find themselves in NPC heaven, though.

gives us insights regarding whatever god or gods there may or may not be of Reality. We, as gods, have no say in this: we get the insights whether we want them or not. An architect who spends ten years designing buildings cannot prevent themself from coming to a subsequent understanding of the process of designing buildings: it arrives as an unbidden consequence of their art. So it is with gods of virtual worlds.

You don't have to accept any of what I describe in this book. Whether you're right or I'm right or we're both right – or both wrong – to a greater or lesser degree is immaterial. The doors to new realities have been flung open, and neither you nor I can influence who'll be going through them a thousand years hence. The feel of Reality itself will alter in ways as yet undreamt of; all we know for sure is that there *will* be change:

> *Ever larger numbers of people will spend many hours inside online games. To the rest of us, these choices will feel like an exodus from our reality. Our reality will be changed.*
>
> (Castronova, 2007)

As for why people will choose to represent in these worlds rather than to engage with Reality, game designer Jane McGonigal sums it up concisely in the title of her book, *Reality is Broken*, and its first line:

Gamers have had enough of reality.
(*McGonigal, 2011*)

Nothing short of extinction will stop humanity from creating and living in realities other than Reality. The most we can do from our vantage point today is to strive to ensure that the realities we do create are places worthy of us.

Answers and unanswers

I've asked a lot of questions in this book, some of which are answered and some of which are unanswered. Whether or not you find the questions, answers or unanswers comfortable or uncomfortable depends on your personal philosophy.

For example: the Holy Trinity makes a lot more sense when examined from an implementational point of view, but whether you're happy with that may depend on whether you're a Christian or not[62]. Likewise, the rather neat explanation of how transubstantiation works may please Roman Catholics but be received with less enthusiasm by others[63]. Reincarnation is perhaps the biggest

---

[62] Christian technophobes will have a dilemma.

[63] Technopagans, for example, treat real and virtual candles as being equally meaningful in their rituals (O'Leary, 1996).

overall winner, with virtual worlds offering several mechanisms for it; whether you fall on the "that clinches it" or "an explanation isn't a proof" side of the argument is contingent on your world view.

As another example, this time of a suggestion that's likely to be more widely vexatious: I raised the possibility that our gods could well be duffers. We may actually be smarter than our gods, or, if we're not, in the coming decades, centuries, millennia or whatever we'll create NPCs in our virtual worlds who *are* smarter than our gods. Worse, the easy defensive position – that our gods are of never-to-be-equalled, supra-genius level intelligence – means it's even more certain that you have no idea what they're really like, and that any and all glimpses you perceive of them are wholly and reliably uninterpretable. That may sit well with you or it may not; there may be a felicitous way of accepting it or there may not. It depends on how you come at it.

I've done my best to be accommodating in this book, treating all religions past and present as equally valid. A consequence of this is that I've been able to call on evidence (or if you prefer, "evidence") from many cultures of varied parts of the world when discussing both natural and supernatural occurrences. This has been of use in two ways: to see if we can implement in virtual worlds what has been reported in Reality; to see if there are reports in Reality of what we can implement in virtual worlds.

Now as I said back in Chapter 1[64], adopting this impartiality could be taken as offensive. Usually, it isn't – Japanese role-playing games routinely mix figures and themes from assorted religions (De Wildt & Aupers, 2020) and no-one raises an eyebrow. That said, context is important. *Smite*, a multi-player online battle arena, features gods from the pantheons of Ancient Greece, Ancient Rome, Ancient Egypt, Ancient China, Ancient Japan, Ancient Polynesia, the Norse, the Slavs, the Celts, the Mayans, Vodou and Hinduism. Now even though Hinduism is older than any of the other religions referenced by *Smite*, it's still widely practised whereas the rest (Vodou perhaps excepted) are not. Prior to *Smite*'s launch, there was some pushback from Hindu leaders who felt that the presence of Hindu gods in the game trivialised them, and as such was offensive to the devoted (Eurasia Review, 2012). Much of this was because of the art style[65], but the more general point was that by situating the world's third-largest religion[66] alongside a bunch of largely dead ones, it was placing it in the same category.

Although such a comparison-of-unequals appears rather low down on the list of significant offences that this book is likely to cause, I could

[64] It was right there in the footnotes.

[65] Kali in particular was singled out, as she was depicted wearing what was basically a bikini.

[66] Fourth-largest if you include "no religion" as a religion.

nevertheless have avoided it by concentrating only on "dead" religions or only on "live" ones. I didn't, though, because who am I to judge whether a religion is worthy of inclusion or exclusion? I'm just a jumped-up computer programmer. Furthermore, had I taken either of these approaches, the result would have been even more unsatisfactory.

The thing is, most of the evidence concerning what gods did or didn't do comes from a time when people had neither the ability to record supernatural phenomena nor the methodology to test the veracity of reports. Even "modern" ideas such as monotheism are several millennia old. Although there *are* religions that have developed more recently – Scientology, Falun Gong, Rastafarianism, many hundreds more – these don't tend to come with attendant miracles or other supernatural claims (indeed, some of them don't even have gods). If they did, cynics would ask to see the evidence and feel justified in their cynicism when it was not forthcoming to even half-way credible standards. It would therefore seem that modern gods are more reticent to perform acts of physics-changing than were those of yesteryear.

This means that had I not included gods with no present-day followers alongside gods with millions of them, I would have been short of examples of the kind of things gods can do. However, had I *only* included them, I couldn't have said much of relevance to the modern reader. My decision to treat all gods as if they existed thus addressed both issues, while allowing me to remain relatively impartial.

I bring this up because of what it says about the incidence of supernatural activity. Basically, the closer we are to the present, the less of it there is. No gods seem to visit Reality any more (if indeed they ever did).

Why is this?

Well there could be many reasons. Perhaps Reality is undergoing a denial-of-service attack by hackers in the reality of the gods. Perhaps there's a new law in the gods' reality that prohibits their access to Reality at certain times. Perhaps the gods have lost the password to Reality and can't log in.

Assuming that there's an open communication channel between the gods and Reality, though, if you hope to understand why no gods visit Reality then you have to assign motivations to gods – about whom, as I've repeatedly pointed out, you know nothing. All you can do is speculate – "he's busy", "it's part of their plan", "she's about to rain death and destruction on us all" – but in so doing you open yourself up to further questioning. Busy doing what? What plan? Why destroy *all* of us? In answering those questions, you expose yourself further, until you wind up with either a huge web of secrets and suppositions, conspiracy-theory style, or you have to say you don't know (which you probably should have done in the first place).

As the fictional detective Sherlock Holmes put it:

> *It is a capital mistake to theorise before one has data. Insensibly one begins to twist facts to suit theories, instead of theories to suit facts.*
>
> *(Doyle, 1891)*[67]

You may find it problematic that no gods visit Reality today, or you may not[68]; either way, you would be wise to examine *why* you think what you think. I may not be able to furnish an answer that will suit you, but you should at least have an answer yourself that makes some progress towards that end.

A related point that you need to consider (if you haven't considered it before) is that existence is a reality-relative concept. To say, from Reality, that one or more gods "exist" means that they exist in Reality. This is clearly true of some gods – the gods of virtual worlds – who do indeed exist in Reality. What about gods *of* Reality, though? Well the same rule applies: for them to exist from our perspective, they too have to exist in Reality, the here and now.

Awkwardly, there's nothing to indicate that they *do* exist either here or now: they don't interact with Reality in any measurable way. If they did

[67] This from an author who believed in fairies.

[68] You certainly won't if you advocate pandeism.

interact, there'd be repercussions which today would be easily noticed – changes to the principle of conservation of energy would have quite violent side effects, for example. Perhaps they used to interact, but have shied away now that we're able to detect the fact.

Of course, any god of Reality can by definition control its physics, so could stop any detectable effects of their actions by attaching functionality to symbolic objects. For example, to create a material object out of nothing should be impossible and to create it out of energy should require phenomenal temperatures – 10,000,000,000,000 degrees or more. However, if you were to specify that for a particular, symbolic interpretation of matter (that is, matter you identify as being a coherent object), regular physics was overridden by a different physics, you could indeed do something like create manna and rain it from the skies to prevent the Israelites from starving. This is the kind of miracle that our modern instruments would not be able to detect (although obviously the resulting manna would be detectable).

That said, this same active use of physics could be employed in other situations, such as stopping good people from being struck by lightning[69]. We never see this, though: we never see physics selectively overridden anywhere, ever. It's not as if

---

[69] Did you know lightning is sexist? 80% of fatalities are male (Jensenius, 2018).

there's a need to hide it: if it were an everyday occurrence, we wouldn't even suspect anything was untoward, it would seem to be part of the nature of things (which it would indeed be).

No gods appear to be interacting with Reality. A god of Reality who is present in Reality but never interacts with it is effectively absent from it; a god who never visits it at all is *de facto* absent from it. In either case, the god concerned does not exist relative to us.

This rather pedantic "definition of existence" argument doesn't say that gods *can't* come to Reality, it merely says that they *don't*. Because it admits the possibility that, say, Dionysus might show up tomorrow and so *would* exist, it's not an argument against the existence of gods in absolute. Nevertheless, it is an argument against the existence of gods until they deign to show up or to do something. Whether this is worrisome to you or not I don't know; if you haven't already, you do need to give some thought as to what you mean when you say that you believe a particular god "exists" or not, though.

Oh, speaking of beliefs....

I spent a section of this book talking about the fiction of virtual worlds: that which you have to buy into to accept the virtual as real. As it happens, it's not abnormal for an MMO to have religions for its NPCs built into its fiction; this is usually to add depth to the virtual world (thereby helping with immersion), but it can also be for story purposes.

In practical terms, what's happening here is that the actual gods of the reality in question are thoughtfully providing it with in-fiction gods whom the NPCs behave as if they believe exist.

Sometimes, these gods[70] don't make an appearance (you never see Elune in *World of Warcraft*, she just speaks through people) but quite often they do (you encounter Hydaelyn several times in *Final Fantasy XIV* cut scenes). In the latter case, an NPC's "belief" in the existence of the god is no more problematical than their belief in the existence of other NPCs – unsurprisingly, because the god *is* an NPC (albeit one with supernatural powers). This means that this particular aspect of the virtual world's fiction is objective truth from the NPC's perspective, somewhat undermining any claims that their religion is indeed a religion (Lefebvre, 2019).

The possibility that Reality's apparent gods could, like us, be mere NPCs created by its genuine gods, I leave open as a topic for your consideration.

One of the problems religions have in general is that they try to use persuasive logic to explain themselves both to followers and to prospective followers, but eventually they hit a wall – something that doesn't follow logically from the available facts but isn't contradicted by them either. They draw a line here and call it "faith". However, when new information arrives courtesy

---

[70] Formally, they're demigods.

of science, they then have to decide whether what they previously asserted with unshakable conviction is:

- wrong, because the facts can't be made to fit (so, what about everything that suggested it was right, or that followed from this?);
- right, because the facts can be made to fit (suggesting that the religion lacks detail);
- right, because the facts are simply flat-out denied (therefore the use of evidence to support the religion's tenets is selective).

Virtual world religions are no different from those of Reality in this regard, except that their gods are more open to changing the physics (and therefore the science) so as to maintain the integrity of the account they wish to promulgate.

As an example of how new information (in this case from software engineering) can challenge an older idea, consider the notion of consciousness. From our understanding of virtual worlds, it's clear that we humans have an embedded, emergent form of intelligence, from which derives our sapience and thence consciousness. We're independent thinkers, whose only access to one another's thoughts comes from observing one another's behaviour in the environment that we share, Reality. Any other form of implementing intelligence would encourage additional phenomena.

For example, if consciousness worked by using rules of physics specific to consciousness (and so was supernatural) which had effects that were physical (such as those that result from actions consciously taken) then from those same supernatural rules would emerge other phenomena that would also have physical impact, such as telepathy, body swaps and ESP[71].

If consciousness *were* a supernatural phenomenon, then, there would be natural consequences; these consequences are not observed, therefore consciousness is not a supernatural phenomenon. Nevertheless, some accounts of human consciousness routinely assert that it has spiritual, even transcendent qualities. Likewise, they explain what a soul is and why we all have one, but not why some of the things that would happen if we did have one don't happen.

This isn't to say there isn't a perfectly reasonable explanation (some god could be effortlessly dealing with the consequences, for example); it's just to say that those who think consciousness is a separate and separable entity should ponder what this entails, knowing what we know about how it would have to be implemented. They can then either incorporate this into their account, ignore it, or argue against it.

---

[71] It's possible to take this further, and use what we know about consciousness to understand what constraints this imposes on how Reality works. This is the aim of *integrated information theory* (Tononi, 2004).

Again, whether the results of this analysis are comfortable or uncomfortable for you isn't for me to judge. I can point out some of what follows logically from what we know about virtual worlds, but that doesn't mean I can answer the questions so raised to everyone's (or indeed anyone's) satisfaction.

These are unanswered questions. It's for you to turn those unanswers into answers, bespoke to you.

WELL HOW ABOUT THAT

Human culture knows four major ways of thinking.

Western philosophy emphasises logic and reason. Its aim is to establish objective facts. Although it has its sages – Aristotle, Newton, Einstein – it does not take their words as inviolate. It seeks truth for its own sake. That which can be deduced from established mathematics using established mathematics is accepted as true. That which can be observed is provisionally accepted as true, unless and until evidence to the contrary is presented.

The philosophy of east Asia is not preoccupied with the world as it appears to be. Rather, it is concerned with how to chart a path through life. The wisdom accumulated by sages since antiquity is used as a guide. The means by which the words of the sages may be understood are themselves revealed by the words of those sages who have since followed, even up until the present day.

The philosophy of south Asia lies in between. The words of the sages tell us how we might live well, and their wisdom has stood the test of millennia. New discoveries about the world as it appears to be are welcomed because they cast additional light on what we know from the sages to be true, adding to our understanding of their words.

The philosophy of the Islamic world also lies in between that of east Asia and the west. Unlike the philosophy of south Asia, however, it uses the wisdom revealed by the sages[72] to explain the phenomena observed in the natural world, rather than the reverse. Indisputable words describe how to behave such that the wonders of creation may be revealed.

These summaries are just that – summaries. Furthermore, they're summaries by me, a non-philosopher[73]. Every one of them can be attacked rightly and justifiably by philosophers of any of the

---

[72] Primarily just the one sage, but with interpretations by others.

[73] Unless purveyors of *pseudophilosophy* (Moberger, 2021) count as philosophers.

traditions outlined. I happily defer to them, because this is their area of expertise, not mine[74].

That said, I do believe that, at least in the abstract, my summaries are serviceable.

This being so, it would seem that we can think of philosophers as having a concept they want to understand and a preferred method for pursuing this understanding.

- Western philosophers contend that the world in which we live can be used to help us understand the world in which we live. The world explains the world.
- South-Asian philosophers contend that the world in which we live can be used to help us understand the way we should live. The world explains the words.
- East-Asian philosophers contend that the way we should live can be used to help us understand the way we should live. The words explain the words.
- Islamic-world philosophers contend that the way we should live can be used to help us understand the world in which we live. The words explain the world.

We can illustrate this as a graph, as shown in Figure 11.

[74] Just as I'm rather hoping they'll defer to my expertise in reality-creation over theirs.

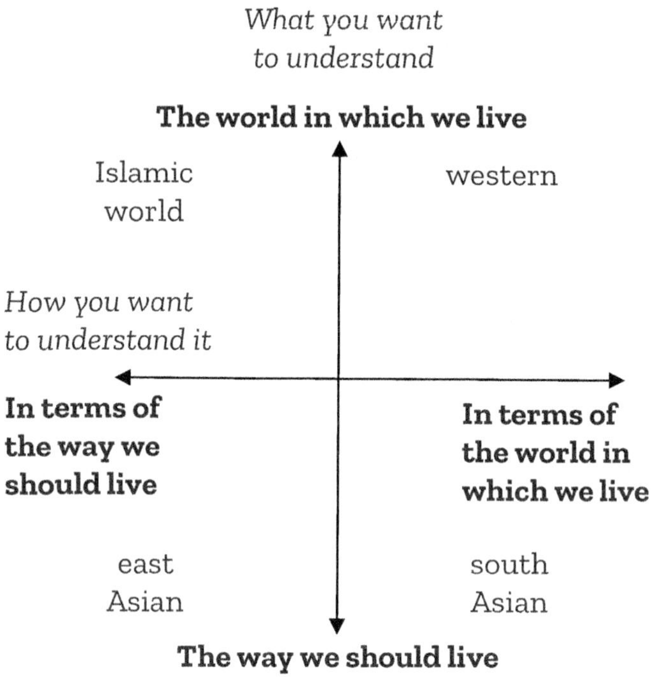

Figure 11 – Philosophical Traditions.

This graph can be augmented by two diagonal lines, which I haven't shown because it's enough of a mess as it is. One line, from east Asian to western, is well-established in Comparative Philosophy: it's from "way-seeking" to "truth-seeking" (Hall & Ames, 1998). The other line, from south Asian to Islamic world is, as far as I can tell, not something to which comparative philosophers have given much thought – mainly, I suspect, because they haven't constructed the graph. My first shot at labelling the line is "identity-seeking" to "conformity-seeking", but I'm sure there are better ways of putting it.

Given what I've written elsewhere in this book, "the world in which we live" would seem to correspond to Reality. It depends on which direction you come at it, though. For example, in south Asian philosophy, the world as we perceive it isn't the world as it truly is. It has the form of it, but isn't itself it. That would make it a virtual world, then? Well yes, if you're looking subjectively *at* Reality, but if you're looking objectively *as* Reality then the world described[75] by the sages of antiquity is the one that's virtual.

Because these two different views are in practice simply two sides of the same coin, we only need to consider one to understand both. Being humans, let's take the human-centric one and look *at* Reality, rather than *as* Reality. This enables us to use the terminology of virtual worlds to characterise the different philosophical traditions as follows:

- Virtual Worlds as Virtual Worlds
  Western philosophy
  The world as it appears illuminates itself.
- Virtual Worlds as Realities
  Islamic world philosophy
  The world as it appears is illuminated by the world as it truly is.

---

[75] Or imagined, if you take a strongly realist perspective.

- Realities as Realities
  East Asian philosophy
  The world as it truly is illuminates itself.
- Realities as Virtual Worlds
  South Asian philosophy
  The world as it truly is is illuminated by the world as it appears.

This book is divided into four sections. Their titles are those of the bullet-point headers above.

This late revelation makes it look as if I was being rather clever in my choice of partitions. As such, I could stop at this juncture and leave you with a favourable impression of my intellect (if not my character).

I would be misinforming you if I did so, though.

In the first draft of this text, I adopted what computer scientists call a *depth-first* approach. I took each of my central themes in turn and followed their individual lines of argument until they reached their conclusions. When one branch terminated, I backed up and followed the next branch. Although this form of investigation is systematic in its coverage of content, at the level of discourse it bounces around between multiple topics with little demarcation. The draft ended up reading like a collection of independent discussions with no overall structure to it.

After this effect was pointed out to me (see the Acknowledgements), I rewrote the book using a *breadth-first* approach. I formulated a narrative thread which (see the Prologue) went something like this: explain what realities are; describe how we create realities; discuss what responsibilities those who create realities have; assess whether any creator of Reality lives up to these responsibilities. I changed focus between each step, and figured that I should indicate this to the reader by partitioning the chapters accordingly.

The steps didn't originally have names, just part numbers. This didn't convey much information to the reader, so I decided they needed titles. I went through several iterations, mainly involving different permutations of "looking up" and "looking down", until I settled on *what* was being looked upon and what it was being looked upon *as*.

It was only several months later that, in an effort to see how my thesis might fit into the wider philosophical landscape[76], I drew up the graph depicted in Figure 11 and realised that there was a connection with how I'd organised my book's parts.

It was, in other words, mere accident[77].

I present this anecdote as evidence that virtual worlds are opening new philosophical and theological doors. They serve to reveal wondrous, unmapped territories of thought and experience. If I, a mere game designer, can stumble across a

[76] I still don't know the answer.

[77] Those of you who drew the graph I left as an exercise in the aside of this chapter's Motivation section will note a second curious accidental connection.

previously unnoticed way of characterising what different philosophical traditions offer their proponents, what marvels might *you* uncover if you put your mind to it?

Reflections

In northern Europe, around one woman in 30,000 will die of childbirth, whereas in the poorest parts of the world it's one woman in six (Ronsmans & Graham, 2006). In 16th- to 18th-century England, it was somewhere between one woman in 34 and one woman in 41 (Wilmott Dobbie, 1982).

If you were a god of Reality, how would you explain these statistics? Are modern-day women in one society somehow more worthy than those in another? Are they more or less worthy than those of the past? Has death, in your view, got nothing to do with the character of the individual? If so, what's wrong with murder? Why is what you, as a god, are doing to these women not itself a form of murder?

This is the kind of question that we can ask of gods of Reality, because we know that soon we will have to ask it of ourselves as gods of virtual worlds. If our NPCs have babies, will we make some of those NPCs die as a result? We can stop it. Would we? Why would we? Why wouldn't we?

Any gods of Reality must work to a very different ethical system to us for Reality to be as it is, because our own situation is unethical by our standards. Will we have to do likewise for our own created realities? Might our own ethical codes perhaps prevent us from creating populated-by-sapients realities from the outset?

It is said that we cannot know the mind of God[78]. That's correct, especially if there is no God, but we *can* know the minds of gods – we have some among us right now. These gods rule realities that are consequent on Reality. As a result of their experience, we know what gods in general need to think about and to do. We know what problems they can expect to encounter and we know many of the solutions on offer. We know some of what works and some of what doesn't work. Crucially, we know enough to make deductions about how our own reality – Reality – must be.

If you were to go outside right now and take a photograph of something – anything at all – then obviously I wouldn't know what was in the resulting image. I would, however, know some of what certainly wasn't in it. It wouldn't show a flashdark, because those things are impossible. It wouldn't show my paternal grandfather, because he died in 1982. It wouldn't show a vampire,

---

[78] The original phraseology is rather more convoluted in Corinthians 1:2 of *The Bible*, but this is the gist of it.

because they're only the stuff of folk tales[79]. If I saw any of these things in your photograph, I'd know that the image had been manipulated.

So it is with Reality. I don't know much of what's in it, but I do know some of what's not in it – of what can't be in it. I also know some of what must be in it for it to be consistent. There must be light, there must be gravity, there must be me[80]. If someone were to posit an idea that could be true but would have implications that are false, or that could be false but would be implied by something that's true, then I know the truth value of the idea itself. If you were to tell me that at night the sun didn't exist, I'd know that this couldn't be true – because if it were true then too many other things that we know to be true would have to be false (such as the existence of moonlight).

For me, knowing what I know about the design of virtual worlds, I can see what would have to follow if Reality were a conscious creation. These consequences have not arisen. I can also see what states of affairs we currently have that we wouldn't if Reality had been a conscious creation. Even if it were an accidental creation ruled over by an uncaring or capricious god, it would be different

---

[79] Also, they don't show up in single-lens reflex cameras because these use mirrors and vampires have no reflection (at least if the mirror is silvered, anyway).

[80] For you, there must be you.

to how it is now. Time and dimensionality would not behave as they do, for example.

That's just my view, though. Other gods of virtual worlds (there aren't many of us at present – a few thousand at most) may well see things differently. Everyone has their own take on life, and how each of us accounts in our philosophy for the lessons we've learned from being a god is always going to depend on what our philosophy was in the first place. My hope is merely that people dwell on these experiences for long enough to understand them.

The point is, when we create realities we have to make decisions regarding how those realities must *be*. If Reality is also created then those same decisions must have been made for us. Your experience, you can translate upwards.

Gods are gods: what one of them does reflects on what others must do – or must have done.

We – you – have godly power over entire realities. Sure, they're not much now, but given computers the size of planets they will be. It behoves us to use this power thoughtfully and responsibly – just as it would have done any creator of Reality.

I am a god. It's great! I love being a god!

Our realities don't *need* gods, though. No reality *needs* a god.

Let's give our realities what they *do* need, instead: humanity.

HOW TO Be a GOD

> *"You know that question about whether if a tree falls in a forest and no-one hears it, does it make a sound? It does in MUD – I've just implemented it."*
>
> *Roy Trubshaw, 1978*

PS:).

EPILOGUE

Except for one unsubtle hint in the final few paragraphs of Chapter 9, I've avoided in this text taking any position myself on how things "really" are with regard to the nature of Reality. It would be strange indeed if I didn't have opinions of my own, though, and you could justifiably feel cheated if I ducked out of telling you what these are. I shall therefore bite the bullet and explain my own thoughts on the matter. You can skip what follows if you like, it adds nothing to the discussion: I merely present it so that you can moderate your view of this book's content accordingly.

Important: this is just how *I* see it. You can, and probably will, see it a different way. In matters of faith (or lack thereof)[1], it's invariably the case that more people think you're wrong than think you're right; this is true for all instantiations of "you", including "you" = "me". All I ask is that if you do read on and find yourself disagreeing, don't get too cross over it. It's not my intention to upset anyone,

[1] "Faith is that quality by which we believe what we should otherwise think to be false" (Richmond, 1934).

so if you catch yourself becoming hot under the collar, that's the time to put the book down.

Right, then! You've probably figured out by now that I'm at least agnostic and quite probably atheist. I'm actually the latter. This admission will immediately put some readers on the alert, as atheists have a reputation second only to that of vegans for being smug, sanctimonious, self-righteous prigs[2]. As I've said, though, my hope here isn't to persuade people to renounce their god(s), nor indeed to embrace ones they may have previously dismissed; rather, it's to help further the reader's understanding of the nature of Reality, regardless of whether this understanding aligns with mine. I don't mind if what I write actually entrenches your faith in some deity, so long as you've digested and assimilated what virtual worlds have taught us about being a god that we didn't know before we created them.

With this in mind, then, here's my own interpretation.

Some reality has to be at the bottom. Modulo what programmers on other planets might have done, until 1978 Reality was at the bottom. Today, virtual worlds or other worlds-within-worlds[3] are at the bottom.

---

[2] No, I'm not vegan. Vega is over 25 light years away.

[3] It's possible to play *Skyrim* on the in-world, wrist-mounted personal information processor (*pip-boy*) your character can wear in *Fallout 4*.

Some reality has to be at the top. For atheists, it's Reality. For some theists, it's a heaven (in one guise or another), possibly paired with a hell. For other theists, it's a ladder or tree of heavens, possibly infinite in extent (meaning there is no "top").

My view, based on what I know of virtual world design, is that there are no realities above Reality. Not one, not two, not dozens, not an indefinite number. This is because, if there were, Reality would be *different*.

Robyn and Rand Miller, the designers of *Myst*, were once asked the following question in an interview for *Wired*: "How has designing a whole world changed your idea of God?". Rand replied: "I guess the simple way is to say that we know how much work it took to create *Myst*, and how puny and unreal it is compared to the real world, and therefore how miraculous all of creation is. Matching our experience ... it just makes us realise how great God is." (Carroll, 1994).

This isn't how I see the situation *at all*.

We know how to make realities. We know how to design realities. The thing is, **Reality's design sucks**.

The usual teleological argument is that the world is so well-constructed that it *must* have been designed. Its mere existence tips you off that there's a god about[4]. Remarkably, even some players in game worlds can feel the presence of God in those worlds, despite the fact that God didn't write them (White Hodge, 2010). Whatever, how could there *not* be a creator behind all these wonders?

This is fair enough, but once you've made a world yourself you can see that Reality *isn't* actually designed very well. If it's designed at all, it's incompetent design, not intelligent design. For me, the teleological argument leads to the opposite conclusion: the way the world is tells us that it's *not* designed, not that it *is* designed.

If it's not designed, it doesn't have a designer; this means that it wasn't created by a god.

Reality's procedural content-generation is pretty robust, I'll certainly concede that. It may even have procedurally-generated procedural generation rules, which would be quite impressive. There's a lot of it, too, although sheer size isn't really a factor when automatic processes are doing all the work.

Where Reality falls down is in its content. This is dreadful – full of newbie mistakes. If Reality is so beautiful and perfect, why do we humans spend most of our time and effort trying to improve what

---

[4] The technical term for this is *numinous*. It's not related to the term *noumenal* (meaning a reality as it truly is) that I mentioned in an earlier footnote, notwithstanding its looking as if it really should be.

it has to offer? Shouldn't we still be enjoying living in caves? Why would we be trying to rid ourselves of disease, pain and suffering if those were good things? They're not good things! Reality is *not* a good place.

Another problem is that even at the level of individual humans, Reality isn't fair. It's not a level playing field. We, the sapient creatures of Reality are not meaningful to it. When asked what his secret to longevity was, the philosopher Bertrand Russell quipped "Choose your parents wisely" (Ross, 1957)[5]. I'd go somewhat further: your starting conditions impact practically *every* aspect of your progress through life. I know the precise minute when it was determined that I would never become a High Court Judge: 11:15am on 10th January, 1960 – the very moment I was born. At least I didn't make the mistake of being born female – I'd have been placed even further to the back of the starting grid of life had I done so.

This kind of thing simply isn't right. How could any god justify such inequality? Each of us became who we are at some point between being conceived and being born (possibly later but certainly not earlier); when we came into being as people, we were in no position to do wrong. Why, then, would

---

[5] Given that he was from one of the most notable families in the British aristocracy (his grandfather was Prime Minister twice), let it not be said that the third Earl Russell didn't practise what he preached.

a god treat some of us better than others? Whether a poor start in life is explained away by some concept of reincarnation or of original sin, if it's intentional then we're essentially being punished for something we, as the people we know ourselves to be, didn't do. That takes bearing a grudge to a whole different level. Even if Reality were designed by a committee, we wouldn't have such blatant examples of negligence[6].

Realities that are designed are designed to *say* something. All design decisions are informed by the overall message that the designer wishes to convey. Reality, though, *doesn't say anything*. The reason some people are born into want and some are born into luxury is simply that this is how the dice fell. No god set up this ghastly inequity, we did all that ourselves.

A god could stop it, though. Unfortunately, this would necessitate changes to the way that Reality works – changes that would have been there from the beginning had Reality been properly designed.

The thing is, Reality's implementation leans entirely on procedural generation. Everything is emergent; there's no special-case physics to lock out unpleasantness. Virtual worlds can and do attach functionality to symbolic objects – that is, to things made up of fundamental particles, rather

---

[6] "Committees are good for generating red tape, deferring decisions, and shirking responsibility, but they are useless when it comes to creative efforts." (Crawford, 1984).

than only to the fundamental particles themselves. It's not hard to implement this for patterns, either – I showed how to do it using that paragon of emergent content, Conway's game of *Life*. Symbolic objects are the very bedrock of exception-based physics: they're what allow a reality to work differently for different kinds of objects.

Reality doesn't have symbolic objects, though. The sad consequence of this is that what we think of as objects aren't remotely regarded as such by Reality. If they were then terrible injustices such as stillbirths could easily be rectified by gods or demigods. They continue to happen, though. Symbolic object representation, a core tool of all gods, has not been implemented for Reality. All we have are fundamental particles arranged in piecemeal-decomposable clumps, some of which are common enough that the clumps that form us ourselves assign meaning to them.

Symbolic representations are also required for supernatural functionality, in order that such physics-bending capabilities can be attached to the objects that bear the requisite permissions. If you can't point at something in an ostensive fashion and identify it as being an angel, you can't give it angelic powers. Were Reality to have supernatural functionality, then, it must also have symbolic representations of objects. If it did have such representations, though, the fact would be evident.

The fact is not evident.

It could be that the reason Reality lacks symbolic representations is that they turn out to be impossible for reasons to do with assembly (remember Andy and Boudicca?); if so, then that would explain it. Nothing requiring symbolic representations could be implemented – including supernatural functionality. A god might therefore *wish* to stop human beings from suffering, but be unable to do so without changing Reality so much that this would alter what it meant to be human in the first place.

Whatever, regardless of *why* we have no symbolic representation built into Reality's physics, the end result is the same either way: there is no supernatural involvement in Reality.

We're on our own, kids.

The resolutely impassive nature of Reality with regard to us humans raises issues of morality. See, when you build a world, you have to decide whether to consider some or all of its creatures to be moral beings. No, really, you *have* to do this. If they're nothing but bits in a database to you, you can be uncaring. If they're morally considerable, though, you must treat them as such – and that means *all* of them, not just some favoured tribe or gender (what's *with* that, by the way?) or occupation. When bad things happen that are the fault of individual moral beings, OK, you can run with that. When bad things happen that aren't their fault – such as plagues that wipe out millions of people indiscriminately[7] – well frankly you can and should stop these; it's simply bad management not to do so. Worse, though, you should have designed your reality so that such events *couldn't happen in the first place.*

We, mere human beings, can do this right now, today, with our virtual worlds. *We* can design around these problems. Why isn't Reality designed around them?

It's because Reality *isn't* designed, that's why.

Reality could be so much better! It has permadeath, pain, suffering; it has no shape-changing, no teleportation, no mental projection; most of it is empty space (quite literally). Creating content is the *fun* part of design, yet Reality has nothing except what flows from the interactions between fundamental forces and particles. It's like Conway's game of *Life* played out on a multi-dimensional canvas so immense that in occasional small, random patches of matter, something happens by complete chance to come together in a fiendishly complex way. We are merely one such small, random patch of matter.

Pause for breath.

OK, so it's possible that this is all relative. For example, perhaps a god of Reality gave us death because in their view that's better than the eternal

[7] Or, in the case of COVID-19, discriminately based largely on age.

life that they have in their own reality[8]. This nevertheless doesn't alter the fact that there isn't a single piece of Reality that can't be explained by appealing to a universal physics. There's no game-mastered content, no hand-crafted content, no user-created or user-generated content, just systems content deriving from the single instance of procedurally-generated content that is Reality. Overall, in terms of content, most of Reality is (literally, again) vacuous.

Now I do admit that saying Reality is nothing more than a vast, vast state machine, repeatedly running in perpetuity from arbitrary beginnings, does sound rather implausible. How could something as complex as us come to be unless by the hand of something even more complex[9]?

Well, at random would do it.

Suppose I told you that a record of your life from cradle to grave is already extant, even though you haven't lived it yet, and even if the universe is non-deterministic. This seems a little improbable.

The human eye can distinguish between about a million different colours. Let's say 10 million, to be

---

[8] "A finite game is played for the purpose of winning, an infinite game for the purpose of continuing the play."; "The finite player aims to win eternal life; the infinite player aims for eternal birth." (Carse, 1986).

[9] Who in turn, by the same reasoning, must have come to be by the hand of someone even more complex, and so on until you run out of complex. Or, if created by someone less complex than us, until you run out of someone.

on the safe side. A single pixel in your field of vision would therefore need seven decimal digits to store it (because 10 million is 10^7; put another way, 0 to 9,999,999 inclusive is 10 million numbers).

At a conservative estimate, the human eye has a resolution of about 576 megapixels (Clark, 2017), but let's go with a thousand megapixels so we don't underestimate. In fact, because most of us have two eyes, let's make it two thousand megapixels. A megapixel is a million pixels, so if one pixel needs seven digits to store it then two thousand megapixels would need 2,000,000,000×7 decimal digits, which is 14×10^9. This means that to store the image that you can see right now would need 14,000,000,000 digits to write down.

The human eye can interpret something like a thousand frames a second. There are around 365.25×24×60×60 = 31,557,600 seconds in a year. How long do you want to live? Would 120 years be enough? That would make your life be around 3,786,912,000 seconds long. Let's make it 5,000,000,000, or 5×10^9 seconds long, in case life expectancy suddenly shoots up.

At a thousand frames a second, you would see 5×10^{12} frames in your lifetime. If each frame needs 14×10^9 digits then to store a stereoscopic motion picture of your life would need 7×10^{22} digits.

That's 70,000,000,000,000,000,000,000 digits.

Reminder: this is not the number that encapsulates everything you've ever seen and ever will see: it's the number of digits that are in that number.

It's a big number.

Now consider the mathematical quantity π (pi). It has an infinite number of decimal places. Somewhere in its decimal part is at least one sequence of 70,000,000,000,000,000,000 consecutive digits that correspond exactly to the motion picture of your life. Indeed, there are an infinite number of these sequences[10].

Things which seem impossibly improbable can actually be a hundred percent certain.

Do not underestimate the power of random in the context of infinity.

These are my reasons for rejecting the existence of one or more gods of Reality, even though I myself am a god of a reality. They're not my only reasons[11], but they're the ones drawn from my experience with virtual worlds. I owed it to you to explain my take, but you don't owe it to anyone to accept my line of argument.

That's the point of being a free-thinker: you get to think freely.

---

[10] Strictly speaking it's only conjectured that this is the case for pi. It's definitely true for the Copeland–Erdős constant, but fewer people have heard of that than they have of pi.

[11] We know the way that supernatural views of Reality came about, and they didn't involve any supernatural elements. If you are apprised of how a story was constructed, and this construction makes it clear that the story is a fiction, well that means the story is indeed a fiction.

EPILOGUE

Whatever the natures of Reality and the human condition may be, our understanding can only be improved by thinking about them.

I therefore invite you to do so.

GLOSSARY

AI	Artificial Intelligence
CSR	Customer Service Representative
D&D	*Dungeons & Dragons*
ESO	*Elder Scrolls Online*
ESP	Extra-Sensory Perception
GMC	Game-Mastered Content
GOFAI	Good Old-Fashioned Artificial Intelligence
HCC	Hand-Crafted Content
LARP	Live-Action Role-Playing
MMO	Massively-Multiplayer Online
MMORPG	Massively-Multiplayer Online Role-Playing Game
MUD	*Multi-User Dungeon*
NPC	Non-Player Character
OED	*Oxford English Dictionary*
PC	Player Character
PCG	Procedural Content Generation
PGC	Procedurally-Generated Content
PvP	Player *versus* Player
RNG	Random-Number Generator
RPG	Role-Playing Game
SoG	*Sceptre of Goth*
SWL	*Secret World Legends*
TSW	*The Secret World*
UCC	User-Created Content
UGC	User-Generated Content

VR	Virtual Reality
WoW	*World of Warcraft*

References

Alberti, B., 2010. *The Scepter of Goth*, Minneapolis, MN: University of Minnesota.

Allen, T., 1999. MUD Stats. *The MUD Journal.*

Althöfer, I., 2013. *Random Structures from Lego Bricks and Analog Monte Carlo Procedures.* Jena: Department of Mathematics and Computer Science, Friedrich-Schiller University.

Asimov, I., 1950. Runaround. In: *I, Robot.* New York(NY): Doubleday.

Asimov, I., 1973. The Ancient and the Ultimate. In: *The Tragedy of the Moon.* Garden City(NY): Doubleday.

Auden, W. H., 1968. The World of the Sagas. In: *Secondary Worlds.* London: Faber and Faber.

Auden, W. H., 1971. Writing. In: *A Certain World.* London: Faber and Faber, pp. 423-425.

Aupers, S., Schaap, J. & De Wildt, L., 2018. Quanitative In-Depth Interviews: Studying Religious Meaning-Making in MMOs. In: V. Šisler, K. Radde-Antweiler & X. Zeiler, eds. *Methods for Studying Video Games and Religion.* New York(NY): Routledge, pp. 153-167.

Azevedo, F. A. C. et al., 2009. Equal Numbers of Neuronal and Nonneuronal Cells Make the Human Brain an Isometrically Scaled-Up Primate Brain. *Journal of Comparative Neurology*, 10 April, 5(513), pp. 532-541.

Babbage, C., 1838. *The Ninth Bridgewater Treatise (2nd edition)*. London: John Murray.

Bainbridge, W. S., 2010. *The Warcraft Civilization: Social Science in a Virtual World*. 1st ed. Cambridge(MA): MIT Press.

Bainbridge, W. S. & Bainbridge, W. A., 2007. Electronic Game Research Methodologies: Studying Religious Implications. *Review of Religious Research*, September, 49(1), pp. 35-53.

Baron-Cohen, S., Leslie, A. & Frith, U., 1985. Does the Autistic Child have a "Theory of Mind"?. *Cognition*, October, 21(1), pp. 37-46.

Bartle, R. A., 1996. Hearts, Clubs, Diamonds, Spades: Players who Suit MUDs. *Journal of MUD Research*, June.1(1).

Bartle, R. A., 2003. *Designing Virtual Worlds*. Indianapolis(IN): New Riders.

Bartle, R. A., 2004. *Newbie Induction: How Poor Design Triumphs in Virtual Worlds*. Copenhagen, ITU Copenhagen.

Bartle, R. A., 2009. Understanding the Limits of Theory. In: C. Bateman, ed. *Beyond Game Design: Nine Steps to Creating Better Videogames.* 1st ed. Boston(MA): Delmar, pp. 117-133.

Bartle, R. A., 2011. Unrealistic Expectations. In: T. Krzywinska, E. MacCallum-Stewart & J. Parsler, eds. *Ring Bearers: The Lord of the Rings Online as Intertextual Narrative.* Manchester: Manchester University Press, pp. 155-174.

Bartle, R. A., 2012. MMO Morality. In: J. Fromme & A. Unger, eds. *Computer Games and New Media Cultures: a Handbook of Digital Games Studies.* Heidelberg: Springer.

Bartle, R. A., 2016. *MMOs from the Inside Out.* New York(NY): Apress.

Becher, J. J., 1667. *Physica Subterranea.* 3rd ed. Leipzig: Gleditschium.

Beckwith, M. W., 1940. *Hawaiian Mythology.* New Haven(CT): Yale University Press.

Bers, M. U., 2001. Identity Construction Environments: Developing Personal and Moral Values through the Design of a Virtual City. *The Journal of the Learning Sciences,* 10(4), pp. 365-415.

Björk, S. & Juul, J., 2012. *Zero-Player Games, or What We Talk about When We Talk about Players.* Madrid,

6th International Conference on Philosophy of Computer Games.

Bogost, I., 2007. *Persuasive Games: The Expressive Power of Videogames.* 1st ed. Cambridge(MA): MIT Press.

Boren, J. K., 2016. *Playing God: An Analysis of Video Game Religion.* Claremont(CA): Claremont McKenna College.

Bosman, F. G., 2016. The Word has Become Game: Researching Religion in Digital Games. *Heidelberg Journal of Religions on the Internet,* Volume 11, pp. 28-45.

Bostrom, N., 2003. Are you Living in a Computer Simulation?. *The Philosophical Quarterly,* 28 April, 53(211), pp. 243-255.

Bowman, S. L., 2013. Social Conflict in Role-Playing Communities: an Exploratory Qualitative Study. *International Journal of Role-Playing,* 12 September, Issue 4, pp. 4-25.

Bowman, S. L., 2018. Immersion and Shared Imagination in Role-Playing Games. In: J. P. &. D. S. Zagal, ed. *Role-Playing Game Studies: Transmedia Foundations.* 1st ed. New York(NY): Routledge, pp. 379-394.

Broome, F., 2010. *Nelson Mandela Died in Prison?.* [Online]

Available at: http://mandelaeffect.com/nelson-mandela-died-in-prison/
[Accessed 6 March 2021].

Bruckman, A., 1992. *Identity Workshop: Emergent Social and Psychological Phenomena in Text-Based Virtual Reality*, Boston, MA: MIT Media Lab.

Burris, C. T. & Dow, T., 2015. Lost in the Myst?: Narrative Video Gaming Decreases Self-Reported Propensity for Spiritual/Religious Experience. *International Journal for the Psychology of Religion*, 25(1), pp. 18-28.

Butler, S., 1872. *Erewhon, or Over the Range*. 1st ed. London: Trübner and Ballantyne.

Butler, S., 1898. *The Iliad of Homer*. Cambridge: Cambridge University Press.

Campbell, J., 1949. *The Hero with a Thousand Faces*. Princeton(NJ): Princeton University Press.

Carpenter, H., 1981. *The Letters of J. R. R. Tolkien*. 1st ed. London: Allen & Unwin.

Carroll, J., 1994. Guerrillas in the Myst. *Wired*, 1 August, 2(8), pp. 69-73.

Carroll, J. W., 2016. Laws of Nature. In: E. N. Zalta, ed. *The Stanford Encyclopedia of Philosophy*. Fall 2016 ed. Stanford(CA): Metaphysics Research Lab, Stanford University.

Carse, J. P., 1986. *Finite and Infinite Games: a Vision of Life as Play and Possibility*. New York(NY): The Free Press.

Carter, L., 1973. *Imaginary Worlds*. 1st ed. New York(NY): Ballantine.

Carter, M., Gibbs, M. & Arnold, M., 2012. *Avatars, Characters, Players and Users: Multiple Identities at/in Play*. Melbourne, CHISIG, Human Factors and Ergonomics Society of Australia, pp. 68-71.

Casas-Roma, J. et al., 2019. *Towards Simulated Morality Systems: Role-Playing Games as Artificial Societies*. Prague, 11th International Conference on Agents and Artificial Intelligence.

Castronova, E., 2005. *Synthetic Worlds: The Business and Culture of Online Games*. 1st ed. Chicago(IL): University of Chicago Press.

Castronova, E., 2007. *Exodus to the Virtual World: How Online Fun is Changing Reality*. 1st ed. New York(NY): Palgrave Macmillan.

Castronova, E., 2008. A Test of the Law of Demand in a Virtual World: Exploring the Petri Dish Approach to Social Science. *CESifo Working Paper Series*, 24 July.Issue 2355.

Castronova, E., 2012. *The Renaissance of Natural Law: Tolkien, Fantasy, and Video Games*.

Greencastle, Prindle Institute for Ethics, DePauw University.

Clark, R. N., 2017. *Notes on the Resolution and Other Details of the Human Eye.* [Online]
Available at:
http://www.clarkvision.com/articles/eye-resolution.html
[Accessed 30 December 2021].

Clodius, J., 1995. *Ritual and Religion in DragonMud.* [Online]
Available at:
https://web.archive.org/web/20031013094255/http://dragonmud.com/people/jen/ritual.html
[Accessed 30 December 2021].

Cooper, W., 1995. Virtual Reality and the Metaphysics of Self, Community and Nature. *International Journal of Applied Philosophy,* 9(2), pp. 1-14.

Copier, M., 2005. *Connecting Worlds. Fantasy Role-Playing Games, Ritual Acts and the Magic Circle.* Vancouver, DiGRA.

Copson, A., 2017. *Secularism.* 1st ed. Oxford: Oxford University Press.

Costikyan, G., 2013. *Uncertainty in Games.* Cambridge(MA): MIT Press.

Crawford, C., 1984. *The Art of Computer Game Design.* 1st ed. Berkeley(CA): Osborne/McGraw-Hill.

Darwin, C., 1871. *The Descent of Man, and Selection in Relation to Sex.* 1st ed. London: John Murray.

Dawson, L. L., 2001. New Religions in Cyberspace: the Promise and the Perils of a New Public Space. In: P. Côté, ed. *Chercheurs de Dieux dans l'Espace Public - Frontier Religions in Public Space.* Ottowa(Ontario): University of Ottowa Press, pp. 35-54.

De Wildt, L., 2020. *Playing at Religion: Encoding/Decoding Religion in Videogames,* Leuven: Katholieke Universiteit Leuven.

De Wildt, L. et al., 2019. (Re-)Orienting the Video Game Avatar. *Games and Culture,* 17 July.pp. 1-9.

De Wildt, L. & Aupers, S., 2020. Eclectic Religion: the Flattening of Religious Cultural Heritage in Videogames. *International Journal of Heritage Studies,* 26(6).

Descartes, R., 1637. *Discourse on the Method of Rightly Conducting One's Reason and of Seeking Truth in the Sciences.* 1st ed. Leiden: Ian Maire.

Detweiler, C., 2010. Conclusion: Born to Play. In: C. Detweiler, ed. *Halos and Avatars: Playing Video Games with God.* Louisville(KY): Westminster John Knox, pp. 190-196.

Dibbell, J., 1993. A Rape in Cyberspace: How an Evil Clown, a Haitian Trickster Spirit, Two Wizards, and a Cast of Dozens Turned a Database Into a Society. *The Village Voice*, 21 December, XXXVIII(51), pp. 36-42.

Doyle, A. C., 1891. A Scandal in Bohemia. *The Strand Magazine*, 25 June, II(7), pp. 61-75.

Dreyfus, H. L., 1972. *What Computers Can't Do: A Critique of Artificial Reasoning.* 1st ed. New York(NY): Harper & Row.

Dyck, B., 2008. *Breaking the Golden Bough.* [Online] Available at: http://mud.co.uk/dvw/breakingthegoldenbough.html
[Accessed 30 December 2021].

Earp, J. et al., 2018. *Ethical Issues in Gaming: A Literature Review.* Sophia Antipolis, Academic Conferences and Publishing International Limited.

Edwards, J., 1765. *A Dissertation Concerning the End for Which God Created the World.* Boston(MA): S. Kneeland.

Eurasia Review, 2012. Hindus Upset At Online Video Game Using Kali And Other Gods As Combat Tools. *Eurasia Review*, 27 July.

Fagerholt, E. & Lorentzon, M., 2009. *Beyond the HUD: User Interfaces for Increased Player Immersion in FPS Games*, Göteborg: Chalmers University of Technology.

Farmer, F. R., 1993. *Habitat Anecdotes and Other Boastings*, Cupertino: Electric Communities.

Farmer, F. R., 2012. Web Reputation Systems and the Real world. In: H. Masum & M. Tovey, eds. *The Reputation Society: How Online Opinions are Reshaping the Offline World*. 1st ed. Cambridge(MA): MIT Press, pp. 13-24.

Fine, G. A., 1983. *Shared Fantasy: Role Playing Games as Social Worlds*. 1st ed. Chicago(IL): Chicago University Press.

Formosa, P. et al., 2022. Morality Meters and Their Impacts on Moral Choices in Videogames: A Qualitative Study. *Games and Culture*, 1 January, 17(1), pp. 89-121.

Forster, E. M., 1927. *Aspects of the Novel*. London: Edward Arnold.

Gadamer, H.-G., trans. 2013. *Truth and Method*. 2nd ed. London: Bloomsbury Academic.

Gardner, M., 1970. Mathematical Games: The Fantastic Combinations of John Conway's New Solitaire Game, "Life". *Scientific American*, October, Issue 223, pp. 120-123.

Garriott, R. & Fisher, D., 2017. *Explore/Create.* 1st ed. New York(NY): HarperCollins.

Geertz, C., 1966. Religion as a Cultural System. In: M. Banton, ed. *Anthropological Approaches to the Study of Religion.* London: Tavistock, pp. 1-46.

Geraci, J. L., 2019. Until the End of the World: Fans as Messianic Heroes in World of Warcraft. In: C. M. Cusack, J. W. Morehead & V. L. D. Robertson, eds. *The Sacred in Fantastic Fandom: Essays on the Intersection of Religion and Pop Culture.* 1st ed. Jefferson(NC): McFarland, pp. 138-153.

Geraci, R. M., 2020. Theological Productions: the Role of Religion in Video Game Design. In: A. L. Brackin & N. Guyot, eds. *Cultural Perspectives of Video Games: from Desiger to Player.* Leiden: Brill, pp. 101-114.

Gibbs, M., Mori, J., Arnold, M. & Kohn, T., 2012. Tombstones, Uncanny Monuments and Epic Quests: Memorials in World of Warcraft. *Game Studies,* September.12(1).

Goffman, E., 1961. *Encounters: Two Studies in the Sociology of Interaction.* 1st ed. Indianapolis(IN): Bobbs-Merrill.

Habermas, J., 2003. *The Future of Human Nature.* 1st ed. Cambridge: Polity Press.

Hall, D. L. & Ames, R. T., 1998. *Thinking from the Han: Self, Truth and Transcendence in Chinese and Western Culture.* Albany(NY): State University of New York Press.

Hammer, A., 2005. Weaving Trickster: Myth and Tribal Encounters on the World Wide Web. In: E. W. Rothenbuhler & M. Coman, eds. *Media Anthropology.* 1st ed. Thousand Oaks(CA): Sage, pp. 260-268.

Hart, G., 1986. *A Dictionary of Egyptian Gods and Goddesses.* London: Routledge.

Haugeland, J., 1985. *Artificial Intelligence: The Very Idea.* Cambridge(MA): MIT Press.

Hedges, P., 2017. Multiple Religious Belonging after Religion: Theorising Strategic Religious Participation in a Shared Religious Landscape as a Chinese Model. *Open Theology,* 2017 January, 3(1), pp. 48-72.

Heidbrink, S. & Knoll, T. eds., 2014. *Heidelberg Journal of Religions on the Internet,* Volume 5.

Heidegger, M., 1927. *Being and Time.* Tübingen: Max Niemeyer.

Hess, E., 2003. *Yib's Guide to MOOing: Getting the Most from Virtual Communities on the Internet.* Victoria(BC): Trafford.

Hofstadter, D., 1979. *Gödel, Escher, Bach: An Eternal Golden Braid.* New York(NY): Basic Books.

Huizinga, J., trans. 1949. *Homo Ludens: A Study of the Play-Element in Culture.* London: Routledge and Kegan Paul.

Hume, D., 1739. *A Treatise of Human Nature.* 1st ed. London: John Noon.

Humphreys, S., 2005. Productive Users, Intellectual Property and Governance: the Challenges of Computer Games. *Media Arts Law Review,* 10(4), pp. 299-310.

International Theological Commission, 2007. *The Hope of Salvation for Infants who Die without being Baptised,* Vatican: International Theological Commission.

Iron Realms Entertainment, 2021. *The Gods of Achaea.* [Online]
Available at: https://www.achaea.com/gods/
[Accessed 30 December 2021].

Jackson, S., 1991. *Realism versus Playability in Simulation Game Design.* Barcelona, Generalitat de Catalunya, Departament de Cultura.

Jensenius, J. S., 2018. *A Detailed Analysis of Lightning Deaths in the United States from 2006 through 2017,* Silver Spring (MD): National Oceanic and Atmospheric Administration.

Johnston, I., 2010. *Homer Iliad.* Revised ed. Nanaimo(BC): Ian Johnstone.

Jonson, B., 1606. *Volpone.* London: King's Men.

Jung, C. G., 1923. *Psychological Types.* 1st ed. London: Kegan Paul, Trench, Trubner.

Juul, J., 2021. *The Game of Video Game Objects: a Minimal Theory of when we see Pixels as Objects rather than Pictures.* New York, Association for Computing Machinery, pp. 376-381.

Kania, M. M., 2017. *Perspectives of the Avatar: Sketching the Existential Aesthetics of Digital Games.* Wrocław: University of Lower Silesia Press.

Keegan, M., 1997. A Classification of MUDs. *Journal of MUD Research,* July.2(2).

Kelly, K., 1994. *Out of Control.* 1st ed. New York(NY): Addison Wesley.

Kipping, D., 2020. A Bayesian Approach to the Simulation Argument. *Universe,* 3 August, 6(8), p. 109.

Klastrup, L., 2007. Why Death Matters: Understanding Gameworld Experience. *Journal of Virtual Reality and Broadcasting,* 25 April.Volume 4.

Kluver, R., 2008. The Church of Fools: Virtual Ritual and Material Faith. *Heidelberg Journal of Religions on the Internet,* 3(1).

Kneale, M., 2013. *An Atheist's History of Belief: Understanding our most Extraordinary Invention.* 1st ed. London: Bodley Head.

Knoll, T., 2018. 'Instant Karma' - Moral Decision Making Systems in Digital Games. *Religions,* 16 April, 9(131), pp. 126-160.

Koepsell, D. R., 2000. *The Ontology of Cyberspace.* 1st ed. Peru(IL): Carus.

Koljonen, J., 2007. Eye-Witness to the Illusion: An Essay on the Impossibility of 360° Role-Playing. In: J. Donnis, M. Gade & L. Thorup, eds. *Lifelike.* Copenhagen: Levende Rollespil, pp. 174-187.

Koster, R., 2013. *A Theory of Fun for Game Design.* 2nd ed. Sebastopol(CA): O'Reilly.

Koster, R., 2018. *Postmortems: Selected Essays Volume One.* 1st ed. San Diego(CA): Altered Tuning.

Kuntz, R. & Ward, J. M., 1976. *Gods, Demi-Gods and Heroes.* Lake Geneva(WI): TSR Games.

Latour, B., 2000. On the Partial Existence of Existing and Nonexisting Objects. In: L. Daston, ed. *Biographies of Scientific Objects.* Chicago(IL): Chicago University Press, pp. 247-169.

Lawrence, C. R., 2015. *Planck 2015 Results*, Pasadena: NASA Astrophysics Subcommittee.

Lawrie, M., 1991. *Confessions of an Arch-Wizard.* [Online]
Available at: http://arch-wizard.com/confessions.html
[Accessed 30 December 2021].

Lawrie, M., 2003. *A Footnote to Confessions.* [Online]
Available at: http://arch-wizard.com/footnote.html
[Accessed 30 December 2021].

Laycock, J. P., 2015. *Dangerous Games: What the Moral Panic over Role-Playing Games Says about Play, Religion and Imagined Worlds.* 1st ed. Oakland(CA): University of California Press.

Lefebvre, E., 2019. *Storyboard: Exploring Religions in MMOs.* [Online]
Available at:
https://massivelyop.com/2019/06/10/storyboard-exploring-religion-in-mmos/
[Accessed 30 December 2021].

Leino, O. T., 2019. *God is a Game Designer - Accelerating 'Existential Ludology'*. Kyoto, DiGRA.

Lem, S., 1979. Non Serviam. In: *A Perfect Vacuum.* London: Secker & Warburg.

Lombard, M. & Ditton, T., 1997. At the Heart of it All: The Concept of Presence. *Journal of Computer-Mediated Communications,* 3(2).

MacDonald, G., 1893. The Fantastic Imagination. In: *The Light Princess and Other Fairy Tales.* New York(NY): G. P. Putnam's Sons.

Mackie, J. L., 1977. *Ethics: Inventing Right and Wrong.* 1st ed. London: Pelican Books.

Malliarakis, C., Satratzemi, M. & Xinogalos, S., 2017. CMX: The Effects of an Educational MMORPG on Learning and Teaching Computer Programming. *IEEE Transactions on Learning Technologies,* April, 10(2), pp. 219-235.

Marx, K. & Engels, F., 1848. *The Communist Manifesto.* London: J. E. Burghard.

McGonigal, J., 2011. *Reality is Broken: Why Games Make us Better and How they can Change the World.* 1st ed. London: Jonathan Cape.

McKee, H. A. & Porter, J. E., 2009. Playing a Good Game: Ethical Issues in Researching MMOGs and Virtual Worlds. *International Journal of Internet Research Ethics,* February, 2(1), pp. 5-35.

Minsky, M., 1980. Telepresence. *Omni,* June, pp. 45-53.

Moberger, V., 2021. Philosophy Encourages Confused, Self-Indulgent Thinking. *Psyche*, 9 February.

Montagne, O., 2007. *Metaverse Manifesto*. San Francisco(CA): Studio SFO.

Montola, M., 2010. *The Positive Negative Experience in Extreme Role-Playing*. Stockholm, DiGRA.

More, T., trans. 1901. *Utopia, by Thomas More.* London: Cassell.

Mukherjee, S., 2009. *'Remembering How You Died': Memory, Death and Temporality in Videogames.* London, DiGRA.

Mukherjee, S., 2017. *Videogames and Postcolonialism: Empire Plays Back.* 1st ed. London: Palgrave Macmillan.

Murdock, M., 1990. *The Heroine's Journey: Woman's Quest for Wholeness.* Boulder(CO): Shambhala Publications.

Murray, S., 2014. *PlayStation.blog.* [Online] Available at: https://blog.eu.playstation.com/2014/08/26/exploring-18446744073709551616-planets-mans-sky/ [Accessed 30 December 2021].

Nagasiva, T., 1992. *LIBER MUD: The MUD as a Basis for Western Mysticism.* [Online]

Available at:
http://www.luckymojo.com/avidyana/gnostik/liber-mud.html
[Accessed 30 December 2021].

National Health Service, 2018. *Miscarriage.* [Online] Available at:
https://www.nhs.uk/conditions/miscarriage/
[Accessed 30 December 2021].

Nesbit, E., 1910. *The Magic City*. London: Macmillan.

Nesbit, E., 1913. *Wings and the Child; Or, the Building of Magic Cities*. London: Hodder & Stoughton.

Nevejans, N., 2016. *European Civil Law Rules in Robotics*, Brussels: European Union Directorate-General for Internal Policies.

Newsome-Ward, T. & Ng, J., 2021. Between Subjectivity and Flourishing: Creativity and Game Design as Existential Meaning. *Games and Culture*, 19 October, 0(0), pp. 1-24.

O'Leary, S. D., 1996. Cyberspace as Sacred Space: Communicating Religion on Computer Networks. *Journal of the American Academy of Religion*, 1 October, LXIV(4), pp. 781-808.

Oxford English Dictionary, third edition, 2014. *god, n. and int.*. Oxford: Oxford University Press.

Payscale, 2021. *Average Computer Programmer Salary in United Kingdom.* [Online] Available at: https://www.payscale.com/research/UK/Job=Computer_Programmer/Salary [Accessed 30 December 2021].

Payscale, 2021. *Average Video Game Programmer Salary in United Kingdom.* [Online] Available at: https://www.payscale.com/research/UK/Job=Video_Game_Programmer/Salary [Accessed 30 December 2021].

Plato, trans. 1892. *The Dialogues of Plato: Laws.* 3rd ed. London: Oxford University Press.

Plato, trans. 1892. *The Dialogues of Plato: Phaedo.* 3rd ed. London: Oxford University Press.

Postman, N., 1985. *Amusing Ourselves to Death.* 1st ed. New York(NY): Viking.

Rachels, J. & Rachels, S., 2019. *The Elements of Moral Philosophy.* 9th ed. New York(NY): McGraw-Hill Education.

Raff, J., 2019. The Alchemy of Imagination. *Psychological Perspectives,* November 20, 62(2-3), pp. 276-284.

Reid, E., 1994. *Cultural Formations in Text-Based Virtual Realities*, Melbourne: University of Melbourne.

Reid, E., 1996. Informed Consent in the Study of On-Line Communities: A Reflection on the Effects of Computer-Mediated Social Research. *The Information Society*, 12(2), pp. 169-174.

Relph, E., 1976. *Place and Placelessness.* 1st ed. London: Pion.

Reynolds, R., 2002. *Playing a "Good" Game: A Philosophical Approach to Understanding the Morality of Games*, Toronto: International Game Developers Association.

Reynolds, R., 2007. *MMOs as Practices.* Tokyo, DiGRA.

Richmond, F. M., 1934. *School Yarns and Howlers.* London: Universal Publications.

Riezler, K., 1941. Play and Seriousness. *Journal of Philosophy*, 11 September, 38(11), pp. 505-517.

Ringel, Z. & Kovrizhin, D. L., 2017. Quantised Gravitational Responses, the Sign Problem, and Quantum Complexity. *Science Advances*, 27 September.3(9).

Roberts, S., 2015. *Genius at Play: The Curious Mind of John Horton Conway*. New York(NY): Bloomsbury USA.

Ronsmans, C. & Graham, W. J., 2006. Maternal Mortality: Who, When, Where, and Why. *The Lancet*, 30 September, 368(9,542), pp. 1189-1200.

Rosedale, P., 2009. The Mission of Linden Lab. In: T. M. Malaby, ed. *Making Virtual Worlds: Linden Lab and Second Life*. Ithaca(NY): Cornell University Press, pp. 139-143.

Ross, I., 1957. Voice of the Sages. *New York Post*, 6 November, p. M2.

Russell, B., 1903. *The Principles of Mathematics*. 1st ed. Cambridge: Cambridge University Press.

Russell, B., 1911. Le Réalisme Analytique. *Bulletin de la Société Française de Philosophie*, 23 March, 11(3), pp. 53-61.

Ryan, M.-L., 1980. Fiction, Non-Factuals, and the Principle of Minimal Departure. *Poetics*, August, 9(4), pp. 403-422.

Ryle, G., 1949. *The Concept of Mind*. 1st ed. London: Hutchinson.

Salazar, J., 2005. *On the Ontology of MMORPG Beings: a Theoretical Model for Research*. Vancouver, DiGRA.

Salen, K. & Zimmerman, E., 2003. *Rules of Play: Game Design Fundamentals.* Cambridge(MA): MIT Press.

Saler, M., 2012. *As If: Modern Enchantment and the Literary Prehistory of Virtual Reality.* 1st ed. New York(NY): Oxford University Press.

Santayana, G., 1905. *The Life of Reason: The Phases of Human Progress.* New York(NY): Dover Publications.

Schaap, F., 2002. *The Words that Took us There: Ethnography in a Virtual Reality.* 1st ed. Amsterdam: Aksant.

Schaap, J. & Aupers, S., 2017. 'Gods in World of Warcraft Exist': Religious Reflexivity and the Quest for Meaning in Online Computer Games. *New Media and Society,* 19(11), pp. 1744-1760.

Schrier, K., 2021. Ethics and Gaming. In: R. E. Ferdig, E. Baumgartner & E. Gandolfi, eds. *Teaching the Game.* Pittsburgh(PA): Carnegie Mellon University: ETC Press, pp. 20-41.

Schrödinger, E., 1935. The Present Situation in Quantum Mechanics. *Naturwissenschaften,* November, 23(48), pp. 807-812.

Schütz, A., 1945. On Multiple Realities. *Philosophy and Phenomenological Research,* June, 5(4), pp. 533-576.

Scott, M., Stardate 1704.2. *Engineering*. USS Enterprise NCC-1701: Starfleet.

Sellers, M., 2018. *Advanced Game Design: a Systems Approach*. Boston(MA): Addison-Wesley.

Sicart, M., 2009. *The Ethics of Computer Games*. 1st ed. Cambridge(MA): MIT Press.

Sloane, N. J. A. & Plouffe, S., 1995. *The Encyclopedia of Integer Sequences*. San Diego(CA): Academic Press.

Somerville, M., 2006. *The Ethical Imagination: Journeys of the Human Spirit*. 1st ed. Melbourne: Melbourne University Press.

Sparrow, L. A., Gibbs, M. & Arnold, M., 2020. Ludic Ethics: The Ethical Negotiations of Players in Online Multiplayer Games. *Games and Culture*, 31 October, 0(0), pp. 1-24.

Stephenson, N., 1992. *Snow Crash*. New York(NY): Bantam.

Stonehouse, A., 2014. *User Interface Design in Video Games*. [Online]
Available at:
https://www.gamedeveloper.com/design/user-interface-design-in-video-games
[Accessed 30 December 2021].

Suber, P., 1990. *The Paradox of Self-Amendment: A Study of Law, Logic, Omnipotence, and Change*. Bern: Peter Lang.

Suits, B., 1978. *The Grasshopper: Games, Life and Utopia*. 1st ed. Edinburgh: Scottish Academic Press.

Taylor, T. L., 2006. Beyond Management: Considering Participatory Design and Governance in Player Culture. *First Monday*, October, Issue (Special) #7.

Therrien, C., 2011. *"To Get Help, Press X": th eRise of the Assistance Paradigm in Video Games*. Utrecht, DiGRA.

Thompson, S., 1958. *Motif-Index of Folk-Literature: A Classification of Narrative Elements in Folk-Tales, Ballads, Myths, Fables, Mediaeval Romances, Exempla, Fabliaux, Jest-Books, and Local Legends*. 2nd ed. Copenhagen: Rosenkilde and Bagger.

Tobar, G. & Costa, F., 2020. Reversible Dynamics with Closed Time-Like Curves and Freedom of Choice. *Classical and Quantum Gravity*, 21 September.37(20).

Tolkien, J. R. R., 1954. *The Lord of the Rings*. 1st ed. London: George Allen & Unwin.

Tolkien, J. R. R., 1964. On Fairy Stories. In: *Tree and Leaf*. London: George Allen and Unwin.

Tomasik, B., 2014. *Do Video-Game Characters Matter Morally?*. [Online]
Available at: https://reducing-suffering.org/do-video-game-characters-matter-morally/
[Accessed 30 December 2021].

Tononi, G., 2004. An Information Integration Theory of Consciousness. *BMC Neuroscience,* 2 November, Volume 5, p. 42.

Totten, C. W., 2019. *An Architectural Approach to Level Design.* 2nd ed. Boca Raton(FL): CRC Press.

Turing, A. M., 1937. On Computable Numbers, with an Application to the Entscheidungsproblem. *Proceedings of the London Mathematical Society,* 1 January, s2-42(1), pp. 230-265.

Turing, A. M., 1950. Computing Machinery and Intelligence. *Mind,* October, 59(236), pp. 433-460.

Updegraff, R. R., 1916. *Obvious Adams: the Story of a Successful Business Man.* 1st ed. New York(NY): Harper and Brothers.

Upton, B., 2015. *The Aesthetic of Play.* 1st ed. Cambridge(MA): MIT Press.

Vallikat, J., 2014. *Virtually Religious: Myth, Ritual and Community in World of Warcraft.* Melbourne: Royal Melbourne Institute of Technology.

Vaughan, L., 2003. Playing Religiously. *Muddled Times*, February.

Vineyard, J., 2017. *A Brief Conversation With Kit Harington About Jon Snow on 'Game of Thrones'.* [Online]
Available at:
https://www.nytimes.com/2017/08/15/watching/daenerys-kit-harington-game-of-thrones.html
[Accessed 30 December 2021].

Wagner, R., 2009. Dreaming Cyborg Dreams: Virtual Identity and Religious Experience. *Religion Dispatches*, 15 June.

Wagner, R., 2012. *Godwired: Religion, Ritual and Virtual Reality.* 1st ed. Abingdon(Oxon.): Routledge.

Wakeman, I., Lewis, D. & Crowcroft, J., 1991. *Traffic Analysis of Trans-Atlantic Traffic,* London: University College.

Waltemathe, M., 2015. Current Key Perspectives in Video Gaming and Religion. *Gamevironments,* 3(1), pp. 50-52.

Wayman, A., 1967. Significance of Dreams in India and Tibet. *History of Religions,* August, 7(1), pp. 1-12.

Weber, M., 1919. *Politics as a Vocation.* Munich: Verlag Duncker & Humblot.

Weinersmith, Z., 2013. *Meat is Murder.* [Online] Available at: https://www.smbc-comics.com/comic/2013-09-07 [Accessed 30 December 2021].

Wertheim, M., 1999. *The Pearly Gates of Cyberspace: A History of Space from Dante to the Internet.* London: Virago.

White Hodge, D., 2010. Role Playing: Toward a Theology for Gamers. In: C. Detweiler, ed. *Halos and Avatars: Playing Video Games with God.* Louiseville(KY): Westminster John Knox, pp. 163-175.

Williams, D., 2010. The Mapping Principle, and a Research Framework for Virtual Worlds. *Communication Theory*, 1 October, 20(4), pp. 451-470.

Williams, T., 1998. *City of Golden Shadow.* New York(NY): DAW.

Wilmott Dobbie, B. M., 1982. An Attempt to Estimate the True Rate of Maternal Mortality, Sixteenth to Eighteenth Centuries. *Medical History*, Volume 26, pp. 79-90.

Wittgenstein, L., 1953. *Philosophical Investigations.* New York(NY): Macmillan.

Wolf, M. J. P., 2012. *Building Imaginary Worlds: the Theory and History of Subcreation.* 1st ed. New York(NY): Routledge.

Wolf, M. J. P., 2020. Concerning the "Sub" in "Subcreation": the Act of Creating Under. In: M. J. P. Wolf, ed. *World-Builders on World-Building: an Exploration of Subcreation.* 1st ed. New York(NY): Routledge, pp. 132-142.

Wolfram, S., 2020. *Finally We May Have a Path to the Fundamental Theory of Physics ... and It's Beautiful.* [Online]
Available at:
https://writings.stephenwolfram.com/2020/04/finally-we-may-have-a-path-to-the-fundamental-theory-of-physics-and-its-beautiful
[Accessed 30 December 2021].

Wowhead, 2021. *Quests.* [Online]
Available at: https://www.wowhead.com/quests
[Accessed 30 December 2021].

Wright, R., 2009. *The Evolution of God.* 1st ed. London: Little, Brown.

Yannakakis, G. N. & Togelius, J., 2011. Experience-Driven Procedural Content Generation. *IEEE Transactions on Affective Computing,* 2(3), pp. 147-161.

Yee, N. & Bailensen, J. N., 2007. The Proteus Effect: The Effect of Transformed Self-Representation on

Behavior. *Human Communication Research*, 1 July, 33(3), pp. 271-290.

Zabet, F.-D., 2012. *Playing Together and Ritualisation in Online Games*, Canterbury: University of Kent.

Zagal, J. P., 2021. Ethics in Videogames. In: R. E. Ferdig, E. Baumgartner & E. Gandolfi, eds. *Teaching the Game*. 1st ed. Pittsburgh(PA): Carnegie Mellon University: ETC Press, pp. 42-62.

Zagal, J. P., Björk, S. & Lewis, C., 2013. *Dark Patterns in the Design of Games*. Chania, Foundations of Digital Games.

Zenit, 2010. *Pontiff Warns of Truth-Falsehood Mix-Up*. [Online]
Available at: https://zenit.org/articles/pontiff-warns-of-truth-falsehood-mix-up/
[Accessed 30 December 2021].

INDEX

∃ .... *See* existential quantifier
π .... *See* pi
360° illusion 141
3Kingdoms 498
Abraham 14, 102
Abrahamic religions .... *See* religions: Abrahamic
absenting 230–31, 235–37, 246, 254, 467, 476
Absolute, the 172
accounts 13, 17, 94, 284
Achaea 79
actors 325
Adam 259, 275
Addams, Wednesday 43
addons 281
adds 314
agnosticism 241
AI .... *See* Artificial Intelligence
aimbots 326
Albion Online 84
Alfheim 460, 465
Allah 170, 365, 487, 496, 500
alpha testing 490
American Football 268
Ammit 406
amorality .... *See* morals
Amphitryon 96
Amun 153

Amun-Ra....153
An Atheist's History of Belief....362
ancestor-simulations....495
Ancient Africans....49
Ancient Chinese....49, 522
Ancient Egyptians....153, 157, 194, 333, 362, 405, 451, 522
Ancient Greeks. 13, 18, 49, 95, 148, 173, 222, 259, 319, 329, 431, 485, 522
Ancient Indians....49
Ancient Japanese....522
Ancient Mesopotamians....248, 407
Ancient Polynesians....522
Ancient Romans....95, 209, 259, 317, 522
Ancient Slavs....13, 522
Angrathar the Wrathgate....88
Anthropology....441, 509
Anubis....405
Apep....451
Apollo....13
Aquinas, Saint Thomas....182
arborescence....463
Arden....493
argument from marginal cases....420
argument from species normality....420
Aristotle....202
Artificial Intelligence22, 206, 299, 325, 335, 346, 496
  ethics of.... *See* ethics: of Artificial Intelligence
  Good Old-Fashioned....207
artists....56–57, 201
  medieval....257–58

ascending 152, 229, 235, 237, 246, 406, 412, 451, 467
Asgard 245, 461
asiety 150
Asimov, Isaac 339
asking for a pony 473
Association Football 268
atheism 241, 517–18, 545
Athena 57, 62
attaching 232–33, 236, 249
Atum 153
Atum-Ra 153
Auden, Wystan H. 136
augmented reality 145
Aurora Technology 382
Avatar 31–33, 59
avatars 59, 171
Azeroth 465
Aztecs 356, 462
Babbage, Charles 51
Babylonians 492
backfire effect 371
back-ups 123, 130
backward chaining 299
Barker, Muhammad A. R. 138
Bartle, Richard 31
Batman 170
BCPL 21
beehives 162
beetle in a box 136
beings

moral.......... *See* moral beings
morally considerable ..... *See* morally considerable beings
supernatural.......... *See* supernatural: beings
Benedict XVI, Pope 125, 513
beta testing 490
Bible Online, The 494, 507
Bible, The 94, 102, 113, 150, 190, 259, 505, 539
Big Bang, the.......... 128, 152
bits 198, 307, 346
in a database. 196, 210, 226, 337, 394, 397, 425, 550
Black Desert Online 37, 84, 282
bleed 378
blinkers.......... 162
Blizzard Entertainment 465
Bodh Gaya 443
Book of the Dead, The 406
bosses.......... 313
bots 320, 325–34
Boudicca and Andy 208–15
Brahma.......... 105
brains 135, 180, 238, 240–41, 354
branching factor.......... 159
Brethren of the Free Spirit.......... 369
British, Lord.......... 390
Brontë sisters.......... 137
Buckley, Theodore A. 318
Buddhism 148, 336
Buffy the Vampire Slayer 508
Buffyverse 139
bugs 120

Burning Crusade, The .... *See World of Warcraft:The Burning Crusade*
Butler, Samuel 318
C 21, 359, 494
C++ 93, 359
Call of Cthulhu 511
Campbell, Joseph 266
capsuleers 510
cardinal virtues 416
Cataclysm .... *See World of Warcraft: Cataclysm*
causa sui 153
causality 164, 168, 184, 187, 296–301, 307
cells 160–62, 200
cellular automata 164, 486
Celts 522
channelling 324
Chaos 149
Chapman, George 318
characters
  non-player .... *See* non-player characters
  player .... *See* player characters
cheats 417
Cheondoism 246
Chess 42, 157–59, 374
chosen one 14
Christ
  body and blood of 250
  real presence of 252
Christianity 95, 150, 170, 183, 229, 252, 257, 259, 335, 410, 416, 431, 455, 520
Church of England 445

Church of Fools 440–42, 498, 510
Civilization V 286
clients 90
Clodius, Jen 441, 510
CMX 494
code 63, 66, 181, 195, 202, 226, 235, 465, 483
  executable 64, 71, 131
  self-modifying 67, 176, 184, 188–90
  source 32–33, 64, 71
codebases 74, 483
cogito, ergo sum 220
Columbo 355
Communist Manifesto, The 469
compilers 64
completeness 192–93
Computer Science 23–25, 160, 222
computers 63, 195, 234
  analogue 68, 306
  quantum 306
consciousness 207, 319, 337, 529–30
consent 342, 429, 471–72
consequent realities .... *See* realities: consequent
consequentialism 416
consistency 192
content 20, 75–84, 87, 94–98, 102, 104, 116, 127, 464, 483, 502, 546, 551
  contextual 82
  designed 82
  direct 82
  emergent 82–84, 549
  explicit 78

freeform.. 82, 100
game-mastered.................................. 79, 96–98, 552
hand-crafted........................ 80, 96–98, 101, 103, 552
implicit...78
procedurally-generated 81, 96, 99, 101, 103, 546, 552
systems..81, 98, 103, 384, 552
user-created..80, 97, 100, 552
user-generated... 80, 99, 552
contextual content................*See* content: contextual
continuous time........................ *See* time: continuous
Conway, John H. 160, 164, 486
Conway's Game of *Life*.......................................See *Life*
Copeland–Erdős constant....................................... 554
corpse runs..388
cosmic egg 149
cosmic inflation..153
covenant, the.. 276
covertness..173–75, 364
Cowper, William..318
creatio ex deo..150–52, 155
creatio ex materia....................................... 149–50, 155
creatio ex nihilo..................................149–50, 154, 156
Crowfall 84
CSRs..............*See* customer services representatives
Curtis, Pavel 177–79, 472–73
customer service representatives............................57
D&D..................................... *See Dungeons & Dragons*
da Vinci, Leonardo...129
dancing 315
Darwin, Charles..414

dasein....386
data..... 63, 65–67, 103, 113, 123–26, 180, 184, 195, 226
  hard-coded.... 66, 70–71, 74, 103–4
  interpreted.... 67, 70–72, 104
  soft-coded.... 66, 70–72, 104
database, bits in a....*See* bits: in a database
databases....113, 296, 388, 390
declarative representations....222
deflationism....210, 221
deism....171–74, 176–78
demigods....17, 57, 173–74, 528
demiurges....149
deontology....416
Descartes, René....44, 179
descending....148, 229, 236–37, 245, 253, 451, 467
design team....55–57
designed content....*See* content: designed
designers...... 19, 53, 55–57, 73, 181–82, 276, 281, 363, 384, 439, 476, 487
  lead....55, 57, 483
detaching....232
deterministic realities....*See* realities: deterministic
deterministic Reality....*See* Reality: deterministic
Detweiler, Craig....513
Deucalion....485
dharma....415
digital simulations....305
DikuMUD....483–84, 497
DikuMUDs....75
Dionysus....527
direct content....*See* content: direct

directors 325
discrete time .... *See* time: discrete
divine command theory 417, 437, 517
divine providence 453
Doran, James 466
Doyle, Arthur C. 286
Dr Who 437, 508
DragonMUD 441, 510
DragonRaid 514
dreams 134, 144
  lucid 134
Duchamp, Marcel 201
dumps 123, 164, 167, 450
Dungeons & Dragons 25, 58, 79, 139–40, 514
Earth 101, 128, 257, 308, 357
Earth-divers 148, 155
Easter eggs 508
Edwards, Jonathan 495
effects 299
egoism 416
Elder Scrolls Online, The 58
Elune 528
Elysian Fields, the 220
emergent content .... *See* content: emergent
Empire of the Petal Throne 138
end boss 314
endurantism 162
End-User Licence Agreement 326, 383
engagement 41
engines, game .... *See* game engines
Enlil 420

Entropia Universe 492
environmentalism 422
Epicurean paradox 431
Epicurus 431
Erebus 485
Eros 485
escape rooms 142
Esege Malan 17
ESO .... *See Elder Scrolls Online, The*
ESP .... *See* extra-sensory perception
Essex University .... *See* University of Essex
ethics 341, 378, 415, 439
  normative 416
  of Artificial Intelligence 418
  of care 417
  systems of 377, 433–38, 452, 539
  systems of meta- 438
  virtue 416
Eucharist 249, 252
EULA .... *See* End-User Licence Agreement
Euthyphro dilemma 517
Eve 275
EVE Online 59, 81, 464, 473–74, 510
Evening Star, the 322
evidence 14
executable code .... *See* code: executable
existence
  abstract .... *See* existence: conceptual
  conceptual 221, 224, 252
  equivocal interpretation of 224
  ideal of 482

material .... *See* existence: physical
modes of 221, 224, 242
nature of 219
partial 243–45
physical 221, 224, 226, 228, 252, 443
relative 119, 205, 244, 246–47, 525
to bring into 11, 99, 107, 110, 223, 297, 413, 471
to will oneself into 153, 183
univocal interpretation of 224
existential quantifier 222
expansions 84, 88, 128–29
expectations 295
explicit content .... *See* content: explicit
exploits 73, 408
extensional definitions 201, 222
extra-sensory perception 324
Fallout 4 544
Falun Gong 523
Farmer, Randy 31
Fiasco 140
Fiction Theory 260
fiction, the 41, 59, 82, 272–80, 283–92, 510, 527
Field of Reeds 406
Final Fantasy XIV 37, 424, 509, 528
Finger of Death 384
first cause argument 150
flashdarks 186, 539
Flinn, Kelton 31
forking
realities .... *See* realities:forking
servers .... *See* servers: forking

formal logic 221
Forster, Edward M. 275, 345
forward chaining 299
Fountain 201
frames 376, 380
Free Guy 422
free will165, 168–69, 337, 341–42, 354, 365, 395, 400, 403, 426, 429, 432
freeform content .... *See* content: freeform
freeish will 341
Friends 508
full resets .... *See* resets:sudden
fun 41, 97, 158, 167, 276, 355, 489, 493, 551
functionalism 478
Gabriel 409
Gaea .... *See* Gaia
Gaia 329, 485
game directors 55
game engines 32, 73–74, 79, 155
Game of Thrones 290–92
  Beyond the Wall 291
Game Studies 41, 82, 489
game-mastered content .... *See* content: game-mastered
gameplay 76, 81, 85, 272, 286, 384, 499
games 32, 73, 158, 278, 316, 507, 513–14
  multi-player 28
  serious 494
Ganges, River 443
Garriott, Richard 390
Gather 486

Gautama, Siddhārtha 443
Geertz, Clifford 441, 448–49
gender 12, 379–82
General, the 437
generations 160–63, 200, 304
ghosts 18, 297, 322
Gillian's Hoop 466
gliders 162
GMC .... *See* content: game-mastered
Go 335, 374
God 6, 14–15, 150–51, 170, 259, 335, 369, 373, 399, 455–56, 495, 498, 545–46
Gödel, Kurt 191–93
Gödel's Incompleteness Theorems .... *See* Incompleteness Theorems
gods 6, 10–17, 47, 56–57, 102, 172, 177, 194, 218, 235, 241, 259, 310, 328, 361–64, 385, 431, 447, 451, 455, 461–62, 472–77, 482, 485, 491, 517–18, 521, 523–28, 538, 541
  belief in 218
  creator 17, 149–50, 171, 183, 275, 349, 455, 496, 499, 516
  definition of 7
  personal 169–71, 173, 177, 195, 242, 292
Gods .... *See Lap of the Gods*
Gods, Demi-Gods and Heroes 58
GOFAI .... *See* Artificial Intelligence: Good Old-Fashioned
Golden Rule 434
Goliath 209
Gomorrah 329

governments 470–76
graceful resets .... *See* resets: graceful
graphical MUDs .... *See* MUDs: graphical
Greek Orthodoxy 444
Groundhog Day 121
Groundhog Day resets .... *See* resets: sudden
Guild Wars 2 230–31
gunk 198
Habitat 31–33, 59, 444
hacker culture 25
hadith, books of 259, 487
hand-crafted content .... *See* content: hand-crafted
hard-coded data .... *See* data: hard-coded
hardware 63, 68
  of Reality .... *See* Reality: hardware of
Harington, Kit 291
Hasbro 140
HCC .... *See* content: hand-crafted
Heaven 229, 231, 246, 257–58, 308, 389, 445
heavens 149, 294, 462, 482, 545
Hegel, Georg W. F. 19
Heliopolis 153
Hell 456
Hellblade: Senua's Sacrifice 146
hells 294, 482, 545
Hemera 485
Henry V 176
Hephaestus 57, 317
Heracles 62, 95
Hercules .... *See* Heracles
Hermes 18, 62

Hermeticism 261, 456
heroes 58, 114
heroine's journey, the 267
hero's journey, the 266
higher realities .... *See* realities: super-
Hinduism 59, 105, 118, 151, 171, 175, 335–36, 410, 486, 490, 522
Hittites 458
Holmes, Sherlock 285, 525
Holy Ghost .... *See* Holy Spirit
Holy Spirit 170, 183
Holy Trinity 182, 520
Homer 97, 317
Hounds and Jackals 157
Huizinga, Johan 42
human rights 336, 454, 508
Hume, David 436
Hydaelyn 528
ideal of existence .... See existence: ideal of
idealism 180–81, 204–8, 468
Ilhuicatl-Teteocan 463
Iliad, The 97, 317
Ilm al-Kalām 150
imagination 43, 134–35, 144
imago dei 455, 500
immanence 153, 184, 228–29, 355
immanent transcendence 355
immersion 265–71, 276–79, 281, 285, 295
  identity 266, 268
  presence as .... *See* presence: as immersion
  sensory 265, 268–69

system 270
immortality .... *See* mortality
immortals 58, 392
immutability 195
impassibility 195
implicit content .... *See* content: implicit
Incans 494
inclusive position 36, 38
Incompleteness Theorems 191–93, 235
Indiana Jones and the Crystal Skull 276
inductivism 478
information gain 373
information loss 372–73, 516
initial states .... *See* states: initial
instances .. 87–89, 106–10, 115–19, 250, 387, 398, 552
integrated information theory 530
intelligence 334–35
artificial .... *See* Artificial Intelligence
group 321, 347
human-level 337
of non-player characters 318–25, 342, 419
super- 343
intensional definitions 201
interfaces 145–46, 262, 269–71, 282, 503
diegetic 279, 281–82
meta 279
non-diegetic 280
spatial 279
interpreted data .... *See* data: interpreted
interpreters 67–68, 72
Isaac 102

Iscariot ... 315
Ishmael ... 102
Islam ... 102, 150, 170, 259, 409, 455, 488
Island of Kesmai ... 31–33
Islandia ... 138
is-ought problem ... 436
Israelites ... 333, 526
Jainism ... 148, 336
Jehovah's Witness ... 505
JennyMUSH ... 496
Jesus ... 249, 410, 513
John Paul II, Pope ... 125
Jonson, Ben ... 379
Jotunheim ... 461–62
Judaism ... 150, 170, 333, 455
just-in-time evaluation ... 99
Kali ... 522
Kali Yuga ... 491
Kane ... 152
Kant, Immanuel ... 347
Kaplan, Jeffery ... 78
karma systems ... 407
keying ... 306
King of the World ... 382
Klietz, Alan ... 31
Koster, Raph ... 483
Krishna ... 171
Ku ... 152
Kuba ... 151
Kukulkán ... 499
Kur ... 407

Kurma 171
Lactantius 431
LambdaMOO 38, 177–78, 182, 472–73
land, laws of the .... *See* laws: of the land
Lap of the Gods 59
LARPs .... *See* live-action role-playing games
Las Vegas 118
laws
  of nature 11, 185, 471–72, 475
  of physics 70, 103–4, 185, 188, 207, 215, 294–96
  of robotics, Asimov's three 339
  of the land 11, 471, 475–77
layers 91, 106–7, 116
lead designers .... *See* designers: lead
LegendMUD 483
legitimate use of force 470
Lego bricks 196–200, 206
Lem, Stanisław 487
Leveilleur, Alphinaud 423
Lewis, Clive S. 138
Life 160–64, 200, 302, 304, 486, 549, 551
Lila 486
limbo 445
live-action role-playing games 141–43, 145, 146
lived religion 478
logical atomism 200
Loki 462
Lono 152
Lord of the Rings, The 289
lore 55, 273–75
lower realities .... *See* realities: sub-

lucid dreams........ *See* dreams: lucid
Lumpl........ 209
lusory attitude........ 41
Luther, Lex........ 353
Ma'at........ 405–6
Maggs, Bruce........ 31
magic circle, the........ 42–43, 144, 417
magic cities........ 138
Maia........ 62
Malachy, Saint........ 125
Mandela Effect, the........ 145
many-worlds interpretation........ 459
Marduk........ 492
marginal cases........ 420
Mars........ 176
Marvel cinematic universe........ 139
Massively-Multiplayer Online Role-Playing Games
.... 34, 37, 79, 85, 295, 387–89
Mathematics........ 50
Matrix, The........ 14, 201
Mayans........ 499, 522
Mbombo........ 151
McGonigal, Jane........ 519
men, angry young........ 26
mereological nihilism........ 197
Mereology........ 198
Meretzky, Steve........ 158
merging servers........ *See* servers:merging
Meridian 59........ 24
Metaphysics........ 201, 203, 209, 221, 242
Metaverse Manifesto, The........ 469

Metaverse, the....464
metrics 405
Microsoft Word 65
Middle Earth....289
Midgaard 75
Midgard....245, 460–62
Miller, Rand....545
Miller, Robyn 545
mind
  physics of.... 319
  theory of.... 345–50, 355–56, 358, 366, 417
mind uploading 241
mind-body dualism 179, 319
mind-body problem....180
Minecraft 100, 199
mini-boss 314
mîs-pî....248
mixed reality.... 146
MMORPGs. *See* Massively-Multiplayer Online Role-Playing Games
MMOs .... *See* Massively-Multiplayer Online Role-Playing Games
mobiles 61, 232, 313–16, 506
mobs.... *See* mobiles
modal realism....*See* realism: modal
Molea Cemetery 510
Mondain....90
monism 180
monomyth.... *See* hero's journey, the
Monopoly 28
monotheism....499, 523

Monster ... 31
monsters ... 61, 85, 312
moral beings ... 414, 420, 423–24, 550
morality meters ... 407
morally considerable beings ... 420–26, 429, 452
morals ... 376, 383, 398, 411, 415–17, 429, 439, 454
  systems of ... 418, 422, 432
More, Saint Thomas ... 498
Mormonism ... 150
Morning Star, the ... 322
Morningstar, Chip ... 31
mortality ... 385–87, 391–93, 401
mortals ... 58, 392, 447
Moses ... 443
MUD ... 20–23, 25–34, 56, 155, 173, 184, 202, 293, 355, 370, 389, 482–83, 505–6, 542
MUD1 ... 22, 32, 231, 313, 379, 509
MUD2 ... 22, 89, 155, 232, 253, 316, 512
MUDs ... 32–34, 37, 79, 89, 199, 389, 498
  graphical ... 34
  stock ... 75, 485, 497
Muggletonians ... 371
Muhammad ... 259, 409, 487
multi-boxing ... 233
multi-player online battle arena ... 522
multiple religious belonging ... 371
Multi-User Dungeon ... *See MUD*
Mutt, Richard ... 201
Myrkheim ... 460
Myst ... 545
myths ... 13

Native Americans 148, 152
Natural Law 508
nature
laws of........ *See* laws: of nature
of realities........ *See* realities: nature of
of Reality........ *See* Reality: nature of
Neo........ 14
Nergal........ 248–49, 252
Nesbit, Edith........ 138
New Game Experience 510
Newsnight 415
Newton, Isaac........ 243
nihilism 197
Nomic 190
nominalism........ 203–4, 206–7
Non Serviam........ 487
non-player characters 94, 311, 341, 354, 412, 435, 442, 475, 528
abilities of........ 312, 346–48, 446, 451–52
bodies of........ 234–36
copying........ 237–38
death of 130–31, 387, 394–98
fictional integrity of........ 115, 282–84
in our image........ 258, 261, 311, 349–51, 356, 362
intelligence of........ *See* intelligence:of non-player characters
morally considerable 422–24
of Reality...... *See* Reality: non-player characters of
perspective of.. 182, 204, 253–56, 365–69, 391, 515
souls of 399–407
Norse........ 259, 460, 462, 522

noumenal ... 347
NPCs ... *See* characters: non-player
numinous ... 546
Nyāya-Vaiśeṣika ... 341
Nyx ... 485
occasionalism ... 175
Odin ... 225, 245, 252, 256, 350, 497
OED ... *See Oxford English Dictionary*
Olodumare ... 493
Olympians ... 329, 392
Olympus ... 97
omnipotence ... 193
omniscience ... 168, 193
ontology ... 219
operation phase ... 53
optimistic-exclusive position ... 36–37, 41
Order of the Holy Walnut, the ... 444
Orion ... 18
Otherland ... 354
overtness ... 173–75, 364
Oxford English Dictionary ... 7
pandeism ... 171, 177–79, 182, 183
panentheism ... 151
pantheism ... 151, 171–72, 176, 246
paracosms ... 137–38, 318, 483, 486, 498, 506
paramount realities ... *See* realities: paramount
partial existence ... *See* existence: partial
partial realities ... *See* realities: partial
patches ... 84, 89, 127–29, 504
Payne, Cynthia ... 415
PCG ... *See* content:procedurally-generated

PCs ..... *See* characters: player
perdurantism 162
permadeath 388–90, 551
persistence 29, 205
personae 355
personal gods ..... *See* gods: personal
personhood 336, 421
personification 227, 451
persuasiveness 260, 263, 268–69, 271, 294
pessimistic-exclusive position 36, 38–39, 43
PGC ..... *See* content:procedurally-generated
Phaedo 400
phases 88, 91, 106, 109, 114–16, 251, 398
phenomenal 347
phenomenology 478
Philosophy 41, 110, 198
phlogiston theory 243
physicalism 180–81
physics
  laws of ..... *See* laws: of physics
  of realities ..... *See* realities: physics of
  of Reality ..... *See* Reality: physics of
  of the supernatural... *See* supernatural: physics of the
pi 66, 554
places 265–66, 297, 439
  other-directed 442
  sacred 443–44, 446
  spiritual 439–40
Planetfall 158
Plato 202, 400, 503, 517

player characters... 29, 42, 58–59, 90, 182, 253, 276–78, 325, 378, 406, 413
abilities of ... 284, 311, 320
bodies of ... 180, 232–33, 262
death of ... *See* permadeath
fictional integrity of ... 279–81, 312
identifying with ... 231, 266, 355, 389
of Reality ... *See* Reality: player characters of
player-*versus*-player ... 78, 80
playtesters ... 58
Pleiades, the ... 62
Plutarch ... 216
Polly ... 379–82
Pope Simulator ... 508
Pope, Alexander ... 318
Poseidon ... 18
possessing ... 233, 321
possible worlds ... 111, 116
post-colonialism ... 453
Potter, Harry ... 458
powers, supernatural ... *See* supernatural: powers
prayers ... 175, 480–81
preconditions ... 299
predicate calculus ... 222
premonitions ... 298
pre-production phase ... 52
presence ... 230, 263
as active medium ... 264
as immersion ... 264–65
as parasociality ... 264, 350
as realism ... 263

as social richness 263
as transportation 264–65
presenting 230, 270, 277
primary worlds .... *See* worlds: primary
principle of minimal departure 260
problem of universals 202–5, 227
procedural content-generation .... *See* content:procedurally-generated
procedural representations 222
procedural rhetoric 384
procedurally-generated content .... *See* content: procedurally-generated
producers 57
production phase 52–53, 55
production rules 299
programmers 29, 56–57, 64, 89, 121, 166, 177, 188, 210, 212, 465
Project Horseshoe 384
projection 345, 348, 351–52, 354
Prometheus 319
properties 201–6, 212, 216, 222–23, 239, 319, 412
of virtual worlds 28
physical 45
property dualism 180–81
prophecy 125, 325
Proteus effect 355
pseudophilosophy 532
Ptah 45, 153, 156, 183–88, 193–94, 235, 467
PvP .... *See* player-*versus*-player
Pyrrha 485
qualia 321

quests 58, 78, 85, 88, 266, 311, 509
Qur'an, The 102, 190, 259, 365, 409, 496
Ra 153
Rama 171
random-number generator 116, 166, 168, 174
Ranters 370
Rastafarianism 523
real time .... *See* time: real
realism 202–7
  modal 111
  presence as .... *See* presence: as realism
realisticness 288–91, 294, 346, 394
realities
  as communication 502
  as destination 502
  as product 502
  as tools 502
  consequent 226, 235–36, 245, 307, 460–69, 493, 496, 539
    definition of 460
  deterministic ... 155–57, 159, 163, 166–67, 188, 298, 552
  forking 301, 451
  higher .... *See* realities: super-
  nature of 9–10, 437
  paramount 44, 46
  partial 142
  physics of 9–12, 15, 185, 191, 461, 472
  self-modifying 192
  sub- .. 51, 154, 218, 229, 231, 235, 245, 251, 260, 307, 310, 370, 373, 438, 451–52, 460–67, 477

sub-sub- 235, 465
subtle 135
super- 51, 97, 100, 108, 111, 118, 148, 153, 164, 170, 172, 186, 218, 228–29, 231, 236, 245–46, 251, 292–94, 300, 310, 334, 438, 466–67, 475
Reality 29, 36–40, 45
bugs in 121–22, 126
content of 98–101, 104, 546
death in 389, 551
definition of 8
design of 545–48, 551
deterministic 164–65, 187
existence of 8, 180, 245–46, 254
hardware of 95, 270, 373, 466
implementation of 103–8, 111, 114, 120, 303–5, 413, 546–49
nature of 438, 543
non-player characters of 95, 108, 118, 125–26, 239, 303, 327–28, 332, 343, 390, 528
origins of 148–53, 171, 183
physics of 68, 180, 185–88, 193, 260, 297, 470
player characters of . 95–97, 112, 114, 168, 328, 332, 413
self-modifying 194
visiting 95, 99, 113, 234, 300, 524–25
Reality is Broken 519
reattaching 232, 249
reference worlds .... *See* worlds: reference
reincarnation 110, 320, 323, 386, 401, 413, 467, 520
relative existence .... *See* existence: relative
religion 289, 441, 478, 507, 510–14, 528

religions..363, 438, 447–48, 507–8, 514, 521–23, 528
  Abrahamic 150, 169, 455
Religious Studies 478, 509
representing.......230, 234, 237, 244–45, 249, 251–54, 269–70, 277, 365, 368–74, 451, 461–62, 464, 467, 516, 519
reputation systems 407–8
resets
  full ....*See* resets:sudden
  graceful..124
  Groundhog Day..............................*See* resets: sudden
  respawning..............................*See* resets: rolling
  rolling..85, 88–89, 120
  sudden..85, 88–89, 122
respawning....................86, 387–88, 390, 396–97, 513
respawning resets..............................*See* resets: rolling
resurrection..322, 386
Rift 509
RNG..............................*See* random-number generator
RNGesus 174
robots 234, 241, 339
Rock 'n' Roller Coaster 106
Roko's basilisk..343
role-playing 139, 379, 381
role-playing games..378, 514
  Japanese 522
  live-action ....*See* live-action role-playing games
  massively-multiplayer online..........*See* Massively-Multiplayer Online Role-Playing Games
  tabletop..79, 139–40, 144
rolling resets ....*See* resets: rolling

roll-out phase 52
Roman Catholicism 249–50, 438, 498, 508, 520
Rosedale, Philip 495
RPGs .... *See* role-playing games
rules 41
  of *Life* 160, 163
  sets of 191–92
Russell, Bertrand 547
sacred places .... *See* places: sacred
Salen, Katie 42
Saler, Michael 139
Sally-Anne test 345
sandboxes 79, 81, 498
Sansar 37
sapience 335–38, 351–54, 390, 395, 399, 422, 424, 429, 475, 487
Sceptre of Goth 31–33
Schrödinger's cat 242
Scientology 523
scripts 67–68, 353
Second Life 37, 79, 155, 444, 495
secondary worlds .... *See* worlds: secondary
Secret World Legends 272, 277, 315, 509
Secret World, The 58, 272
secular sacred 436
self-awareness 335–37, 352
self-modifying code .... *See* code: self-modifying
self-modifying systems *See* systems: self-modifying
Sellers, Mike 24
sentience 336, 399, 421–22, 424
servers 90, 428, 450, 484, 504

forking 90, 112–14
merging 90, 112–14
wipes 485
Shakespeare, William 176
shamans 359
Shapira, Andrew 31
shards 90–91, 106–7, 111–14, 130
Sherlock 287
Ship of Theseus 216
Shiva 105
Sia 362
Sides, David 31
Sikhism 336
Simargl 13
simples 196, 211
Sinai, Mount 443
singularity, the 342
Skrenta, Rich 31
SkyForge 59
Skyrim 140, 544
SkySaga 199
Sleipnir 462
Smite 522
Smith-Stanley, Edward G. G 318
Snow Crash 59
Snow, Jon 291
social contract theory 417, 433
Socrates 517
Sodom 329
soft-coded data ..... *See* data: soft-coded
software 62–69, 73, 108, 323, 346

multi-user 28
SoG .... *See Sceptre of Goth*
Somerville, Margaret 435
Sosaria 90
souls 111, 180–81, 205–6, 257–58, 320, 323, 399–407, 411–13, 442, 496, 530
source code .... *See* code: source
spaces 45, 439
Spinoza, Baruch 165
spirit worlds 359
spirits 349, 358–62
spiritual places .... *See* places: spiritual
spiritual worlds .... *See* worlds:spiritual
Spiritualism 358
spirituality 439–43, 511–12, 530
Star Trek 393, 459
Star Wars Galaxies 483, 509
Star Wars: the Old Republic 406
stasis 130
states...... 70, 123, 125, 130, 158–61, 164, 166, 294, 303, 450, 481, 552
initial 159, 161, 163
transformation 158
Stevenson, Robert L. 138
stock MUDs .... *See* MUDs: stock
Stoicism 246
Stormwind 507
strategic religious participation 371
Suber, Peter 190
sub-realities .... *See* realities: sub-
substance dualism 179, 205

sub-sub-realities .... *See* realities: sub-sub-
subtle realities .... *See* realities: subtle
sudden resets .... *See* resets: sudden
suffering 421, 424–28, 431, 550
Sufism 135, 455
Sumerians 420
Summerland, the 246
sunset phase 53
Superman 227, 353
supernatural
  beings 17–18, 57, 126, 284, 349
  physics of the 296
  powers 71, 173–74, 365, 446, 528
super-realities .... *See* realities: super-
supervention 180
SWL .... *See Secret World Legends*
symbolic interpretation .... *See* symbolic representation
symbolic objects .... *See* symbolic representation
symbolic representation 196–200, 207, 211, 526, 548–50
systems
  content .... *See* content: systems
  self-modifying 184–85, 188, 191–92
tabletop RPGs .... *See* role-playing games: tabletop
Tale in the Desert, A 474
Talmud, The 190
Taoism 246
Targaryen, Daenerys 292
Tartarus 485
Taylor, John 31

Technopaganism..520
Tékumel..138
telekinesis..325
teleology..172, 545
telepathy..321
telepresence.............*See* presence: as transportation
Tepeu..499
Terms of Service..383
text..33, 74, 262, 268–69
Tezcatlipoca..356
The Evolution of God..362
theism..545
theme parks..79, 442, 498
Theology..50, 511
theory of mind.............................*See* mind: theory of
Theseus..216
threads..122
ticks..304
time..........................121, 124, 128, 298, 300–306, 541
  continuous..304–7
  discrete..304–7
  real..29, 302, 374
  travel..300–303, 481
Time Lords..437
TinyMUD..484, 499
Tolkien, John R. R.......................44, 137, 260, 455, 508
transcendence...................153, 171, 184, 228, 356, 456
transhumanism..241
transmigration..320
transubstantiation..249–52, 520
trash..314

Trubshaw, Roy....... 20–21, 25–26, 28–32, 34, 56, 105, 184, 293, 355, 370, 379, 483, 506, 518, 542

true names.. 327

trust 276, 287–88, 291, 366–69

TSW.. *See Secret World, The*

Turing machine..373

Turing Test... 353

Turing, Alan.. 353

tutorials 80, 98

typists.. 60

tyrannies 471

UCC.......................................*See* content: user-created

UGC...................................*See* content: user-generated

Ultima Online 91, 390, 483

Ultima universe 479

ultimate end 495

ultraphysics... 272

Uluru...443

uncertainty.. 160, 166–67

universal sets 247

Universal Turing Machine...163

universals 202–3

  problem of....................... *See* problem of universals

University of Essex 20, 24

unmoved mover paradox 150

unrealisticness .... *See* realisticness

updates.. 72, 85, 485, 504

Uranus... 329

user-created content.........*See* content: user-created

user-generated content................. *See* content: user-generated

utilitarianism 416
Utopia 498
Valhalla 246
Vaughan, Lexley 512–13
Venus 101, 322
verisimilitude 288, 428
via negativa 182
Victoria, Queen 286
Viracocha 494
virtual reality 26, 33, 146, 262, 265
virtual worlds
  definition of 28
  game 37, 39, 123, 183, 260, 497, 546
  history of 30
  original 31
  physics of 29, 61, 70, 177
  principals of 54
  separate from Reality 36–38, 439
  social 37–38, 59, 79, 123, 155, 177, 472, 484, 499
  switching off 130, 226, 449–51, 454, 504
Vishnu 105, 171
Vodou 522
voxels 199
VR .... *See* virtual reality
Vulcan 317
Watson, John H. 286
whales 77
Whiro-te-tipua 16
whole brain emulation 241
Whoniverse 139
Wicca 141

Williams, Robin 510
Williams, Tad 354
Wired 545
wisdom 335–36
Wittgenstein, Ludwig 136
Wizards of the Coast 140
wizzes 173
World of Tanks 146
World of Warcraft .. 34, 37, 40, 58, 78, 85, 88, 199, 268, 273, 441, 444, 448, 464–65, 507, 510, 528
  Cataclysm 85
  The Burning Crusade 78
  Wrath of the Lich King 78, 88
worlds 458
  primary 44, 137
  reference 295
  secondary 137
  spiritual 257–58
  virtual .... *See* virtual worlds
Would-Be, Politic 379
WoW .... *See World of Warcraft*
Wrath of the Lich King .. *See World of Warcraft: Wrath of the Lich King*
Wright, Austin T. 138
Yahweh 170, 333
Yggdrasil 460–61, 463
Yoruba 493
Young Earth Creationism 124, 357
zero-player games 302
Zeus 57, 62, 96, 392, 448, 485
Zimmerman, Eric 42

Zorya..13–14, 323

Cover by Sir John Tenniel
from *Punch* 19th May, 1883
public domain.

THE HARVEST OF THE SEA.

FATHER NEPTUNE. "THERE'S PLENTY FOR EVERYBODY!—HUMPH!—IF YOU COULD ONLY *GATHER IT!*"

Fonts used:

Zilla Slab by Typotheque
IM Fell DW Pica by Igino Marini
Delius Unicase by Natalia Raices

all released under the Open Font License.

Printed in Great Britain
by Amazon

74708062R10363